M. TVLLI
IN L. CALPVR
OR

EDITED WITH
TEXT, INTRODUCTION, AND
COMMENTARY BY
R. G. M. NISBET

CLARENDON PRESS · OXFORD

Oxford University Press, Walton Street, Oxford OX2 6DP

Oxford New York Toronto
Delhi Bombay Calcutta Madras Karachi
Petaling Jaya Singapore Hong Kong Tokyo
Nairobi Dar es Salaam Cape Town
Melbourne Auckland

and associated companies in
Berlin Ibadan

Oxford is a trade mark of Oxford University Press

Published in the United States
by Oxford University Press, New York

© *Oxford University Press 1961*

First published 1961
Reprinted 1974, 1975
First issued in Clarendon paperbacks 1987
Reprinted 1989

All rights reserved. No part of this publication may be reproduced,
stored in a retrieval system, or transmitted, in any form or by any means,
electronic, mechanical, photocopying, recording, or otherwise, without
the prior permission of Oxford University Press

This book is sold subject to the condition that it shall not, by way
of trade or otherwise, be lent, re-sold, hired out or otherwise circulated
without the publisher's prior consent in any form of binding or cover
other than that in which it is published and without a similar condition
including this condition being imposed on the subsequent purchaser

British Library Cataloguing in Publication Data
Cicero, Marcus Tullius
in L. Calpurnium Pisonem oratio.
I. Title   II. Nisbet, R. G. M.
875'.01   PA6281.P4
ISBN 0–19–872131–5

Library of Congress Cataloging in Publication Data
Cicero, Marcus Tullius.
M. Tulli Ciceronis In L. Calpurnium Pisonem oratio.
Latin text; commentary in English.
Reprint. Originally published: Oxford: Clarendon Press, 1961.
Bibliography: p.
Includes indexes.
1. Piso Caesoninus, Lucius Calpurnius.   I. Nisbet,
R. G. M. (Robin George Murdoch)   II. Title.   III. Title:
In L. Calpurnium Pisonem oratio.
PA6281.P4 1987   875'.01   87–5514
ISBN 0–19–872131–5 (pbk.)

Printed in Great Britain
by the Ipswich Book Company Ltd., Suffolk

EDITOR'S NOTE

I HAVE many obligations to record. Mr. Gordon Williams read the whole book while it was being put together; he has discussed many problems with me, and given unfailing help in every difficulty. Professor W. S. Watt has read the completed commentary and made improvements on every page; as if this were not enough, he has corrected the proofs with equal vigilance. I have consulted Professor R. A. B. Mynors on the manuscripts, Mr. M. W. Frederiksen and Mr. F. A. Lepper on historical matters, always to my great profit. I owe a special word of thanks to Professor Eduard Fraenkel, who has taken an interest in my work from the start, and has come to my rescue on a number of occasions. Professor A. Campana has generously allowed me to quote the unpublished readings of Poggio's manuscript, which he has recently rediscovered. I have been helped in various ways by Mr. E. Courtney, Miss Margaret Hubbard, Dr. R. W. Hunt, Professor S. Mariotti, Mr. L. D. Reynolds, and Mr. S. Weinstock. I have received every assistance from the authorities of the Vatican Library, the Hospital at Kues, l'Institut de Recherche et d'Histoire des Textes; and not least from the staff of the Clarendon Press.

R. G. M. N.

Corpus Christi College, Oxford
September, 1960

CONTENTS

INTRODUCTION
    I. The historical background   v
    II. Clausulae   xvii
    III. The manuscripts   xx
    IV. Bibliography   xxix

TEXT   1

COMMENTARY   51

APPENDICES
    I. Piso's proconsulship of Macedonia   172
    II. Piso and Catullus   180
    III. Piso and Philodemus   183
    IV. Piso and the Villa of the Papyri   186
    V. Gabinius   188
    VI. The *in Pisonem* as an invective   192
    VII. Piso and the *Invectiva in Ciceronem*   197
    VIII. The date of delivery and publication   199

INDICES   203

INTRODUCTION

I. THE HISTORICAL BACKGROUND

CICERO wrote this invective in 55 B.C. against L. Calpurnius Piso Caesoninus, the consul of 58, the proconsul of Macedonia 57–55, the father of the Calpurnia who married Julius Caesar. Piso belonged to a noble plebeian family which came to prominence in the second century B.C., though it implausibly claimed descent from Calpus, son of Numa.[1] His great-grandfather was probably the consul of 148; his grandfather was consul in 112 (frag. ix n.). Cicero depicts his father[2] as a profiteer who superintended the manufacture of arms in the Social War (§ 87); he may in fact have been praetor in 90[3] and author of the *lex Calpurnia* which extended the citizenship. He seems to have been a man of wide sympathies; at any rate he married the daughter of one Calventius, a rich merchant from Placentia, who is unkindly portrayed in our speech as a Gallic auctioneer (frag. ix n.).

As the consul of 58 Piso cannot have been born later than 101. He won the consulship at the first attempt (§ 2), and in view of Cicero's reticence in that passage one would suppose that he was elected at the earliest possible age. Yet elsewhere it is said that he was a *grandis puer* during the Social War (§ 87), and this might almost suggest that he was born about 104 or 105. Piso married the daughter of a certain Rutilius Nudus (Asc. 4 KS), perhaps the P. Rutilius Nudus[4] who commanded Cotta's fleet in 73. His early career was undistinguished,[5] according to Cicero (§ 1); yet he became quaestor,

---

[1] E. A. Sydenham, *Coinage of Roman Rep.*, no. 1032, Hor. *a.p.* 292 'Pompilius sanguis', *laus Pis.* 3 and 15.

[2] Quaestor perhaps in 100 (Broughton, *Mag. Rom. Rep.* i. 578).

[3] R. Syme, *Historia*, iv, 1955, 58, quoting Sisenna frag. 17.

[4] App. *Mith.* 71, Oros. vi. 2. 13, J. Bingen, *BCH* lxxviii, 1954, 84.

[5] It cannot be proved that he was the L. Piso who at some date before

v

INTRODUCTION

aedile, and praetor at the first attempt (§ 2). There is no evidence that he governed a province at this stage. Valerius Maximus (viii. 1. 6) mentions a L. Piso who was prosecuted by 'L. Claudius Pulcher'; some have supposed that he is referring to Piso Caesoninus and P. Clodius, but Cicero could hardly have kept quiet about the episode if it had involved his two enemies.[1]

In 59 B.C. Rome was dominated by the alliance of Pompey, Caesar, and Crassus, who had combined to control and manipulate the institutions of the Republic. The senate, expecting that the consuls of 58 would favour this formidable cabal, did not make them the usual allocation of provinces (12. 21 n.). The elections were postponed till October 59 (*Att*. ii. 20. 6), but in the end Piso was elected with Pompey's partisan Gabinius; Cicero, writing in April, foresaw the election of Gabinius, but did not mention Piso's name (*Att*. ii. 5. 2). During the same year Caesar married Piso's daughter Calpurnia; she was perhaps a distant relative through her mother Rutilia.[2] It is uncertain whether the wedding came before or after the election,[3] but as Caesar supported Piso (§ 3) he must in any case have made a bargain with him. It is true that Caesar needed a friend in the consulship to match Gabinius, yet Piso had claims of his own on the office, and must have won considerable support from the senate.

Up to this time Piso had been on good terms with Cicero. He had approved his energy in 63 (§ 72), though he was related to the Catilinarian Cethegus (*in sen*. 10, *dom*. 62); yet he probably regarded the execution of the conspirators as imprudent (§ 14). He was supported by Cicero in his own

70 prosecuted P. Gabinius for extortion in Achaea (*Caecil*. 64). If he was, Cicero has missed some opportunities for comedy.

[1] Perhaps Piso's grandfather is meant (R. Syme, *Classica et Mediaevalia*, xvii, 1956, 133).

[2] F. Münzer, *Römische Adelsparteien* (Stuttgart, 1920), p. 327.

[3] Suet. *Jul*. 21, App. *b.c*. ii. 14, Dio xxxviii. 9. 1 (against Plut. *Caes*. 14. 8) put the election first, but on such a point the sources cannot be trusted.

vi

INTRODUCTION

candidature, and in the early days of his consulship he treated Cicero with respect (11. 17 n.). Yet in a few weeks Cicero was in exile, and his friendship with Piso had turned to venomous hostility.

The pretext for Cicero's exile was his execution of the Catilinarian conspirators in 63 without trial.[1] He could point to the *senatusconsultum ultimum* and the precedent of Opimius, who was acquitted after the suppression of C. Gracchus; but even Opimius had acted at a time of actual disorder and not merely of threatened disturbance. Cicero claimed that the Catilinarians had ceased to be citizens, but that sophism could be used to justify murder. It could be argued more reasonably that the consuls' supreme duty was the defence of the established order, without a timid respect for technicalities. The expediency of the execution is in fact doubtful, as the Catilinarians fought to the last man; but in the confusion of the moment there must have seemed a real threat of civil war, and there were rumours of a move to rescue the prisoners. Cicero had a difficult decision to make, and after the recent trial of Rabirius (4. 7 n.) he knew the risks involved for himself (*Cat.* iv. 9, *Sest.* 47). He cautiously consulted the senate, no doubt in more guarded terms than in the published Fourth Catilinarian (Plut. *Cic.* 21. 3). In his politically weak position as a *novus homo* he could hardly have done otherwise, but after Cato's speech it was impossible to draw back. Yet the senate was morally committed to his support (§ 14). It did not fail him.

A more immediate reason for Cicero's exile was his vendetta with P. Clodius Pulcher. Cicero's account of his enemy is vague and incoherent, without even the merits of a good caricature. Clodius was a cultured and witty aristocrat, and a brilliant political tactician. Like other demagogues (even Roman ones) he may have been partly convinced by his own

---

[1] Greenidge, *Legal Procedure*, pp. 397 ff., E. G. Hardy, *Some Problems in Roman History* (Oxford, 1924), pp. 35 ff. (= *JRS* iii, 1913, 53 ff.), H. Last, *JRS* xxxiii, 1943, 93 ff.

vii

INTRODUCTION

slogans; certainly many ordinary people regarded him as their champion and lamented his murder in 52 (Asc. 28 KS). After that has been said the fact remains that his ambition and irresponsibility brought disaster to his own class and to the whole Republican system. In December 62 Clodius was detected[1] in Caesar's house disguised as a woman; the mysteries of the Bona Dea were being held, which no male was allowed to attend. He acted out of bravado and curiosity; the story of an intrigue with Caesar's wife Pompeia need not be true. Cicero, as a patriotic Roman, was enjoyably indignant (*Att.* i. 12. 3), though less so than other more pious senators (*Att.* i. 13. 3); and when Clodius produced an alibi he gave evidence to break it. When Clodius was acquitted he regarded the verdict as a slight on his own honour and pursued his enemy with imprudent epigrams. Clodius was too proud to submit, and saw the advantages of counter-attack. There was a genuine feeling that Cicero in 63 had ignored a cherished right of Roman citizens;[2] if Clodius could exploit this attitude he would win popularity and revenge. But first he needed to become a tribune, and here he was impeded by the misfortune of patrician birth.

Clodius alone could not have defied a united senate; the intervention of Caesar was decisive. Cicero deplored the *rapprochement* of Caesar and Pompey, and he was still a dangerous and crafty opponent. He had lost credit, it is true, with the *plebs* of Rome, and his vanity and sarcasm had offended some powerful *nobiles* (Plut. *Cic.* 27, Dio xxxviii. 12. 5–7), but he could still claim powerful support among the *equites*, in Italy, and surely also in the senate. Caesar offered him a place with Pompey and Crassus in the inner ring (*Att.* ii. 3. 3, *prov. cons.* 41, *Pis.* 79), but Cicero declined, and in his defence of Antonius in the spring of 59 commented indiscreetly on the

[1] Plut. *Caes.* 10, *Cic.* 28, Schol. Bob. p. 89 Stangl, E. Ciaceri, *Cicerone e i suoi tempi* ii² (Genova, 1941), 20 ff.

[2] *Verr.* v. 163 'o nomen dulce libertatis! o ius eximium nostrae civitatis! o lex Porcia legesque Semproniae!'

viii

INTRODUCTION

triumvirate. Caesar, with his usual speed, introduced a bill the same day, with Pompey's support, transferring Clodius to the *plebs* (*dom.* 41, *Sest.* 16); though the Bona Dea incident concerned him more closely than Cicero he did not let it affect his political judgement. He continued to make offers to Cicero, a seat on his agrarian board, a *libera legatio*, a *legatio* on his own staff (*Att.* ii. 18. 3, ii. 19. 4–5). But Cicero still refused: he was unwilling to sacrifice his principles, he was sensitive to senatorial opinion, and he misjudged the danger (*prov. cons.* 42). There were rumours that Caesar and Clodius had quarrelled (*Att.* ii. 12. 2); Pompey promised his support and obtained guarantees from Clodius (*Att.* ii. 20. 2, ii. 22. 2, Dio xxxviii. 15). The consuls-designate gave every satisfaction (*Q.f.* i. 2. 16): Gabinius was controlled by Pompey, and Piso's face inspired trust.

Clodius became tribune on 10 December 59, towards the end of Caesar's consulship, and on the same day promulgated four bills (*Sest.* 55, *Pis.* 9. 5 n.–10 n., Asc. 7–8 KS). One secured the support of the urban poor by authorizing a free corn ration; in the *in Pisonem* Cicero discreetly forgets this popular and justifiable measure (Asc. 7 KS). A second abolished the *leges Aelia et Fufia* by which the auspices had been manipulated against Caesar. A third restored the right to form *collegia*, a useful instrument for bribery or violence. A fourth limited the power of the censors to expel persons from the senate. On 4 January 58 (9. 5 n.) the laws were passed. Cicero unreasonably blames the new consuls rather than Caesar; he does not mention that he had himself been tricked into acquiescence by lying promises from Clodius (Dio xxxviii. 14. 2, cf. *Att.* iii. 15. 4). In the period that followed Clodius enrolled *collegia* and established an armoury in the forum (11. 5 n.–7 n.).

Caesar's province needed him and his patience was exhausted. His legislation of 59 was in danger; early in 58, at an inconvenient moment for both Caesar and Cicero, its

ix

INTRODUCTION

validity was challenged by the new praetors Memmius and Domitius (*Sest.* 40, *Pis.* 79, Suet. *Jul.* 23. 1). The departure of Cicero would win the support of Clodius, who controlled the electoral machine; this was vital for Caesar, as he had quarrelled with the senate, and could not trust Pompey for a moment. At the same time the senate would be taught the realities of power; Cicero was unpopular in powerful circles, and could perhaps be detached without causing undue distress. Pompey concurred, in spite of all his promises; the settlement of his veterans depended on Caesar's legislation. In late January or February[1] Clodius promulgated two bills: the first (*de capite civis Romani*) interdicted from fire and water anybody who had put a Roman citizen to death without trial; the second assigned Macedonia to Piso and Cilicia[2] to Gabinius (*dom.* 23), in both cases with extraordinary powers (pp. 172, 189). It is difficult to avoid Cicero's conclusion that the consuls' neutrality had been bought; the bills were synchronized (*Sest.* 25, *Pis.* 21) to prevent double-crossing. Piso could do nothing to save Cicero, and in politics, as he knew, everybody had to think of himself (§ 12).

Cicero won much support from the propertied classes in Rome and Italy (*quir.* 8, *Sest.* 32, *Pis.* 11). The senate appealed to Gabinius without result; it then went into mourning, but was forced to desist by a consular edict (*in sen.* 12, *Sest.* 26–27, 32, *Pis.* 17–18). L. Aelius Lamia, who was inciting the *equites* to make demonstrations, was relegated by Gabinius 200 miles from Rome (*Sest.* 29, *Pis.* 23, 64). A deputation of prominent senators waited on Pompey, who evasively referred them to the consuls (*Sest.* 41, *Pis.* 77). Piso told them, very sensibly, that if Cicero fought there would be no end of bloodshed (§ 78). Cicero himself approached Pompey, but was

[1] M. Gelzer, *RE* viiA. 914, suggests that January was the date because *in sen.* 16 refers to Piso's edicts, and Piso was presiding consul in the odd months of the year (*in sen.* 17). But these edicts were issued by both consuls jointly.

[2] Later changed to Syria, perhaps because of events in Egypt.

INTRODUCTION

rebuffed (76. 25 n.); he then called on Piso, but though received politely, he could not forget that Piso was getting a province out of the transaction (§ 12, Plut. *Cic.* 31. 4). Meanwhile Clodius threatened the senate with the army which Caesar was mobilizing for his province (*in sen.* 32, *Sest.* 39, *har. resp.* 47, *Pis.* 21); the threat was decisive, but augured no good for Republican institutions. At one *contio*, held outside the *pomerium* for Caesar's benefit, Clodius questioned Piso and Gabinius, and they expressed their disapproval of execution without trial (*in sen.* 13, 17, *Pis.* 14, Dio xxxviii. 16. 6). Cicero does not mention that Caesar said the same, though he insincerely declined to support Clodius's bill (Dio xxxviii. 17. 1).

Cicero now withdrew into exile, probably in early March (22. 13 n.). During the bitter year that followed he blamed his advisers for cowardice or treachery (*Att.* iii. 15), but after his return gave himself great credit for self-sacrifice (*dom.* 63–64, 98–99, *Sest.* 43–50, *Pis.* 21). In fact he had no choice. Clodius saw his two bills passed (*Sest.* 53, *Pis.* 21), and soon promulgated a stronger measure, *de exsilio Ciceronis.* This accused Cicero by name of executing citizens without trial (§§ 30, 72), and ordered the confiscation of his property. Meanwhile his Palatine house and Tusculan villa were looted (*dom.* 62, *Pis.* 26); on the site of the former, in a prominent position overlooking the city, Clodius, by an imaginative stroke, erected a Shrine of Liberty (*dom.* 100, 110–12, *Pis.* 72).[1] He also arranged that Cato should be sent to annex Cyprus (*dom.* 22, 52, 65, *Sest.* 60); Cicero, with a natural eagerness to find companions in misfortune, represents this mission as virtual exile.

But Clodius's alliance with the dynasts did not last long. His policy was always opportunistic, and he may have felt himself undervalued; his natural connexions and future hopes lay with the *optimates.*[2] About April 58 he arranged the escape

---

[1] Cf. W. Allen, *TAPA* lxxv, 1944, 1 ff.
[2] For his friendship with some *optimates* in the period 58–56 see *prov. cons.* 47, *har. resp.* 46, 48, 50, *fam.* i. 9. 19.

xi

INTRODUCTION

of Tigranes, who was held in Rome as Pompey's prisoner (*Att.* iii. 8. 3, *dom.* 66, Dio xxxviii. 30. 1); and Pompey began to show more sympathy with Cicero's cause (*dom.* 25, *Sest.* 67, *Pis.* 27). Gabinius soon followed suit, but his fasces were broken and he himself was stoned (§ 28, Dio xxxviii. 30. 2); finally Clodius consecrated his property (*dom.* 124). Clodius even denounced the validity of Caesar's bills, which had been passed against the auspices (*dom.* 40, *har. resp.* 48). It was a strange manœuvre, as his own transference to the *plebs*, and hence all his legislation, was equally vulnerable; perhaps he hoped that his new senatorial friends would not press the point. Yet at the worst he stood to lose little, for he had already gained the support of the *plebs*; Cicero had been irretrievably humiliated, and it was not Clodius's only aim to keep him in exile for ever.[1] The climax was reached on 11 August, when a slave of Clodius's dramatically dropped a dagger in the vestibule of the temple of Castor, where the senate was meeting; Pompey, who had a morbid dread of assassination, took the hint, and to Cicero's ill-concealed satisfaction stayed at home till December (*Sest.* 69, *har. resp.* 49, *Pis.* 16, 28–29, Asc. 41 KS).

Caesar was not yet ready to let Cicero return, and so Piso did nothing against Clodius (*dom.* 66, *Pis.* 28). Little is known of the consuls' other activities during the year. Like other magistrates of the period they took repressive measures against the Egyptian cults in Rome (Tert. *nat.* i. 10, *apol.* 6. 8, *RE* ix. 2103). They also sponsored the *Lex Gabinia Calpurnia*, giving customs exemption to Delos (p. 189). Meanwhile Cicero's friends were doing their best to bring about his recall. The consuls refused to introduce a motion as they felt bound by a clause in the *lex de exsilio* forbidding senatorial discussion (*Att.* iii. 23. 2, *in sen.* 4, 8, *dom.* 70, *Pis.* 29. 21 n.). The senate

---

[1] For other views see L. G. Pocock, *CQ* xviii, 1924, 59 ff., xix, 1925, 182 ff. Yet it is hard to suppose either that Cicero was completely deceived by Clodius's new policy, or that he completely misrepresented its drift.

xii

INTRODUCTION

in turn refused to discuss other business till Cicero's case was dealt with (*Att*. iii. 24. 2, *Pis*. 29). On 1 June L. Ninnius's proposal in the senate was passed unanimously but vetoed (*in sen*. 3, *Sest*. 68). On 29 October a bill was promulgated by eight tribunes, and supported by Pompey, but again vetoed (*Att*. iii. 23, *Sest*. 69). In November Cicero moved from Thessalonica to Dyrrachium; he did not want to run into Piso, who was going to Thessalonica as proconsul of Macedonia (31. 7 n., *fam*. xiv. 1. 3).

On 1 January 57 new consuls appeared and Cicero's hopes revived. Lentulus Spinther raised his case in the senate, with the grudging consent of his colleague Metellus Nepos (*in sen*. 5, *Pis*. 34); the discussions were postponed by an un-friendly tribune (*quir*. 12, *Sest*. 74). On 23 January a tribuni-cian *rogatio* was thwarted by Clodius's gangs (*Sest*. 75–80); Sestius and Milo battled for Cicero with hooligans of their own. Caesar now agreed to Cicero's return, at the price of guarantees which limited his independence (*fam*. i. 9. 9, *Pis*. 80). Pompey, who was *duumvir* of Capua, obtained a favour-able resolution from the local council, where no veto was possible (*in sen*. 29, *Pis*. 25, *Mil*. 39). Other *municipia* fol-lowed suit, and the *equites* and business corporations passed honorary decrees (*dom*. 74, *Pis*. 41). The senate thanked the cities which had received Cicero, commended him to the magistrates in the provinces, and summoned loyal citizens to Rome (*in sen*. 24, *dom*. 85, *Sest*. 128, *Pis*. 34, *Planc*. 78). Finally (in July) it decreed that a bill should be brought before the *comitia centuriata*; anybody who interfered would be re-garded as a public enemy (*in sen*. 26–27, *Sest*. 129, *Pis*. 35). The bill was promulgated by all the magistrates except one praetor, Appius Claudius, and two tribunes (35. 9 n.). Lentulus and others held *contiones* in Rome, and Pompey spoke on Cicero's behalf (*quir*. 16–17, *Sest*. 107, *Pis*. 34, 80). On 4 August the *comitia* passed the motion unanimously (*in sen*. 28, *quir*. 25, *dom*. 75, *Pis*. 36). Cicero proceeded up the

INTRODUCTION

Appian Way in triumph, and entered Rome by the *porta Capena* on 4 September (*Att.* iv. 1. 4–5, *Sest.* 131, *Pis.* 51–52). His house was rebuilt at the public expense (*Att.* iv. 2. 2–5, *har. resp.* 12–16, *Pis.* 52).

Piso's government of Macedonia is discussed in Appendix I; many of Cicero's charges can be rebutted, and there are positive indications that he was an able proconsul. Cicero, after his return, was eager to recall his enemy (*quir.* 21, *prov. cons.* 13), and in June 56 in the *de provinciis consularibus* pressed his attack strongly (88. 4 n.). Piso was duly superseded, but did not leave Macedonia till the summer of 55 (Appendix VIII); when he reached Rome he complained in the senate about Cicero's attacks (Asc. 2 KS). He mentioned with complacency his own electoral victories (§ 2), asked why Cicero had needed his help in 58 (§ 18), ridiculed Cicero's undignified flight (§§ 31, 34) and tactless verses (§§ 72–74), correctly observed that he ought to hate Caesar and Pompey more than himself (§ 78), and challenged him to prosecute (§§ 82, 94). In the senatorial debate there was a lively *altercatio* between Piso and Torquatus (§§ 47, 92), and Cicero renewed his onslaught; this speech he worked up into the *in Pisonem* (p. 202). Piso retorted with a pamphlet of his own,[1] which Cicero mentions in September 54 (*Q.f.* iii. 1. 11): 'alterum est de Calventi Mari[2] oratione quod scribis; miror tibi placere me ad eam rescribere, praesertim cum illam nemo lecturus sit si ego nihil rescripsero, meam in illum pueri omnes tamquam dictata perdiscant.'

Piso's later career was moderate and statesmanlike. He became censor in 50 against his will (Dio xl. 63. 2); he was still at this time an enemy of Cicero's (*fam.* viii. 12. 2). In 49 he supported Curio's proposal that both Caesar and Pompey should lay down their commands (Plut. *Pomp.* 58. 7), and offered to go on an embassy to Caesar (Caes. *b.c.* i. 3. 6).

---

[1] Wrongly identified by some with Pseudo-Sallust, *in Ciceronem* (cf. Appendix VII).   [2] i.e. Piso; cf. 20. 14 n.

xiv

INTRODUCTION

When Caesar marched on Rome he left the city rather than meet him, and Cicero writes 'amo etiam Pisonem' (*Att.* vii. 13. 1, cf. *fam.* xiv. 14. 2). In 46 he intervened on behalf of Marcellus (*fam.* iv. 4. 3). When Caesar was killed he insisted on a public funeral, and rebuked the arrogance of the tyrannicides (App. *b.c.* ii. 135–6). On 1 August 44 he attacked Antony in the senate, but found no support (*Phil.* i. 10); Cicero says that he was the only consular worthy of the republic (*Phil.* i. 14). But at the beginning of 43 he insisted that Antony should not be condemned without a trial (App. *b.c.* iii. 50–60); he pointed out the legal strength of Antony's position, and the danger of driving him into extreme measures. Piso was sent with Servius Sulpicius and Philippus on an unprofitable mission to Antony, much to Cicero's disgust (*fam.* xii. 4. 1). In March together with Fufius Calenus he proposed that another deputation should be sent (*Phil.* xii. 3), but Cicero wrecked the scheme. And there he vanishes from history.[1]

The memorable caricature of Piso, repeated in several speeches (cf. *in sen.* 13–16, *Sest.* 19–24) follows the conventions of ancient invective (Appendix VI), and should not be taken too seriously. With his rugged forehead and bushy eyebrows (1. 16 n.) Piso was a formidable personage; Appian describes how he overawed the senate by his presence (*b.c.* iii. 54). He was cautious and sensible in 49 and 44–43, but Cicero's charge of cynical selfishness in 58 has some justification. In his private life Cicero describes him as a drunkard and a voluptuary (cf. Catull. xlvii, below, p. 180); the same could be said, or invented, about many Roman noblemen. It is more important that Piso was the patron and disciple of the Epicurean Philodemus (Appendix III); among the Romans Epicureanism did not inhibit political activity.[2] It is also possible that he was the owner of the opulent villa and artistic bronzes found in the eighteenth century at Herculaneum

---

[1] For activities at Pola, attributed by some to his old age, see 92. 4 n.

[2] A. Momigliano, *JRS* xxxi, 1941, 151 ff.

INTRODUCTION

(Appendix IV). Yet his magnificence should not be exaggerated; Cicero says that he was dull in manner (*in sen.* 14, *Pis.* frag. viii, §§ 1, 19) and dressed plainly (*Sest.* 19), and this account cannot be completely untrue. Piso seems to have combined an interest in Greek culture with the ponderous gravity of a Roman; his political moderation depended on native common sense rather than on philosophical theory. In his varied talents he resembles his son,[1] L. Piso *pontifex*, prefect of the city and patron of literature, conqueror of Thrace and boon-companion of Tiberius; one might say of the father as Velleius said of the son 'vix quemquam reperiri posse qui aut otium validius diligat aut facilius sufficiat negotio' (ii. 98. 3).

The *in Pisonem* is a masterpiece of misrepresentation. In spite of all Cicero's rhetoric, his exile was a disaster from which he never recovered, politically or psychologically. He won his return by making humiliating promises, renewed in 56 after the conference of Luca. Cicero felt dutiful gratitude to Pompey for bringing him back, but in his more candid moments recognized that he had previously betrayed him.[2] Besides, Clodius and Pompey had been reconciled (Dio xxxix. 29. 1), a fact carefully concealed in our speech. As for Caesar, Cicero must have hated him intensely, but now could only speak of him with urbane insincerity (*prov. cons.* 18–25, 40–47, *Pis.* 79–82). But he had given no guarantees to the dynasts' underlings; an attack on them would relieve his feelings and give warning that he was still dangerous. Above all, Piso's *dignitas* to some extent affected that of his son-in-law;[3] the uncontrolled onslaught on Piso is in part a calculated thrust

---

[1] Tac. *ann.* vi. 10. 3, *Prosop. imp. Rom.*[2] C 289. C. Cichorius, *Römische Studien*, p. 341, points out difficulties in the identification, but they seem preferable to the assumption that Tacitus has made a mistake.

[2] *Att.* ix. 5. 2, ix. 13. 3, ix. 19. 2, x. 4. 3, App. *b.c.* ii. 16 Κικέρων μὲν δὴ διὰ Πομπήιον ἐκπεσὼν διὰ Πομπήιον κατῄει.

[3] Caesar showed satisfaction when he avenged the death in Gaul of Piso's grandfather, the consul of 112 (*b.G.* i. 12. 7). Cicero himself claims that he refrains from prosecuting Piso in order to save Caesar anxiety (§ 82).

xvi

INTRODUCTION

at Caesar. But Cicero went too far, and in 54 was called to order; in the *pro Vatinio* and *pro Gabinio* he was forced to atone for his imprudence.

II. CLAUSULAE[1]

Cicero's prose (except in most letters) is formal and rhetorical, and has the intricacy and balance which in modern languages is expected only in poetry. In particular he writes rhythmically; in this he follows the Greek orators, especially late orators of the 'Asiatic' school, and some of his Roman predecessors. His rhythm is most pronounced in the clausulae, i.e. in the phrases which occur at the ends of cola (the major divisions of a sentence).[2] These clausulae tend to conform to a limited number of metrical patterns.

The following are the clausulae most often used by Cicero. The last syllable is common in every case. The rules for elision are the same as in verse.

    1 (Cretic-trochee). $- \cup - - \smile$ (*ĕssĕ vĭdĕātŭr* is a variation of this type).

    2 (Double-cretic). $- \cup - - \cup \smile$ ($- - - - \cup \circ$ is also frequent).

    3 (Double-trochee). $- \cup - \smile$ (often preceded by $- \cup -$ or $- - -$).

    4 (Cretic-iambus). $- \cup - \cup \smile$ (less frequent than the other three).

Cicero's method may be illustrated from §§ 1–2 of the *in Pisonem*. The ends of cola (as they appear to me) are marked

---

[1] This account gives only the most elementary facts. There are useful introductions by W. H. Shewring in the *Oxford Classical Dictionary*, pp. 738 ff., S. F. Bonner in M. Platnauer's *Fifty Years of Classical Scholarship* (Oxford, 1954), pp. 358 ff. Zielinski's *Clauselgesetz* (see below, p. xxxi) is an indispensable source, but his methods are too complicated and often misleading. H. D. Broadhead's *Latin Prose Rhythm* (Cambridge, 1922) discusses many important questions.

[2] Some authorities use the word clausula only of the cadence at the end of a sentence; I have found the above definition more convenient.

B   xvii

INTRODUCTION

with a vertical stroke. The rhythm of the clausula has only been marked where it belongs to one of the four main patterns mentioned above (sometimes we find a long syllable resolved into two short syllables). Sometimes a rhythmical phrase has been marked before a pause too slight to be regarded as the end of a colon.

Iamne vides, belua, iāmnĕ sēntīs | quae sit hominum querēlā frōntīs tŭāē. | Nemo queritur Syrum nescio quem de grege noviciorum factum ēssĕ cōnsŭlĕm. | Non enim nos color īstĕ sērvīlĭs, | nōn pĭlōsāē gĕnāē, | non dentes putridi deceperunt: | oculi supercilia frons voltus denique totus, qui sermo quidām tăcĭtūs mēntĭs ēst, | hic in frāūdem hŏmĭnēs īmpŭlĭt, | hic eos quibus eras ignotus decepit fefēllĭt īndūxĭt. | Pauci ista tua lutulenta vĭtĭă nōrāmŭs, | pauci tārdĭtātem īngĕnī, stuporem debilitatēmquĕ līnguāē. | Numquam erat audītă vōx īn fŏrō, | numquam periculūm fāctūm cōnsĭlī, | nullum nōn mŏdo īnlūstrĕ sed ne notūm quĭdēm fāctum aut militiae aut domi. | Obrepsisti ad honores errore hominum, commendatione fumosārum īmāgĭnŭm, | quarum simile habes nihil praetēr cŏlōrĕm. | Is mihi etiam glōrĭābātŭr | se omnis magistratus sine repulsa ādsĕcūtŭm? | Mihi ista licet de me vera cum gloria prāēdĭcārĕ; | omnis enim honores populus Romanus mihi ipsi non nōmĭnī dētŭlĭt. | Nam tu cum quāēstŏr ēs fāctŭs, | etiam qui tē nūmquăm vīdĕrānt | tamen illum honorem nomini māndābānt tŭō. | Aedīlĭs ēs fāctŭs: | Piso est a populo Romano factus, non īstĕ Pīsō. | Praetura item maioribŭs dēlāta ēst tŭīs: | noti erānt īllī mōrtŭī, | te vivum nondum nŏvĕrāt quīsquăm. | Me cum quaestorem in primis, aedilēm prĭōrēm, praetorem primum cunctis suffragiis populus Romanus faciebat, | homini ille honorem non generi, | moribus non maiōrĭbŭs mĕīs, | virtuti perspectae non auditae nobilitati dēfĕrēbăt. |

Sometimes opinions will differ about where the cola end;[1]

---

[1] See Cic. *orator*, 221–6, E. Fraenkel, *Nachr. Gött. Ges.* 1932, pp. 197 ff., ibid. 1933, pp. 319 ff., Broadhead, op. cit., pp. 10 ff.

INTRODUCTION

indeed, it may occasionally seem arbitrary to draw a precise distinction between cola and articuli (the smaller units of a sentence). The punctuation of modern texts is not a reliable guide. In the present edition I have not ventured to introduce the ancient system of colometry, though this ought some day to be attempted; so punctuation will often be found after short phrases in the middle of cola. Moreover, the ends of some cola cannot be indicated by punctuation without a risk of confusing some English readers; see for instance 4. 10 'ea condicione fortunae', 6. 7 'dubitatione iuravi', 9. 11 'nefariisque versato', 18. 24 'inops fuerit umquam', 28. 3 'religiosus et sanctus', 61. 21 'cognoris intelleges', 79. 26 'et virtutis putavit'.

The rhythm of the clausula often helps one to decide between variant readings. In the following passages, for instance, it is relevant, though not always the only or the most important factor. The rejected alternative is given in brackets. § 9 'Fufia eversa est (versa est)', § 9 'censura (severitas) sublata est', § 18 'auxilio fuissem (fuerim)', § 20 'crotala (cymbala) fugi', § 21 'urbis ipsa (ipsa urbis) lugerent', § 34 'consularibus (consularibusque) litteris', § 39 'iam mea (mea iam) refert', § 42 'in cibo et (et in) vino', § 52 'progredi (procedere) visa est', § 53 'quem ad modum ingressus es (venisti)', § 54 'sed quid ego numero (ego enumero)', § 61 'revocare possis (possis revocare)', § 62 'alteri mors peremit (praeripuit)', § 95 'poena permansit (remansit)'.

Again, in § 55 the rhythm entitles us to read 'defendendum reprendit', in § 71 'detrahi nil volo', in § 73 'versu reprendas', though the shortened forms *reprend-* and *nil* have no manuscript authority. Genitive singulars of nouns in *-ium* are given in the short form in this edition (*ingeni* not *ingenii*), usually against the manuscripts; prose rhythm is one of the factors that make it clear that this was the Republican pronunciation. Where an emendation gives a good clausula its attractiveness is increased (cf. § 2 'non nomini detulit'); where it destroys a good clausula it must be regarded with great suspicion (e.g.

INTRODUCTION

§ 80 'adiutorem C. Caesarem adiunxit', where Bake deleted *C. Caesarem*). Where a rare clausula is given by the manuscripts, one must be on the look-out for corruption; but a rare clausula by itself will not normally be a sufficient ground for rejecting the tradition. 'Hexameter-endings' ($-\cup\cup-\cup$), for instance, are notably uncommon in the clausula; but even they occasionally occur (cf. 70. 9 n., 73. 15 n., 82. 1 n.).

III. THE MANUSCRIPTS

The text of the *in Pisonem* has come down from antiquity in three channels. The principal manuscripts are of exceptional interest, and illustrate the transmission of the Latin classics at every important stage.

(1) The oldest manuscript (*P*) belonged to the ancient world. This was the Turin palimpsest A. II. 2, written in rustic capitals of the fifth century; it was a fine book containing at least ten speeches, and came perhaps from one of the great cities of northern Italy. In the seventh century it found its way to Bobbio, the famous Irish monastery founded in 614 by Columbanus on the Trebbia (near the north end of the Apennines). There the codex was broken up, and on top of the *in Pisonem* were superimposed St. Augustine's disputations with the Arian bishop Maximinus. *P* was removed to Turin in the seventeenth century, and in 1820 Amadeo Peyron, with the help of chemicals, deciphered the hidden text of Cicero.[1] *P*'s long history came to an end in 1904, when it was destroyed by fire, with other valuable MSS., in the Biblioteca Nazionale at Turin.

The parts of the *in Pisonem* discovered by Peyron were contained in 8 folios, with 2 columns of 21 lines. In ff. 5, 6, and 7 only the top 12 lines survived; hence there are four lacunae in each of these

[1] See A. Peyron, *Ciceronis orationum fragmenta inedita* (Stuttgardiae et Tubingae, 1824), C. Cipolla, *Codici Bobbiesi* (Milano, 1907).

xx

INTRODUCTION

folios. The layout was as follows (cf. A. C. Clark, *Descent of Manuscripts*, p. 140):

Perhaps ten folios missing, containing the lost opening of the speech as well as §§ 1–17.

f. 1. § 17 *-to enim . . .* § 20 *alia enim cau-*
f. 2. § 20 *-sa praestantissimi . . .* § 23 *aut te*
Four folios missing.
f. 3. § 33 *-rentur male . . .* § 36 *esse visam*
Four folios missing.
f. 4. § 47 *-am in quam . . .* § 50 *ille si non*
Four folios missing.
f. 5. § 61 *-terea mi Caesar . . .* § 63 *iam vides quo-* (with lacunae[1])
f. 6. § 64 *num etiam . . .* § 66 *nolite* (with lacunae)
Three folios missing.
f. 7. § 75 *quorum quidem . . .* § 79 *ego C.* (with lacunae)
f. 8. § 79 *-vit non sum . . .* § 82 *montes rese-*
Seven folios missing.

For facsimiles see Peyron, op. cit., Cipolla, op. cit., tav. ii. 2, E. Chatelain, *Paléographie*, pl. xxix. 2, E. A. Lowe, *Cod. Lat. Ant.* iv. 442 (who also gives a description and bibliography). *P*'s readings are quoted by Peyron, op. cit.; important corrections are added by E. Ströbel, *Blätter f. d. bayerische Gym.* xxv, 1889, 381 ff., *Festschrift zum 150 jähr. Bestehen der Universität Erlangen* (Nürnberg, 1893), pp. 28 ff., *Philol.* lxx, 1911, 442 ff.

(2) The chief representative of the second branch of the tradition is *V*, i.e. cod. H. 25 in the Archive of St. Peter's (in the Vatican Library). This unusual manuscript was written in the ninth century during the Carolingian renaissance, and is the oldest extant manuscript of Cicero apart from palimpsests. It contains three columns to the page; this feature is most unexpected at this date, and suggests that *V* was copied from an ancient original. The part containing the *in Pisonem* is written in uncials, another striking sign of archaism; apparently the writer wished to add dignity to his manuscript by imitating the script of his exemplar. However, the other speeches in the book are written more normally in Caroline

[1] See the apparatus criticus.

xxi

INTRODUCTION

minuscules, though the writer of both parts may have been the same. *V* belonged to Cardinal Giordano Orsini (died 1439), whose arms are on f. 1; it was used by Poggio in 1428, evidently soon after its discovery.[1]

At the beginning of *V* 8 folios have been lost (p. 51). Ff. 1–8ᵛ contain *Pis.* § 32 *tamen misericordia* . . . § 74 *oratione hoc*. Then 32 folios have been lost. The rest of the MS. contains parts of *pro Flacco* and *pro Fonteio*, and almost all of the *Philippics*. For a facsimile of §§ 40–42, description, and bibliography, see Lowe, op. cit. i. 3; for a facsimile of §§ 43–44 see Chatelain, op. cit., pl. xxvi. Some details are given by A. C. Clark, *Descent of Manuscripts*, pp. 162 ff., and by Ströbel in the three articles cited above (p. xxi).

Extracts from the *in Pisonem* are contained in a florilegium (*C*) in cod. 52 (formerly C. 14 or 37) in the Hospital at Kues (opposite Bernkastel on the Mosel). This manuscript was written in the twelfth century; the florilegium appears to be the composition of Sedulius Scottus,[2] the Irish scholar and poet who worked at Liège in the middle of the ninth century. One of Sedulius's couplets reads 'cedite vos tenebrae, frontis nubecula cedat; dum iubar est praesens cedite vos tenebrae':[3] Traube[4] pointed out the reminiscence of *Pis.* 20 'frontis tuae nubeculam'. *C* belonged to Nicolaus Cusanus (1401–64), and was left by him to his hospital at Kues. The Ciceronian fragments were discovered by Theodor Oehler in 1843, but not published till 1866.[5]

C contains extracts from *in Pisonem*, *pro Flacco*, *pro Fonteio*, and *Philippics*, exactly the speeches which are found in *V*, and it normally reproduces *V*'s idiosyncratic readings. It

---

[1] Cf. R. Sabbadini, *Le scoperte dei codici latini e greci*, i. 127, ii. 212, A. C. Clark, *praefatio* to text, p. iii.

[2] See M. Manitius, *Geschichte der lat. Lit. des Mitt.* i. 315 ff., M. L. W. Laistner, *Thought and Letters in Western Europe* (London, 1957), pp. 251 ff., 315 ff., 347 ff.

[3] ii. 10. 3 f. (*Monum. Germ. Hist.* iii. 178).

[4] *O Roma nobilis*, *Abhand. Bayer. Akad.* xix. 2, 1891, 364 ff.

[5] When Oehler died, his brother refused to reveal the whereabouts of the MS.; cf. Halm ap. Orelli ii². i. 465.

xxii

INTRODUCTION

looks as if *V*, before its mutilation, was the actual MS. used by Sedulius. At *Pis*. 70 *C* agrees with *V* in reading *ut nihil* (*nihil ut* Ω, rightly); this crucial passage has been misreported.[1]

C has two columns to the page and about 70 lines to the column. The florilegium is contained in ff. 246–74ᵛ, the extracts from the *in Pisonem* in f. 261ʳ. For *C*'s contents and readings see J. Klein, *Über eine Handschrift des Nicolaus von Cues* (Berlin, 1866); for an important discussion see S. Hellmann, *Quellen und Untersuchungen zur lat. Phil. des Mitt.* i, heft 1, 1906, 92 ff.

(3) The third branch of the tradition includes all the other extant MSS. All have lost the same part at the opening of the speech, and are therefore derived from a common source, called Ω in this edition. They may be subdivided into a German family (whose common source is here called α) and an Italian family.

The most important member of the German family is *E*, a twelfth-century Berlin manuscript, lat. fol. 252, previously of Erfurt, at present to be found in the Universitätsbibliothek at Tübingen. This is the most comprehensive medieval manuscript of Cicero, and contains many speeches as well as some philosophical works and part of the *epistulae ad familiares*. We know that such a collection was made by Wibald, who was abbot of Corvey on the Weser from 1146 to 1158, and one of the most important men in the Germany of Conrad III and Frederick Barbarossa. He writes to the abbot of Hildesheim, 'nec . . . pati possumus quod illud nobile ingenium [Cicero], illa splendida inventa, illa tanta rerum et verborum ornamenta oblivione et negligentia depereant; set ipsius opera universa, quantacumque inveniri poterunt, in unum volumen confici volumus'.[2] The frontispiece of *E* shows three saints, Vitus, Stephen, and Justin; at their feet a cleric is handing over

---

[1] Note however *Pis*. 57 *animis V*: *animi C*Ω, rightly.
[2] Ph. Jaffé, *Bibl. rer. Germ.* i. 327.

xxiii

INTRODUCTION

a book; below Cicero is portrayed with the insignia of a consul. As St. Vitus was patron of Corvey the MS. evidently belonged to that abbey, and is presumably the very one mentioned by Wibald; the figure with the book may be Wibald himself.[1]

E has 203 folios and was even larger at one time; the *in Pisonem* is contained in ff. 125^r–32^r (the number 127 is repeated in error). For an account see especially P. Lehmann, op. cit., also E. Wunder, *Variae Lectiones* (Lipsiae, 1827); a complete lithographic facsimile of *pro Milone*, with a list of abbreviations, was published by W. Freund (Vratislaviae, 1838).

Also descended from α are two fifteenth-century German manuscripts. *e* = cod. Vaticanus Palatinus latinus 1525, written in 1467. As its name shows, it was part of the famous library transferred in 1623 from Heidelberg, the capital of the Palatinate, to the Vatican. *f* = cod. Erlangensis 618 (formerly 38 or 847). It also was written at Heidelberg, as appears from the note on the last page: 'comparatus est hic praesens liber per fratrem conradum haunolt in studio heydelbergensi pro VI quasi fl. vel ultra anno etc. LXVI°' (i.e. 1466). *e* and *f* are very close to each other. They mostly agree with *E*, but include a large number of mistakes and a few good readings not found in *E*.

The *in Pisonem* is contained in ff. 215^r–24^v (wrongly marked 234) of *e*, in ff. 51^r–63^v of *f*. For *e* see K. Halm, *Neue Jahrbücher für Phil.* Supp. xv, 1849, 165 ff.; for a facsimile from *pro Caecina* see Chatelain, op. cit., pl. xxv. For a description of *f* see *Katalog der Handschriften der Universitätsbibliothek Erlangen*, 1936, ii. 322 ff.; there is a short account in Pease's edition of *de natura deorum*, i. 73. I have not investigated the readings added by Pithou to a text of Cicero[2] at Heidelberg, many of which are reported to agree with *ef*; cf. C. Halm, *Zur Handschriftenkunde der Ciceronischen Schriften* (München, 1850), p. 22.

---

[1] P. Lehmann, *Corveyer Studien, Abhand. Bayer. Akad.* xxx, 1919, 5 Abh., 35.   [2] ed. Lambinus (Argentorati, 1581).

xxiv

INTRODUCTION

The *in Pisonem* is contained in a large number of fifteenth-century Italian MSS.; it has long been recognized that this family is derived from one of Poggio's most interesting discoveries. In 1417, in a tour of France and Germany, Poggio found eight speeches of Cicero which were unknown at that date: *pro Caecina, pro Roscio comoedo, de lege agraria* (three speeches), *pro Rabirio perduellionis reo, in Pisonem, pro Rabirio Postumo*.[1] Of these *pro Caecina* came from Langres, the others perhaps from Cologne cathedral; Niccoli writes 'in ecclesia cathedrali colonie sunt due bibliotece quarum Poggius noster vidit illam que est vulgatior, in qua repperiit quasdam Ciceronis orationes'.[2] Poggio made his own copy, to which he refers in various letters.[3] Unfortunately this copy disappeared from view, and scholars have had a complicated task in trying to reconstruct its readings from its numerous descendants.

Professor A. Campana has now rediscovered Poggio's autograph manuscript in the Vatican Library (cod. Vaticanus lat. 11458, called X in the present edition).[4] With extreme generosity he has allowed me to quote its readings, which are hitherto unpublished; he himself intends to give a full account in due course. At the end of the *in Pisonem* X has the following colophon (which is already known from other MSS., including cod. Laurent. Conv. Soppr. 13): 'Has septem M. tullii orationes, que antea culpa temporum apud italos deperdite erant, Poggius florentinus, perquisitis plurimis gallie germanieque biblyotheci summo cum studio ac diligentia biblyothecis, cum latentes comperisset in squalore et sordibus in lucem solus extulit, ac in pristinam dignitatem decoremque restituens latinis musis dicavit.'

[1] E. Walser, *Poggio Florentinus* (Leipzig–Berlin, 1914), pp. 58 f., A. C. Clark, *Inventa Italorum* (Anecdota Oxoniensia, Oxford, 1909).
[2] Walser, op. cit., p. 58, n. 2.
[3] A. C. Clark, *praefatio* to text, p. v.
[4] See the catalogue of *Codices Vaticani Latini*, recens. J. Ruysschaert, 1959, pp. 93 ff.

xxv

INTRODUCTION

Professor Campana's important discovery will greatly simplify the textual criticism of this group of speeches, as Poggio's readings no longer have to be reconstructed from those of later MSS. It also transpires that some readings of the Italian family, hitherto accepted as part of the tradition, are in fact marginal or interlinear additions in X; see for instance § 16 *mentes* αX: *manes* X (*marg.*); § 46 *veniret* $V\alpha X$: *venerat* X^2. At other places plausible emendations are made by X^2 which have hitherto been attributed to other MSS.

The symbol ς is used in the apparatus to describe interesting readings found in fifteenth-century MSS. which are not found in V, E, e, f, X, or Asconius. I have made no attempt to trace the affiliations of the *recentiores*; but it seems likely that these readings are due to emendation.

A complicating factor is the MS. found in 1426 at Cologne by Nicolaus Cusanus.[1] Clark[2] traced its influence in some Italian MSS. which mainly follow X, but have important readings not found in X. These readings for the most part agree with the α family, to which Nicolaus's MS. must have been related; others seem to have been interpolated from V or Asconius. The rest may be emendations; to this category belong § 14 *caesoninus*, § 20 *epicuro*, § 29 *tu te*, § 74 *intelligi*, § 79 *cur ego*, § 80 *sibi aliquando*, § 81 *imperium*, § 82 *infirmo*, § 87 *esse*. Admittedly the reading in § 79 seems very good for an emendation, but it has not yet been proved that this group of MSS. contains any good tradition that cannot be found elsewhere.

The text of Asconius is the only source for some of the fragments of the *in Pisonem*. The lost Sangallensis, discovered by Poggio in 1416, is represented by three descendants, copied from it immediately or at one remove. S = cod. Pistoriensis, Forteguerri 37, written by Zomino (Sozomeno). P = cod. Matritensis X. 81, written by Poggio. M = cod.

---

[1] R. Sabbadini, *Scoperte*, i. 109 ff.
[2] *Inventa Italorum*, pp. 23 ff.

xxvi

INTRODUCTION

Laurentianus LIV. 5, copied by a scribe from the apograph of Bartolomeo da Montepulciano.

S is the most reliable of the three; *P* has been emended and supplemented by Poggio; *M* is unreliable, and includes some of Poggio's interpolations found in *P*. The consensus of *SP* or *SM* is a good guide to the reading of the Sangallensis; the consensus of *PM* is not authoritative in the same way.[1] Lacunae of approximately the right size are left in the three MSS. where there were holes or damaged patches in the Sangallensis. It is particularly difficult to supplement these lacunae as the Sangallensis sometimes left gaps between words and sometimes did not.[2]

Of the three main sources for the text none is free from mistakes, though *P* and *V* have fewer than Ω.[3] *C* has many absurd mistakes, few of which are recorded in this edition; it is only of real importance where no other manuscript is available. Readings found in *PV* or *P*Ω or *V*Ω were probably widely diffused in the ancient world, but though they have a *prima facie* plausibility they are not necessarily right. For instance *P*Ω are probably wrong at § 21 *his*, § 48 *praesidium tu populi Romani*, § 50 *aut senatus*, § 65 *maioribus suis*, *V*Ω at § 33 *tempus profectionis*, § 39 *tabulas*, § 44 *absens*, § 53 *referri, adventus tuus, venisti*, § 57 *levis*, § 65 *paratissimi*, § 67 *solio*; *PV*Ω all seem to be wrong at § 64 *desperatissimo*.

I have collated *VCEefX* from the original manuscripts or from microfilms; reports of *P* are derived from Peyron and Ströbel, of Asconius from Stangl's edition. Most of the readings marked ς are given by Clark or by Ströbel, op. cit. (1893), pp. 37 ff. The apparatus criticus does not aim at completeness; not only are peculiarities of spelling omitted, but also some other trivial variants which cause no doubt about the true reading.

Certain other readings have been excluded, as they can be

[1] T. Stangl, *Philol.* lxix, 1910, 490, C. Giarratano's edition (Roma, 1920), p. xvi.

[2] Cf. Kiessling–Schoell's edition, p. xxii.

[3] Note the glosses in Ω (or α) which have been incorporated in the text.

xxvii

INTRODUCTION

eliminated from the tradition.[1] The relationship of Ω's descendants may be set out as follows:

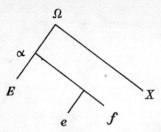

The readings of α are deduced from the agreement of *Eef*, *Ee*, or *Ef*; where *e* disagrees with *Ef* or *f* with *Ee* the discrepancy is not usually recorded in the apparatus. The readings of Ω are deduced from the agreement of *EX*; variants found only in *e* or *f* or *ef* are ignored unless where they are of exceptional interest.[2] In theory one might also derive Ω from the consensus of *efX*, but it has seemed unwise to obscure the readings of *E*;[3] therefore the symbol Ω is only used where *E* and *X* give the same reading. But a number of variants in *E* which have no plausibility in themselves, and are contradicted by *efX*, have been omitted. Where *P* or *V* agrees with *X* against α it is clear that Ω must have agreed with *X* rather than with α; in such cases a textual note has not normally been included. In the same way when *P* or *V* agrees with α against *X*, *X* loses its authority, but in this case it has seemed desirable to give fuller reports.

In general the method of the 'negative apparatus' has been adopted; that is to say, at 51. 22 the note 'concursum Ω' implies

[1] Cf. P. Maas, *Textual Criticism* (Oxford, 1958), pp. 5 ff.

[2] For good readings in *ef* not found in *EX* see 8. 2, 34. 14, 61. 14. These are not of such a kind as to rule out the stemma offered here.

[3] There is a risk that *e* and *f* may be derived from more than one source, as they are in other speeches (cf. A. Klotz, *Rh. Mus.* lxviii, 1913, 503, *praefatio* to Teubner text vol. vii, pp. xxix ff.). Note *Pis.* 18 *potestatis tuae crudelitatis PE*: *crudelitatis tuae potestatis efX*; the former is certainly right.

INTRODUCTION

that *concursus*, the reading in the text, is in *V*. But in all places where a textual note is given *P* and *C*, if available, are explicitly cited; their readings never have to be inferred from the silence of the apparatus.

IV. BIBLIOGRAPHY

ABRAM, N. Commentarius in tertium volumen orationum Ciceronis. Lutet. Paris., 1631.

ACCAME, S. Il Dominio romano in Grecia dalla guerra acaica ad Augusto. Roma, 1946.

AUSTIN, R. G. M. Tulli Ciceronis pro M. Caelio oratio. 3rd edition. Oxford, 1960.

BAKE, J. *Mnemosyne* ix, 1860, 211 ff.

—— Scholica hypomnemata, iv. 298 ff. Leyden, 1852.

BLOCH, H. L. Calpurnius Piso Caesoninus in Samothrace and Herculaneum (*American Journal of Archaeology*, xliv, 1940, 485 ff.).

BOTSFORD, G. W. The Roman Assemblies. New York, 1909.

BROUGHTON, T. R. S. The Magistrates of the Roman Republic, vol. ii. New York, 1952.

BUTLER, H. E., and CARY, M. M. Tulli Ciceronis de provinciis consularibus oratio ad senatum. Oxford, 1924.

CAMMELLI, E. M. Tullio Cicerone, L'Orazione 'In L. Calpurnium Pisonem'. Milano. (Elementary commentary.)

CLARK, A. C. M. Tulli Ciceronis orationes, vol. iv. Oxonii, 1909.

DELACY, P. Cicero's Invective against Piso (*Transactions of American Philological Association*, lxxii, 1941, 49 ff.).

DRUMANN, W., and GROEBE, P. Geschichte Roms. 2nd edition. Leipzig, 1899–1929.

ERNESTI, J. A. Ciceronis opera. Halis Saxonum, 1774–7.

FRANCKEN, C. M. *Mnemosyne* N.S. xii, 1884, 62 ff.

GARATONI, G. Ciceronis opera xi. Neapoli, 1788. (Variorum edition, mainly as in Graevius.)

GELZER, M. M. Tullius Cicero. *RE* viiA. 827 ff.

GRAEVIUS, J. G. Ciceronis orationes III. i. Amstelodami, 1699. (Variorum edition including useful material, notably from Abram.)

GREENIDGE, A. H. J. The Legal Procedure of Cicero's Time. Oxford, 1901.

xxix

INTRODUCTION

HAND, F. Tursellinus. 4 vols. Lipsiae, 1829–45. [Hand.]

HANDFORD, S. A. The Latin Subjunctive. London, 1947.

HOFMANN, J. B. Lateinische Umgangssprache. 3rd edition. Heidelberg, 1951.

KLOTZ, A. M. Tulli Ciceronis scripta, fasc. 24. Lipsiae, 1916 (for praefatio see vol. vii, 1919).

KÜHNER, R., and STEGMANN, C. Ausführliche Grammatik der lateinischen Sprache: Satzlehre. 2 vols. 2nd edition. Hannover, 1912–14. (Or 3rd edition. Leverkusen, 1955.) [K.–S.]

LANDGRAF, G. Kommentar zu Ciceros Rede pro Sex. Roscio Amerino. 2nd edition. Leipzig, 1914.

LEBRETON, J. Études sur la langue et la grammaire de Cicéron. Paris, 1901. [Lebreton.]

LEUMANN, M., and HOFMANN, J. B. Lateinische Grammatik (5th edition of Stolz–Schmalz). München, 1928. [L.–H.]

LÖFSTEDT, E. Syntactica. Lund: Teil i², 1942; Teil ii, 1933.

MADVIG, J. N. Adversaria critica. 3 vols. Hauniae, 1871–84.

—— Opuscula academica. 2nd edition. Hauniae, 1887.

MALCOVATI, H. Oratorum Romanorum fragmenta. 2nd edition. Torino, 1955.

MARQUARDT, J. Das Privatleben der Römer. 2nd edition by A. Mau. Leipzig, 1886.

—— Römische Staatsverwaltung. 3 vols. 2nd edition. Leipzig, 1881–5. [*St.-V.*]

MAY, J. Kritische Bemerkungen zu den Reden des Demosthenes nebst einem Anhang über Ciceros Rede in Pisonem. Durlach, 1914. (Inaccessible to me.)

MERGUET, H. Lexikon zu den Reden des Cicero. 4 vols. Jena, 1877–84. Lexikon zu den philosophischen Schriften des Cicero. 3 vols. 1887–94.

MOMMSEN, Th. Römisches Staatsrecht. 3 vols. (i and ii, 3rd edition). Leipzig, 1887–8. [*St.-R.*]

MÜLLER, C. F. W. Ciceronis opera II. iii. Lipsiae, 1893.

MÜNZER, F. L. Calpurnius Piso. *RE* iii. 1387 ff.

NÄGELSBACH, K. F. Lateinische Stilistik. 9th edition. Nürnberg, 1905. [Nägelsbach.]

NISBET, R. G. M. Tulli Ciceronis de domo sua ad pontifices oratio. Oxford, 1939.

ORELLI, J. C. Ciceronis orationes II. ii. Turici, 1826. 2nd edition (ed. C. Halm) Turici, 1856.

xxx

INTRODUCTION

OTTO, A. Die Sprichwörter und sprichwörtlichen Redensarten der Römer. Leipzig, 1890. [Otto.]

PARZINGER, P. Beiträge zur Kenntnis der Entwicklung des Ciceronischen Stils. Landshut, 1911–12.

PEASE, A. S. M. Tulli Ciceronis de natura deorum, vol. i. Cambridge, Mass., 1955.

PLUYGERS, W. G. *Mnemosyne* x, 1861, 106 ff.

ROSTOVTZEFF, M. The Social and Economic History of the Hellenistic World. Oxford, 1941.

SEYFFERT, M. Scholae Latinae. 3rd edition. Leipzig, 1870–2.

—— and MÜLLER, C. F. W. M. Tullii Ciceronis Laelius. 2nd edition. Leipzig, 1876.

SYME, R. The Roman Revolution. Oxford, 1939.

VOLKMANN, R. Die Rhetorik der Griechen und Römer. 2nd edition. Leipzig, 1885. [Volkmann.]

WATTS, N. H. Cicero, the speeches, with an English translation: pro Milone, in Pisonem, etc. (Loeb). London, 1931. (Inaccurate.)

WERNER, E. Stilistische Untersuchungen zur Pisoniana. Leipzig, 1933.

WUILLEUMIER, P. Cicéron, discours, tome xiii. Au sénat, au peuple, sur sa maison (Budé). Paris, 1952.

WUNDER, E. Variae lectiones. Lipsiae, 1827.

ZIELINSKI, T. Das Clauselgesetz in Ciceros Reden. Leipzig, 1904 (= *Philologus*, Supp.–Bd. ix, 1904, 589 ff.).

This bibliography makes no attempt at completeness. Most abbreviations follow the system of *L'Année philologique*; note also the following.

ALL	Archiv für lateinische Lexicographie.
D.–S.	Daremberg–Saglio, *Dictionnaire des antiquités.*
K.–S.	Kühner–Stegmann.
L.–H.	Leumann–Hofmann.
RE	Pauly–Wissowa, *Realencyclopädie.*
St.-R.	Mommsen, *Staatsrecht.*
Thes. L. L.	*Thesaurus Linguae Latinae.*

SIGLA

P = palimpsestum Taurinense A. II. 2, saecl. v, nunc deperditum (continebat fere §§ 17–23, 33–36, 47–50, 61–66, 75–82)

V = cod. tabularii Basilicae Vaticanae H. 25, saecl. ix (continet §§ 32–74)

C = excerpta Sedulii Scotti, servata in codice Cusano 52, saecl. xii

Ω = fons communis codd. α et X

α = fons communis codd. E et ef

E = Berolinensis (olim Erfurtensis) lat. fol. 252, saecl. xii

e = Vaticanus Palat. lat. 1525, saecl. xv

f = Erlangensis 618, saecl. xv

X = Vaticanus lat. 11458, saecl. xv

P^2, V^2 et similia manum correctricem indicant

ς = codicum deteriorum coniecturae

Asconii cod. S = Pistoriensis, Forteguerri 37

cod. P = Matritensis X. 81

cod. M = Laurentianus LIV. 5

M. TVLLI CICERONIS
IN L. CALPVRNIVM PISONEM ORATIO

FRAGMENTA

i (= Cl. 1, Kl. 1). Pro di inmortales! qui hic inluxit dies, mihi quidem, patres conscripti, peroptatus, ut hoc portentum huius loci, monstrum urbis, prodigium civitatis viderem!

ii (= Cl. 2, Kl. 2). Equidem nihil malui: vos fortasse consumptum istum cruciatu aut demersum fluctibus audire malletis.

iii (= Cl. 19). Quid quod miser, cum loqui non posset, tacere non potuit?

iv (= Cl. 3, Kl. 3). Perturbatio istum mentis et quaedam scelerum offusa caligo et ardentes Furiarum faces excitaverunt.

v (= Cl. 4, Kl. 4). Quem enim iste in scopulum non incidit, quod in telum non inruit?

vi (= Cl. 5, Kl. 5). Quid est negare ausus, aut potius quid non confessus?

vii (= Cl. 6, Kl. 6). Quid enim illo inertius, quid sordidius, quid nequius, quid enervatius, quid stultius, quid abstrusius?

viii (= Cl. 8, Kl. 12). Quod minimum specimen in te ingeni? Ingeni autem? immo ingenui hominis ac liberi? qui

---

Frag. i pro . . . dies *Quintilianus* ix. 4. 76, *Charisius, GL* i. 235 (= *p*. 305 *Barwick*), *Diomedes, GL* i. 468, *Sacerdos, GL* vi. 447 *frag.* iii *Quintilianus* viii. 5. 18; qui cum loqui . . . potuit *Gellius* i. 15. 16; Pisoniano vitio cum loqui nesciret tacere non potuit *Hieronymus, epist.* 69. 2. 5 *frag.* iv *Quintilianus* ix. 3. 47 *frag.* viii *Asconius*

C (*frag.* i, ii, iv, v, vi, vii)] 8 potuit *Gell.*: poterat *Quint.* 10 excitaverunt *C, Quint.*: -tarunt *Quint.* (*var. lect.*)

M. TVLLI CICERONIS

colore ipso patriam aspernaris, oratione genus, moribus nomen.

ix (= Cl. 11, Kl. 15). Insuber quidam fuit, idem mercator et praeco. Is cum Romam cum filia venisset, adulescentem nobilem, Caesonini hominis furacissimi filium, ausus est appellare * * * homini levi et subito filiam conlocavit. * * * Calventium aiunt eum appellatum.

x (= Cl. 9, Kl. 13). Hoc non ad contemnendam Placentiam pertinet, unde se is ortum gloriari solet; neque enim hoc mea natura fert, nec municipi, praesertim de me optime meriti, dignitas patitur.

xi (= Cl. 10, Kl. 14). Hic cum †adom . . . . Placentiae forte consedit, et pauci⟨s post annis⟩ in eam civitatem—nam tum erat . . . .—ascendit. Prius enim Gallus, dein Gallica⟨nus fuit, ad⟩ extremum Placentinus haberi . . . . est.

xii (= Cl. 7, Kl. 7). Turbulenti seditiosi factiosi perniciosi.

xiii (= Cl. 13, Kl. 16). Lautiorem . . . . pater tuus socerum quam C. Piso . . . . †in illo luctu . . . . . . †Non enim† filiam meam conlocavi, quem ego ⟨si mihi⟩ potestas tum omnium fuisset, unum potissimum delegissem.

xiv (= Cl. 14, Kl. 9). Te tua illa nescio quibus a terris apportata mater pecudem ex alvo, non hominem effuderit.

---

frag. ix (*om.* homini . . . subito) *Asconius*; homini . . . conlocavit *Arusianus, GL* vii. 462   *frag.* x *et* xi *et* xiii *Asconius*   *frag.* xiv quae te

---

C(*frag.* xii, xiii unum . . . delegissem, xiv)]   3 Insuber *ed. Ven.*: intuber *Asc.*   4 filia *Manutius*: filio *Asc.*   5 Caesonini *Mommsen*: -oniani *Asc.*   6 subito *Arus.*: subdolo *Watt*   7 Calventium *ed. Ald.*: -tinum *Asc.*   12 adom . . . . (*lac.* 6 *litt. cod. M*) *Asc.*: advena *Stangl*   forte *Manutius*: foret *Asc.*   13 consedit et *Asc.*: consedisset *Manutius*   paucis post annis *Manutius*: pauci . . . . *Asc.*   14 erat peregrinus *Mommsen*   Gallicanus fuit *Kiessling–Schoell*: gallica . . . . . . *Asc. cod.* S (*lac.* 4 *litt.* P, *sine lac.* M)   15 ad extremum *Kiessling–Schoell*: extremus *Asc.*   *lac.* 9 *litt. Asc. codd.* PM, 12 *litt.* S: coeptus *Beraldus*   17 *lac.* 7 *litt. Asc. codd.* PM, *sine lac.* S   18 *post* Piso *lac.* 10 *litt. Asc. codd.* SM, 12 *litt.* P   *post* luctu *lac.* 6 *litt. Asc. cod.* P, *sine lac.* SM   non enim *Asc. codd.* SM, non ei P: nam ei *Ernesti*   19 collocavi *ed. Ven.*: colloca . . . *Asc. cod.* S (*sine lac.* PM)   si mihi *Rau*: *lac.* 9 *litt. Asc. cod.* S, 7 *litt.* PM: licet mihi *Mommsen*

2

IN L. PISONEM ORATIO

xv (= Cl. 12, Kl. 18). Maiorem sibi Insuber ille avus adoptavit.

xvi (= Cl. 15, Kl. 17). Cum tibi tota cognatio serraco advehatur.

5 **xvii** (= Cl. 16, Kl. 10). Simulata ista ficta fucata sunt omnia.

xviii (= Cl. 17, Kl. 11). Putavi austerum hominem, putavi tristem, putavi gravem; sed video adulterum, video ganeonem, video parietum praesidio, video amicorum sordibus, video 10 * * tenebris occultantem libidines suas.

xix (= Kl. 19). †Prope me est†.

[**xx**. Non me debes lacerare, quia non ego te in exilium misi, sed Caesar et Pompeius.]

[**xxi** (= Cl. 18). Neque adsidere Gabinium aut adloqui in 15 curia quisquam audebat.]

———————

Iamne vides, belua, iamne sentis quae sit hominum querela **1** frontis tuae? Nemo queritur Syrum nescio quem de grege **1** noviciorum factum esse consulem. Non enim nos color iste servilis, non pilosae genae, non dentes putridi deceperunt: 20 oculi supercilia frons voltus denique totus, qui sermo quidam tacitus mentis est, hic in fraudem homines impulit, hic eos quibus eras ignotus decepit fefellit induxit. Pauci ista tua lutulenta vitia noramus, pauci tarditatem ingeni, stuporem

———————

beluam ex utero non hominem fudit *Servius, Aen.* viii. 139   *frag.* xv *Arusianus, GL* vii. 496   *frag.* xvi *Quintilianus* viii. 3. 21   *frag.* xviii putavi gravem video . . . ganeonem *Grillius, Rhet. Lat. Min. p.* 599 *frag.* xix *Diomedes, GL* i. 410   *frag.* xx *Grillius, ed. Martin, p.* 72 *frag.* xxi *Arusianus, GL* vii. 452
16 iam vides . . . 17 tuae *Arusianus, GL* vii. 504   20 voltus . . . 22 induxit *Gellius* xiii. 25. 23

———————

C (frag. xvii, xviii, 16 iamne vid- . . . 17 tuae), Ω *(incip.* 16)]   10 noctis (lustrorum *Halm*) ten- *A. Klotz*   16 iam ne vides *C*: iam vides Ω, *Arus.*   hominum querela *CX, Arus.*: quer- hom- α   19 putidi *efX* 22 eras *var. Junt.*: erat Ω, *Gell.*

3

1 1] M. TVLLI CICERONIS

debilitatemque linguae. Numquam erat audita vox in foro, numquam periculum factum consili, nullum non modo inlustre sed ne notum quidem factum aut militiae aut domi. Obrepsisti ad honores errore hominum, commendatione fumosarum imaginum, quarum simile habes nihil praeter colorem. 5
2 Is mihi etiam gloriabatur se omnis magistratus sine repulsa adsecutum ? Mihi ista licet de me vera cum gloria praedicare; omnis enim honores populus Romanus mihi ipsi non nomini detulit. Nam tu cum quaestor es factus, etiam qui te numquam viderant tamen illum honorem nomini mandabant tuo. 10 Aedilis es factus: Piso est a populo Romano factus, non iste Piso. Praetura item maioribus delata est tuis: noti erant illi mortui, te vivum nondum noverat quisquam. Me cum quaestorem in primis, aedilem priorem, praetorem primum cunctis suffragiis populus Romanus faciebat, homini ille honorem non 15 generi, moribus non maioribus meis, virtuti perspectae non
3 auditae nobilitati deferebat. Nam quid ego de consulatu loquar, parto vis anne gesto ? Miserum me! cum hac me nunc peste atque labe confero ? Sed nihil comparandi causa loquar, ac tamen ea quae sunt longissime disiuncta comprendam. Tu 20 consul es renuntiatus—nihil dicam gravius quam quod omnes fatentur—impeditis rei publicae temporibus, dissidentibus consulibus [Caesare et Bibulo], cum hoc non recusares eis a quibus dicebare consul, quin te luce dignum non putarent, nisi nequior quam Gabinius exstitisses. Me cuncta Italia, me 25 omnes ordines, me universa civitas non prius tabella quam
2 voce priorem consulem declaravit. Sed omitto ut sit factus

---

14 praetorem me populus Romanus primum fecit, consulem priorem *Ausonius, grat. act.* 12. 58

Ω] 4 famosarum X 6 gloriabitur Ϛ: gloriatur Ϛ   8 non nomini *lib. Vrsini*: homini Ω: *del. Halm*   9 tu Ϛ: tum Ω   15 ille] illi α
16 perspectae Ϛ: perfectae Ω   20 ac tamen] attamen fX comprendam X^2: -pendam Ω   23 Caesare et Bibulo *del. Manutius* his α   24 luce dignum] dignum luce E

4

IN L. PISONEM ORATIO [2 3

uterque nostrum; sit sane Fors domina Campi. Magnificentius est dicere quem ad modum gesserimus consulatum quam quem ad modum ceperimus.

Ego Kalendis Ianuariis senatum et bonos omnis legis 4
5 agrariae maximarumque largitionum metu liberavi. Ego agrum Campanum, si dividi non oportuit, conservavi, si oportuit, melioribus auctoribus reservavi. Ego in C. Rabirio, perduellionis reo, xl annis ante me consulem interpositam senatus auctoritatem sustinui contra invidiam atque defendi.
10 Ego adulescentis bonos et fortis, sed usos ea condicione fortunae ut si essent magistratus adepti, rei publicae statum convolsuri viderentur, meis inimicitiis, nulla senatus mala gratia comitiorum ratione privavi. Ego Antonium conlegam cupi- 5
dum provinciae, multa in re publica molientem, patientia
15 atque obsequio meo mitigavi. Ego provinciam Galliam senatus auctoritate exercitu et pecunia instructam et ornatam, quam cum Antonio commutavi, quod ita existimabam tempora rei publicae ferre, in contione deposui, reclamante populo Romano. Ego L. Catilinam, caedem senatus, interitum urbis
20 non obscure sed palam molientem, egredi ex urbe iussi, ut a quo legibus non poteramus, moenibus tuti esse possemus. Ego tela extremo mense consulatus mei intenta iugulis civitatis de coniuratorum nefariis manibus extorsi. Ego faces iam accensas ad huius urbis incendium comprehendi protuli
25 exstinxi. Me Q. Catulus, princeps huius ordinis et auctor $\frac{3}{6}$
publici consili, frequentissimo senatu parentem patriae nominavit. Mihi hic vir clarissimus qui propter te sedet, L. Gellius,

---

1 M. Tullius dicit magnificentius esse dicere quemadmodum ⟨gesserit quam quemadmodum⟩ ceperit consulatum *historia Augusta* xxvii. 13. 4
7 ego . . . 9 defendi *Asconius*   27 propter te iuxta te: mihi hic vir . . . Gellius *Arusianus, GL* vii. 502   mihi Quintus Gellius qui propter te sedet et civicam coronam decrevit *adnot. super Lucanum* i. 358

Ω] 4 ego] ergo α   17 commutavi Ϛ: communicavi Ω   22 mense (s. decembri *add. in mg.*) X: mense decembri α   25 me Q.] meq. α
27 propter X, *Arus., adnot. super Luc.*: iuxta α   sedit X

5

3 6] M. TVLLI CICERONIS

his audientibus civicam coronam deberi a re publica dixit. Mihi togato senatus, non ut multis bene gesta, sed ut nemini conservata re publica, singulari genere supplicationis deorum immortalium templa patefecit. Ego cum in contione abiens magistratu dicere a tribuno pl. prohiberer quae constitueram, 5 cumque is mihi tantum modo ut iurarem permitteret, sine ulla dubitatione iuravi rem publicam atque hanc urbem mea unius 7 opera esse salvam. Mihi populus Romanus universus illa in contione non unius diei gratulationem sed aeternitatem immortalitatemque donavit, cum meum ius iurandum tale atque 10 tantum, iuratus ipse, una voce et consensu approbavit. Quo quidem tempore is meus domum fuit e foro reditus ut nemo, nisi qui mecum esset, civium esse in numero videretur. Atque ita est a me consulatus peractus ut nihil sine consilio senatus, nihil non approbante populo Romano egerim, ut semper in 15 rostris curiam, in senatu populum defenderim, ut multitudinem cum principibus, equestrem ordinem cum senatu coniunxerim.

4
8 Exposui breviter consulatum meum: aude nunc, o furia, de tuo dicere! Cuius fuit initium ludi compitalicii tum primum 20 facti post L. Iulium et C. Marcium consules, contra auctoritatem huius ordinis; quos Q. Metellus—facio iniuriam fortissimo viro mortuo, qui illum cuius paucos paris haec civitas tulit cum hac importuna belua conferam—sed ille designatus consul, cum quidam tribunus pl. suo auxilio magistros ludos 25 contra senatus consultum facere iussisset, privatus fieri vetuit, atque id quod nondum potestate poterat obtinuit auctoritate.

---

4 ego ... 8 esse salvam *Asconius*   22 quos ... 26 vetuit *Asconius*

Ω] 1 civicam] de quercu civi eam α   2 gesta ... conservata r.p. X^2: gestae ... conservatae r.p. Ω   5 dicere a tr. pl. Ω, *Asc. cod. S*: a tr. pl. dicere *Asc. cod. P*   quae Ω, *Asc. cod. S*: eaque *Asc. codd. PM* 6 cumque] cum *Asc.*   ut iurarem] iurare *Asc.*   10 tale] tacite α 21 Iulium *Turnebus* (*cf. Asc.*): luscellum Ω   Marcium *f*: marium Ω 22 Q.] quae (*vel* que) α, *Asc.*   Metellus] fieri vetuit add. *Asc.*   24 designatos consules (cons *ef*) α   25 magistros] magis *Asc. cod. S*: magnos *Asc. codd. PM, Xmg*.

6

IN L. PISONEM ORATIO [4 8

Tu cum in Kalendas Ianuarias compitaliorum dies incidisset, Sex. Cloelium, qui numquam antea praetextatus fuisset, ludos facere et praetextatum volitare passus es, hominem impurum ac non modo facie sed etiam osculo tuo dignissimum. Ergo 9 his fundamentis positis consulatus tui, triduo post, inspectante et tacente te, a fatali portento prodigioque rei publicae lex Aelia et Fufia eversa est, propugnacula murique tranquillitatis atque oti; conlegia non ea solum quae senatus sustulerat restituta, sed innumerabilia quaedam nova ex omni faece urbis ac servitio concitata. Ab eodem homine in stupris inauditis nefariisque versato vetus illa magistra pudoris et modestiae censura sublata est, cum tu interim, bustum rei publicae, qui te consulem tum Romae dicis fuisse, verbo numquam significaris sententiam tuam tantis in naufragiis civitatis.

Nondum quae feceris, sed quae fieri passus sis dico. Neque $\genfrac{}{}{0pt}{}{5}{10}$ vero multum interest, praesertim in consule, utrum ipse perniciosis legibus, improbis contionibus rem publicam vexet, an alios vexare patiatur. An potest ulla esse excusatio, non dicam male sentienti, sed sedenti cunctanti dormienti in maximo rei publicae motu consuli? Centum prope annos legem Aeliam et Fufiam tenueramus, cccc iudicium notionemque censoriam. Quas leges ausus est non nemo improbus, potuit quidem nemo convellere, quam potestatem minuere, quo minus de moribus nostris quinto quoque anno iudicaretur, nemo tam effuse

1 tu . . . 3 passus *Asconius*   4 ergo . . . 12 sublata est (*om.* nova) *Asconius*   16 nihil interest utrum ipse consul improbis contionibus perniciosis legibus rem publicam . . . 18 patiatur *Martianus Capella* v. 497, *additamentum in nonnullis Cassiodori codicibus* (*cf. inst. ed. Mynors p.* 166)

Ω] 1 incidisset *Asc.*: -ent Ω 2 cloelium *ef, Asc. codd. PM*: clodium *EX, Asc. cod. S*   ante *Asc.*   4 ac] atque *X*   osculo *Luterbacher*: oculo Ω 5 triduo post *X, Asc.*: post triduo α 6 et tacente te] te et tacente *Asc.*   a *X, Asc.*: clodio a α 7 eversa *Asc.*: versa Ω 9 faece *X, Asc.*: face α 12 censura *Asc., Xmg.*: severitas Ω 15 sis *om. X*   16 vero *om. X*   21 notionem *Manutius*: rationem Ω 22 est α, *Xmg.*: esse *X*   24 quoquo *X*

7

5 10]   M. TVLLI CICERONIS

11 petulans conatus est, haec sunt, o carnifex, in prooemio
sepulta consulatus tui. Persequere continentis his funeribus
dies. Pro Aurelio tribunali, ne conivente quidem te (quod
ipsum esset scelus), sed etiam hilarioribus oculis quam solitus
eras intuente, dilectus servorum habebatur ab eo qui nihil 5
sibi umquam nec facere nec pati turpe [esse] duxit. Arma in
templo Castoris, o proditor templorum omnium, vidente te
constituebantur ab eo latrone cui templum illud fuit te consule
arx civium perditorum, receptaculum veterum Catilinae militum, castellum forensis latrocini, bustum legum omnium ac 10
religionum. Erat non solum domus mea sed totum Palatium
senatu, equitibus Romanis, civitate omni, Italia cuncta re-
fertum, cum tu non modo ad eum [Ciceronem]—mitto enim
domestica quae negari possunt, haec commemoro quae sunt
palam—non modo, inquam, ad eum cui primam comitiis tuis 15
dederas tabulam praerogativae, quem in senatu sententiam
rogabas tertium, numquam aspirasti, sed omnibus consiliis
quae ad me opprimendum parabantur non interfuisti solum
verum etiam crudelissime praefuisti.

6   Mihi vero ipsi coram genero meo, propinquo tuo, quae 20
12   dicere ausus es ? [Egere] foris esse Gabinium, sine provincia
stare non posse; spem habere a tribuno plebis, si sua consilia
cum illo coniunxisset, a senatu quidem desperasse; huius te
cupiditati obsequi, sicuti ego fecissem in conlega meo; nihil
esse quod praesidium consulum implorarem, sibi quemque 25
consulere oportere. Atque haec dicere vix audeo; vereor ne

---

2 persequere . . . 6 duxit *Asconius*   3 pro Aurelio tribunali
dilectus servorum habebatur *Arusianus, GL* vii. 501

Ω] 1 prooemio *Madvig*: gremio Ω   2 continentes *Asc.*: connexos
(conexus *E*) Ω   3 ne conveniente α: nec an veniente *Asc. archetypum*
5 habebatur Ω, *Arus., Asc. codd. PM*: -bantur ⸖, *Asc. cod. S*   eo *X*,
Asc.: eo clodio α   6 esse Ω: om. *Asc.*   duxit *X, Asc. cod. P*:
dixit α, *Asc. codd. SM*   13 Ciceronem *del. Wunder*   16 dederas]
desideras α   21 egere *del. A. Klotz*   22 plebis clodio antonio α
sua] tua *X²*   23 coniunxisset *Halm*: coniunxeris sed Ω

8

IN L. PISONEM ORATIO [6 12

qui sit qui istius insignem nequitiam frontis involutam integumentis nondum cernat; dicam tamen. Ipse certe agnoscet
et cum aliquo dolore flagitiorum suorum recordabitur. Memi- 13
nistine, caenum, cum ad te quinta fere hora cum C. Pisone
5 venissem, nescio quo e gurgustio te prodire involuto capite
soleatum, et cum isto ore foetido taeterrimam nobis popinam
inhalasses, excusatione te uti valetudinis, quod diceres vinu-
lentis te quibusdam medicaminibus solere curari? Quam nos
causam cum accepissemus—quid enim facere poteramus?—
10 paulisper stetimus in illo ganearum tuarum nidore atque fumo;
unde tu nos cum improbissime respondendo, tum turpissime
ructando eiecisti. Idem illo fere biduo productus in contionem 14
ab eo cui †sic equatum† praebebas consulatum tuum, cum
esses interrogatus quid sentires [eis] de consulatu meo, gravis
15 auctor, Calatinus credo aliquis aut Africanus aut Maximus,
et non Caesoninus Semiplacentinus Calventius, respondes
altero ad frontem sublato, altero ad mentum depresso supercilio, crudelitatem tibi non placere. Hic te ille homo dignis- 7
simus tuis laudibus conlaudavit. Crudelitatis tu, furcifer,
20 senatum consul in contione condemnas? non enim me qui
senatui parui; nam relatio illa salutaris et diligens fuerat
[bona] consulis, animadversio quidem et iudicium senatus.
Quae cum reprehendis, ostendis qualis tu, si ita forte accidisset, fueris illo tempore consul futurus: stipendio me hercule
25 et frumento Catilinam esse putasses iuvandum. Quid enim 15
interfuit inter Catilinam et eum cui tu senatus auctoritatem, salutem civitatis, totam rem publicam provinciae praemio vendidisti? Quae enim L. Catilinam conantem consul

---

3 meministine . . . 6 soleatum *Arusianus, GL* vii. 491

Ω] 4 te hora V *Arus.* 5 te e gurgustio prodire *Arus.* 7 in-
hiasses X 11 responderes X 12 ructando *Lambinus*: eruct- Ω
13 sic equatum] quasi addictum *Halm* (sic add- *Ernesti*): emancipatum
Kayser 14 eis *om.* $\mathcal{S}$ 16 caesoninus $\mathcal{S}$: cesonius Ω 18 ille
om. X 22 bona Ω: *del.* X^2: boni $\mathcal{S}$ 23 si ita] iusticia α
28 quae] qua α

9

7 15] M. TVLLI CICERONIS

prohibui, ea P. Clodium facientem consules adiuverunt. Voluit
ille senatum interficere, vos sustulistis; leges †incendere, vos
abrogastis; vi terrere patriam, [vos adiuvistis] quid est vobis
consulibus gestum sine armis? Incendere illa coniuratorum
manus voluit urbem, vos eius domum quem propter urbs 5
incensa non est. Ac ne illi quidem, si habuissent vestri
similem consulem, de urbis incendio cogitassent; non enim se
tectis privare voluerunt, sed his stantibus nullum domicilium
sceleri suo fore putaverunt. Caedem illi civium, vos servitutem
expetistis. Hic vos etiam crudeliores; huic enim populo ita 10
fuerat ante vos consules libertas insita ut emori potius quam
16 servire praestaret. Illud vero geminum consiliis Catilinae et
Lentuli, quod me domo mea expulistis, Cn. Pompeium
domum suam compulistis; neque enim me stante et manente
in urbis vigilia, neque resistente Cn. Pompeio, omnium 15
gentium victore, umquam se illi rem publicam delere posse
duxerunt. A me quidem etiam poenas expetistis quibus
coniuratorum manis mortuorum expiaretis; omne odium
inclusum nefariis sensibus impiorum in me profudistis.
Quorum ego furori nisi cessissem, in Catilinae busto vobis 20
ducibus mactatus essem. Quod autem maius indicium ex-
spectatis nihil inter vos et Catilinam interfuisse quam quod
eandem illam manum ex intermortuis Catilinae reliquiis
concitastis, quod omnis undique perditos conlegistis, quod
in me carcerem effudistis, quod coniuratos armastis, quod 25
eorum ferro ac furori meum corpus atque omnium bonorum
8 vitam obicere voluistis? Sed iam redeo ad praeclaram illam
17

12 illud . . . 13 expulistis *Arusianus, GL* vii. 477   21 quod . . . 22
interfuisse *Arusianus, GL* vii. 482

Ω]   2 incendere] exstinguere *Müller*: *alii alia*   3 vi terrere α:
interire *X*: interimere ς: vim inferre (patriae) *Kayser*   vos adiuvistis
del. Ernesti: vos adflixistis *Schütz*   7 consules *E*: coss *ef*   11
emori] ei mori *Halm*   16 illi] ille *E*   18 manes *Xmg.*: mentes Ω
19 inclusum in *Halm*   24 concitastis (-atis *E*) αX²: exc- X¹   26 ac
furori *om. X*

10

IN L. PISONEM ORATIO   [8 17

contionem tuam. Tu es ille cui crudelitas displicet? qui cum
senatus luctum ac dolorem suum vestis mutatione declaran-
dum censuisset, cum videres maerere rem publicam amplissimi ordinis luctu, o noster misericors, quid facis? Quod nulla
5 in barbaria quisquam tyrannus. Omitto enim illud, consulem
edicere ut senatus consulto ne obtemperetur, quo foedius nec
fieri nec cogitari quicquam potest; ad misericordiam redeo
eius cui nimis videtur senatus in conservanda patria fuisse
crudelis. Edicere est ausus cum illo suo pari, quem tamen 18
10 omnibus vitiis superare cupiebat, ut senatus contra quam ipse
censuisset ad vestitum rediret. Quis hoc fecit ulla in Scythia
tyrannus ut eos quos luctu adficeret lugere non sineret?
Maerorem relinquis, maeroris aufers insignia; eripis lacrimas
non consolando sed minando. Quod si vestem non publico
15 consilio patres conscripti sed privato officio aut misericordia
mutavissent, tamen id his non licere per interdicta potestatis
tuae crudelitatis erat non ferendae: cum vero id senatus frequens censuisset, et omnes ordines reliqui iam ante fecissent,
tu ex tenebricosa popina consul extractus, cum illa saltatrice
20 tonsa, senatum populi Romani occasum atque interitum rei
publicae lugere vetuisti. At quaerebat etiam paulo ante de 9
me quid suo mihi opus fuisset auxilio, cur non meis inimicis
meis copiis restitissem. Quasi vero non modo ego, qui multis
saepe auxilio fuissem, sed quisquam tam inops fuerit umquam
25 qui isto non modo propugnatore tutiorem se sed advocato aut
adstipulatore paratiorem fore putaret. Ego istius pecudis ac 19
putidae carnis consilio scilicet aut praesidio niti volebam, ab

19 tonsae compositae, ut Cicero 'cum saltatrice tonsa' *Servius auct.
georg.* iii. 21

P (*incip.* 5 -to enim), C (19 tu . . . popina abstractus), Ω]   1 qui *ed.
Ven.*: cui Ω   3 in amplissimi *Williams*   5 illud P^1 Ω: illum P^2
6 senatus $P\alpha$: senatus senatus X   obtemperetur P: obtemperet Ω
11 fecit $P\varsigma$: facit Ω   13 relinquis PX^2: non relinquis Ω   16 his
$P\alpha$: iis X   pot- tuae crud- PE: crud- tuae pot- *efX*   18 et omnes
P: om. Ω   19 extractus PΩ: abstractus C   24 fuissem] fuerim
P   27 putidae *PefX*: putridae E   niti volebam] volebam niti P

11

9 19]   M. TVLLI CICERONIS

hoc eiecto cadavere quicquam mihi aut opis aut ornamenti
expetebam? Consulem ego tum quaerebam, consulem inquam, non illum quidem quem in hoc maiali invenire non
possem, qui tantam rei publicae causam gravitate et consilio
suo tueretur, sed qui tamquam truncus atque stipes, si stetisset 5
modo, posset sustinere tamen titulum consulatus. Cum enim
esset omnis causa illa mea consularis et senatoria, auxilio mihi
opus fuerat et consulum et senatus; quorum alterum etiam ad
perniciem meam erat a vobis consulibus conversum, alterum
rei publicae penitus ereptum. Ac tamen si consilium exquiris 10
meum, neque ego cessissem et me ipsa suo complexu patria
tenuisset, si mihi cum illo bustuario gladiatore et tecum et cum
20 conlega tuo decertandum fuisset. Alia enim causa praestantissimi viri Q. Metelli fuit, quem ego civem meo iudicio cum
deorum immortalium laude coniungo; qui C. illi Mario, 15
fortissimo viro et consuli et sextum consuli, et eius invictis
legionibus, ne armis confligeret, cedendum esse duxit. Quod
mihi igitur certamen esset huius modi ? cum C. Mario scilicet
aut cum aliquo pari, an cum altero barbaro Epicuro, cum
altero Catilinae lanternario consule ? Neque hercule ego 20
supercilium tuum neque conlegae tui crotala fugi, neque tam
fui timidus ut qui in maximis turbinibus ac fluctibus rei
publicae navem gubernassem, salvamque in portu conlocas-

---

2 consulem, consulem, inquam, quaerebam quem in isto maiali invenire non poteram *Cassiodorus, inst.* ii. 3. 15 (*p.* 125 *Mynors*), *Isidorus,*
etym. ii. 30   16 inde Cicero de Mario sic ait 'sextum consul' *Augu-*
stinus, GL v. 517   22 ut qui ... 2 (*p.* 13) pertimescerem *Martianus*
Capella v. 512

P (*deerat* 18 esset ... Mar-), Ω]   2 quaerebam *P, Cassiod., Isid.*: re-
quir- Ω   3 maiali *P, Cassiod., Isid.*: animali Ω   8 consulum *E*:
coss *X*: cōs *ef*: consulis *P*   12 illo *PX*: clodio illo α   tecum *P*Ω:
non t- *X²*   13 gabinio collega *P*   14 Q.] quae *P*α   19 barbaro *P*Ω: barbato ϛ   epicuro ϛ: Epicureo *P*Ω   20 consule *P*: quod
α: quos *X*   hercule ego] ego hercule *P*   21 crotalia Ω: cinbala
(*vel* cymb-) *P, Xmg.*   22 in *P*α, *Mart.*: om.*X*   turbinibus *P*Ω:
tempestatibus *Mart.*

12

IN L. PISONEM ORATIO [9 20

sem, frontis tuae nubeculam aut conlegae tui contaminatum
spiritum pertimescerem. Alios ego vidi ventos, alias pro- 21
spexi animo procellas, aliis impendentibus tempestatibus non
cessi sed [his] unum me pro omnium salute obtuli. Itaque
5 discessu tum meo omnes illi nefarii gladii de manibus crude-
lissimis exciderunt, cum quidem tu, o vaecors et amens, cum
omnes boni abditi inclusique maererent, templa gemerent,
tecta urbis ipsa lugerent, complexus es funestum illud animal
ex nefariis stupris, ex civili cruore, ex omni scelerum impor-
10 tunitate et flagitiorum impuritate concretum, atque eodem in
templo, eodem et loci vestigio et temporis, arbitria non mei
solum sed patriae funeris abstulisti.

Quid ego illorum dierum epulas, quid laetitiam et gratu- **10**
lationem tuam, quid cum tuis sordidissimis gregibus intem- **22**
15 perantissimas perpotationes praedicem ? quis te illis diebus
sobrium, quis agentem aliquid quod esset libero dignum, quis
denique in publico vidit ? cum conlegae tui domus cantu et
cymbalis personaret, cumque ipse nudus in convivio saltaret;
in quo cum illum suum saltatorium versaret orbem, ne tum
20 quidem fortunae rotam pertimescebat: hic autem non tam concinnus helluo nec tam musicus iacebat in suorum Graecorum
foetore atque vino; quod quidem istius in illis rei publicae
luctibus quasi aliquod Lapitharum aut Centaurorum convivium ferebatur; in quo nemo potest dicere utrum iste plus

20 rotam fortunae *Tacitus, dial.* 23. 1

P (*deerat* 4 -um salute obtuli, 13 et gratulationem tu-, 22 -re . . .
quidem), *C* (20 hic autem in suorum . . . 22 fetore et caeno, 23 quasi . . .
24 ferebatur), Ω] 1 aut *P*: tum Ω: et *Mart.* 4 his *PX*: sic his α: bis
Mommsen: *del. Wunder*: *fort.* iis 6 o *PX*: *om.* α 8 urbis ipsa] ipsa
urbis *P⌒* fun- illud *P*: illud fun- Ω 9 omni *Pe*: omnium Ω
10 et flag- impuritate *Halm*: et flag- impunitate *X*: et flag- α: *om. P*
conceptum *P* 11 et loci] loci *P* 13 dierum *P*α: dicam *X* 14
intemperant- *P²*α: intemperat- *P¹X* 18 cumque] cum quidem *P*
19 illum suum *X*: suum (situm *E*) illum α: illum *P* ne tum quidem
hoc loco hab. P, post in quo Ω 21 suorum *PC*: suo Ω 22 atque
vino Ω, *vestigia in P exstabant*: et caeno *C* 23 aut *PC*Ω: ac *Garatoni*:
et *Sauppe* convivium *P*Ω: conv- esset *C*

13

10 22]　　M. TVLLI CICERONIS

23 biberit [an vomuerit] an effuderit. Tune etiam mentionem
facies consulatus tui, aut te fuisse Romae consulem dicere
audebis ? Quid ? tu in lictoribus, in toga [et] praetexta esse
consulatum putas ? quae ornamenta etiam in Sex. Cloelio te
consule esse voluisti. Huius tu Clodiani canis insignibus con- 5
sulatum declarari putas ? Animo consulem esse oportet,
consilio fide gravitate vigilantia cura, toto denique munere
consulatus omni officio tuendo, maximeque, id quod vis
nominis ipsa praescribit, rei publicae consulendo. An ego
consulem esse putem qui senatum esse in re publica non 10
putavit, et sine eo consilio consulem numerem sine quo Romae
ne reges quidem esse potuerunt ? Etenim illa iam omitto. Cum
servorum dilectus haberentur in foro, arma in templum Castoris luce [et] palam comportarentur, id autem templum sublato aditu revolsis gradibus a coniuratorum reliquiis atque a 15
Catilinae praevaricatore quondam, tum ultore, armis tene-
retur, cum equites Romani relegarentur, viri boni lapidibus
e foro pellerentur, senatui non solum iuvare rem publicam sed
ne lugere quidem liceret, cum civis is quem hic ordo ad-
sentiente Italia cunctisque gentibus conservatorem patriae 20
iudicarat nullo iudicio, nulla lege, nullo more servitio atque
armis pelleretur, non dicam auxilio vestro, quod vere licet
dicere, sed certe silentio : tum Romae fuisse consules quisquam
24 existimabit ? Qui latrones igitur, si quidem vos consules, qui
praedones, qui hostes, qui proditores, qui tyranni nomina- 25
11 buntur ? Magnum nomen est, magna species, magna dignitas,

---

6 consulem animo esse . . . 8 consulatus *Marius Victorinus, de defin.*
p. 25 *St.*　　　8 maximeque . . . 9 consulendo *ibid. p.* 15; rei p. consulendo *Arusianus, GL* vii. 460　　　14 id . . . 18 pellerentur *Asconius*

P (defic. post 2 aut te), *C* (21 nullo iud- . . . more servato), Ω]
1 an vomuerit *PX*: aut vom- α: *del. Wunder*　　tune *P*: tum α: tun *X*
2 tui *om. P*　　dicere α*X*²: *om. X*¹　　　3 in toga *Turnebus*: in toga et
Ω: et in toga *vel* et *Garatoni*　　4 Cloelio *Shackleton Bailey*: clodio Ω
8 tuendo . . . 9 an *om. X*　　13 haberetur *X*　　templo *X*　　14 et Ω:
om. ⌠　　15 adito *efX*　　reliquis *Asc.*　　17 releg- ⌠: relig- Ω

14

IN L. PISONEM ORATIO [11 24

magna maiestas consulis; non capiunt angustiae pectoris tui,
non recipit levitas ista; non egestas animi, non infirmitas
ingeni sustinet, non insolentia rerum secundarum tantam
personam, tam gravem, tam severam. Seplasia me hercule,
5 ut dici audiebam, te ut primum aspexit, Campanum consulem
repudiavit. Audierat Decios Magios et de Taurea illo Vibellio
aliquid acceperat; in quibus si moderatio illa quae in nostris
solet esse consulibus non fuit, at fuit pompa, fuit species, fuit
incessus saltem Seplasia dignus et Capua. Gabinium denique 25
10 si vidissent duumvirum vestri illi unguentarii, citius agno-
vissent. Erant illi compti capilli et madentes cincinnorum
fimbriae et fluentes purpurissataeque buccae, dignae Capua,
sed illa vetere; nam haec quidem quae nunc est splendidis-
simorum hominum, fortissimorum virorum, optimorum civi-
15 um mihique amicissimorum multitudine redundat. Quorum
Capuae te praetextatum nemo aspexit qui non gemeret de-
siderio mei, cuius consilio cum universam rem publicam, tum
illam ipsam urbem meminerant esse servatam. Me inaurata
statua donarant, me patronum unum asciverant, a me se
20 habere vitam fortunas liberos arbitrabantur, me et praesentem
contra latrocinium tuum suis decretis legatisque defenderant,
et absentem principe Cn. Pompeio referente et de corpore rei
publicae tuorum scelerum tela revellente revocarunt. An tum 26
eras consul cum in Palatio mea domus ardebat non casu aliquo
25 sed ignibus iniectis instigante te ? Ecquod in hac urbe maius
umquam incendium fuit cui non consul subvenerit ? At tu illo

4 Seplasia . . . 6 repudiavit *Asconius* (*om.* ut dici audiebam), *Festus*
458 *L* (= 340 *M*)   11 Cicero in Gabinium 'fibrae cincinnorum
madentes' *Servius auct. georg.* i. 120   18 me . . . 19 donarunt *Arusi-*
anus, GL vii. 463   19 a me habere . . . 20 arbitrabantur *ibid.* 477
25 ecquod . . . 2 (*p.* 16) sedebas *Asconius*

Ω] 3 secundarum] sclarium *E*   6 taureia *E*   vibellio *ef*: iubellio
X: in bello *E*   8 at fuit *om. E*   12 purpurissataeque *Halm*:
pulsataeque Ω: cerussataeque ϛ   14 hominum *om. E*   18 memi-
nerint α   19 donarunt α, *Arus.*   23 revocarant *Lambinus*
25 ecquod *Victorius*: et quod Ω, *Asc.*   26 subveniret *Asc.*

15

11 26] M. TVLLI CICERONIS

ipso tempore apud socrum tuam prope a meis aedibus, cuius
domum ad meam domum exhauriendam patefeceras, sedebas
non exstinctor sed auctor incendi, et ardentis faces furiis
12 Clodianis paene ipse consul ministrabas. An vero reliquo
tempore consulem te quisquam duxit, quisquam tibi paruit, 5
quisquam in curiam venienti adsurrexit, quisquam consulenti
respondendum putavit ? Numerandus est ille annus denique
in re publica, cum obmutuisset senatus, iudicia conticuissent,
maererent boni, vis latrocini vestri tota urbe volitaret, neque
civis unus ex civitate sed ipsa civitas tuo et Gabini sceleri 10
furorique cessisset ?
27 Ac ne tum quidem emersisti, lutulente caeso, ex miserrimis
naturae tuae sordibus, cum experrecta tandem virtus clarissimi viri celeriter et verum amicum et optime meritum civem
et suum pristinum morem requisivit, neque est ille vir passus 15
in ea re publica quam ipse decorarat atque auxerat diutius
vestrorum scelerum pestem morari; cum tamen ille qualiscum-
que est, qui est ab uno te improbitate victus, [Gabinius] conlegit ipse se vix, sed conlegit tamen, et contra suum Clodium
primum simulate, deinde non libenter, ad extremum tamen 20
pro Cn. Pompeio vere vehementerque pugnavit. Quo quidem
in spectaculo mira populi Romani aequitas erat: uter eorum
perisset, tamquam lanista in eius modi pari lucrum fieri
putabat, immortalem vero quaestum si uterque cecidisset.

---

4 an vero . . . 5 duxit, 6 quisquam in . . . 7 putavit *Marius Victorinus,
de defin. p.* 24 *St.*   12 ac . . . 13 sordibus *Donatus, eun.* 555; ac . . .
15 requisivit (*om.* clarissimi viri) *Asconius*

Ω] 1 prope. . . aedibus *om. Asc.*   cuius domum ad meam domum] cui
domum meam *Asc.*   5 duxit (*vel* duxerit) *Mar. Vict.:* dixit Ω   tibi
paruit Ϛ: disparuit Ω   6 ven- in cur- *Mar. Vict.*   12 ac α, *Asc.*:
at *X*: *variant Donat. codd.*   ceso Ω, *Asc. codd. PM, Donat.:* caesone
Asc. cod. S: Caesonine *Manutius*   ex Ω, *Donat.:* e *Asc.*   13 experrecta *Asc.:* experta Ω   18 Gabinius *del. Muretus*   21 vero
X   22 p.r. α: r.p. *X*

16

IN L. PISONEM ORATIO [12 28

Sed ille tamen agebat aliquid: tuebatur auctoritatem summi 28
viri. Erat ipse sceleratus, erat gladiator, cum scelerato tamen
et cum pari gladiatore pugnabat. Tu scilicet homo religiosus
et sanctus foedus quod meo sanguine in pactione provinciarum
5 iceras frangere noluisti; caverat enim sibi ille sororius adulter
ut si tibi provinciam, si exercitum, si pecuniam ereptam ex rei
publicae visceribus dedisset, omnium ut suorum scelerum
socium te adiutoremque praeberes. Itaque in illo tumultu
fracti fasces, ictus ipse, cotidie tela lapides fugae, deprehensus
10 denique cum ferro ad senatum is quem ad Cn. Pompeium
interimendum conlocatum fuisse constabat. Ecquis audivit **13**
non modo actionem aliquam aut relationem sed vocem omnino **29**
aut querelam tuam ? Consulem tu te fuisse putas, cuius in imperio qui rem publicam senatus auctoritate servarat, †idemque
15 in Italia, qui omnis omnium gentium partis tribus triumphis
devinxerat, is se in publico tuto statuit esse non posse ? An tum
eratis consules cum quacumque de re verbum facere coeperatis
aut referre ad senatum, cunctus ordo reclamabat, ostende-
batque nihil esse vos acturos, nisi prius de me rettulissetis ?
20 cum vos quamquam foedere obstricti tenebamini, tamen
cupere vos diceretis, sed lege impediri. Quae lex privatis 30
hominibus esse lex non videbatur, inusta per servos, incisa per
vim, imposita per latrocinium, sublato senatu, pulsis e foro
bonis omnibus, capta re publica, contra omnis leges nullo
25 scripta more, hanc qui se metuere dicerent consules non dicam
animi hominum, sed fasti ulli ferre possunt ? Nam si illam
legem non putabatis, quae erat contra omnis leges indemnati
civis atque integri capitis bonorumque tribunicia proscriptio,

21 quae . . . 22 videbatur *Quintilianus* ix. 3. 67

Ω] 5 iceras *Ascensius*: ieceras (icc- *f*) Ω   7 ut *om. X*   8 tumultu
om. α   9 ipsa α   11 ecquis *Manutius*: et quis Ω   13 tu Ϛ: tum Ω
14 idemque] is se *Manutius*: idem se *Mommsen*: *fort.* is quidem   22
inusta] iussa *Ernesti*   25 hos consules *E*

5993   D   17

13 30] M. TVLLI CICERONIS

ac tamen obstricti pactione tenebamini, quis vos non modo
consules sed liberos fuisse putet, quorum mens fuerit oppressa
praemio, lingua astricta mercede ? Sin illam vos soli legem
putabatis, quisquam vos consules tunc fuisse aut nunc esse
consularis putet, qui eius civitatis in qua in principum numero 5
voltis esse non leges, non instituta, non mores, non iura
31 noritis ? An cum proficiscebamini paludati in provincias vel
emptas vel ereptas, consules vos quisquam putavit ? Itaque,
credo, si minus frequentia sua vestrum egressum ornando
atque celebrando, at ominibus saltem bonis ut consules, non 10
tristissimis ut hostes aut proditores prosequebantur.

14 Tune etiam, immanissimum ac foedissimum monstrum,
ausus es meum discessum, illum testem sceleris et crudelitatis
tuae, ⟨in⟩ maledicti et contumeliae loco ponere ? Quo quidem
tempore cepi, patres conscripti, fructum immortalem vestri in 15
me et amoris et iudici; qui non admurmuratione sed voce et
clamore abiecti hominis ac semivivi furorem petulantiamque
32 fregistis. Tu luctum senatus, tu desiderium equestris ordinis,
tu squalorem Italiae, tu curiae taciturnitatem annuam, tu silen-
tium perpetuum iudiciorum ac fori, tu cetera illa in maledicti 20
loco pones quae meus discessus rei publicae volnera inflixit ?
Qui si calamitosissimus fuisset, tamen misericordia dignior
quam contumelia et cum gloria potius esse coniunctus quam
cum probro putaretur, atque ille dolor meus dumtaxat, vestrum quidem scelus ac dedecus haberetur. Cum vero—forsitan 25
hoc quod dicturus sum mirabile auditu esse videatur, sed certe
id dicam quod sentio—cum tantis a vobis, patres conscripti,
beneficiis adfectus sim tantisque honoribus, non modo illam
calamitatem esse non duco, sed si quid mihi potest a re publica

---

V (*incip.* 22 tamen), *C* (12 o imman- . . . monstrum, 18 tu luctus senatus
tu squalor icurie italiae tu), Ω]   1 ac *Wunder*: hac Ω   10 at] atque
α   ominibus *X*: omnibus α   11 prosequ- ϛ: persequ- Ω   14 in
suppl. Halm   16 adm- *X*: abm- α   17 ac] et *X*   semiviri ϛ
22 qui si ϛ: quasi Ω   24 *fort.* dolor dumtaxat meus   25 cum] tum
X   28 que *om.* Ω   29 dico *VE*¹

IN L. PISONEM ORATIO [14 32

esse seiunctum, quod vix potest, privatim ad meum nomen
augendum, optandam duco mihi fuisse illam expetendamque
fortunam. Atque ut tuum laetissimum diem cum tristissimo 33
meo conferam, utrum tandem bono viro et sapienti optabilius
5 putas sic exire e patria ut omnes sui cives salutem incolumi-
tatem reditum precentur, quod mihi accidit, an quod tibi pro-
ficiscenti evenit, ut omnes exsecrarentur, male precarentur,
unam tibi illam viam et perpetuam esse vellent ? Mihi me dius
fidius in tanto omnium mortalium odio, iusto praesertim et
10 debito, quaevis fuga quam ulla provincia esset optatior.

Sed perge porro. Nam si illud meum turbulentissimum 15
tempus tuo tranquillissimo praestat, quid conferam reliqua,
quae in te dedecoris plena fuerunt, in me dignitatis ? Me 34
Kalendis Ianuariis, qui dies post obitum occasumque [vestrum]
15 rei publicae primus inluxit, frequentissimus senatus, concursu
Italiae, referente clarissimo ac fortissimo viro, P. Lentulo,
consentiente atque una voce revocavit. Me idem senatus
exteris nationibus, me legatis magistratibusque nostris auctoritate sua consularibus litteris, non ut tu Insuber dicere
20 ausus es, orbatum patria, sed ut senatus illo ipso tempore
appellavit, civem servatorem rei publicae commendavit. Ad
meam unius hominis salutem senatus auxilium omnium civium
cuncta ex Italia, qui rem publicam salvam esse vellent, consulis voce et litteris implorandum putavit. Mei capitis con-
25 servandi causa Romam uno tempore quasi signo dato Italia

6 an quod . . . 7 evenit *Arusianus, GL* vii. 470 19 non ut . . .
20 patria *Arusianus, GL* vii. 496

P (incip. 7 -rentur male), *V*Ω] 2 dico *Bake* 5 e] a Ω 6 *ante*
tibi *add.* in provinciam *V*² (*in mg.*) 10 quaevis *PV, Xmg.*: eius Ω
quam *PV*: potius quam Ω 12 tempus *P*: tempus profectionis *V*Ω
14 vestrum *PVE*: nostrum *X*: *om. ef* 15 concursu (-us *E*) Italiae
*PV*Ω: *del. Francken* 17 consentiente *PV*: cons- p.r. Ω 19 consularibus *P*Ω: -busque *V* Insuber *Turnebus*: insuper *P*Ω, *Arus.*: super
*V*¹(?): semper *V*² 21 servatorem (-emque *V*) *PV*: conservatorem
(-emque *ef*) Ω 22 hominis *PV*: *om.* Ω civium *P*Ω: *om. V* 24 con-
servandi *P*: serv- *V*Ω

19

15 34]　　　M. TVLLI CICERONIS

tota convenit. De mea salute P. Lentuli, praestantissimi viri
atque optimi consulis, Cn. Pompei, clarissimi atque invictis-
simi civis, ceterorumque principum civitatis celeberrimae et
35 gratissimae contiones fuerunt. De me senatus ita decrevit,
Cn. Pompeio auctore et eius sententiae principe, ut si quis 5
impedisset reditum meum, in hostium numero putaretur,
eisque verbis ea de me senatus auctoritas declarata est ut
nemini sit triumphus honorificentius quam mihi salus resti-
tutioque perscripta. De me cum omnes magistratus promul-
gassent, praeter unum praetorem a quo non fuit postulandum, 10
fratrem inimici mei, praeterque duos de lapide emptos tribunos, legem comitiis centuriatis tulit P. Lentulus consul, de
conlegae Q. Metelli sententia, quem mecum eadem res publica
quae in tribunatu eius disiunxerat in consulatu virtute optimi
ac iustissimi viri sapientiaque coniunxit. Quae lex quem ad 15
modum accepta sit quid me attinet dicere ? Ex vobis audio
nemini civi ullam quo minus adesset satis iustam excusationem esse visam; nullis comitiis umquam neque multitudinem hominum tantam neque splendidiorem fuisse; hoc certe
video, quod indicant tabulae publicae, vos rogatores, vos diri- 20
bitores, vos custodes fuisse tabularum, et quod in honoribus
vestrorum propinquorum non facitis vel aetatis excusatione vel
honoris, id in salute mea nullo rogante vos vestra sponte fecistis.
16
37 Confer nunc, Epicure noster ex hara producte non ex schola,
confer, si audes, absentiam tuam cum mea. Obtinuisti pro- 25

---

9 de me . . . 12 consul *Asconius*　　　　10 praeter . . . postulandum
11 praeterque . . . tribunos *Arusianus, GL* vii. 499　　　24 ex hara . . .
non schola *Nonius* 173 *L* (= 120 *M*)　　　25 confer . . . mea *Arusianus,
GL* vii. 462; τόλμα audacia . . . Cicero in Pisonem: confer si audes ausen-
tia tuam cum mea *Corpus Gloss. Lat.* ii. 457

P (defic. post 18 visam), *V*Ω] 　6 putaretur *P*Ω: reput- *V*　　7 eisque *V*:
iisque (*vel* usque) Ω: hisque *P*　　ea de me *P*Ω: eadem *V*　　8 nemini *P*Ω:
-nis *V*　　9 perscripta *P*Ω: prae- *V*　　11 tribunos *P*Ω, *Asc., Arus.*:
tribunos P.L.B. *V*　　13 Q. *P*Ω: om. *V*　　14 disiunxerat *V*Ω: dilux-
P: diiunx- ϛ　　16 recepta *P*　　18 neque *V*: nec Ω　　20 distribu-
tores Ω　　21 tabellarum ϛ　　24 conferte *V*

20

IN L. PISONEM ORATIO [16 37

vinciam consularem finibus eis quos lex cupiditatis tuae, non
quos lex generi tui pepigerat. Nam lege Caesaris iustissima
atque optima populi liberi plane et vere erant liberi, lege autem
ea quam nemo legem praeter te et conlegam tuum putavit
5 omnis erat tibi Achaia Thessalia Athenae cuncta Graecia
addicta; habebas exercitum tantum quantum tibi non senatus
aut populus Romanus dederat, sed quantum tua libido con-
scripserat; aerarium exhauseras. Quas res gessisti imperio 38
exercitu provincia consulari? Quas res gesserit quaero? Qui
10 ut venit statim—nondum commemoro rapinas, non exactas
pecunias, non captas, non imperatas, non neces sociorum,
non caedis hospitum; non perfidiam, non immanitatem, non
scelera praedico; mox, si videbitur, ut cum fure, ut cum sacri-
lego, ut cum sicario disputabo; nunc meam spoliatam for-
15 tunam conferam cum florente fortuna imperatoris. Quis
umquam provinciam cum exercitu obtinuit qui nullas ad
senatum litteras miserit? tantam vero provinciam cum tanto
exercitu, Macedoniam praesertim, quam tantae barbarorum
gentes attingunt ut semper Macedonicis imperatoribus idem
20 fines provinciae fuerint qui gladiorum atque pilorum; ex qua
aliquot praetorio imperio, consulari quidem nemo rediit, qui
incolumis fuerit, quin triumpharit. Est hoc novum; multo
illud magis. Appellatus est hic volturius illius provinciae, si
dis placet, imperator: ne tum quidem, Paule noster, tabellas 17
25 Romam cum laurea mittere audebas? 'Misi,' inquit. Quis 39
umquam recitavit, quis ut recitarentur postulavit? Nihil enim
iam mea refert utrum tu conscientia oppressus scelerum

23 appellatus . . . 25 audebas *Asconius*   23 vulturius illius provinciae *Charisius, GL* i. 147 (= *p.* 187 *Barwick*)

---

*V*Ω] 3 erant *om. V*   8 in imperio Ω   10 non ex-] nondum ex-
X   12 caedem Ω   14 ut *om. X*   15 *fort.* confero floren-
tem fortunam *V*   18 quae tantis barbarorum gentibus attingitur Ω
19 macedonibus *X*   21 consularis *X*   redit *V*   qui] quin *V*   22
quin] qui non Ω   24 tabellas *Asc.*: tabulas *V*Ω   25 cum laurea
Romam *Asc.*   27 iam mea] mea iam *V*

21

17 39] M. TVLLI CICERONIS

tuorum nihil umquam ausus sis scribere ad eum ordinem quem
despexeras, quem adflixeras, quem deleveras, an amici tui
tabellas abdiderint idemque silentio suo temeritatem atque
audaciam tuam condemnarint; atque haud scio an malim te
videri nullo pudore fuisse in litteris mittendis, [an] amicos tuos 5
plus habuisse et pudoris et consili, quam aut te videri pudentiorem fuisse quam soles, aut tuum factum non esse condemna-
40 tum iudicio amicorum. Quod si non tuis nefariis in hunc
ordinem contumeliis in perpetuum tibi curiam praeclusisses,
quid tandem erat actum aut gestum in tua provincia de quo 10
ad senatum cum gratulatione aliqua scribi abs te oporteret?
vexatio Macedoniae, an oppidorum turpis amissio, an sociorum
direptio, an agrorum depopulatio, an munitio Thessalonicae,
an obsessio militaris viae, an exercitus nostri interitus ferro
fame frigore pestilentia? Tu vero qui ad senatum nihil scri- 15
pseris, ut in urbe nequior inventus es quam Gabinius, sic in
41 provincia paulo tamen quam ille demissior. Nam ille gurges
atque helluo, natus abdomini suo non laudi et gloriae, cum
equites Romanos in provincia, cum publicanos nobiscum et
voluntate et dignitate coniunctos omnis fortunis, multos fama 20
vitaque privasset, cum egisset aliud nihil illo exercitu nisi ut
urbis depopularetur, agros vastaret, exhauriret domos, ausus
est—quid enim ille non audeat?—a senatu supplicationem per
18 litteras postulare. O di immortales! tune etiam atque adeo
vos, geminae voragines scopulique rei publicae, vos meam 25
fortunam deprimitis, vestram extollitis, cum de me ea senatus
consulta absente facta sint, eae contiones habitae, is motus
fuerit municipiorum et coloniarum omnium, ea decreta publicanorum, ea conlegiorum, ea denique generum ordinumque

---

V, C (25 vos ... publicae), Ω]   3 tabulas Ω   5 an *del. Graevius*:
et *Lambinus*: at *Clark*   6 habuisse et] habuisset *V¹*: habuisse
V²   prudentiorem *VE*   10 tua] illa Ω   16 ut *om. V*   18 et]
atque Ω   21 illo] in illo Ω   23 ille non audeat] non ille auderet Ω
24 tune] tunc Ω   27 sunt Ω   eae] hae (*vel* hee) α: ḥ eae *X*   28 ea
om. V¹

22

IN L. PISONEM ORATIO [18 41

omnium quae non modo ego optare numquam auderem
sed cogitare non possem, vos autem sempiternas foedissimae
turpitudinis notas subieritis ? An ego si te et Gabinium cruci 42
suffixos viderem, maiore adficerer laetitia ex corporis vestri
5 laceratione quam adficior ex famae ? Nullum est supplicium
putandum quo adfici casu aliquo etiam boni viri fortesque
possunt. Atque hoc quidem etiam isti tui dicunt voluptarii
Graeci—quos utinam ita audires ut erant audiendi; numquam
te in tot flagitia ingurgitasses. Verum audis in praesepibus,
10 audis in stupris, audis in cibo et vino.—Sed dicunt isti ipsi qui
mala dolore, bona voluptate definiunt, sapientem, etiam si in
Phalaridis tauro inclusus succensis ignibus torreatur, dictu-
rum tamen suave illud esse seque ne tantulum quidem com-
moveri; tantam virtutis vim esse voluerunt ut non posset esse
15 umquam vir bonus non beatus. Quae est igitur poena, quod 43
supplicium ? Id mea sententia quod accidere nemini potest
nisi nocenti, suscepta fraus, impedita et oppressa mens,
bonorum odium, nota inusta senatus, amissio dignitatis. Nec 19
mihi ille M. Regulus quem Carthaginienses resectis palpebris
20 inligatum in machina vigilando necaverunt supplicio videtur
adfectus, nec C. Marius quem Italia servata ab illo demersum
in Minturnensium paludibus, Africa devicta ab eodem expulsum et naufragum vidit. Fortunae enim ista tela sunt non
culpae; supplicium autem est poena peccati. Neque vero ego,
25 si umquam vobis mala precarer, quod saepe feci, in quo di
immortales meas preces audierunt, morbum aut mortem aut

---

8 numquam ... 9 ingurgitasses *Eutyches, GL* v. 461   10 sed ...
12 torreatur (*om.* inclusus) *Charisius, GL* i. 130 (= *p.* 165 *Barwick*)

---

*V*Ω]   1 non modo ego] ego non modo *X*   5 famae] fama α: infamia
X   est] esse *X*[1]   6 viri *om. X*   9 te *om. V*[1]   10 vino *Vf*: in
vino Ω   13 seseque Ω   commovere *V*[1]   14 vim esse] esse vim Ω
esse umquam] umquam esse Ω   17 mens conscientia Ω   18 bonorum omnium odium Ω   nota ... senatus *del. Williams*   inusta
Faernus: iusta *V*: iussu α: iusti *X*   a senatu *Faernus*   21 C. *om. V*
22 Ment- *V*   26 audiverunt Ω

23

19 43] M. TVLLI CICERONIS

cruciatum precarer. Thyestea est ista exsecratio, poetae volgi animos non sapientium moventis, ut tu naufragio expulsus uspiam 'saxis fixus asperis, evisceratus latere penderes,' ut ait
ille, 'saxa spargens tabo sanie et sanguine atro.' Non ferrem omnino moleste, si ita accidisset; sed id tamen esset humanum. 5
M. Marcellus, qui ter consul fuit, summa virtute pietate gloria militari, periit in mari; qui tamen ob virtutem gloria et laude vivit. In fortuna quadam est illa mors non in poena putanda. Quae est igitur poena, quod supplicium, quae saxa, quae cruces ? Esse duos duces in provinciis populi Romani, habere 10 exercitus, appellari imperatores; horum alterum sic fuisse infrenatum conscientia scelerum et fraudum suarum ut ea ex provincia quae fuerit ex omnibus una maxime triumphalis nullam sit ad senatum litteram mittere ausus. Ex qua provincia modo vir omni dignitate ornatissimus, L. Torquatus, 15 magnis rebus gestis me referente ab senatu imperator est appellatus, unde his paucis annis Cn. Dolabellae, C. Curionis, M. Luculli iustissimos triumphos vidimus, ex ea te imperatore nuntius ad senatum adlatus est nullus. Ab altero adlatae
litterae, recitatae, relatum ad senatum. Di immortales! idne 20 ego optarem ut inimicus meus ea qua nemo umquam ignominia notaretur, ut senatus is qui in eam iam benignitatis consuetudinem venit ut eos qui bene rem publicam gesserint novis honoribus adficiat et numero dierum et genere verborum, huius unius litteris nuntiantibus non crederet, postulantibus 25

---

3 saxis ... latere pendens saxa ... atro *Ennius, scaen.* 362–3 (*cf. Cic. Tusc.* i. 107, *Non.* 651*L* = 405*M*) 6 Marcellus ... 8 vivit (*om. virtute*) *Asconius*

V, C (15 vir ... ornatissimus), Ω] 1 est ista ex-] ista ex- est Ω
4 et *V, Cic. Tusc., Non.*: *om.* Ω ferrem omnino] omnino ferrem *V*
6 M. *om. V*[1], *Asc.* 7 perit *V*α, *Asc.* gloria et *Asc.*: gloriae Ω: in gloria et *V* 8 in poena] poena *X* 10 esse] ecce Ω duo α
11 infirmatum Ω 12 fraudium Ω ea ex] ex ea *V* 13 ex *om. V*
14 nullas ... litteras Ω 15 L. *om. V* 16 ab senatu *Manutius*: absens (aps- *V*) *V*Ω est] sit *X*: *om.* α 20 litterae *om. V*[1]
22 iam *om. V*

24

IN L. PISONEM ORATIO [19 45

denegaret ? His ego rebus pascor, his delector, his perfruor, 20
quod de vobis hic ordo opinatur non secus ac de acerrimis
hostibus, quod vos equites Romani, quod ceteri ordines, quod
cuncta civitas odit, quod nemo bonus, nemo denique civis est,
5 qui modo se civem esse meminerit, qui vos non oculis fugiat,
auribus respuat, animo aspernetur, recordatione denique ipsa
consulatus vestri perhorrescat. Haec ego semper de vobis 46
expetivi, haec optavi, haec precatus sum; plura etiam acci-
derunt quam vellem; nam ut amitteretis exercitum, numquam
10 hercule optavi. Illud etiam accidit praeter optatum meum,
sed valde ex voluntate: mihi enim numquam veniret in mentem
furorem et insaniam optare vobis in quam incidistis. Atqui
fuit optandum. Me tamen fugerat deorum immortalium has
esse in impios et conscleratos poenas certissimas. Nolite enim
15 ita putare, patres conscripti, ut in scaena videtis, homines
consceleratos impulsu deorum terreri furialibus taedis ardentibus. Sua quemque fraus, suum facinus, suum scelus, sua
audacia de sanitate ac mente deturbat; hae sunt impiorum
furiae, hae flammae, hae faces. Ego te non vaecordem, non 47
20 furiosum, non mente captum, non tragico illo Oreste aut
Athamante dementiorem putem, qui sis ausus primum facere—
nam id est caput—deinde paulo ante, Torquato, gravissimo
et sanctissimo viro, premente, confiteri te provinciam Macedoniam, in quam tantum exercitum transportasses, sine ullo
25 milite reliquisse ? Mitto de amissa maxima parte exercitus (sit
hoc infelicitatis tuae): dimittendi vero exercitus quam potes
adferre causam ? Quam potestatem habuisti, quam legem,
quod senatus consultum, quod ius, quod exemplum ? Quid est

28 quid est ... 2 (*p.* 26) suum *Marius Victorinus, de defin. p.* 25 *St.*

P (*incip.* 24 -am in quam), *V, C* (1 his ego ... perfruor, 18 hae sunt ...
21 putem, 26 qua causa. qua lege. qua potestate. qua auctoritate. quo iure.
quo exemplo. qua ratione), Ω] 2 de acerrimis] deterr- α: de deterr- *X*
6 recordationem ... ipsam α 10 me hercule Ω 11 numquam
om. Ω veniret *V*Ω: venerat *X*²: venit *Bake* 14 certissimas constitutas Ω 15 ita *om.* Ω 16 furiarum Ω 20 aut Athamante
om. C 22 grav- et sanct-] sanct- et grav- *V* 23 praesente *V*

25

20 47]   M. TVLLI CICERONIS

aliud furere ? Non cognoscere homines ? non cognoscere leges,
non senatum, non civitatem. Cruentare corpus suum ? maior
48 haec est vitae famae salutis suae volneratio. Si familiam tuam
dimisisses, quod ad neminem nisi ad ipsum te pertineret,
amici te constringendum putarent: praesidium tu rei publicae, 5
custodiam provinciae iniussu populi Romani senatusque
21 dimisisses, si tuae mentis compos fuisses ? Ecce tibi alter
effusa iam maxima praeda quam ex fortunis publicanorum,
quam ex agris urbibusque sociorum exhauserat, cum partim
eius praedae profundae libidines devorassent, partim nova 10
quaedam et inaudita luxuries, partim etiam in illis locis ubi
omnia diripuit emptiones, partim permutationes ad hunc
Tusculani montem exstruendum; cum iam egeret, cum illa
eius intermissa intolerabilis aedificatio constitisset, se ipsum,
fascis suos, exercitum populi Romani, numen interdictumque 15
deorum immortalium, responsa sacerdotum, auctoritatem
senatus, iussa populi, nomen ac dignitatem imperi regi
49 Aegyptio vendidit. Cum finis provinciae tantos haberet
quantos voluerat, quantos optaverat, quantos pretio mei
capitis periculoque emerat, eis se tenere non potuit, exercitum 20
eduxit ex Syria: qui licuit extra provinciam ? Praebuit se
mercennarium comitem regi Alexandrino: quid hoc turpius ?
In Aegyptum venit, signa contulit cum Alexandrinis: quando
hoc bellum aut hic ordo aut populus susceperat ? Cepit
Alexandriam: quid aliud exspectamus a furore eius nisi ut 25

P, V, C (7 tuae mentis conpos esto), Ω]   1 homines $PV\Omega$, *Mar. Vict.*:
homines ? gravius est *Madvig*: homines ? immo *Watt*   2 suum $P\Omega$
(*post* suum *defic. Mar. Vict.*): suum leve est V 5 te PV: te tui Ω
r.p. V: populi r. (*vel* p.r.) $P\Omega$ 6 Romani] R. PV: om. Ω 9 quam
P: om. $V\Omega$ partim $P\Omega$: partem V 10 praedae PV: praedam Ω
12 partim permutationes Ω: partim mut- V^2: om. PV^1 13 Tusculani
(-culani *in rasura ante* 6 *litt. spatium add.* V^2) PV: tusculani (*vel* -lam)
in montem α: tusculanum X cum iam egeret PV: om. Ω cum
illa $P\Omega$: cui illa V 14 intermissa PV: inmissa Ω 17 populi]
P.R. P 19 optarat P pr(a)etio mei capitis PV: mei cap- pret- Ω
20 periculoque $P\Omega$: om. V iis V: is P: his Ω 21 praebuit se P:
praebuisse V: tribuit se Ω 22 Alexandrino PV: -dro Ω

IN L. PISONEM ORATIO [21 49

ad senatum tantis de rebus gestis litteras mittat ? Hic si mentis 50
esset suae, nisi poenas patriae disque immortalibus eas quae
gravissimae sunt furore atque insania penderet, ausus esset—
mitto exire de provincia, educere exercitum, bellum sua sponte
5 gerere, in regnum iniussu populi Romani ac senatus accedere,
quae cum plurimae leges veteres, tum lex Cornelia maiestatis,
Iulia de pecuniis repetundis planissime vetat—sed haec omitto;
ille si non acerrime fureret, auderet quam provinciam P.
Lentulus, amicissimus huic ordini, cum et auctoritate senatus
10 et sorte haberet, interposita religione sine ulla dubitatione
deposuisset, eam sibi adsciscere, cum etiam si religio non im-
pediret, mos maiorum tamen et exempla et gravissimae legum
poenae vetarent ?

Et quoniam fortunarum contentionem facere coepimus, de 22
15 reditu Gabini omittamus, quem etsi sibi ipse praecidit, ego 51
tamen os ut videam hominis exspecto; tuum, si placet, reditum
cum meo conferamus. Ac meus quidem is fuit ut a Brundisio
usque Romam agmen perpetuum totius Italiae viderit; neque
enim regio ulla fuit nec municipium neque praefectura aut
20 colonia ex qua non ad me publice venerint gratulatum. Quid
dicam adventus meos, quid effusiones hominum ex oppidis,
quid concursus ex agris patrum familias cum coniugibus ac
liberis, quid eos dies qui quasi deorum immortalium festi atque
sollemnes apud omnis sunt adventu meo redituque celebrati ?
25 Vnus ille dies mihi quidem immortalitatis instar fuit quo in 52
patriam redii, cum senatum egressum vidi populumque universum, cum mihi ipsa Roma prope convulsa sedibus suis ad

12 et gravissimae . . . 13 vetarent *Arusianus, GL* vii. 502

P (*defic. post* 8 si non), *V*Ω]   2 disque *PV²*Ω: dis *V¹*   5
Romani] R. *P*: *om. V*Ω   ac *V*: aut *P*Ω   6 Cornelia maiestatis]
mai- Corn- *P*   7 vetat *PV*: vetant Ω   9 et Ω: ex *V*   14
et] sed Ω   17 a] e *V*   18 viderit] viderem Ω: viderim *Garatoni*
19 ulla fuit nec] fuit ulla neque Ω   20 ad me publicae *V*: publice ad
me Ω   22 concursum Ω   24 apud omnis α: apud homines *V*:
om. X   25 quo] cum *V*   26 populumque R. Ω

22 52] M. TVLLI CICERONIS

complectendum conservatorem suum progredi visa est. Quae
me ita accepit ut non modo omnium generum aetatum ordinum omnes viri ac mulieres omnis fortunae ac loci, sed etiam
moenia ipsa viderentur et tecta urbis ac templa laetari. Me
consequentibus diebus in ea ipsa domo qua tu me expuleras, 5
quam expilaras, quam incenderas, pontifices consules patres
conscripti conlocaverunt, mihique, quod ante me nemini,
pecunia publica aedificandam domum censuerunt.

53 Habes reditum meum: confer nunc vicissim tuum, quando
quidem amisso exercitu nihil incolume domum praeter os illud 10
tuum pristinum rettulisti. Qui primum qua veneris cum
laureatis tuis lictoribus quis scit? Quos tu maeandros, dum
omnis solitudines persequeris, quae deverticula flexionesque
quaesisti? Quod te municipium vidit, quis amicus invitavit,
quis hospes aspexit? Nonne tibi nox erat pro die, solitudo pro 15
frequentia, caupona pro oppido, non ut redire ex Macedonia
nobilis imperator sed ut mortuus infamis efferri videretur?
23 Romam vero ipsam [foedavit adventus tuus], o familiae non
dicam Calpurniae sed Calventiae, neque huius urbis sed
Placentini municipi, neque paterni generis sed bracatae cogna- 20
tionis dedecus, quem ad modum ingressus es? Quis tibi non
dicam horum aut civium ceterorum sed tuorum legatorum
54 obviam venit? Mecum enim L. Flaccus, vir tua legatione
indignissimus atque eis consiliis quibus mecum in consulatu
meo coniunctus fuit ad conservandam rem publicam dignior, 25
mecum fuit tum cum te quidam non longe a porta cum lictori-

---

4 me . . . 8 censuerunt (*om.* quam expilaras *et* conscripti) *Asconius*
18 Romam vero ipsam o . . . Calpurniae sed huius urbis . . . municipi et
bracatae . . . 21 ingressus es *Arusianus, GL* vii. 483 (*propter* ingressus)

V, C (2 me roma ita . . . 4 templa retari, 15 nonne . . . 16 oppido),
Ω] 1 progredi] procedere Ω 7 collocarunt *Asc.* ante me] antea
Asc. 8 pecuniam publicam ad aed- *Asc.* 11 tuum pristi-
num] prist- tuum Ω 12 quis] qui Ω 13 quae *om. V* 15
solitudo *VC*: non sol- Ω 17 efferri ϛ: referri *V*Ω 18 foedavit
adventus tuus Ω: adv- tuus *V*: *om. Arus.* o *V²*Ω, *Arus.*: *om. V¹* 21
ingressus es *Arus.*: venisti *V*Ω 22 sed tuorum] aut *V* 23 enim]
enim tum Ω

28

IN L. PISONEM ORATIO [**23** 54

bus errantem visum esse narrabat; scio item virum fortem, in
primis belli ac rei militaris peritum, familiarem meum Q.
Marcium, quorum tu legatorum opera in proelio imperator
appellatus eras cum longe afuisses, adventu isto tuo domi
5 fuisse otiosum. Sed quid ego numero qui tibi obviam non
venerint, cui dico venisse paene neminem ne de officiosissima 55
quidem natione candidatorum, cum volgo essent et illo ipso
et multis ante diebus admoniti et rogati? Togulae lictoribus
ad portam praesto fuerunt; quibus illi acceptis sagula reiece-
10 runt, catervam imperatori suo novam praebuerunt. Sic iste
a tanto exercitu, tanta provincia, triennio post, Macedonicus
imperator, in urbem se intulit ut nullius negotiatoris obscuris-
simi reditus umquam fuerit desertior. In quo me tamen, qui
esset paratus ad se defendendum, reprendit. Cum ego eum
15 Caelimontana introisse dixissem, sponsione me ni Esquilina
introisset homo promptus lacessivit; quasi vero id aut ego
scire debuerim aut vestrum quisquam audierit aut ad rem
pertineat qua tu porta introieris, modo ne triumphali, quae
porta Macedonicis semper consulibus ante te patuit; tu in-
20 ventus es qui consulari imperio praeditus ex Macedonia non
triumphares.

At audistis, patres conscripti, philosophi vocem: negavit se **24**
triumphi cupidum umquam fuisse. O scelus, o pestis, o labes! 56
cum exstinguebas senatum, vendebas auctoritatem huius ordi-
25 nis, addicebas tribuno pl. consulatum tuum, rem publicam
evertebas, prodebas caput et salutem meam una mercede
provinciae, si triumphum non cupiebas, cuius tandem te rei

V, C (23 o scelus . . . labes), Ω] 1 narraret *V*   3 martium *X*   opera
in *om.* Ω   4 cum non longe Ω   5 enumero Ω   6 cui] qui Ω:
quin *Jeep*: *del. Ernesti*   7 illo ipso] ipso illo *V*   8 admoniti . . . lictoribus *om. V*   10 et catervam Ω   11 a *om.* Ω   tantae provinciae
V   12 ut *V²*Ω: uti *V¹*   nullius] ne ullius *V*   14 reprehendit *V*Ω
eum *om.* Ω   15 cael- porta Ω   responsione me menia esqu- introisse
Ω   16 promptissimus Ω   17 quispiam Ω   19 proconsulibus
Naugerius   26 una *om. V¹*   27 cuius tandem] tandem cuius *V*
te rei] rei te (rei *ef*) Ω

24 56] M. TVLLI CICERONIS

cupiditate arsisse defendes? Saepe enim vidi qui et mihi et
ceteris cupidiores provinciae viderentur triumphi nomine
tegere atque celare cupiditatem suam. Hoc D. Silanus consul
in hoc ordine, hoc meus etiam conlega dicebat. Neque enim
potest quisquam exercitum cupere aperteque petere, ut non 5
57 praetexat cupiditatem triumphi. Quod si te senatus populusque Romanus aut non appetentem aut etiam recusantem
bellum suscipere, exercitum ducere coegisset, tamen erat
angusti animi atque demissi iusti triumphi honorem digni-
tatemque contemnere. Nam ut levitatis est inanem aucupari 10
rumorem et omnis umbras etiam falsae gloriae consectari,
sic est [levis] animi lucem splendoremque fugientis iustam
gloriam, qui est fructus verae virtutis honestissimus, repudiare.
Cum vero non modo non postulante atque cogente, sed invito
atque oppresso senatu, non modo nullo populi Romani studio, 15
sed nullo ferente suffragium libero, provincia tibi ista manu-
pretium fuerit eversae per te et perditae civitatis, cumque
omnium tuorum scelerum haec pactio exstiterit ut si tu totam
rem publicam nefariis latronibus tradidisses, Macedonia tibi
ob eam rem quibus tu velles finibus traderetur: cum exhau- 20
riebas aerarium, cum orbabas Italiam iuventute, cum mare
vastissimum hieme transibas, si triumphum contemnebàs,
quae te, praedo amentissime, nisi praedae ac rapinarum
58 cupiditas tam caeca rapiebat? Non est integrum Cn. Pompeio
consilio iam uti tuo; erravit enim, non gustarat istam tuam 25
philosophiam, ter iam homo stultus triumphavit. Crasse,
pudet me tui; quid est quod confecto per te formidolosissimo

V, C (10 ut . . . 13 repudiare, 25 nolumus istam tuam gustare philosophiam), Ω] 1 cup- te *V* 3 velare Ω hoc modo decimus (dic- α)
Ω: hoc dicebat (t *in ras.*) *V* 5 potest quisquam] quis- pot- Ω
7 que *om. V* 9 dimissi Ω iusti] iussi α: *om. X* dignita-
temque] atque dignitatem Ω 11 et *VC*: ut Ω 12 est levis *VC*: levis
est Ω: est *Lambinus* animi *C*Ω: animis *V* 16 suffragia *V*[2] 17
non eversae . . . sed perd- Ω 18 tu *om. V* 20 velles finibus]
fin- vell- Ω traderetur *Faernus*: uttrad- (*primum* t *sup. lin. m. 1*) *V*:
redd- Ω 22 transiebas *V* 23 praedae] praeda Ω 27 quid est]
quidem *V* per te *om. X*

30

IN L. PISONEM ORATIO [**24** 58

bello coronam illam lauream tibi tanto opere decerni volueris
a senatu ? P. Servili, Q. Metelle, C. Curio, L. Afrani, cur hunc
non audistis tam doctum hominem, tam eruditum, prius quam
in istum errorem induceremini ? C. ipsi Pomptino, necessario
5 meo, iam non est integrum; religionibus enim susceptis impe-
ditur. O stultos Camillos Curios Fabricios Calatinos Scipiones
Marcellos Maximos! o amentem Paulum, rusticum Marium,
nullius consili patres horum amborum consulum, qui triumpharint!

10 Sed quoniam praeterita mutare non possumus, quid cessat **25**
hic homullus ex argilla et luto fictus [Epicurus] dare haec **59**
praeclara praecepta sapientiae clarissimo et summo imperatori genero suo ? Fertur ille vir, mihi crede, gloria; flagrat
ardet cupiditate iusti et magni triumphi. Non didicit eadem
15 ista quae tu. Mitte ad eum libellum, et si iam ipse coram con-
gredi poteris, meditare quibus verbis incensam illius cupiditatem comprimas atque restinguas. Valebis apud hominem
volitantem gloriae cupiditate vir moderatus et constans, apud
indoctum eruditus, apud generum socer. Dices enim, ut es
20 homo factus ad persuadendum, concinnus perfectus politus
ex schola: 'quid est, Caesar, quod te supplicationes totiens
iam decretae tot dierum tanto opere delectent ? in quibus
homines errore ducuntur, quas di neglegunt; qui ut noster
divinus ille dixit Epicurus, neque propitii cuiquam esse solent

---

6 o stultos . . . 9 triumpharunt *Asconius*   11 homullus . . . fictus
Priscianus, GL ii. 109   21 quid . . . 22 delectant *anon., Rhet. Lat.
Min. p.* 72

V, C (20 homo . . . 21 schola), Ω] 1 auream *V*   tantopere Ω   2 C.
*om. V*¹   luci afrane *V*: P. affricane (*vel* afr-) Ω   hunc non] non hunc
Ω   4 pontino Ω   6 Curios] furios *Asc.*   calatinos Ω, *Asc.*:
palantinos *V*   7 marcellum *Asc.*   o amentem *X*: camertem α: orna-
mentum *Asc.*: amentem *V*   8 triumpharint *V*: -arunt Ω, *Asc.*   11
homullus *V*²Ω, *Prisc.*: humillus *V*¹   fictus Ω, *Prisc.*: factus *V*   epicurus *V*: epicureus Ω: *del. Müller*   12 praeclara] parate clara α:
parate *X*   14 ardet *del. Baiter*   15 et si iam] sed iam si Ω
20 factus *V*¹: facetus *V*²*C*Ω   21 e *C*Ω   22 iam *om.* Ω, *anon.*
delectant *X, anon.*: -antur α   tantopere Ω, *anon.*   24 ille div- Ω

31

25 59] M. TVLLI CICERONIS

neque irati.' Non facies fidem scilicet, cum haec disputabis;
60 tibi enim et esse et fuisse videbit iratos. Vertes te ad alteram
scholam; disseres de triumpho: 'quid tandem habet iste currus,
quid vincti ante currum duces, quid simulacra oppidorum,
quid aurum quid argentum, quid legati in equis et tribuni, 5
quid clamor militum, quid tota illa pompa ? Inania sunt ista,
mihi crede, delectamenta paene puerorum, captare plausus,
vehi per urbem, conspici velle. Quibus ex rebus nihil est quod
solidum tenere, nihil quod referre ad voluptatem corporis
61 possis. Quin tu me vides qui ex qua provincia T. Flamininus, 10
L. Paulus, Q. Metellus, T. Didius, innumerabiles alii levitate
et cupiditate commoti triumpharunt, ex ea sic redii ut ad
portam Esquilinam Macedonicam lauream conculcarim, ipse
cum hominibus duodecim male vestitis ad portam Caelimontanam sitiens pervenerim? quo in loco mihi libertus praeclaro 15
imperatori domum ex hac die biduo ante conduxerat; quae
vacua si non fuisset, in campo Martiali mihi tabernaculum
conlocassem. Nummus interea, mi Caesar, neglectis ferculis
triumphalibus, domi manet et manebit. Rationes ad aerarium
rettuli continuo, sicut tua lex iubebat, neque alia ulla in re 20
legi tuae parui. Quas rationes si cognoris intelleges nemini
plus quam mihi litteras profuisse. Ita enim sunt perscriptae
scite et litterate ut scriba ad aerarium, qui eas rettulit, perscriptis rationibus secum ipse caput sinistra manu perfricans
commurmuratus sit: "ratio quidem hercle apparet, argentum 25
οἴχεται."' Hac tu oratione non dubito quin illum iam escendentem in currum revocare possis.

25 *Plautus, trinummus* 419

P (18 -terea . . . 23 scr-, 26 -bito . . . 27), *V, C* (3 quid . . . 8 velle), Ω] 2
videbit] deos videbis Ω 8 ex] ex e *V* 10 quin tu] quid tum *V*
T. *om. V*¹ flamininus *E*: -minius *VfX* 11 lev- et] levi Ω 13
-arim *X*: -arem *V*: -ari(t) α 14 xii *ef*: xv *EX*: quindecim α *V* 17
marciali *V*: martio Ω 18 mi *P*: mihi *V*Ω ferc- *PV*: vehic- Ω
20 ret(t)uli cont- . . . iub- *P*Ω: cont- . . . iub- detuli *V* ulla *om. P*
21 -oris *PV*²Ω: -overis *V*¹ 26 oechetae *V, Xmg.*: et doctum te thece Ω
tu] tua *V* iam *om. P* esc- *P*: asc- *V*Ω 27 rev- p- *PV*: p- rev- Ω

IN L. PISONEM ORATIO [26 62

O tenebrae, o lutum, o sordes, o paterni generis oblite, **26**
materni vix memor! ita nescio quid istuc fractum, humile, **62**
demissum, sordidum inferius etiam est quam ut Mediolanensi
praecone, avo tuo, dignum esse videatur. L. Crassus, homo
5 sapientissimus nostrae civitatis, specillis prope scrutatus est
Alpis, ut ubi hostis non erat, ibi triumphi causam aliquam
quaereret; eadem cupiditate vir summo ingenio praeditus,
C. Cotta, nullo certo hoste flagravit. Eorum neuter triumphavit, quod alteri illum honorem conlega, alteri mors peremit.
10 Inrisa est abs te paulo ante M. Pisonis cupiditas triumphandi,
a qua te longe dixisti abhorrere. Qui etiam si minus magnum
bellum gesserat, ut abs te dictum est, tamen istum honorem
contemnendum non putavit. Tu eruditior quam Piso, pru-
dentior quam Cotta, abundantior consilio ingenio sapientia
15 quam Crassus, ea contemnis quae illi 'idiotae', ut tu appellas,
praeclara duxerunt ? Quos si reprehendis quod cupidi coronae **63**
laureae fuerint, cum bella aut parva aut nulla gessissent, tu
tantis nationibus subactis, tantis rebus gestis, minime fructum
laborum tuorum, praemia periculorum, virtutis insignia con-
20 temnere debuisti. Neque vero contempsisti, sis licet Themista
sapientior, sed os tuum ferreum senatus convicio verberari
noluisti.

Iam vides—quoniam quidem ita mihimet fui inimicus ut
me tecum compararem—et digressum meum et absentiam et
25 reditum ita longe tuo praestitisse ut mihi illa omnia immor-

---

7 eadem . . . 13 Piso (*om.* 8 flagravit, 12 ut . . . tamen) *Asconius*

P (1 . . . 5 sapientis-, 9 -phavit . . . 13 putavit, 17 parva . . . **23** vides
quo-), V, C (1 o tenebre . . . surdes), Ω] 1 o lutum o sordes $VC\Omega$:
lutum sordes P 2 o materni P istuc $P\Omega$: istud V 5 specillis *Madvig*: pecullis (-ulis V^2) V: spiculis (spec- $f)\Omega$ 8 C.
om. Asc.   cocta eX 9 quod $P\Omega$: quorum V peremit V, *Asc.
cod.* S: ademit (*vel* ed-) Ω, *Asc. codd.* PM: praeripuit P 10 abs
(*vel* aps) $PV\Omega$: a *Asc.*   M. $P\Omega$: *om.* V 13 contemnendum $PV\Omega$:
omittendum *Asc.*   14 cocta efX 15 ea *om.* V 16 quos]
quod Ω 17 fuerunt Vef 20 sis PV: *om.* Ω 21 sed PV:
si Ω verberari $PV\alpha$: -are X 23 quoniam (quo/P) $PV\alpha$: qm̄ X^1:
qñ $Xmg.$ mihimet Ω (*vestigia in P exstabant*): met mihi V

5993   **E**   33

26 63] M. TVLLI CICERONIS

talem gloriam dederint, tibi sempiternam turpitudinem in-
64 flixerint. Num etiam in hac cotidiana adsidua urbanaque vita
splendorem tuum, gratiam, celebritatem domesticam, operam
forensem, consilium, auxilium, auctoritatem, sententiam sena-
toriam nobis, aut ut verius dicam, cuiquam es infimo ac 5
27 despicatissimo antelaturus ? Age, senatus odit te—quod eum
tu facere iure concedis—adflictorem ac perditorem non modo
dignitatis et auctoritatis sed omnino ordinis ac nominis sui;
videre equites Romani non possunt, quo ex ordine vir prae-
stantissimus et ornatissimus, L. Aelius, est te consule rele- 10
gatus; plebs Romana perditum cupit, in cuius tu infamiam
ea quae per latrones et per servos de me egeras contulisti;
Italia cuncta exsecratur, cuius idem tu superbissime decreta
65 et preces repudiasti. Fac huius odi tanti ac tam universi periculum si audes. Instant post hominum memoriam apparatis- 15
simi magnificentissimique ludi, quales non modo numquam
fuerunt, sed ne quo modo fieri quidem posthac possint possum
ullo pacto suspicari. Da te populo, committe ludis. Sibilum
metuis ? ubi sunt vestrae scholae ? Ne acclametur times ? ne
id quidem est curare philosophi. Manus tibi ne adferantur ? 20
dolor enim est malum, ut tu disputas, existimatio dedecus
infamia turpitudo verba atque ineptiae. Sed de hoc non dubito: non audebit accedere ad ludos. Convivium publicum non
dignitatis causa inibit, nisi forte ut cum patribus conscriptis,

15 instant . . 18 suspicari *Asconius*

P (2 num . . . 6 quod, 10 -legatus . . . 16 lu-, 20 -dem est . . . 24 conscriptis), V, C (1 haec congressio mihi immortalem gloriam conparat,
tibi sempiternam turpitudinem infligit), Ω]   2 num PV: nunc Ω assi-
dua PV: assiduaque Ω 4 forense P 5 ut P^2V: *om.* $P^1\Omega$ es
$P\Omega$: *om.* V infimo PV: infirmissimo Ω 6 despicat- *var. Junt.*:
desperat- $PV\Omega$: despect- $\mathcal{S}$ ante- $P\Omega$: sis ante- V 7 tu facere
Ω (*vestigia in P exstabant*): facere tu V ac VEf: et eX 9 nolunt
non possunt V 10 -legatus PV: -ligatus Ω 12 et per $P\Omega$:
per V 13 idem $P\Omega$: item V 15 appar- P, *Asc.*: par- $V\Omega$
19 times V: *om.* Ω 20 afferantur V: adferantur times $P\Omega$ 21
ut tu P (*sup. lin.*): ut $V\Omega$ 22 verba PV: verba sunt Ω atque *om.* P^1
de hoc non dub- $P\Omega$: haec non dub- nam V 24 patribus conscriptis
$PV\alpha$: p.c. X: P. Clodio *Naugerius*

34

IN L. PISONEM ORATIO [27 65

hoc est cum amatoribus suis, cenet, sed plane animi sui causa: ludos nobis 'idiotis' relinquet. Solet enim in disputationibus 66 suis oculorum et aurium delectationi abdominis voluptates anteferre. Nam quod vobis iste tantum modo improbus, 5 crudelis, olim furunculus, nunc vero etiam rapax, quod sordidus, quod contumax, quod superbus, quod fallax, quod perfidiosus, quod impudens, quod audax esse videatur, nihil scitote esse luxuriosius, nihil libidinosłus, nihil posterius, nihil nequius. Luxuriem autem nolite in isto hanc cogitare: est 67 10 enim quaedam, quamquam omnis est vitiosa atque turpis, tamen ingenuo ac libero dignior. Nihil apud hunc lautum, nihil elegans, nihil exquisitum; laudabo inimicum, ne magno opere quidem quicquam praeter libidines sumptuosum. Toreuma nullum, maximi calices, et hi, ne contemnere suos videa- 15 tur, Placentini; exstructa mensa non conchyliis aut piscibus, sed multa carne subrancida. Servi sordidati ministrant, non nulli etiam senes; idem coquus, idem atriensis; pistor domi nullus, nulla cella; panis et vinum a propola atque de cupa; Graeci stipati quini in lectulis, saepe plures; ipse solus; bibitur 20 usque eo dum de †solio ministretur. Vbi galli cantum audivit, avum suum revixisse putat; mensam tolli iubet.

Dicet aliquis 'unde haec tibi nota sunt ?' Non me hercules **28** contumeliae causa describam quemquam, praesertim ingeni- 68 osum hominem atque eruditum, cui generi esse ego iratus ne

5 olim . . . rapax *Priscianus, GL* ii. 109

P (1 cum maior-, suis ce-, 4 -tum modo . . . 9 nolite), *V, C* (5 olim . . . rapax, 11 nihil apud . . . 12 exquisitum), Ω] 1 amatoribus *V*: maior-*P*Ω: amor- *Manutius* 2 enim *V*: om. Ω 3 abdomini *X* 5 *aut ante aut post* quod sordidus *aliquid excidisse credo* 8 esse *P*Ω: om. *V* nihil libidiniosius nihil proterb *in ras. vel inter lin. V²* posterius *P*Ω: proterbius *V²* 9 luxuriem (lux *deerat*) *P*: luxuriam *V*Ω nolite in isto (*post* nolite *defic. P*) *PV*: in isto nolite Ω *post* hanc *lacunam susp. Faernus* 10 quaedam Ω: quaedam quae *V* 11 est tamen *Clark* 12 ne] cui ne *V* 14 ii ﬅ 18 propola *ed. Rom.*: -pula *V*: -pala Ω 19 lectis *V* bibitur . . . dum] bibiturus qu(a)e eodem Ω 20 solio *V*Ω: dolio *Ant. Augustinus* ministrentur Ω 22 me hercule (-cle *E*) Ω 24 esse ego] ego esse *efX*

35

28 68]　　　M. TVLLI CICERONIS

si cupiam quidem possum. Est quidam Graecus qui cum isto
vivit, homo, vere ut dicam—sic enim cognovi—humanus, sed
tam diu quam diu aut cum aliis est aut ipse secum. Is cum
istum adulescentem iam tum hac distracta fronte vidisset, non
fastidivit eius amicitiam, cum esset praesertim appetitus; dedit 5
se in consuetudinem sic ut prorsus una viveret nec fere ab isto
umquam discederet. Non apud indoctos sed, ut ego arbitror,
in hominum eruditissimorum et humanissimorum coetu loquor.
Audistis profecto dici philosophos Epicureos omnis res quae
sint homini expetendae voluptate metiri; rectene an secus, 10
nihil ad nos, aut si ad nos, nihil ad hoc tempus; sed tamen
lubricum genus orationis adulescenti non acriter intellegenti
69 et saepe praeceps. Itaque admissarius iste, simul atque audivit
voluptatem a philosopho tanto opere laudari, nihil expiscatus
est: sic suos sensus voluptarios omnis incitavit, sic ad illius 15
hanc orationem adhinnivit, ut non magistrum virtutis sed
auctorem libidinis a se illum inventum arbitraretur. Graecus
primo distinguere et dividere, illa quem ad modum dicerentur;
iste, 'claudus' quem ad modum aiunt 'pilam', retinere quod
acceperat, testificari, tabellas obsignare velle, Epicurum diser- 20
tum decernere. Et tamen dicit, ut opinor, se nullum bonum
70 intellegere posse demptis corporis voluptatibus. Quid multa ?
Graecus facilis et valde venustus nimis pugnax contra sena-
29 torem populi Romani esse noluit. Est autem hic de quo loquor
non philosophia solum sed etiam ceteris studiis quae fere 25
ceteros Epicureos neglegere dicunt perpolitus; poema porro

1 est quidam . . . 3 secum *Asconius*

　　V, C (26 poema . . .), Ω] 　2 vere ut Ω, *Asc.*: ut vere *V* 　3 quam-
diu *om. Asc.* 　　aut cum *V, Asc.*: cum Ω 　4 tum] tum cum Ω 　dis-
tracta] diis irata Ω 　　5 fastidivit] fugit Ω 　　6 ab isto umquam]
umquam ab eo *V* 　　10 sunt Ω 　　rectene an *Garatoni*: recte-
neant *V*: recte nam (an *Xmg.*) Ω 　　12 adulescentis *V* 　　13 et
Pluygers: est *V*: *om.* Ω 　　14 tantopere Ω 　　16 adhinniit Ω 　　18
et] atque Ω 　　19 quem ad modum] quomodo Ω: *om.* ς: *fort.* quod
20 epicureum *V* 　diserte α 　　21 decernere] dicere *V* 　et tamen] est
tamen *V*: is autem *Müller*: is tamen *A. Klotz* 　dicit ut] dictum Ω
23 senatorem] imperatorem *V* 　　25 ceteris studiis quae] litteris quod Ω

36

IN L. PISONEM ORATIO [29 70

facit ita festivum, ita concinnum, ita elegans, nihil ut fieri
possit argutius. In quo reprehendat eum licet si qui volet,
modo leviter, non ut improbum, non ut audacem, non ut
impurum, sed ut Graeculum, ut adsentatorem, ut poetam.
5 Devenit autem seu potius incidit in istum eodem deceptus
supercilio Graecus atque advena quo tot sapientes et tanta
civitas; revocare se non poterat familiaritate implicatus, et
simul inconstantiae famam verebatur. Rogatus invitatus
coactus ita multa ad istum de isto quoque scripsit ut omnis
10 hominis libidines, omnia stupra, omnia cenarum genera conviviorumque, adulteria denique eius delicatissimis versibus
expresserit, in quibus si qui velit possit istius tamquam in 71
speculo vitam intueri; ex quibus multa a multis et lecta et
audita recitarem, ni vererer ne hoc ipsum genus orationis quo
15 nunc utor ab huius loci more abhorreret; et simul de ipso qui
scripsit detrahi nil volo. Qui si fuisset in discipulo comparando
meliore fortuna, fortasse austerior et gravior esse potuisset;
sed eum casus in hanc consuetudinem scribendi induxit philosopho valde indignam, si quidem philosophia, ut fertur, vir-
20 tutis continet et offici et bene vivendi disciplinam; quam qui
profitetur gravissimam mihi sustinere personam videtur. Sed 72
idem casus illum ignarum quid profiteretur, cum se philoso-
phum esse diceret, istius impurissimae atque intemperantis-
simae pecudis caeno et sordibus inquinavit.
25 Qui modo cum res gestas consulatus mei conlaudasset, quae
quidem laudatio hominis turpissimi mihi ipsi erat paene turpis,
'non illa tibi' inquit 'invidia nocuit sed versus tui.' Nimis

7 familiaritate implicatus *Priscianus, GL* ii. 473

V, C (1 ... 2 argutius), Ω] 1 nihil ut] ut ni(c)hil *VC* 2 volet
modo] modo vult *V* 3 non ut impurum *post* audacem *V, post*
leviter Ω 5 autem seu] aut Ω 6 tot sapientes] tam (tñ
E) sapiens Ω 7 revocare se] se revocare *X* 9 isto] ipso
Ernesti quoque *om.* Ω 10 hominis *om. V* omnia stupra *om.*
Ω genera conv-] conv- genera *V* 11 denique *om.* Ω 13 et
lecta] lecta Ω 14 ni] nisi Ω 16 nihil volo *V*: volo α: nolo *X*
21 confitetur *V* mihi sustinere] sust- mihi *V* 25 cum *om. X*
26 conlaudatio *V* 27 illa] ulla Ω

37

29 72] M. TVLLI CICERONIS

magna poena te consule constituta est sive malo poetae sive
libero. 'Scripsisti enim: "cedant arma togae". ' Quid tum ?
'Haec res tibi fluctus illos excitavit.' At hoc nusquam opinor
scriptum fuisse in illo elogio quod te consule in sepulcro rei
publicae incisum est: 'VELITIS IVBEATIS VT QVOD M. CICERO 5
30 VERSVM FECERIT,' sed 'QVOD VINDICARIT.' Verum tamen,
73 quoniam te non Aristarchum sed Phalarim grammaticum
habemus, qui non notam apponas ad malum versum, sed
poetam armis persequare, scire cupio quid tandem in isto
versu reprendas, 'cedant arma togae'. 'Tuae dicis' inquit 10
'togae summum imperatorem esse cessurum.' Quid nunc te,
asine, litteras doceam ? non opus est verbis sed fustibus. Non
dixi hanc togam qua sum amictus, nec arma scutum et
gladium unius imperatoris, sed quia pacis est insigne et oti
toga, contra autem arma tumultus atque belli, poetarum more 15
locutus hoc intellegi volui, bellum ac tumultum paci atque
74 otio concessurum. Quaere ex familiari tuo Graeco illo poeta:
probabit genus ipsum et agnoscet, neque te nihil sapere mira-
bitur. 'At in altero illo' inquit 'haeres, "concedat laurea
laudi".' Immo me hercule habeo tibi gratiam; haererem 20
enim nisi tu me expedisses. Nam cum tu timidus ac tremens
tuis ipse furacissimis manibus detractam cruentis fascibus
lauream ad portam Esquilinam abiecisti, iudicasti non modo
amplissimae sed etiam minimae laudi lauream concessisse.
Atque ista oratione hoc tamen intellegi, scelerate, vis, Pom- 25
peium inimicum mihi isto versu esse factum, ut si versus
mihi nocuerit, ab eo quem is versus offenderit videatur mihi

---

2 cedant arma togae *Cicero, de consulatu suo*   4 in eo elogio . . . 5
incisum est *Arusianus, GL* vii. 487   19 concedat laurea laudi *Cicero,
de consulatu suo*

V (*defic. post* 25 hoc), Ω]   1 a malo *V*   2 enim versus Ω   5
ut *VX*¹: ut non α*X*²   9 in isto *Vef*: isto in Ω   10 rephendas *V*:
reprehendas Ω   13 *fort.* ⟨togam⟩ hanc togam   et] aut *V*   14
quia] quae α: q *X*   15 poetarum more] more poetarum Ω   16 lo-
cutus] conloc- *V*: tum loc- *Lambinus*   19 altero illo] illo altero Ω
22 detractam e *V*   23 indicasti ⌐   25 ratione *X*   intellegi
⌐:-gis Ω   27 non nocuerit α

38

IN L. PISONEM ORATIO [30 74

pernicies esse quaesita. Omitto nihil istum versum pertinuisse 75
ad illum; non fuisse meum, quem quantum potuissem multis
saepe orationibus scriptisque decorassem, hunc uno violare
versu. Sed sit offensus primo: nonne compensavit cum uno
5 versiculo tot mea volumina laudum suarum? Quod si est
commotus, ad perniciemne non dicam amicissimi, non ita de
sua laude meriti, non ita de re publica, non consularis, non
senatoris, non civis, non liberi, in hominis caput ille tam
crudelis propter versum fuisset? Tu quid, tu apud quos, tu 31
10 de quo dicas intellegis? Complecti vis amplissimos viros ad
tuum et Gabini scelus, neque id occulte; nam paulo ante
dixisti me cum eis confligere quos despicerem, non attingere
eos qui plus possent, quibus iratus esse deberem. Quorum
quidem—quis enim non intellegit quos dicas?—quamquam
15 non est una causa omnium, tamen est omnium mihi probata.
Me Cn. Pompeius, multis obsistentibus eius erga me studio 76
atque amori, semper dilexit, semper sua coniunctione dignissimum iudicavit, semper non modo incolumem sed etiam
amplissimum atque ornatissimum voluit esse. Vestrae fraudes,
20 vestrum scelus, vestrae criminationes insidiarum mearum,
[vestrae cupiditates provinciarum effecerunt] illius periculorum nefarie fictae, simul eorum qui familiaritatis licentia
suorum improbissimorum sermonum domicilium in auribus
eius impulsu vestro conlocarant, ⟨vestrae cupiditates provin-
25 ciarum effecerunt⟩ ut ego excluderer, omnesque qui me, qui
illius gloriam, qui rem publicam salvam esse cupiebant, sermone atque aditu prohiberentur; quibus rebus est perfectum 77
ut illi plane suo stare iudicio non liceret, cum certi homines
non studium eius a me alienassent, sed auxilium retardassent.
30 Nonne ad te L. Lentulus, qui tum erat praetor, non Q. Sanga,

P (13 quorum ... 19 amplis-, 22 -miliaritatis ... 28 cum cer-), Ω]
2 meum] eum α   3 violarem α   4 compensavit *R. Klotz*: -abit Ω
5 est] esset *Schütz*   9 quid] quidem *efX*   tu de] de *X*   10
complecti vis] complecteris *X*   12 me cum eis] mecum hos α   15 una
causa] causa una *P*   16 eius erga me] erga me eius *P*   21 vestrae ...
effecerunt Ω: *del. Angelius*   24 colocarant *P*: collocaverunt Ω: collocaverunt vestrae ... effecerunt *Angelius*   28 suo stare] stare in suo *P*

39

31 77] M. TVLLI CICERONIS

non L. Torquatus pater, non M. Lucullus venit? qui omnes
ad eum multique mortales oratum in Albanum obsecratumque
venerant ut ne meas fortunas desereret cum rei publicae salute
coniunctas. Quos ille ad te et ad tuum conlegam remisit, ut
causam publicam susciperetis, ut ad senatum referretis; se 5
contra armatum tribunum pl. sine publico consilio decertare
nolle: consulibus ex senatus consulto rem publicam defenden-
78 tibus se arma sumpturum. Ecquid, infelix, recordaris quid
responderis? in quo illi omnes quidem, sed Torquatus praeter
ceteros furebat contumacia responsi tui: te non esse tam fortem 10
quam ipse Torquatus in consulatu fuisset aut ego; nihil opus
esse armis, nihil contentione; me posse rem publicam iterum
servare si cessissem; infinitam caedem fore si restitissem.
Deinde ad extremum neque se neque generum neque conlegam suum tribuno pl. defuturum. Hic tu hostis ac proditor 15
32 aliis me inimiciorem quam tibi debere esse dicis? Ego C.
79 Caesarem non eadem de re publica sensisse quae me scio; sed
tamen, quod iam de eo his audientibus saepe dixi, me ille sui
totius consulatus eorumque honorum quos cum proximis com-
municavit socium esse voluit, detulit invitavit rogavit. Non 20
sum ego propter nimiam fortasse constantiae cupiditatem ad-
ductus ad causam; non postulabam ut ei carissimus essem
cuius ego ne beneficiis quidem sententiam meam tradidissem.
Adducta res in certamen te consule putabatur utrum quae
superiore anno ille gessisset manerent an rescinderentur. Quid 25
loquar plura? Si tantum ille in me esse uno roboris et virtutis putavit ut quae ipse gesserat conciderent si ego restitissem, cur ego non ignoscam si anteposuit suam salutem meae?

P (2 in Albanum . . . 7 defendentibus, 11 fuisset . . . 16 ego C., 20
-vit non . . . 28), Ω] 3 ut *P: om.* Ω   6 publico consilio *P*: con- pub-
Ω   7 consulibus] se cons- *P*: sed cons- *R. Klotz*   8 ecquid ς:
haec quid *E*: et quid *efX*   9 responderis] his resp- α   12 esse]
esset *P*   contione *P*   rem p. iterum *P*: iterum r.p. Ω   13 servare *P*α: salvare *X*   14 se . . . suum *P*Ω: te . . . tuum *Garatoni*
15 tribunum pl. *P*: tr ñ (*vel* nō) pl α: tr. pl. non *X*   21 ego *om. P*
23 ne ben- *P*: ben- Ω: ben- ne *X²*   27 quae *P*: ea quae Ω   28 cur
ego *P*ς: cur Ω

40

IN L. PISONEM ORATIO [**32** 80

Sed praeterita omitto. Me ut Cn. Pompeius omnibus suis 80
studiis laboribus vitae periculis complexus est, cum municipia
pro me adiret, Italiae fidem imploraret, P. Lentulo consuli,
auctori salutis meae, frequens adsideret, senatus sententiam
5 praestaret, in contionibus non modo se defensorem salutis
meae sed etiam supplicem pro me profiteretur, huius volun-
tatis eum quem multum posse intellegebat, mihi non inimicum
esse cognorat, socium sibi et adiutorem C. Caesarem adiunxit.
Iam vides me tibi non inimicum sed hostem, illis quos describis
10 non modo non iratum sed etiam amicum esse debere; quorum
alter, id quod meminero, semper aeque mihi amicus fuit ac
sibi, alter, id quod obliviscar, aliquando sibi amicior quam
mihi. Deinde hoc ita fit ut viri fortes, etiam si ferro inter se 81
comminus decertarint, tamen illud contentionis odium simul
15 cum ipsa pugna armisque deponant. Neque me ille odisse
potuit umquam, ne tum quidem cum dissidebamus. Habet
hoc virtus, quam tu ne de facie quidem nosti, ut viros fortis
species eius et pulchritudo etiam in hoste [posita] delectet.
Equidem dicam ex animo, patres conscripti, quod sentio, 33
20 et quod vobis audientibus saepe iam dixi. Si mihi numquam
amicus C. Caesar fuisset, si semper iratus, si semper aspernaretur amicitiam meam seque mihi implacabilem inexpia-
bilemque praeberet, tamen ei, cum tantas res gessisset
gereretque cotidie, non amicus esse non possem; cuius ego
25 imperium, non Alpium vallum, contra ascensum transgres-
sionemque Gallorum, non Rheni fossam gurgitibus illis red-
undantem Germanorum immanissimis gentibus obicio et
oppono; perfecit ille ut si montes resedissent, amnes exaruis- 82
sent, non naturae praesidio sed victoria sua rebusque gestis
30 Italiam munitam haberemus. Sed cum me expetat diligat

P (1 ... 28 rese-), Ω]   1 mitto P suis studiis] studiis suis P
4 senatus P: senatui Ω 11 amicus $P\alpha$: *om*. X 12 aliquando
(*vel* aliquo) sibi Ω: sibi aliquando $P\varsigma$ 15 deponant P: pon- Ω
neque $P\alpha$: atque X 16 potuit umquam P: numquam (um- E) potuit
Ω 18 posita $P\Omega$: *om*. ς: proposita *Francken*   21 fuisset si $P\alpha$:
fuisset sed X semper asp- P: asp- Ω 22 seque P: seseque Ω
25 imperium $P\varsigma$: imperio Ω

41

33 82]   M. TVLLI CICERONIS

omni laude dignum putet, tu me [a] tuis inimicitiis ad simultatem revocabis, sic tuis sceleribus rei publicae praeterita fata
refricabis ? Quod quidem tu, qui bene nosses coniunctionem
meam et Caesaris, eludebas, cum a me trementibus omnino
labris, sed tamen cur tibi nomen non deferrem requirebas, 5
quamquam, quod ad me attinet, 'numquam istam imminuam
curam infitiando tibi', tamen est mihi considerandum quantum illi tantis rei publicae negotiis tantoque bello impedito
ego homo amicissimus sollicitudinis atque oneris imponam.
Nec despero tamen, quamquam languet iuventus, nec perinde 10
atque debebat in laudis et gloriae cupiditate versatur, futuros
aliquos qui abiectum hoc cadaver consularibus spoliis nudare
non nolint, praesertim tam adflicto, tam inopi, tam infirmo,
tam enervato reo, qui te ita gesseris ut timeres ne indignus
beneficio videreris, nisi eius a quo missus eras simillimus 15
exstitisses.

34   An vero tu parum putas investigatas esse a nobis labis
83 imperi tui stragisque provinciae ? quas quidem nos non vestigiis odorantes ingressus tuos sed totis volutationibus corporis
et cubilibus persecuti sumus. Notata a nobis sunt et prima 20
illa scelera in adventu, cum accepta pecunia a Dyrrachinis ob
necem hospitis tui Platoris, eius ipsius domum devertisti cuius
sanguinem addixeras, eumque servis symphoniacis et aliis
muneribus acceptis timentem multumque dubitantem con-
firmasti, et Thessalonicam fide tua venire iussisti. Quem ne 25
maiorum quidem more supplicio adfecisti, cum miser ille
securibus hospitis sui cervices subicere gestiret, sed ei medico
quem tecum [tu] eduxeras imperasti ut venas hominis inci-

6 quamquam . . . 7 tibi *Asconius* (numquam . . . tibi *Accius, trag.* 234)

Ω] 1 a *del. Garatoni*   simultatem C. Caesaris *Lambinus*   2
sic *del. Pluygers*   3 quod] in quo *Koch*   tu] cū α: çū tu *X*
5 tibi] ibi α   11 debeat *X*   13 nolit *X*   inopi *Halm*: opimo Ω
infirmo ς: infimo Ω   20 notata *Angelius*: notanda Ω   22 devertisti *Mommsen*: evert- Ω   24 accepisti trementem α   28 tu *del.*
Naugerius: tum *Halm*

42

IN L. PISONEM ORATIO [34 83

deret; cum quidem tibi etiam accessio fuit ad necem Platoris 84
Pleuratus eius comes, quem necasti verberibus summa sene-
ctute confectum. Idemque tu Rabocentum, Bessicae gentis
principem, cum te trecentis talentis regi Cotto vendidisses,
5 securi percussisti, cum ille ad te legatus in castra venisset, et
tibi magna praesidia et auxilia a Bessis peditum equitumque
polliceretur; neque eum solum sed etiam ceteros legatos qui
simul venerant, quorum omnium capita regi Cotto vendidisti.
Denseletis, quae natio semper oboediens huic imperio etiam
10 in illa omnium barbarorum defectione Macedoniam C. Sentio
praetore tutata est, nefarium bellum et crudele intulisti, eisque cum fidelissimis sociis uti posses, hostibus uti acerrimis
maluisti. Ita perpetuos defensores Macedoniae vexatores ac
praedatores effecisti: vectigalia nostra perturbarunt, urbes
15 ceperunt, vastarunt agros, socios nostros in servitutem ab-
duxerunt, familias abripuerunt, pecus abegerunt, Thessalo-
nicensis, cum oppido desperassent, munire arcem coegerunt.
A te Iovis Zbelsurdi fanum antiquissimum barbarorum san- 35
ctissimumque direptum est. Tua scelera di immortales in 85
20 nostros milites expiaverunt; qui cum novo genere morbi
adfligerentur, neque se recreare quisquam posset qui semel
incidisset, dubitabat nemo quin violati hospites, legati necati,
pacati atque socii nefario bello lacessiti, fana vexata hanc
tantam efficerent vastitatem.
25 Cognoscis ex particula parva scelerum et crudelitatis tuae
genus universum: quid avaritiae, quae criminibus infinitis 86
implicata est, summam nunc explicem? Generatim ea quae
maxime nota sunt dicam. Nonne sestertium centiens et

26 quid ... 27 explicem *Priscianus, GL* ii. 473

C (14 vectigalia ... 16 abegerunt), Ω]   1 quidem ς: equidem Ω
2 eius] est *E*   4 Cotto *Beroaldus*: coddo Ω: Cotyi *Garatoni*   6 et
auxilia *X*: auxilia α: *del. Baiter*   8 Cotto *ed. Ven.*: cottho (*vel*
coccho) Ω: Cotyi *Garatoni*   10 Macedoniam *Garatoni*: mace-
donica Ω   sentio p.R. α: sextio pr. *X*   14 praedatores *E*: perdit-
X: p̄dit- *e*: p̄dit- *f*   16 abripuerunt *C*: arr- Ω   18 Svelsurdi *J. H.
Mordtmann*: velsuri Ω   20 novo *Müller*: uno Ω   21 simul α
25 cognoscis Ω: agnoscis *Watt*   27 implicita (-ata *v.l.*) *Prisc.*

43

35 86] M. TVLLI CICERONIS

octogiens, quod quasi vasari nomine in venditione mei capitis
ascripseras, ex aerario tibi attributum Romae in quaestu
reliquisti ? Nonne cum c talenta tibi Apolloniatae Romae
dedissent ne pecunias creditas solverent, ultro Fufidium,
equitem Romanum, hominem ornatissimum, creditorem debi- 5
toribus suis addixisti ? Nonne hiberna cum legato praefectoque tuo tradidisses, evertisti miseras funditus civitates, quae
non solum bonis sunt exhaustae sed etiam nefarias libidinum
contumelias turpitudinesque subierunt ? Qui modus tibi fuit
frumenti aestimandi, qui honorarii ? si quidem potest vi et 10
metu extortum honorarium nominari. Quod cum peraeque
omnes, tum acerbissime Boeotii [et] Byzantii, Cherronensus
Thessalonica sensit. Vnus tu dominus, unus aestimator, unus
36 venditor tota in provincia per triennium frumenti omnis fuisti.
87 Quid ego rerum capitalium quaestiones, reorum pactiones, red- 15
emptiones, acerbissimas damnationes, libidinosissimas libera-
tiones proferam ? tantum locum aliquem cum mihi notum esse
senseris, tecum ipse licebit quot in eo genere et quanta sint
crimina recordere. Quid ? illam armorum officinam ecquid
recordaris, cum omni totius provinciae pecore compulso pel- 20
lium nomine omnem quaestum illum domesticum paternum-
que renovasti ? videras enim grandis iam puer bello Italico
repleri quaestu vestram domum, cum pater armis faciendis
tuus praefuisset. Quid ? vectigalem provinciam, singulis rebus
quaecumque venirent certo portorio imposito, servis tuis [pu- 25
88 blicanis] a te †factam esse meministi ? Quid ? centuriatus palam
venditos, quid ? per tuum servolum ordines adsignatos, quid ?

20 omni pecore compulso *Servius auct. buc.* 7. 2

Ω] 1 quasi *del. Pluygers*   3 cc *X*   apolloniate ς: apolliniate (*vel*
-inate) Ω   7 tuo *om. X*   10 extimandi *X*   12 boetii Ω:
Bottiaei *Madvig*   et *del. Müller*   Cherronensus *Halm*: -enses Ω   13
et Thess- *Halm*   estimator *E*: existim- *ef*: extim- *X*   15 reorum]
rerum *E*   17 esse ς: est (*om. ef*) Ω   19 recordere ς: -dare Ω
armorum ς: marmorum (in arm- *E*) Ω   ecquid] et quid *efX*   24
p.r. provinciam *Clark*   25 servam *Clark*   publicanis *del. Bake*
26 facta *E*

44

IN L. PISONEM ORATIO   [36 88

stipendium militibus per omnis annos a civitatibus mensis
palam propositis esse numeratum ? Quid ? illa in Pontum profectio et conatus tuus, quid ? debilitatio atque abiectio animi
tui Macedonia praetoria nuntiata, cum tu non solum quod
5 tibi succederetur sed quod Gabinio non succederetur exsanguis
et mortuus concidisti, quid ? quaestor aediliciis reiectis praepositus, legatorum tuorum optimus abs te quisque violatus,
tribuni militares non recepti, M. Baebius, vir fortis, interfectus
iussu tuo ? Quid quod tu totiens diffidens ac desperans rebus 89
10 tuis in sordibus lamentis luctuque iacuisti, quod populari illi
sacerdoti sescentos ad bestias amicos sociosque misisti, quod
cum sustentare vix posses maerorem tuum doloremque decessionis, Samothraciam te primum, post inde Thasum cum tuis
teneris saltatoribus et cum Autobulo Athamante [et] Timocle,
15 formosis fratribus, contulisti, quod [cum] inde te recipiens in
villa Euhadiae, quae fuit uxor Execesti, iacuisti maerens
aliquot dies, atque inde obsoletus Thessalonicam omnibus
inscientibus noctuque venisti, quod cum concursum ploran-
tium ac tempestatem querelarum ferre non posses, in oppidum
20 devium Beroam profugisti ? Quo in oppido cum tibi spe falsa,
quod Q. Ancharium non esse successurum putares, animos
rumor inflasset, quo te modo ad tuam intemperantiam, **37**
scelerate, renovasti! Mitto aurum coronarium quod te diutis- 90
sime torsit, cum modo velles, modo nolles; lex enim generi
25 tui et decerni et te accipere vetabat nisi decreto triumpho.
In quo tu acceptam tamen et devoratam pecuniam, ut in

10 quod . . . 11 misisti *Asconius*

Ω] 6 aediliciis reiectis *Gulielmius*: aedilitius reiectus Ω   11 amicos
sociosque] socios stipendiarios quoque *Asc.*   quod *Garatoni*: quid α:
quid quod *X*   12 decessionis Ϛ: decens- *E*: descens- *eX*   13
post *om. X*   Thasum *Turnebus*: tharsum Ω   14 antobulo *efX*   et
del. Madvig   Timocle *Beroaldus*: timode Ω   15 quod *Garatoni*:
quid cum (qui tum *e*) Ω   16 euchadiae *X*   Execesti *Garatoni*:
exegisti Ω   18 quod *Lambinus*: qui Ω   20 perfugisti *X*   21
quod Q.] quodq. α   23 renovasti *Clark*: innov- Ω   25 te *om.* Ϛ
26 acceptam . . . devoratam pecuniam *Abram*: accepta . . . devorata pecunia Ω   tamen] iam *R. Klotz: del. Abram*

45

37 90] M. TVLLI CICERONIS

Achaeorum centum talentis, evomere non poteras, vocabula
tantum pecuniarum et genera mutabas. Mitto diplomata tota
in provincia passim data, mitto numerum navium summam-
que praedae, mitto rationem exacti imperatique frumenti,
mitto ereptam libertatem populis ac singulis qui erant adfecti 5
praemiis nominatim, quorum nihil est quod non sit lege Iulia
91 ne fieri liceat sanctum diligenter. Aetoliam, quae procul a
barbaris disiuncta [est] gentibus, in sinu pacis posita, medio
fere Graeciae gremio continetur, o Poena et Furia sociorum,
decedens miseram perdidisti. Arsinoen Stratum Naupactum, 10
ut modo tute indicasti nobilis urbis atque plenas, fateris ab
hostibus esse captas. Quibus autem hostibus ? nempe eis quos
tu Ambraciae sedens primo tuo adventu ex oppidis Agraeorum
atque Dolopum demigrare et aras et focos relinquere coegisti.
Hoc tu in exitu, praeclare imperator, cum tibi ad pristinas 15
cladis accessio fuisset Aetoliae repentinus interitus, exercitum
dimisisti, neque ullam poenam quae tanto facinori deberetur
non maluisti subire quam numerum tuorum militum reli-
quiasque cognosci.

38
92 Atque ut duorum Epicureorum similitudinem in re militari 20
imperioque videatis, Albucius, cum in Sardinia triumphasset,
Romae damnatus est: hic cum similem exitum exspectaret,
in Macedonia tropaea posuit; ea quae bellicae laudis victoriae-
que omnes gentes insignia et monumenta esse voluerunt noster
hic praeposterus imperator amissorum oppidorum, caesarum 25
legionum, provinciae praesidio et reliquis militibus orbatae ad
sempiternum dedecus sui generis et nominis funesta indicia
constituit; idemque, ut esset quod in basi tropaeorum inscribi
incidique posset, Dyrrachium ut venit decedens, obsessus est
ab eis ipsis militibus quos paulo ante Torquato respondit 30

Ω] 7 liceat] possit *X* 8 est *om.* ⸔ 10 arsinoan Ω Stratum
Turnebus: thracum Ω neopactum *X* 12 his α 13 Agraeorum
Lambinus: aggrinarum Ω: Agrianum *Turnebus* 18 quam quemquam *Madvig* 19 cognosci *Lallemand*: cognoscere Ω 22 exspectaret ⸔: spect- Ω 23 ea que *X*: eaq. α: eaque quae *Naugerius*
27 funesta *om. X* 30 iis ipsis *X*: his ipsis (ipsis his *ef*) α

46

IN L. PISONEM ORATIO [38 92

benefici causa a se esse dimissos. Quibus cum iuratus adfirmas-
set se quae deberentur postero die persoluturum, domum se
abdidit; inde nocte intempesta crepidatus veste servili navem
conscendit Brundisiumque vitavit et ultimas Hadriani maris
5 oras petivit, cum interim Dyrrachii milites domum in qua 93
istum esse arbitrabantur obsidere coeperunt, et cum latere
hominem putarent, ignis circumdederunt. Quo metu commoti
Dyrrachini profugisse noctu crepidatum imperatorem indica-
verunt. Illi autem statuam istius persimilem, quam stare
10 celeberrimo in loco voluerat ne suavissimi hominis memoria
moreretur, deturbant adfligunt comminuunt dissipant. Sic
odium quod in ipsum attulerant, id in eius imaginem ac
simulacrum profuderunt. Quae cum ita sint—non enim dubito 94
quin cum haec quae excellent me nosse videas, non existimes
15 mediam illam partem et turbam flagitiorum tuorum mihi esse
inauditam—nihil est quod me hortere, nihil est quod invites;
admoneri me satis est. Admonebit autem nemo alius nisi rei
publicae tempus, quod mihi quidem magis videtur quam tu
umquam arbitratus es appropinquare. Ecquid vides, ecquid 39
20 sentis, lege iudiciaria lata, quos posthac iudices simus habituri? Neque legetur quisquis voluerit, nec quisquis noluerit
non legetur; nulli conicientur in illum ordinem, nulli eximen-
tur; non ambitio ad gratiam, non †iniquitas ad simulationem
conicientur†; iudices iudicabunt ei quos lex ipsa, non quos
25 hominum libido delegerit. Quod cum ita sit, mihi crede,
neminem invitum invitabis; res ipsa et rei publicae tempus aut
me ipsum, quod nolim, aut alium quempiam aut invitabit aut
dehortabitur.

19 ecquid vides . . . 20 habituri *Asconius*

Ω] 6 arbitrabantur ϛ: -trantur Ω   10 in *om.* α   15 e
turba ϛ   18 mihi quidem *X*: quidem mihi *E*: mihi *ef*   19 ecquid v- *E*: etquid v- *efX, Asc.*   ecquid s- *ed. Ald.*: etquid s- Ω, *Asc.*
20 posthac *X, Asc.*: post haec α   21 neque *Madvig*: non aeque Ω
23 simulationem Ω: simultatem *Lambinus*: aemulationem *Madvig* (non
ad iniquitatem aemulatio *Busche*: non simultas ad iniquitatem *Watt*)
24 conicientur Ω: conitetur *Faernus*   ii *X*: hii *ef*: in *E*   26 invitum
Hotomanus: invitus Ω

47

39 95] M. TVLLI CICERONIS

95 Equidem, ut paulo ante dixi, non eadem supplicia esse in
hominibus existimo quae fortasse plerique, damnationes expul-
siones neces; denique nullam mihi poenam videtur habere id
quod accidere innocenti, quod forti, quod sapienti, quod bono
viro et civi potest. Damnatio ista quae in te flagitatur obtigit 5
P. Rutilio, quod specimen habuit haec civitas innocentiae:
maior mihi iudicum et rei publicae poena illa visa est quam
Rutili. L. Opimius eiectus est e patria, is qui praetor et consul
maximis rem publicam periculis liberarat: non in eo cui facta
est iniuria sed in eis qui fecerunt sceleris et conscientiae poena 10
permansit. At contra bis Catilina absolutus, emissus etiam ille
auctor tuus provinciae, cum stuprum Bonae deae pulvinaribus
intulisset: quis fuit in tanta civitate qui illum incesto libera-
tum, non eos qui ita iudicarunt pari scelere obstrictos arbitra-
40
retur? An ego exspectem dum de te quinque et septuaginta 15
96
tabellae diribeantur, de quo iam pridem omnes mortales
omnium generum aetatum ordinum iudicaverunt? Quis enim
te aditu, quis ullo honore, quis denique communi salutatione
dignum putat? Omnes memoriam consulatus tui, facta mores,
faciem denique ac nomen a re publica detestantur. Legati qui 20
una fuerunt alienati, tribuni militum inimici, centuriones et
si qui ex tanto exercitu reliqui milites exstant, non dimissi
abs te sed dissipati, te oderunt, tibi pestem exoptant, te
exsecrantur. Achaia exhausta, Thessalia vexata; laceratae
Athenae, Dyrrachium et Apollonia exinanita; Ambracia 25
direpta, Parthini et Bullienses inlusi; Epirus excisa, Locri

8 L. Opimius . . . 11 poena remansit *Asconius*

C (17 quis te . . . 20 nomen detestantur, 23 omnes te oderunt . . . 24
execrantur), Ω] 6 haec civitas] hic cuius α: hec civitas maior hic civis
cuius *X* 8 e α: a *X*: *om. Asc.* praetor] et post praeturam *Asc.*:
et praetor *A. Klotz* 9 periculis rem p. *Asc.* 10 iniuria est
Asc. eis *X, Asc.*: his α et α, *Asc.*: ac *X* 11 remansit *X, Asc.*
14 iudicarunt ϛ: -arint Ω: -arant *Ernesti* astrictos *X* 16 diribeantur *Ant. Augustinus*: diripiantur Ω 18 aditu *C*α: auditu *X*
19 putat *C*: putet Ω 21 fuerunt ϛ: fuere Ω militum ϛ: mil. Ω
22 existunt *X* 26 Parthini *Naugerius*: parthenii Ω Bullidenses *Vrsinus*

48

IN L. PISONEM ORATIO [40 96

Phocii Boeotii exusti; Acarnania Amphilochia Perraebia Athamanumque gens vendita; Macedonia condonata barbaris, Aetolia amissa; Dolopes finitimique montani oppidis atque agris exterminati; cives Romani qui in his locis neg-
5 otiantur te unum solum suum depeculatorem vexatorem praedonem hostem venisse senserunt. Ad horum omnium 97 iudicia tot atque tanta domesticum iudicium accessit: sententiae damnationis tuae occultus adventus, furtivum iter per Italiam, introitus in urbem desertus ab amicis, nullae ad
10 senatum e provincia litterae, nulla ex trinis aestivis gratulatio, nulla triumphi mentio; non modo quid gesseris sed ne quibus in locis quidem fueris dicere audes. Ex illo fonte et seminario triumphorum cum arida folia laureae rettulisses, cum ea abiecta ad portam reliquisti, tum tu ipse de te 'FECISSE
15 VIDERI' pronuntiavisti. Qui si nihil gesseras dignum honore, ubi exercitus, ubi sumptus, ubi imperium, ubi illa uberrima supplicationibus triumphisque provincia? Sin autem aliquid speraveras, cogitaras id quod imperatoris nomen, quod laureati fasces, quod illa tropaea plena dedecoris et risus te commen-
20 tatum esse declarant, quis te miserior, quis te damnatior, qui neque scribere ad senatum a te bene rem publicam esse gestam, neque praesens dicere ausus es? An tu mihi cui semper ita **41** persuasum fuerit non eventis sed factis cuiusque fortunam 98 ponderari, [dicere audes] neque in tabellis paucorum iudicum
25 sed in sententiis omnium civium famam nostram fortunamque pendere, [te] indemnatum videri putas quem socii, quem foederati, quem liberi populi, quem stipendiarii, quem negotiatores, quem publicani, quem universa civitas, quem legati,

---

C (4 cives . . . 6 senserunt, 18 ita et imperatoris . . . 20 dampnatior), Ω] 1 acarnania ς: acarnia (ach- X) Ω perrhebia Ω 2 ath- ς: ach- Ω 4 his $C\Omega$: iis *ed. Ven.* 5 solum suum] suum sotiorumque C 7 sententiae X: sententiae et α: nam quid fuerunt nisi sententiae A. *Klotz* sententiae . . . 8 tuae *del. Bake* 13 laurea α 17 aliqς X 18 speraveras *Bake*: sperare volueras Ω: sperare potueras *Madvig* si cogitaras *Naugerius* 20 te est miserior quis dampnatior quis impudentior (im *sup. lin.*) C 24 dicere audes om. ς 26 te *del. Garatoni*

5993 F 49

41 98] IN L. PISONEM ORATIO

quem tribuni militares, quem reliqui milites qui ferrum, qui
famem, qui morbum effugerunt, omni cruciatu dignissimum
putent, cui non apud senatum, non apud ullum ordinem, [non
apud equites Romanos,] non in urbe, non in Italia maximorum
scelerum venia ulla ad ignoscendum dari possit, qui se ipsum 5
oderit, qui metuat omnis, qui suam causam nemini committere
99 audeat, qui se ipse condemnet ? Numquam ego sanguinem
expetivi tuum, numquam illud extremum quod posset esse
improbis et probis commune supplicium legis ac iudici, sed
abiectum, contemptum, despectum a ceteris, a te ipso despe- 10
ratum et relictum, circumspectantem omnia, quicquid increpuisset pertimescentem, diffidentem tuis rebus, sine voce,
sine libertate, sine auctoritate, sine ulla specie consulari, hor-
rentem, trementem, adulantem omnis videre te volui, vidi.
Qua re si tibi evenerit quod metuis ne accidat, equidem non 15
moleste feram; sin id tardius forte fiet, fruar tamen tua et
indignitate et timiditate, nec te minus libenter metuentem
videbo ne reus fias quam reum, nec minus laetabor cum te
semper sordidum, quam si paulisper sordidatum viderem.

10 despecto a ceteris a se ipso desperato *Arusianus, GL* vii. 463
14 adulantem omnes *ibid.* 457; omnes adulantem *Pompeius, GL* v. 234

C (16 fruar . . . 19 viderim), Ω] 2 morbum] mortem *X* 3 putent
Garatoni: -ant Ω non . . . Romanos *del. Halm, post* senatum *posuit
Garatoni* 5 ad ignoscendum *del. Halm* (ulla dari possit ad ignoscendum dari possit *X*) ipse *f* 7 ipsum *X* 8 expetivi *X*²:
expectavi Ω potest *Bake* 16 tamen] vero *C* et indig- et timid-
C: indig- Ω 17 te *C*: *om.* Ω metuentem videbo] videbo metuentem *C* 19 viderim *C*

50

COMMENTARY

THE beginning of the speech survives only in fragments. The size of the missing part can be calculated in two ways (A. Klotz, *praefatio*, p. xli). The quaternion of *V* which contains § 32 *tamen*– § 74 *hoc* is marked at the end with the figure 'ii'. The lost first quaternion must have contained everything before § 32 *tamen*. In the present edition §§ 32–74 contain 526 lines, §§ 1–32 394 lines. Therefore the equivalent of about 130 lines has been lost before § 1.

Secondly, Asconius in his commentary gives references by line. His lines 270, 300, 320, 620(?), and 800 correspond in this text to lines 42, 66, 84, 298, and 435 (counting from § 1). The proportions suggest that the equivalent of about 170 lines of this text has been lost. The calculation from *V* is more accurate as Asconius's figures are approximate and not entirely self-consistent.

Eleven fragments are found in the florilegium *C*, apparently in correct sequence. Five (viii–xi, xiii) are found in Asconius, all but frag. ix in correct sequence. The combination of these two series, and the placing of the other fragments, is a matter for conjecture; it is useful that frag. xiii is found both in *C* and in Asconius.

In frags. i–vi Cicero welcomes Piso's recall from Macedonia and mocks his speech in the senate (introd., p. xiv). In frags. vii–xvi he attacks his abilities and relatives. In frags. xvii–xviii he accuses him of hypocrisy; this leads naturally to § 1. Frag. xix cannot be placed, and frags. xx–xxi probably do not belong to the speech.

Frag. **i**: the opening words of the speech, according to Quintilian and Diomedes. Cicero is paradoxically delighted to see Piso because he has long hoped for his recall. Speeches usually opened with more restraint, but the dramatic note suits an invective (cf. *Cat.* i. 1). Quintilian and Diomedes see a senarius in *pro . . . dies*; they must have pronounced *qui hic* with hiatus. For accidental verses cf. L. Laurand, *Études sur le style des discours de Cicéron* (Paris, 1936–8), ii⁴. 143 ff., Volkmann, pp. 521 ff.

peroptatus: adjectives with the prefix *per-* are particularly common in Cicero's early speeches. They must often have been used in lively conversation, but are not necessarily colloquial; cf. J. André, *REL* xxix, 1951, 121 ff.

viderem: for historic sequence after a true perfect cf. K.–S. ii. 179.

Frag. **ii**: Piso's disgrace is so terrible that it is punishment enough (cf. §§ 42–43, 99).

Frag. **iii**: Piso, though a poor speaker (§ 1), had attacked Cicero

51

Frag. iii–viii] COMMENTARY

in the senate. This fragment, though nowhere specifically assigned to the *in Pisonem*, certainly refers to Piso (cf. the quotation from Jerome in the testimonia); it suits this context well. For the epigram cf. Gell. i. 15. 15 'Epicharmium quoque illud non inscite se habet: οὐ λέγειν τύγ' ἐσσὶ δεινός, ἀλλὰ σιγᾶν ἀδύνατος (frag. 272 Kaibel), ex quo hoc profecto sumptum est: qui cum loqui non posset tacere non potuit'; Otto, p. 338, Mart. vi. 41. 2, Plin. *epist.* vii. 6. 7, Jerome, *epist.* 61. 4. 1, 109. 2. 4, *in Mich.* lib. ii praef., Aug. *retract.* ii. 85. 1.

Frag. **iv:** Piso would not have attacked Cicero if his crimes had not made him mad (cf. 46. 14 n.). This fragment is quoted by Quintilian as an instance of pleonasm.

istum: unemphatic pronouns (and enclitics in general) tend to occupy the second place in the clause in Indo-European languages; cf. J. Wackernagel, *IF* i, 1892, 333 ff. (= *Kleine Schriften*, i. 1 ff.), K.–S. ii. 592 f. For the placing of such a word between a noun and its dependent genitive cf. *Phil.* xiii. 4 'ora vobis eorum ponite ante oculos', *Thes. L.L.* vi. 2739. 67.

scelerum: 'arising from his crimes'. *caligo* refers to mental and moral blindness; cf. *Thes. L.L.* iii. 160. 55. *excitaverunt* suits *faces*, the nearest noun, better than *caligo*.

Frag. **v:** Piso has mentioned topics which in his own interest he ought to have left alone. *incidit* and *inruit* are probably perfect in tense; cf. frag. vi *est ausus*, which belongs to the same context, and perhaps follows immediately after this fragment.

Frag. **vii. quid . . . inertius?:** for this formula (= *ille est omnium inertissimus*) cf. Fraenkel on Aesch. *Ag.* 601, Hofmann, *Umgangssprache*, pp. 89 f.

abstrusius: 'more secretive' (with his thoughts hidden away); Piso is elsewhere described as a hypocrite (p. 195). The only apparent parallel for this usage is Tac. *ann.* i. 24. 1 'abstrusum et tristissima quaeque maxime occultantem'. Yet Cicero uses *tectus* similarly (*Deiot.* 16, *fin.* ii. 54).

Frag. **viii** seems to belong to the same context as frag. vii.

autem: for this use in corrections cf. K.–S. ii. 95, *Thes. L.L.* ii. 1579. 57.

ingenui: assonance (*adnominatio*) is natural in Latin and particularly common in Cicero; cf. § 2 *moribus, maioribus*, § 12 *consulum, consulere*, § 21 *importunitate, impuritate*, § 94 *invitum invitabis*. See further E. Wölfflin, *Sitz. Bayer. Akad.*, Phil.-hist. Kl. 1887, ii. 187 ff., H. Holst, *Die Wortspiele in Ciceros Reden* (Oslo, 1925), pp. 63 ff., Volkmann, p. 479.

colore ipso . . . : Piso's swarthy complexion (§ 1) was unRoman; his inadequacy at public speaking (§ 1, *in sen.* 14) was

52

COMMENTARY [Frag. viii–ix

surprising in a member of this family; his bad character did not suit the name 'Piso', which had a virtuous ring.

moribus nomen: Asconius comments 'non puto vos ignorare hunc Pisonem ex ea familia esse quae Frugi appellata sit'. Cf. also *Sest.* 21 '(Piso) erat eo nomine ut ingenerata familiae frugalitas videretur'. Yet our Piso was not descended from the original Piso Frugi; he is never called Frugi, nor is his son (R. Syme, *JRS* xlvi, 1956, 21). The point seems to be that the name 'Piso', because of its associations with 'Frugi', has itself an air of *frugalitas*. For virtuous Pisones Frugi cf. *Verr.* iv. 56, *Font.* 39, *Flacc.* frag. Bob. x, *fin.* ii. 90, *Tusc.* iii. 16.

Frag. **ix** describes Calventius, Piso's maternal grandfather. This fragment is quoted by Asconius out of sequence; after quoting frag. xiii he comments 'quis fuerit socer Pisonis patris ipse supra dixit his verbis: Insuber quidam fuit . . .'. He would not have given this reminder if frags. ix and xiii had come close together. Frag. ix seems to be the first introduction of Calventius, as is shown by the formula *Insuber quidam fuit* (cf. Caecil. 55 'Agonis quaedam est Lilybaetana' and Richter–Eberhard's note, *Clu.* 21 'Larinas quaedam fuit Dinaea'). Therefore frag. ix comes before frag. xi, which also deals with Calventius; apparently Cicero mentioned his arrival in Rome before his earlier career. Frag. x probably belongs to the same context as frag. xi; so it seems best to put frag. ix before frag. x.

Calventius came from Placentia on the south side of the Po (frags. x, xi, §§ 14, 67); it was already in his time an old and civilized Latin colony. Cicero here pretends that he was an Insuber, i.e. a Gaul living in a tribal society near Mediolanum (so § 62). He even alleges that he was a Transalpine Gaul (frag. xi and Asc. 4 KS, § 53, *in sen.* 15 and Schol. Bob. 'quod vero ait de materno sanguine Transalpino, aequo plenius in ea oratione quae in Pisonem habita est continetur'). For these and similar fictions cf. p. 194, R. Syme, *JRS* xxvii, 1937, 130 f.

The name *Calventius* occurs in 23 inscriptions in *CIL* v (Gallia Cisalpina); this is a much larger proportion than in any other volume. Most of the instances are in the east of the province (Brixia, Verona, Ateste, Tergeste, etc.); there is one case at Mediolanum and two at Comum (also Insubrian), but no inference can be made from such small numbers. No instances are reported from Transalpine Gaul. W. Schulze gives the name an Etruscan origin (*Eigennamen*, p. 139); however that may be, it only occurs 9 times in *CIL* xi. It is found once at Placentia (*CIL* xi. 1243), and also appears in the neighbouring community of Veleia (*CIL* xi. 1147 pag. ii. 57, pag. vi. 83). It may be significant that an inscription to

53

Frag. ix–x] COMMENTARY

Piso's son has been found at Veleia (*ILS* 900); perhaps the Pisones inherited property in the district.

praeco: auctioneers were held in low esteem, and excluded from municipal office in the *tabula Heracleensis* (*ILS* 6085. 94). It was a convention of invective to impute sordid trades to one's enemies' relatives (p. 194).

furacissimi: Piso's paternal grandfather may well be the Piso whose trial for extortion is mentioned *de or.* ii. 265 (cf. ii. 285). The connexion with our passage was suggested by R. Syme, *CP* l, 1955, 137. Rinkes's emendation *frugalissimi* (cf. frag. viii n.) is unnecessary.

appellare: = *adloqui*. Used of matrimonial negotiations by Sen. *cont.* exc. iii. 5 'appellare debui de nuptiis patrem', ibid. exc. viii. 6.

subito: 'hasty', perhaps as shown by his marriage with Calventia. This adjective is not found elsewhere in Cicero, but cf. Tac. *hist.* v. 21. 3 'subitus consiliis'. Professor Watt suggests *subdolo*; he compares *de amic.* 91 'levium hominum atque fallacium'.

Calventium . . . appellatum: Rau rightly assigned these words to Cicero rather than to Asconius. Asconius has no reason to say *aiunt*; but Cicero can pretend to be disdainfully uncertain about a fact so insignificant (Rau compares Plat. *Euthyphr.* 2 b ὀνομάζουσι μέντοι αὐτόν, ὡς ἐγῷμαι, Μέλητον). The sentence probably does not come immediately after *conlocavit*; if it did, *eum* would seem to refer to *homini*, which is absurd. Besides, *appellatum* is a little awkward so soon after *appellare*. A short lacuna is therefore likely.

Frag. **x:** this fragment belongs *circa vers. LXXX* (Asconius), i.e. after the equivalent of over two pages of this text. Cicero has been mocking Piso's association with Placentia (frag. ix n.); he now apologizes to the town. Asconius says that Placentia had passed decrees on Cicero's behalf in 57. Besides, it was inexpedient to insult whole communities (Quintil. xi. 1. 86); for similar caution cf. § 25 on Capua, *Flacc.* 9 on the Greeks.

hoc . . . pertinet: 'this is not said by way of scoffing at Placentia'. Cf. *Balb.* 34 'nec vero oratio mea ad infirmandum foedus Gaditanorum . . . pertinet'.

fert: 'allows'.

municipi: Asconius ad loc. maintains that Placentia was a *colonia*, not a *municipium*. But as a Latin colony it became a *municipium* either by the *lex Iulia* of 90 or by the *lex Pompeia* of 89 (cf. U. Ewins, *PBSR* xxiii, 1955, 77). An inscription from Placentia refers to a *quattuorvir*, the magistrate of a *municipium*

54

COMMENTARY [Frag. x–xiii

(*CIL* xi. 1217 and note ibid., p. 242). Asconius is confused because Placentia later became a Roman colony, perhaps under Augustus. For mistakes in Asconius cf. frag. viii n., 78 KS (Gallius), also his notes on *Mil.* 55, 88, 95.

Frag. **xi** comes 'paulo post' frag. x (Asconius).

hic: Calventius.

cum: Stangl thought that the sentence ran 'such-and-such was happening when Calventius settled . . .'; but this is unlikely. Alternatively *cum* may introduce a subjunctive which has been lost in the lacuna (though there is hardly room); or it may even be a preposition. But perhaps the best solution is Manutius's, who took *cum* with *consedisset* (his emendation for *consedit et*).

adom . . .: Kiessling–Schoell proposed *a domo profectus*, but *a domo* would here be un-Ciceronian (*Thes. L.L.* v. 1. 1962. 54). Stangl, *Philol.* lxix, 1910, 494 proposed *advena*.

forte: *foret* of the MSS. is used only three times in Cicero, and then equals *futurus esset*, never *esset* (L.–H., p. 609).

tum erat . . .: the lacuna is of 9 letters. Mommsen suggested *peregrinus*, or less plausibly *incola* ('resident alien'); but in that case Cicero's comment seems superfluous, especially if *advena* is read above. I have considered *facillimum*.

Gallicanus: an inhabitant of Cisalpine Gaul or Narbonensis who was not a Roman citizen (cf. *Quinct.* 15, 79, *Cat.* ii. 5, Suet. *Ner.* 43. 1, *Vitell.* 18). In the lacuna after *Gallicanus* Kiessling–Schoell add *fuit*; this is consistent with the lacuna in *S*, as *ad* was probably omitted in the archetype. Stangl, *Philol.* lxix. 495, says that a verb is unnecessary at this point; he argues that *prius enim Gallus* means πρότερον μὲν Γάλλος ὤν. Yet the use of *prius* rather than *primum* suggests that there is a marked pause after the first two clauses.

ad extremum: Manutius proposed *extremo*, but this adverb is not used by Cicero. Below, the supplement *coeptus* fits the lacuna in *PM*, but is perhaps not completely convincing in point of sense or rhythm.

Frag. **xii:** this fragment's position in *C* shows that it came after frag. vii and before frag. xiii; Clark places it between frags. vii and viii, which may belong together. The subject of the fragment is quite uncertain.

Frag. **xiii:** 'did your father have a more gentlemanly father-in-law (in Calventius) than C. Piso had (in Cicero) ?' C. Calpurnius Piso Frugi was betrothed to Tullia in 67 (*Att.* i. 3. 3). In 58 he negotiated on Cicero's behalf with L. Piso (§ 13) and Pompey (Plut. *Cic.* 31. 2); he died before Cicero's return from exile.

The sentence is either interrogative or ironic; the former view

55

Frag. xiii–xvi] COMMENTARY

gains support from the next sentence, which is not ironic. Asconius in his note includes the name of Piso's own father-in-law; hence Mommsen supplemented 'lautiorem ⟨igitur et tu et⟩ pater tuus socerum quam C. Piso ⟨invenistis⟩'. But Asconius may possibly be giving superfluous information, in the manner of commentators; he mentions that Tullia later married P. Lentulus (Dolabella), which is certainly irrelevant. So the verb may follow *lautiorem* (e.g. Rau's *invenit*).

in illo luctu: at the end of a sentence this phrase would give an awkward rhythm and word-order; therefore cod. *P* of Asc. may be right in marking a lacuna (of 6 letters) after *luctu*. Even so, *in illo* is obscure and may be corrupt. The drift of the passage might be as follows: 'C. Piso, quem cum nomino luctu conficior'. Elsewhere *ille luctus* refers to Cicero's exile (*Planc.* 73), but such an allusion would be irrelevant here.

non enim: Ernesti's *nam ei* is plausible. Mommsen proposed *nonne ei*, but it is odd to ask even rhetorical questions about one's own preferences. Mommsen apparently took *ei* to be Furius Crassipes, who married Tullia in 56 (he read *iam finito illo luctu nonne ei* . . .). But *tum* surely refers to something more distant than the events of the previous year. For Cicero's high regard for C. Piso cf. *Brut.* 272.

Frag. xiv. apportata: 'imported', like a slave.

pecudem . . . non hominem: for the same contrast cf. Otto, pp. 55 f., C. Weyman, *ALL* xiii. 266; for other expressions of the type κάμινος οὐκ ἄνθρωπος cf. Hofmann, *Umgangssprache*, p. 158, Ellis on Catull. 115. 8.

Frag. xv: quoted by Arusianus to illustrate *sibi adoptare*. Cicero seems to be saying that Calventius adopted his elder grandson, presumably our Piso; his name 'Lucius the son of Lucius' shows that he was his father's eldest son. He cannot have been legally adopted, as then he would have been called 'Calventius Calpurnianus'. Cicero may simply be pretending that he was adopted; elsewhere he refers to Piso as 'Calventius' as if it were his name (14. 16 n.). Alternatively he may be using *adoptavit* in a non-legal sense to indicate that Calventius took Piso into his family as a favourite grandson.

Frag. xvi: Cicero describes Piso's embarrassment when his Gallic relatives appear on a farm-cart; this is comic invention. The *serracum* was a 'genus vehiculi cum humilibus et solidis rotis' (*Corp. Gloss. Lat.* v. 654); it was normally used for heavy loads rather than passengers (Hug, *RE* iiA. 49). Quintilian quotes our fragment to show that 'vim rebus aliquando verborum ipsa humilitas affert'. So Juv. 5. 22 f., with a mixture of mock-heroic and

56

COMMENTARY [Frag. xvi–xxi

bathos, 'illo tempore quo se frigida circumagunt pigri serraca Bootae'.

Frag. **xvii**: Piso's air of gravity was all pretence; cf. *Clu.* 72 'eius fictos simulatosque vultus'. For a possible reminiscence cf. Cyprian, *de mortal.* 20 'si simulata, si ficta, si fucata videntur esse quae dicimus'.

Frag. **xviii** describes Piso's hypocrisy; cf. p. 195. The sentence contains three *putavi* clauses followed by three *video* clauses; the third of the latter clauses (*video parietum . . . libidines suas*) is itself subdivided into three parts. But possibly something such as *video nepotem* has fallen out after *video ganeonem*; then the sentence would break into three groups each of three clauses.

amicorum: Piso's Epicurean friends; cf. 67. 19 n.

Frag. **xix. prope me est:** Diomedes, *GL* i. 410 is giving a list of prepositions: 'ultra, ultra terminum; usque, usque Galliam; prope, prope me est, ut dicit Cicero in Pisonem. dixit item "proximus Pompeium sedebam"'. But Diomedes would not quote the *in Pisonem* by name for anything so common as *prope me est*; his text must be corrupt. A. Klotz suggests a reference to § 6 *propter te sedet*, but Diomedes has already dealt with *propter*. Perhaps a quotation illustrating *propius* with the accusative has fallen out; later on Diomedes illustrates both *propius* and *proximus* with the dative; Priscian, *GL* iii. 292 illustrates *propius* with the accusative.

Frag. **xx:** this fragment is quoted by Grillius (fifth century), *commentum in Ciceronis rhetorica*, ed. J. Martin (Paderborn, 1927), § 16, p. 72. Grillius is discussing *remotio* (diversion of a charge from oneself to someone else); he comments 'ut in Pisoniana ait, cum Pisonem vituperet, "non me debes . . ."'. Clearly *cum Pisonem vituperet* is misleading; if the fragment is genuine, Cicero must be quoting Piso. Yet *oratio recta* would be strange here, and the clausulae are unconvincing. Besides, *exilium* tells against authenticity; Cicero hated to be called an *exul* (cf. *dom.* 72, *Q.f.* iii. 2. 2), and even in quoting his enemy he would hardly have mentioned 'exile' so casually. It looks as if Grillius's source has described Piso's attitude as given in § 75 'paulo ante dixisti . . .' and § 78 'hic tu hostis . . .'; Grillius has taken over the example without understanding the situation.

Frag. **xxi:** the source is missing in Arusianus; Halm assigned the fragment to the *in Pisonem* without much reason. The reference is probably to 58 B.C., when the senate snubbed the consuls (cf. § 26); for reluctance to sit beside somebody in the senate cf. *Cat.* i. 16, ii. 12, Dio lviii. 10. 4. Yet one sees no obvious place for this fragment in the opening sections of the speech.

57

§ 1] COMMENTARY

§§ 1–3: *Cicero maintains that Piso owed the consulship to his appearance of austerity, his distinguished ancestry, and the confused political situation in 59; Cicero, on the other hand, obtained office by his own merits.*

§ **1.** 16. **belua:** 'monster', suggesting foulness and savagery; cf. *bestia*, θηρίον.

quae sit . . . : 'why men are indignant about your brow'. Piso's austere features had made people think that he would be a good consul; they are indignant now that they have discovered the deception. For other comments on Piso's brow cf. *Sest.* 19 'quid ego de supercilio dicam, quod tum hominibus non supercilium sed pignus rei publicae videbatur', *in sen.* 15–16, *prov. cons.* 8, *Pis.* 14, 20, 68.

17. **nemo queritur . . . :** Cicero pretends that Piso is simply a Syrian slave. He says that nobody grumbles that such a man has become consul, because Piso's servile characteristics, unlike his noble brow, involved no deception. The argument is incoherent; for if people had really regarded Piso as a Syrian, his brow could not have deceived them.

Syrum: cf. *in sen.* 14 (also of Piso) 'Cappadocem modo abreptum de grege venalium diceres'. Suggestions of servile origin were common in invective, and seldom serious (p. 194).

18. **noviciorum:** slaves who had only recently been imported, and were therefore even more barbarous than the rest; cf. Ar. *ran.* 731 f. καὶ πονηροῖς κἀκ πονηρῶν εἰς ἅπαντα χρώμεθα ὑστάτοις ἀφιγμένοισιν. *grege* as often is contemptuous.

19. **servilis:** i.e. swarthy. Cf. frag. viii, Lucian, *parasit.* 41 οὐ μέλας δὲ οὐδὲ λευκός, τὸ μὲν γὰρ γυναικί, τὸ δὲ δούλῳ προσέοικεν. D. R. Shackleton Bailey, *Propertiana*, p. 16, contrasts *ingenuus color* (Prop. i. 4. 13).

20. **qui . . . est:** thoughts are usually revealed by the face; cf. Otto, p. 147, Seyffert–Müller, *Laelius*, pp. 421 f., *de or.* ii. 148, iii. 223, *leg.* i. 27, Quintil. xi. 3. 72, xi. 3. 75, Jerome, *epist.* 54. 13. 2.

21. **in fraudem . . . impulit:** 'drove into delusion'; cf. *de amic.* 89 'in fraudem obsequio impellitur', *Att.* iii. 15. 7 'proditus inductus coniectus in fraudem'. Usually *impellere in fraudem* means 'to induce to do wrong'; for phrases in Latin with two different meanings see Madvig on *fin.* ii. 64, Housman on Manil. ii. 617.

22. **quibus eras ignotus:** *eras* is found in some *variae lectiones* printed by Giunta in 1538 (cf. Orelli II[1]. ii. 611 ff.); it is clearly an emendation. This reading gives the required sense, namely 'who did not know your bad character'; for similar uses of *novisse* cf. § 2 'te vivum nondum noverat quisquam', *Verr.* iv. 63, Plancus ap. *fam.* x. 23. 1, Quintil. vi. 3. 98 'tollat te qui non novit'. The MSS. both of Cicero and of Gellius read *erat*; the subject

58

COMMENTARY [§§ 1-2]

could only be *voltus*. The natural meaning would then be 'who did not know you by sight', which is clearly wrong; it would be less easy to interpret 'who did not know the deceptive character of your face'.

decepit fefellit induxit: cf. *Sex. Rosc.* 117 'induxit decepit destituit . . . fefellit'. For such *congeries* (heaping up of synonyms) cf. Volkmann, pp. 451, 472. Gellius xiii. 25. 22 comments 'verba quoque illa M. Ciceronis in L. Pisonem trigemina, etiamsi durae auris hominibus non placent, non venustatem modo numeris quaesiverunt sed figuram simulationemque oris pluribus simul vocibus everberaverunt'.

1. **numquam . . .:** this sentence consists of three cola, parallel in content, with the third colon more expanded than the first two; for this common type of 'tricolon' see E. Lindholm, *Stilistische Studien* (Lund, 1931), pp. 157 ff., Fraenkel on Aesch. *Ag.* 1243. The third colon is here expressed in more general terms than the first two; cf. Nägelsbach, p. 713.

2. **numquam . . . consili:** 'your advice had never been put to the test'.

nullum . . . factum: *nullum* can only be an adjective; therefore *factum* is a noun. *erat* must be understood from the first clause, though there it is part of the verb *erat audita*. *nihil* would have been more normal.

4. **obrepsisti . . .:** 'you crept to office by stealth'; cf. *Planc.* 17 'doceo Cn. Plancium non obrepsisse ad honorem'.

fumosarum: wax images of a Roman nobleman's ancestors were kept in the *atrium* and became black with soot; cf. Juv. 8. 8 'fumosos equitum cum dictatore magistros', Sen. *epist.* 44. 5, Boeth. *cons.* i. 1. 3.

§ 2. 6. At this point there begins a comparison of Cicero and Piso which lasts till § 63. For such comparisons in ancient oratory cf. R. Preiswerk, *De inventione orationum Ciceronianarum* (Basel, 1905), pp. 107 ff.

is: note the abrupt switch from second to third person. Such switches are often made for variety; sometimes the use of the third person is also a sign of contempt. See §§ 16, 22, 31, 78.

mihi: ethic dative. *etiam* is indignant ('actually'); cf. *Thes. L.L.* v. 2. 951. 77.

gloriabatur: the imperfect is sometimes used where the speaker reminds his hearers of somebody's remarks; cf. § 18 'at quaerebat etiam paulo ante de me', *Phil.* ii. 76 'etiam quaerebat cur ego . . . tam subito revertissem', K.–S. i. 124. Some MSS. of no authority read *gloriatur* or *gloriabitur*; cf. *Verr.* II. i. 156 'is mihi etiam queritur ?', *Sest.* 127 'tu mihi etiam commemoras ?', *Verr.* iii. 117 'hic mihi etiam dicere audebit ?'

59

§§ 2–3] COMMENTARY

se: emphatic.

sine repulsa: 'at the first attempt'; so *leg. agr.* ii. 3, *Planc.* 51; contrast *Tusc.* v. 54 *cum repulsa.*

7. **vera cum gloria:** 'with justifiable self-glorification'.

praedicare: Cicero's boasting should be judged by the conventions of his time; in his defence see Quintil. xi. 1. 17 ff., W. Allen, *TAPA* lxxxv, 1954, 121 ff.

8. **non nomini:** *homini*, the reading of the MSS., is impossible. *non nomini* is reported by Ursinus (1581) as the reading 'veteris libri'; it gives good sense, an excellent clausula, and a neat explanation of the corruption (loss of *non* before *nomini*).

11. **Piso . . . :** 'a Piso was made aedile . . ., not that particular Piso'. The first and last words of the clause are the same; this figure is called κύκλος (Volkmann, p. 471).

13. **noverat:** i.e. had not yet known what a scoundrel you were (1. 22 n.). There is a play of words on *noverat* and *noti.*

quaestorem: Cicero was quaestor in 75, aedile in 69, praetor in 66.

14. **in primis:** at elections the candidate who was first in point of time to gain a majority of the tribes or centuries was returned *primus*, or *prior* when there were only two vacancies (*Mur.* 18, *St.-R.* iii. 414). *in primis* (also found Suet. *Vesp.* 2. 3) might mean either 'first equal' or 'among the first two or three'.

cunctis suffragiis: Cicero was elected praetor in the *comitia centuriata* by the votes of all the centuries (*imp. Pomp.* 2). Here *cunctis suffragiis* is most naturally taken with *quaestorem* and *aedilem* as well as with *praetorem*, though this fact about Cicero is not recorded elsewhere. For *cunctis suffragiis* applied to elections for quaestor (i.e. in the *comitia tributa*) cf. *Vat.* 11.

cunctis suffragiis probably means 'by the votes of all the centuries until a majority was obtained'; the lower centuriate classes did not vote unless required (*St.-R.* iii. 413). But in the *comitia tributa* probably the votes of all the tribes were known; cf. P. Fraccaro, *Opuscula* (Pavia, 1957), pp. 249 ff.

15. **homini:** cf. *Verr.* iv. 25 'honorem debitum detraxerunt non homini sed ordini'. For the topic cf. *rhet. ad Her.* iii. 13 'in laude: . . . si humili genere, ipsum in suis non in maiorum virtutibus habuisse praesidium'. See also Anaximenes 35 (Spengel, *Rhet. Gr.* i).

§ 3. 18. parto . . . gesto: 'whether how I won it or how I administered it'. *vis* plays the same part as *dicam* in *imp. Pomp.* 57 'quo . . . indignius videtur obtrectatum esse adhuc, Gabinio dicam anne Pompeio'.

19. **labe:** literally 'fall', 'ruin', hence used of one who causes ruin. *labes* 'a stain' may be a completely different word.

60

COMMENTARY [§§ 3–4

23. [**Caesare et Bibulo**]: the names are superfluous; everybody knew that Caesar and Bibulus were meant. Cicero's criticisms of Caesar are guarded ('nihil dicam gravius quam quod omnes fatentur'); this is not a suitable place for naming him.

cum hoc . . .: 'at a time when you were quite willing that the people who were nominating you consul should count you unfit to live unless you turned out more worthless than Gabinius'. Cicero is thinking primarily of Caesar (introd., p. vi); the comment, though veiled, is unusually critical.

24. **quin**: though in origin *qui nè*, this word can in classical Latin be followed by another negative (L.–H., p. 785). *exstitisses* would have been future-perfect in *oratio recta*.

nisi nequior: for similar insults cf. §§ 18, 82, *prov. cons.* 12.

27. **voce**: cf. *leg. agr.* ii. 4 'meis comitiis non tabellam vindicem tacitae libertatis, sed vocem vivam prae vobis indicem vestrarum erga me voluntatum ac studiorum tulistis'.

priorem: cf. 2. 14 n. Hence Cicero appeared on the *fasti* before his colleague Antonius.

1. **domina**: this name was often applied to the goddess Fortune (*Thes. L.L.* v. 1. 1937. 52, cf. 1903. 24).

Campi: the *comitia centuriata*, which elected consuls, met outside the *pomerium*, normally in the Campus Martius (*St.-R.* iii. 380). Cicero, *de or.* iii. 167, gives *campum pro comitiis* as an instance of *immutatio* or metonymy.

§§ **4–7**. *Cicero describes the main achievements of his own consulship (which would appeal to his senatorial audience).*

§ **4**. 4. **Ego Kalendis . . .**: in *leg. agr.* I. The tribune Rullus had proposed that a fund should be created to buy land for new *coloniae* for the urban plebs; the *ager Campanus*, which was still *ager publicus* and rented to tenants, was also to be used for this purpose. Cicero defeated the scheme by ingenious misrepresentation; cf. Plin. *n.h.* vii. 117 'te dicente legem agrariam, hoc est alimenta sua, abdicarunt tribus'. See E. G. Hardy, *Some Problems in Roman History*, pp. 68 ff., Boulanger's introduction to the Budé edition of *de lege agraria*, H. Strasburger, *Caesars Eintritt in die Geschichte* (München, 1938), pp. 114 f. (who rightly doubts the common view that Caesar was behind the bill).

5. **ego**: anaphora (L.–H., p. 797, Volkmann, p. 467); at 6. 25 *me . . . mihi*, where the case changes, the figure is called 'polyptoton' (L.–H., p. 799, Volkmann, p. 470).

6. **si . . . reservavi**: 'if it was wrong that it should be distributed, I preserved it; if it was right, I kept it for worthier legislators'. Caesar distributed the *ager Campanus* in 59; Cicero

61

§§ 4–5] COMMENTARY

disapproved of his action (*Att.* ii. 16. 1), but in 55 could not say so.

7. C. Rabirio: Rabirius had been involved in the killing of the tribune Saturninus in 100 B.C., after the senate had passed the *consultum ultimum*. In 63 Labienus prosecuted him on the archaic charge of *perduellio* or treason, which included assaults on tribunes. See further E. G. Hardy, *Some Problems in Roman History*, pp. 99 ff., C. Brecht, *RE* xix. 634 ff.; for a summary cf. Boulanger's Budé edition.

8. XL annis . . .: 'the authority of the senate, which had been brought into play forty years before my consulship'. XL is a round number, as Asconius points out.

10. adulescentis: Sulla had debarred from office the sons of his victims in the proscriptions. An attempt was made to annul this provision in 63, but Cicero successfully resisted it; he was afraid that if elected they would begin a general attack on the Sullan constitution. Cf. Quintil. xi. 1. 85, *RE* viiA. 1. 873.

12. nulla . . . mala gratia: 'without the senate's incurring any unpopularity' (*Thes. L.L.* vi. 2222. 65).

13. comitiorum ratione privavi: 'I excluded from consideration by the *comitia*'. Ernesti explains *ratio* as in *rationem habere alicuius*, 'to entertain somebody's candidature' (cf. *St.-R.* i³. 472), and it seems best to accept this view, though the genitive here is of a different type. Others take *ratio* to mean 'department' or 'sphere'; cf. *Sex. Rosc.* 149 'fori iudicique rationem M. Messalla suscepit', H. Nettleship, *Contributions to Latin Lexicography* (Oxford, 1889), p. 564. Elsewhere *ratio comitiorum* seems to mean 'the working of elections'; cf. *Mur.* 35 'quantos aestus habet ratio comitiorum', *Mur.* 36 'nihil fallacius ratione tota comitiorum'.

§ 5. 13. Antonium: Cicero's colleague in 63, son of the orator, uncle of the triumvir; he was exiled in 59 for misgovernment in Macedonia.

14. multa . . . molientem: 'the author of many political intrigues'; cf. *Planc.* 33 'multa in re publica molienti', *Vat.* 21. Cicero thought Antonius an unreliable colleague (cf. *Sest.* 8).

15. provinciam Galliam: the senate had assigned Gallia Cisalpina and Macedonia to the consuls of 63. The lot gave Macedonia (the more lucrative) to Cicero, Cisalpina (which had vital strategic importance) to Antonius; both parties gladly exchanged (Sall. *Cat.* 26. 4, Dio xxxvii. 33. 4, Plut. *Cic.* 12. 4). Cicero was very prudent: Antonius had a difficult military situation to deal with, and lost two important battles (p. 178). Later Cicero renounced Cisalpina; he took great credit for unselfishness, but did not in fact want a province. See W. Allen, *TAPA* lxxxiii, 1952, 233 ff.

COMMENTARY [§§ 5-6]

16. **ornatam:** *ornare provinciam* is the technical term for the voting of supplies by the senate to the governor of a province.

17. **commutavi:** a fifteenth-century emendation of *communicavi*. One might have expected *commutaveram*, but the perfect tense is legitimate (K.–S. i. 129, Lebreton, p. 220). For *commutare* in Cicero with the accusative of the thing received cf. *Sest.* 37 'ut cum patriae caritate constantiae gloriam commutaret'; for *cum* cf. *Thes. L.L.* iii. 1990. 79.

quod . . . ferre: 'because I thought that the national interest so required' (for *ferre* cf. *Thes. L.L.* vi. 549. 46).

20. **non obscure sed palam:** this type of expression is found as early as *Odyss.* xvii. 415 f. οὐ μέν μοι δοκέεις ὁ κάκιστος Ἀχαιῶν ἔμμεναι, ἀλλ' ὥριστος. See E. Schwyzer, *Griech. Gramm.* ii. 704, F. Blass, *Die attische Beredsamkeit*, III². i. 99, L.–H., p. 805; for Cicero cf. P. Parzinger, *Beiträge*, i. 18 ff.

egredi . . . iussi: on 7 November 63; the First Catilinarian purports to be Cicero's speech on that occasion.

21. **moenibus:** the Servian wall still had military significance in the late Republic, notably in the civil wars of 88–87 and 82 (G. Säflund, *Le Mura di Roma repubblicana* (Lund, 1932), pp. 188 f., 213 f.).

22. **extremo mense:** the conspiracy was foiled on 3 December by the information of the Allobroges and the arrest of the conspirators.

23. **faces:** Cicero repeatedly accuses the Catilinarians of planning fires; so also Sall. *Cat.* 43. 2, Plut. *Cic.* 18. 1–3.

§ **6. 25. Q. Catulus:** Q. Lutatius Catulus (cos. 78, cens. 65), a leading aristocrat who resisted Lepidus in 78–77, and opposed the *lex Gabinia* and *lex Manilia* in 67–66. Cicero finely says of him (*Sest.* 101) 'quem neque periculi tempestas neque honoris aura potuit umquam de suo cursu aut spe aut metu demovere'.

princeps huius ordinis: in the late Republic *princeps senatus* was probably not an official title; this is shown by Velleius ii. 43. 3, when he calls Catulus 'omnium confessione senatus princeps'. See *St.-R.* iii. 969 ff.

auctor publici consili: one of the persons responsible for forming national policy; cf. *de or.* i. 211, i. 215, iii. 63, *fam.* xii. 2. 3.

26. **frequentissimo senatu:** a crowded house (cf. J. Stroux, *Philol.* xciii, 1938, 85 ff., J. P. V. D. Balsdon, *JRS* xlvii, 1957, 19 f.).

parentem patriae: the first formal use of the title (Plin. *n.h.* vii. 117). It was later given in a more official form to Julius Caesar, Augustus, and most emperors (*St.-R.* ii³. 779); but cf. Juv. 8. 243 f. 'sed Roma parentem, Roma patrem patriae Ciceronem

63

§ 6]   COMMENTARY

libera dixit'. See further A. Alföldi, *Mus. Helv.* ix, 1952, 204 ff., x, 1953, 103 ff., xi, 1954, 133 ff.

27. propter: 'near'. *X*'s reading is confirmed by Arusianus, who quotes to illustrate *propter*. A senator could sit where he liked (*St.-R.* iii. 933).

L. Gellius: L. Gellius Poplicola (cos. 72, cens. 70) advocated executing the Catilinarians (*Att.* xii. 21. 1); for his praise of Cicero cf. *quir.* 17.

1. his: the senators.

civicam coronam: a wreath of oak-leaves (hence the gloss *de quercu* in α), awarded to a soldier who had killed an enemy and saved a citizen. Augustus was given the decoration in 27 *ob civis servatos*. See further *RE* iv. 1639; for an illustration cf. D.–S. i. 1536.

2. mihi togato: on 3 December 63 on the motion of Cotta (*Phil.* ii. 13) the senate voted Cicero a *supplicatio* (days of thanksgiving to the gods), the first time that this honour had been given to a civilian. See L. Halkin, *La Supplication d'action de graces chez les Romains* (Paris, 1953), pp. 39 ff.

bene gesta . . . conservata re publica: an emendation in *X*; only genitives have authority. The ablative absolute is natural in the citation of military exploits; cf. E. Fraenkel, *Plautinisches im Plautus*, pp. 236 ff., *ILS* 81 'senatus populusque Romanus imp. Caesari . . . republica conservata', *fam.* xv. 4. 11 'mihi supplicationem decrevisti togato, non ut multis re p. bene gesta, sed ut nemini re p. conservata', *Cat.* iii. 15. In favour of the genitive one might quote *Phil.* xiv. 23 'Pharsaliae pugnae triumphum'; but in our passage the construction seems cumbrous, especially since *supplicationis* itself is genitive. At *Cat.* iv. 20 the best MSS. read 'ceteris enim semper bene gestae, mihi uni conservatae rei publicae gratulationem decrevistis'; at *Cat.* iii. 15 some MSS. read genitives (with *supplicationes*). In our passage Lambinus read 'non . . . bene gestae sed . . . conservatae r.p. testimonium dedit, et singulari . . .'; cf. *Att.* ii. 1. 6 'sibi enim bene gestae, mihi conservatae rei publicae dat testimonium', *dom.* 132, *Sest.* 129, *Phil.* ii. 2. But if change is needed, it is simpler to read ablatives.

4. patefecit: Roman temples were kept shut except on special occasions (G. Wissowa, *Religion und Kultus*², pp. 476 f.).

5. tribuno pl.: Q. Caecilius Metellus Nepos, cos. 57, brother of Metellus Celer (8. 22 n.). He became tribune in December 63 and attacked Cicero, saying that only Pompey could save the situation (Dio xxxvii. 43. 1). On 29 December he prevented Cicero from making a speech on leaving office, and only allowed him to take the usual oath 'that he had done nothing against the laws' (*St.-R.*

64

COMMENTARY [§§ 6-8

i³. 625). Cicero retorted by swearing that he had saved the republic (*fam.* v. 2. 7, *Att.* vi. 1. 22, *RE* viiA. 892).

§ 7. 11. iuratus ipse: cf. Plut. *mor.* 801B (when Carbo swore an oath the crowd swore that it did not believe him).

quo quidem tempore . . .: for this honour cf. Quadrigarius ap. Gell. xiii. 29. 1, *Att.* i. 16. 5, Plut. *Cic.* 22. 5.

12. domum: to be taken with the verbal noun *reditus* (K.–S. i. 216); cf. § 22 'cum gregibus perpotationes', § 23 'praevaricatore quondam', § 40 'interitus ferro'.

14. nihil . . .: an eloquent summary of Cicero's ideal of the *consensus omnium bonorum*; cf. *Sest.* 96 ff., H. Strasburger, *Concordia Ordinum* (Leipzig, 1931), pp. 59 ff.

17. principibus: an unofficial term for the leading men in the republic (A. Gwosdz, *Der Begriff des römischen Princeps*, Breslau, 1933).

§§ 8–11. *Having described his own consulship, Cicero turns to Piso's. These sections deal with events early in 58, before the main attack on Cicero was launched.*

§ 8. 20. ludi compitalicii: games held at the Compitalia, the festival of the Lares. The cult of the Lares was performed by *collegia* which contained many freedmen and slaves. In 64 B.C. the senate abolished these *collegia* among many others, and prohibited the holding of the *ludi*. In December 61 a tribune tried to revive the *ludi*, but was prevented by Metellus Celer, then consul-designate. On 4 January 58 P. Clodius had a bill passed restoring the *collegia*. On 1 January 58 Sex. Cloelius anticipated the new bill by holding the *ludi compitalicii*; he was unsuccessfully opposed by the tribune L. Ninnius. See Asc. 6–7 KS (the difficulties of his account cannot be discussed here), S. Accame, *BMIR* xiii. 13 ff. (in *Bull. Comm. Arch. Roma*, 1942).

21. L. Iulium et C. Marcium: consuls in 64 B.C. The MSS. read *L. Luscellum et G. Marium*, but there was no such pair of consuls; Asconius paraphrases *L. Iulio C. Mario*. Hotomanus proposed *L. Metellum et Q. Marcium* (the consuls of 68), but this reading is less close to the MSS. Asconius comments that Clodius restored the collegia (in 58) *post novem annos quam sublata erant*; but *novem* is inconsistent with 68 as well as with 64, and is presumably corrupt. A decisive argument against 68 is given by Asconius 67 KS, who shows that *collegia* were active in 65 at the time of the *pro Cornelio*.

22. Q. Metellus: Metellus Celer, cos. 60, brother of Metellus Nepos (6. 5 n.), husband of the famous Clodia who was probably Catullus's Lesbia; for Cicero's admiration for him cf. *Cael.* 59

5993   G   65

§ 8] COMMENTARY

facio iniuriam . . .: cf. *Verr*. iv. 121 'conferte Verrem, non ut hominem cum homine comparetis, ne qua tali viro mortuo (Marcello) fiat iniuria'. For a similar reluctance to make comparisons cf. Aeschines, *in Ctes*. 182 (from which our passage may be derived) οὐδ' ἐν ταῖς αὐταῖς ἡμέραις ἄξιον ἡγοῦμαι μεμνῆσθαι τοῦ θηρίου τούτου κἀκείνων τῶν ἀνδρῶν, Dein. *in Dem*. 16, Cic. *Pis*. 3, 63.

24. sed: resumptive after a parenthesis (K.–S. ii. 76).

designatus consul: Metellus, though he had not yet the legal power of a consul, used the moral prestige of a consul-designate (cf. *St.-R*. i³. 203, 590 ff.).

25. quidam tribunus pl.: Asconius comments 'cuius tribuni nomen adhuc non inveni'. Of the tribunes who entered office in December 61 L. Flavius and C. Herennius are the only ones whose names are known; the latter was a partisan of Clodius.

suo auxilio: these words go with *facere* and are emphatic. *auxilium* is used of a tribune's protection of citizens against coercion by magistrates (*St.-R*. i³. 278).

magistros: Abram proposed *magistros vicorum*, but the absence of a genitive is confirmed by the lemma of Asconius. After the abolition of the *collegia* the cult of the Lares must have continued in some form; the *magistri* are presumably the persons responsible for this cult; it is not clear whether they were called *magistri vicorum* or *compitorum* or *pagorum*. The MSS. of Asconius, at the end of his note, mention *magistros ludorum*; but as the *ludi* had been prohibited the *magistri ludorum* could hardly have existed in 61.

1. Kalendas Ianuarias: the date of the *compitalia* was fixed every year by the urban praetor; we hear of cases of 29 December, 1 and 2 January (*RE* iv. 791).

2. Sex. Cloelium: Cloelius drafted P. Clodius's laws, organized his riots, and finally in 52 burned his body in the senate-house. The best MSS. read *Sex. Clodium*, the name by which this person is known in all modern books. Dr. D. R. Shackleton Bailey has shown that if one views as a whole the evidence of Cicero and Asconius, manuscript authority overwhelmingly supports *Cloelius* (*CQ* N.S. x, 1960, 41 f.).

praetextatus: the *toga praetexta* (with a purple border) was worn primarily by higher magistrates, but also by persons holding games, even *magistri vicorum*, etc. (*St.-R*. i³. 422, cf. *Pis*. 23). It was also worn by free-born children (Marquardt, *Privatleben*², p. 124 n. 5), even the sons of freedmen in Cicero's day (Macr. *sat*. i. 6. 13); so Cicero is accusing Cloelius of servile origin.

3. volitare: 'to bustle around'; cf. § 26, Landgraf on *Sex. Rosc*. 135.

66

COMMENTARY [§§ 8-9

4. facie: i.e. both Piso (§ 1) and Cloelius were ugly. The remark in itself is not very pointed; it simply prepares the way for the insult in *osculo*.

osculo: Luterbacher's emendation for *oculo* seems the most satisfactory solution; Clark compares *Sest.* 111 (referring to Gellius) 'est me ultus cum illo ore inimicos est meos saviatus'. The implied charge is not made against Piso elsewhere, but was common in invective, and suits Cloelius (*har. resp.* 11, etc.). *oculo* makes a more obvious pair with *facie* than *osculo* does, but has no point here, where there must be an elaboration on *impurum* above.

dignissimum: with *facie* means 'suited to'; cf. *Verr.* iv. 37 'hominem dignissimum tuis moribus', *Thes. L.L.* v.1. 1147. 7. With *osculo* it means 'worthy of'.

§ 9. 5. triduo post: on 4 January 58 (not 3 January). In phrases of this type the inclusive method of counting is inappropriate; cf. C. C. Conrad, *CP* ix, 1914, 78 ff. against J. C. Rolfe, *CP* x, 1915, 82 ff. P. Clodius became tribune on 10 December 59, and must have promulgated his bill the same day. The *trinum nundinum*, or interval between promulgation and voting, was 24 days (*St.-R.* iii. 375 f., *RE* xvii. 1471). From 10 December to 4 January is 24 days, counting inclusively (December had 29 days in the pre-Julian calendar).

inspectante: 'looking on and doing nothing' (*dom.* 114, *Sest.* 33); *inspectante* and *inspectantibus* are the only parts of this verb used by Cicero and Caesar. Piso was actually present when Clodius's bills were passed (*Vat.* 18), yet Cicero's criticisms are misleading (introd., p. ix). The word order of the MSS. is supported against Asconius by *Att.* iii. 15. 7 'inspectante et tacente te'.

6. fatali: 'dire'; cf. Hor. *carm.* i. 37. 21 'fatale monstrum'.

portento prodigioque: P. Clodius. In Latin words beginning with the same letter are often found in pairs; for many examples see E. Wölfflin, *Sitz. Bayer. Akad.*, Phil.-hist. Kl. 1881, ii. 1 ff. (= *Ausgewählte Schriften*, pp. 225 ff.), *ALL* iii. 443 ff.

lex Aelia et Fufia: two laws, not one (*har. resp.* 58, *St.-R.* i³. 111 n. 4, K.–S. i. 55); their date was about 150 B.C. (§ 10, *Vat.* 23); their relation to each other is unknown. They confirmed the right of curule magistrates and tribunes to stop *comitia* by formally reporting (*obnuntiatio*) that they would watch the sky for lightning (W. F. McDonald, *JRS* xix, 1929, 164 ff., S. Weinstock, *JRS* xxvii, 1937, 215 ff.). Bibulus had used this procedure in 59 in an unsuccessful attempt to stop Caesar's legislation. Cicero talks as if Clodius had abolished the laws completely, but *obnuntiatio* is still found after 58. For discussions see *St.-R.* i³. 112 n. 2, McDonald, op. cit., Weinstock, op. cit., J. P. V. D. Balsdon, *JRS* xlvii, 1957,

67

§§ 9–10] COMMENTARY

15 f.; for a summary of the problem cf. R. Gardner's Loeb edition of *pro Sestio*, pp. 309 ff.

8. oti: internal peace (Ch. Wirszubski, *JRS* xliv, 1954, 4 ff.).

conlegia: Clodius restored the *collegia* which had been abolished in 64 (8. 20 n.) and extended the right of association (*Sest.* 55, S. Accame, op. cit. [8. 20 n.], pp. 29 ff., M. I. Henderson, *JRS* xl, 1950, 12).

9. innumerabilia quaedam: 'quite impossible to count'; *quaedam* is intensive (K.–S. i. 643).

10. stupris: cf. §§ 28, 95. Clodius realized that future censors might exclude him from the senate on moral grounds; his law provided reasonably enough that they were not to punish anybody who had not been formally accused before them and pronounced guilty by both (Asc. 8 KS). Dio implies that the censors were deprived of the initiative in making accusations (xl. 57, *St.-R.* ii³. 386 f.). The law was repealed by Metellus Scipio in 52 (Dio, loc. cit.).

11. magistra pudoris: there were censors in 55 B.C., so Cicero's praise of the censorship was both topical and tactful.

12. censura is required by the sense and supported by the clausula. *severitas* is a foolish gloss on *censura*, which in late Latin could mean 'strictness' (*Corp. Gloss. Lat.* iv. 33. 39 and 46, v. 494. 20).

bustum or 'pyre' is somewhat strange when applied to a person, especially here where there is a contrast with *consulem*; 'fax patriae' (*dom.* 102) is distinctly easier. Mr. Williams suggests *o ustor* or *ustor* (an undertaker's disreputable slave); cf. Catull. 59. 5, *Mil.* 90.

§ 10. 15. neque vero ...: for the commonplace Abram compares Sen. *Tro.* 291 'qui non vetat peccare, cum possit, iubet', Dio lxiv. 2. 2, Arnob. *adv. nat.* iv. 32.

19. sedenti implies inactivity (cf. καθῆσθαι).

21. CCCC: the censorship was founded in 443, according to tradition (cf. Broughton, *Mag. Rom. Rep.* i. 54).

iudicium: often applied to the inquiry of the censors, though Cicero elsewhere disapproves of the usage; cf. *Clu.* 117 'sequitur id quod illi iudicium appellant, maiores autem nostri numquam neque iudicium nominarunt neque proinde ut rem iudicatam observarunt, animadversio atque auctoritas censoria', *St.-R.* ii³. 386.

notionemque: 'examination'; cf. the parallel passages *Sest.* 55 'censoria notio et gravissimum iudicium', *prov. cons.* 46 'censorium iudicium ac notionem'. The manuscripts' reading *rationemque* (cf. *Clu.* 118) cannot be defended here. Lambinus proposed *notationemque*; cf. *Clu.* 128, *rep.* iv. 10.

68

COMMENTARY [§§ 10–11

22. quas leges ...: 'laws which some wretch may have boldly attempted, but none has been able, to tear down; an office which nobody has been so unboundedly licentious as to try to impair, in order to prevent judgement being passed on our conduct every five years; all this, you butcher, was swept away at the very beginning of your consulship'. Madvig was the first to see that this forms one sentence; previously *quas ... conatus est* had been joined to the preceding sentence.

ausus est: '*audere* is occasionally used of what is merely attempted or planned' (D. R. Shackleton Bailey, *Propertiana*, p. 172, who quotes parallels).

non nemo: particularly Vatinius, who introduced most of Caesar's legislation in 59; cf. *Vat.* 18 'lex Aelia et Fufia ... quas contra praeter te nemo umquam est facere conatus'. Cicero comes near a direct criticism of Caesar, who introduced his *lex agraria* personally in defiance of Bibulus's use of the *leges Aelia et Fufia*.

potuit quidem: *ausus est ... improbus* and *potuit ... convellere* are contrasted clauses, juxtaposed without a connective; in sense, though not in form, the first clause is subordinate to the second. *quidem* is not in itself adversative, but simply emphasizes *potuit*; for its use in similar contexts cf. K.–S. i. 803.

24. quinto quoque anno: this expression is ambiguous and could mean either 'every fourth year' or 'every fifth year' (cf. C. L. Howard, *CQ* N.S. viii, 1958, 1 ff.). In connexion with the censorship it must mean 'every fifth year' (*St.-R.* ii³. 343 ff., *RE* xiii. 2053).

nemo ... conatus est: = *nemo tam effuse petulans fuit ut conaretur*. Cf. *de or.* i. 226 'quis hoc philosophus tam mollis ... probare posset ?', *Verr.* v. 34, *Deiot.* 37, *Att.* viii. 4. 2, Virg. *georg.* ii. 315, *Aen.* i. 539. Our passage shows that Sulla did not formally abolish the censorship (*St.-R.* ii³. 336 n. 3).

§ 11. 1. carnifex: a term of abuse often used in comedy and political invective; cf. p. 196.

prooemio: Madvig's brilliant emendation (*Adv. crit.* iii. 146). As the word refers to a period of time it suits *centum annos* above and *continentis dies* below. The corruption to *gremio* is explained by the abbreviation of *pro*.

2. persequere: 'trace the course of the days that followed these disasters'. *continentes* (cf. *Thes. L.L.* iv. 710. 61) should be preferred to *connexos*, which is unparalleled in the required sense.

3. pro: 'on the front part of' rather than 'in front of'; cf. *quir.* 13 'cum homines in tribunali Aurelio palam conscribi ... vidissem', *dom.* 54, K.–S. i. 514.

Aurelio tribunali: its position in the Forum is uncertain; cf.

69

§ 11]　　　　COMMENTARY

E. Welin, *Studien zur Topographie des Forum Romanum* (Lund, 1953), pp. 104 ff.

ne conivente quidem te: 'not merely shutting your eyes'; cf. K.–S. ii. 54, 74.

5. **dilectus servorum:** in plain language this means that Clodius enrolled *collegia*; cf. *Sest.* 34 'servorum dilectus habebatur . . . nomine conlegiorum'. There is a deliberate paradox in talking of a 'levy of slaves', for slaves could not be enlisted in the Roman army.

eo: P. Clodius; cf. *Mil.* 73 'eum cui nihil umquam nefas fuit nec in facinore nec in libidine'.

6. **turpe [esse] duxit:** Asconius omits *esse*, and this is not only the more usual construction, but also gives a better rhythm. It is difficult to weigh these arguments against the unreliability of Asconius's text.

7. **templo Castoris:** in the Forum; the three well-known columns are Augustan (Platner and Ashby, *Top. Dict.*, pp. 102 ff.). In 58 Clodius collected weapons and paid his followers there; the steps were removed to prevent access (§ 23, *dom.* 110, *har. resp.* 28).

9. **veterum:** 'veteran'.

Catilinae: Cicero often asserts that Clodius was a friend of Catiline and received his mantle. Clodius helped Catiline at his trial in 65 (23. 16 n.), but in 63 he probably helped Cicero (Plut. *Cic.* 29. 1 against Asc. 44 KS). It is, however, true that both Catiline (Sall. *Cat.* 37. 1) and Clodius won much support from the Roman plebs.

11. **domus mea:** when Cicero was threatened in 58, supporters gathered at his house on the Palatine. The site was on the north side 'in conspectu prope totius urbis' (*dom.* 100), facing the Carinae (*har. resp.* 49). See further W. Allen, *Class. Journ.* xxxv, 1939–40, 134 ff., 291 ff.

13. **eum [Ciceronem]:** it would normally be legitimate for Cicero to name himself in the third person (cf. Landgraf on *Sex. Rosc.* 32, Gudeman on Tac. *dial.* 3. 3). But here the idiom would be unrhetorical; for *ad eum Ciceronem* would be followed in l. 15 by plain *ad eum*.

14. **domestica:** Cicero ignores private tokens of friendship.

sunt palam: cf. *in sen.* 18 'palam factum erat' ('it had become clear'), *Att.* xiii. 21. 3, Hand, iv. 384 f., Hofmann, *Umgangssprache*, p. 166.

15. **comitiis tuis:** at the election which made Piso consul.

16. **tabulam praerogativae:** in the *comitia centuriata*, which elected consuls and praetors, the *centuria praerogativa* was a cen-

70

COMMENTARY [§§ 11–12

tury of the first class, chosen by lot, which voted first; the result often had an influence on the election (*Planc.* 49, C. Meier, *RE* Suppl. viii. 567 ff., L. R. Taylor, *Party Politics in the Age of Caesar* (Berkeley and Los Angeles, 1949), pp. 56 f.). The *tabulae* were boards on which the votes for each candidate were marked; they were put in charge of *custodes*; it was a great mark of favour to act as a *custos* for a candidate (§ 36, *in sen.* 17, *St.-R.* iii. 406 f.).

17. **rogabas tertium:** so *in sen.* 17. Senators were called to speak in the order of their rank (*consulares, praetorii,* etc.), but within each rank the presiding consul was not bound to consult the most senior first (*RE* Suppl. vi. 712 f.). In 61 Pupius Piso adopted the order C. Piso, Cicero, Catulus, Hortensius (*Att.* i. 13. 2); in 59 Caesar began with Crassus at first, but later with Pompey (Gell. iv. 10). Some suppose that Piso put Caesar and Pompey ahead of Cicero, but it is highly probable that Caesar had left the city before 1 January.

numquam aspirasti: 'you did not lift a finger to help me'. *aspirare* means 'to breathe on', hence 'to come near'; sometimes there is an idea of helping (as here) or of harming (*Tusc.* v. 27). In Cicero the verb is found only in negative or quasi-negative sentences. See Nägelsbach, p. 580.

18. **interfuisti ... praefuisti:** these words are combined at *fam.* i. 8. 1, xiii. 29. 4, *Att.* ix. 6. 7.

§§ **12–21.** *Cicero continues his account of Piso's consulship and describes events at the time of his own exile.*

§ **12.** 20. **genero meo:** C. Piso (frag. xiii n.). Cicero emphasizes that he was a relative of L. Piso's, to make the latter's conduct seem more disgraceful (so *in sen.* 17, 38, *Sest.* 68). In fact the connexion was a distant one: C. Piso's great-grandfather was L. Piso Frugi, cos. 133; the great-grandfather of Cicero's enemy was probably L. Piso Caesoninus, cos. 148. The consuls of 148 and 133 may have been cousins, but need not have been blood-relations, as the first Caesoninus was presumably a Caesonius adopted by a Piso. For a conjectural family-tree see Drumann–Groebe, ii. 48.

21. **[egere] foris esse Gabinium:** 'Gabinius was insolvent'. *foris esse* is unlikely to be corrupt in view of *Att.* iv. 18. 3 (54 B.C.) 'candidati consulares omnes rei ambitus. accedit etiam Gabinius; quem P. Sulla, non dubitans quin foris esset, postularat' ('had given notice that he would prosecute'). The meaning of *foris esse* must be deduced from the context of the two passages. A reference to financial difficulties suits both; in the letter the point might be that Gabinius had no money to bribe the jury (cf. Tyrrell–Purser, *Correspondence of Cicero*, ii². 210). The origin of the expression is

71

§§ 12–13]   COMMENTARY

uncertain; Lambinus took it to mean literally 'is not at home when creditors call', but this is unlikely.

A. Klotz proposed the deletion of *egere* as a gloss (*praefatio*, p. lxi). This colourless word does not harmonize with the colloquial *foris esse*, and a single verb balances *stare* much more convincingly. Madvig proposed *egere sordidissime Gabinium*; but the six consecutive iambics make this emendation very unlikely.

sine provincia: cf. *Sest.* 18 '(Gabinius) se etiam invito senatu provinciam sperare dicebat'. In normal circumstances the senate would have assigned provinces to the consuls of 58 before the elections in 59. This passage implies that it failed to do so; it presumably foresaw that the consuls of 58 would favour Pompey and Caesar. Similarly in 60 the senate assigned the worthless provinces *silvae callesque* to the consuls of 59 (Suet. *Jul.* 19. 2). For other instances of the breakdown of the system see E. G. Hardy, *CR* xxxi, 1917, 11 ff.

22. stare: 'avoid ruin'; cf. *Cat.* ii. 21, *Flacc.* 14, Schol. Bob. p. 98 Stangl 'stare eos dicebant veteres qui habebant idoneam rem familiarem'.

tribuno plebis: Clodius.

24. conlega meo: Antonius; cf. 5. 13 n.

nihil esse quod: 'there was no reason why I should . . .' (K.–S. ii. 278). For the assonance *consulum . . . consulere* cf. frag. viii n.

1. qui sit: normally preferred to *quis sit* in order to avoid double *s* (Löfstedt, *Syntactica*, ii. 84 n. 1).

frontis . . . integumentis: 'enveloped by his all-concealing brow'. Cf. *in sen.* 16 'ut . . . frontis tibi integumento ad occultanda tanta flagitia uti non liceret', *Q.f.* i. 1. 15 'multis enim simulationum involucris tegitur et quasi velis quibusdam obtenditur unius cuiusque natura'.

3. flagitiorum: to be taken with *dolore* ('sorrow at his sins'). Classical Latin does not use *recordor* with the genitive (K.–S. i. 472, C. L. Babcock, *Cornell Studies in Class. Phil.* xiv. 6 f.); the construction is, however, found in Minuc. Fel. 33. 2 'priorum . . . recordaris'.

§ 13. 4. quinta fere hora: about 11 a.m. To drink in the morning or early afternoon was reprehensible; cf. *Phil.* ii. 104, Hor. *epist.* i. 19. 5, Juv. 1. 49 (with Mayor's note).

5. gurgustio: a cramped hovel, here a drinking-den. Cf. Ambr. *in psalm.* 43. 23. 2 'in ganeis atque gurgustiis', Pease on *nat. d.* i. 22, T. Kleberg, *Hôtels, restaurants et cabarets dans l'antiquité romaine* (Uppsala, 1957), pp. 10 f.

involuto capite: Piso was muffled up like an invalid (cf.

72

COMMENTARY [§§ 13–14

valetudinis below). Cicero pretends that he had wrapped his head in his cloak to disguise himself while visiting the tavern. Cf. *Phil.* ii. 77, Juv. 8. 145 'tempora Santonico velas adoperta cucullo' and Mayor's note; contrast *aperto capite* (Otto, p. 75).

6. **soleatum:** *soleae* were sandals, partly open on the top (Gell. xiii. 22. 5); cf. Marquardt, *Privatleben²*, pp. 595 f., for illustrations cf. D.–S. iv. 1389. For formal occasions or public appearances *calcei* should have been worn; for disregard of this convention cf. *Verr.* v. 86 'stetit soleatus praetor populi Romani', *Phil.* ii. 76, *Pis.* 92. 3 n. Criticism of dress was common in invective; cf. p. 194.

7. **valetudinis:** Piso's excuse may well have been true; it would explain *Sest.* 26 'nam alter ille horridus et severus (Piso) consulto se domi continebat'. Dio says of Piso at this time τὰ πολλὰ ἠρρώστει (xxxviii. 16. 6), but this may simply be an inference from the present passage.

quod diceres: 'in that you said'; Bake's *cum* is unnecessary. The subjunctive is sufficiently explained by *oratio obliqua* after *meministi*.

9. **quid . . .:** 'what else could we do ?' By the Latin idiom *quid aliud* is unnecessary; cf. Housman, *CQ* vii, 1913, 14.

§ **14.** 12. **illo fere biduo:** 'about a day later'.

productus: when a magistrate or tribune held a public meeting he could summon other persons to the platform to speak or answer questions; this was called *producere in contionem*. A tribune might even bring forward a consul, as here. See *St.-R.* ii³. 313, Botsford, *Roman Assemblies*, p. 146.

13. **eo:** Clodius.

sic aequatum does not give any appropriate meaning. Ernesti proposed *sic addictum* (cf. § 56 'addicebas tribuno plebis consulatum tuum'), but *sic* remains unsatisfactory. Halm proposed *quasi addictum*; he assumed that *cui quasi* was corrupted into *cui sic*. But *quasi* is weak in this common metaphor, and is insufficiently supported by *Tusc.* ii. 5 'certis . . . sententiis quasi addicti'. Kayser proposed *emancipatum*, with a meaning similar to *addictum*; cf. *Phil.* ii. 51 'venditum atque emancipatum tribunatum'. In our passage *emancipatum* is preferable to *addictum* as the longer and more vigorous word. Clark proposed *sicam quandam*; he quoted *Sest.* 24, where the consulship in Piso's hands is compared to a *gladius* in a long and developed simile (ending 'cum hominibus enervatis atque exsanguibus consulatus tamquam gladius esset datus'). He also cited *tog. cand.* frag. 27 (= Asc. 83 KS) 'duas uno tempore conantur in rem publicam sicas destringere', where the *sicae* are Catiline and Antonius. But in our passage *sicam quandam*

73

§ 14]   COMMENTARY

would be intolerably abrupt; *quasi sicam quandam* would be a slight improvement, but remains unconvincing.

15. **Calatinus:** A. Atilius Calatinus, cos. 258 and 254, dict. 249, cens. 247, commanded Roman armies in the first Punic war. *Africanus* refers especially to the elder Scipio Africanus (cf. *de sen.* 61, where Cicero mentions the *auctoritas* of Calatinus, Maximus, the elder Africanus, and others). *Maximus* refers to Q. Fabius Maximus Cunctator.

16. **Caesoninus . . . Calventius:** a derisive name for Piso (so *in sen.* 13, *prov. cons.* 7). Piso perhaps did not use his *agnomen* 'Caesoninus', for it is not normally found in inscriptions (for an exception cf. *CIL* i². 2. 2512); he may not have welcomed a reminder that his ancestors came into the Pisones by adoption (12. 20 n.). For Piso's maternal grandfather Calventius of Placentia see frag. ix n., frag. xv n.

17. **altero . . . :** Piso unsuccessfully tried to assume an air of pretentious gravity; for his eyebrows see 1. 16 n. It was regarded as a fault in an orator if he raised only one eyebrow; cf. Quintil. i. 11. 10 'cum alterum (supercilium) in verticem tenderet, altero paene oculus ipse premeretur', Fortunatianus, *Rhet. Lat. Min.* (ed. Halm), p. 133. For an apparent allusion to our passage cf. Mart. Cap. v. 543.

18. **crudelitatem:** a strong word, applied by Cicero's enemies to the execution of the Catilinarians (*Sull.* 93, *dom.* 75, Ps. Sall. *in Cic.* 5). Yet by making this reply Piso was probably trying to avoid a frontal attack on Cicero. Cicero retorts by accusing Piso himself of *crudelitas* (§§ 14–18).

    ille homo: Gabinius; cf. Dio xxxviii. 16. 6 καὶ ὁ Γαβίνιος ἐρωτηθεὶς τὸ αὐτὸ τοῦτο οὐχ ὅπως ἐκεῖνον (Piso) ἐπήνεσεν . . . . Cicero conceals the important fact that Caesar also spoke at this *contio* (introd., p. xi).

19. **furcifer:** a wooden frame (*furca*) was tied to slaves when they were being flogged; sometimes it was used to make them look ridiculous (*RE* vii. 306). Hence *furcifer* is a term of abuse, frequent in comedy, applied especially to slaves (Hofmann, *Umgangssprache* p. 86).

20. **in contione:** emphatic (as are also *crudelitatis, senatum, consul*); it was particularly objectionable for a consul to criticize the senate in front of a *contio*. Cf. *de or.* iii. 2 '(Livius Drusus) rettulit ad senatum de illo ipso quod consul (Philippus) in eum ordinem tam graviter in contione esset invectus'.

    non enim me: Piso by his general observation about *crudelitas* had avoided criticizing anybody by name; Cicero suggests that his criticism in fact applied to the senate.

21. **relatio:** the laying of a matter before the senate by a

74

COMMENTARY [§§ 14-15]

magistrate for discussion (*St.-R.* iii. 952 f., *RE* Suppl. vi. 709 f.). Cicero refers to the proceedings of 5 December 63, when he consulted the senate about the fate of the Catilinarian conspirators. *diligens* means 'conscientious'.

22. **animadversio:** 'punishment': cf. *Phil.* ii. 18 (also of the Catilinarians) 'animadversio senatus fuit'. Cicero is misleading; the senate could give moral support, but had no executive or judicial power; cf. Greenidge, *Legal Procedure*, pp. 403 f.

23. **qualis ... consul:** for the separation of these words, which lays emphasis on *qualis*, see E. Fraenkel, *Iktus und Akzent*, p. 321 n. 3.

24. **stipendio ... et frumento:** a stock phrase applied to an army commander's supplies (*Thes. L.L.* vi. 1411. 15 and 50).

§ **15.** 26. **eum:** Clodius. For the comparison with Catiline cf. 11. 9 n.

2. **ille:** Catiline.

vos sustulistis: by ignoring the senate's wishes about Cicero (30. 23).

leges incendere: one might compare the metaphors in *Planc.* 95 'ex illo incendio legum', *Vat.* 18 'leges conflagraverunt'; but here *incendere* is more difficult. Or Cicero might mean a literal burning of the *tabularium*, though this intention is not elsewhere imputed to Catiline. Cicero is saying, 'Though Clodius and his friends did not use drastic physical violence like Catiline, in effect they were just as bad.' *incendere* would suit this argument, for like *interficere* it is a literal word of destruction.

Yet *leges incendere* remains an unusual expression, and one's doubts are increased by *incendere* in l. 4. Cicero is often indifferent to repetitions (36. 21 n.), but this case is difficult since l. 4 forms the climax. So *incendere* here may have come from l. 4; in that case the word which it has displaced cannot be recovered.

exstinguere (Müller) and *evertere* (Schwartz) are possible, since they are stronger words than *abrogastis*; *infringere* (A. Klotz) and *inducere* (Brakman) are too weak. *incidere* (Landgraf) would mean 'to engrave', and so is impossible.

vos abrogastis: in particular the *leges Aelia et Fufia* (9. 6 n.).

3. **vi terrere:** if the reading adopted here is correct, *vi* balances *armis* below. *terrere* can be a fairly strong word meaning 'to terrorize'; cf. also *Cael.* 42 'ne quem vi terreat', *Sest.* 88 'vi lacessere et terrere'. *interire* is impossible, as a transitive verb is needed to govern *patriam*. Two *recentiores* read *interimere*, but *interimere patriam* would be an unparalleled expression. Kayser proposed *vim inferre patriae*; this is stronger than *vi terrere patriam*, and therefore an attractive proposal, but I have not ventured to adopt it.

75

§§ 15–16] COMMENTARY

[vos adiuvistis]: these words must be deleted or emended, as Piso and Gabinius did not help Catiline. If they are deleted, *vi terrere patriam* is balanced by *quid . . . armis?* (cf. Madvig ap. Orelli II². ii. 1452). The variation in the structure of the passage by the introduction of a question seems legitimate; for this rhetorical trick cf. Hegesippus v. 22. 1 'ingressus eras ut hostem expelleres, non ut hostem exerceres, ut prohiberes neces, non ut ipse adiungeres, ut latrocinium repelleres, non ut ipse latrocinareris, ut subvenires innocenti populo: cur in ipsum tua arma vertisti ?' In our passage Schütz proposed *vos adflixistis*, but then *quid . . . armis?* interrupts the series of parallel clauses. Vahlen's *vos adtulistis* (sc. *vim*) is unconvincing.

5. eius domum: Cicero's house on the Palatine; cf. § 26.

8. his stantibus: perhaps 'while Rome stood'; cf. *Cat.* iv. 16 'qui non haec stare cupiat', *Sull.* 76 'neque enim est quisquam qui arbitretur illis inclusis in re publica pestibus diutius haec stare potuisse', Nägelsbach, pp. 213 f. The use of the idiom in the ablative is admittedly more difficult. If this explanation is right, *se* is unemphatic, and the main contrast is between *tectis* and *nullum domicilium*. Alternatively one might emphasize *se* and understand *his* (*tectis*) *stantibus*, but *his* does not make a perfect contrast with *se*, and *tectis* does not suit public buildings well. I have considered *his parietibus stantibus*. Hotomanus interpreted *his* as *senatoribus* (cf. *Vat.* 21 'stante non modo maiestate horum sed etiam urbe'), but in the present context *stantibus* surely refers to buildings.

10. hic: = *in hac re* (in seeking to impose slavery).

crudeliores: the omission of the copula in the first and second persons is relatively rare; cf. *Phil.* ii. 96, viii. 2, *rep.* iii. 16, *paradox.* 29, 42, 50, *Att.* iv. 15. 6, ix. 1. 4, xvi. 5. 5, K.–S. i. 12.

11. emori: this word is often found where the thought is 'it is better to die than to experience such-and-such'; cf. Sall. *Cat.* 20. 9 'nonne emori per virtutem praestat quam . . . ?', *off.* iii. 114, *paradox.* 24, *Phil.* ix. 6, Plaut. *asin.* 810. It might be argued that *ei emori* is wanted, to make it clear that the feeling described applies not to everybody but to the Roman people. But after *populo* the sense seems clear enough without another dative. For the sentiment cf. *Phil.* vi. 19, x. 19, Landgraf on *Sex. Rosc.* 26.

potius . . . praestaret: for the pleonasm cf. K.–S. ii. 464.

§ 16. 14. domum . . . compulistis: this is untrue. Clodius was in fact responsible, probably not Piso, certainly not Gabinius (introd., p. xii). For *suam* cf. § 86 *debitoribus suis*, K.–S. i. 604, Lebreton, pp. 133 ff.; the antithesis with *mea* makes the word easier.

18. manis . . . expiaretis: the verb has the rare meaning of

76

COMMENTARY [§§ 16–17

'placate'; cf. *Thes. L.L.* v. 2. 1708. 4. For *mentes* (Ω) cf. *Clu.* 194 'deorum mentes non . . . posse placari', *har. resp.* 23 'mentes deorum . . . placantur', *Balb.* 62 'si certorum hominum mentes nulla ratione . . . placare possumus'. *X* in the margin suggests *manes*, which was conceivably a variant in the archetype; cf. Amm. Marc. xix. 2. 1 'expiare perempti iuvenis manes'. This is an attractive reading; one need have few doubts about the collocation of *manes* and *mortuorum*. *manes* is not elsewhere applied to individual dead in Republican Latin (*RE* xiv. 1056), and *dis manibus* has not been found on Republican tombstones; however, as the usage is found soon after (*ILS* 880, ibid. 8393. 79) one cannot regard this as a decisive argument against *manes* here.

19. **inclusum:** 'bottled up', and growing more intense because it has no outlet; cf. *fam.* i. 9. 20, *Cael.* 75.

21. **mactatus essem:** like a victim sacrificed to the dead (*Thes. L.L.* viii. 22. 70). For similar exaggerations cf. *Flacc.* 95, *Phil.* xiii. 35, Caes. *b.G.* vii. 17. 7, Liv. xxiv. 21. 2. Yet Sulla had actually executed Marius Gratidianus at the tomb of Catulus (*RE* xiv. 1827); for other such episodes cf. Suet. *Aug.* 15, Plut. *Ant.* 22. 6, *RE* xv. 955. After the condemnation of Antonius, whose army had defeated Catiline, ceremonies were held at Catiline's tomb (*Flacc.* 95).

§ **17. 27. redeo . . .:** 'reditus ad propositum'; cf. Seyffert, *Scholae Latinae*, i. 84 f.

1. **tu es ille . . .:** cf. *dom.* 4 ' "tune es ille" inquit "quo senatus carere non potuit ?" '.

2. **vestis mutatione:** 'mourning'; cf. introd., p. x. Magistrates abandoned the *toga praetexta*, senators wore the tunics of *equites* (*St.-R.* i³. 419; cf. *RE* viA. 2229).

3. **maerere . . . luctu:** one would expect the Republic to grieve on its own account, and not simply at the senate's mourning (Madvig, *Adv. crit.* iii. 147). Madvig therefore proposed *maerorem r.p.* (reipublicae), *amplissimi ordinis luctum*. But it spoils the balance of the sentence if *maerorem rei publicae* (which has not been mentioned before) is thus paired with *amplissimi ordinis luctum* (which has been mentioned). One might try to meet Madvig's point by explaining *maerere . . . luctu* as 'to grieve by means of the senate's mourning'; but such an ablative would be somewhat obscure here. Mr. Williams and Professor Watt have independently suggested to me *in amplissimi*.

4. **noster:** cf. § 39 'Paule noster', *Catull.* 13. 6 'venuste noster', Hofmann, *Umgangssprache*, pp. 137, 201.

quid facis ?: so *Verr.* iii. 139.

5. **consulem edicere:** cf. *St.-R.* ii³. 140.

77

§§ 17–18] COMMENTARY

6. **ut . . . ne:** solemn and archaic; cf. L.–H., p. 762, P. Parzinger, *Beiträge*, ii. 1 ff.

obtemperetur: the impersonal passive is very convincing; *-ur* could have been lost in Ω through abbreviation, and a second *senatus* added by X to complete the sense. Yet X's reading, though it has weak authority, finds some support from parallel passages; cf. *Planc.* 87 'qui soli in hac urbe senatum senatui parere non siverint', *Sest.* 32 'quis umquam consul senatum ipsius decretis parere prohibuit ?'

8. **nimis . . . crudelis:** for the hyperbaton cf. *de or.* ii. 288 'sed haec ipsa nimis mihi videor in multa genera discripsisse', C. F. W. Müller, *Rh. Mus.* lv, 1900, 636 f., Seyffert–Müller, *Laelius*, p. 49, E. Löfstedt, *Syntactica*, ii. 397, E. Fraenkel, *Horace*, pp. 84 f.

§ 18. 9. **illo suo pari:** Gabinius.

10. **omnibus vitiis:** cf. *Phil.* ii. 17 'quem (Clodium) . . . doleo a te omnibus vitiis iam esse superatum'.

11. **vestitum:** Francken proposed to insert *suum* after *vestitum*; but Müller compares *Phil.* xiv. 1 'reditum ad vestitum confectae victoriae reservate'.

quis . . . tyrannus: for hyperbaton with *quis* cf. *Phil.* v. 43 'quis tum nobis, quis populo Romano obtulit hunc divinum adulescentem deus?', E. Fraenkel, *Iktus und Akzent*, p. 164.

12. **lugere non sineret:** for the idea that it is the height of cruelty to prohibit the expression of grief cf. *in sen.* 12, *Sest.* 32, *Planc.* 87, Ov. *trist.* v. 1. 55 ff., Sen. *cont.* iii. 8, iv. 1, *paneg. Lat.* ii (xii). 25. 5.

14. **quod si . . .:** 'argumentum a minore'; cf. Volkmann, p. 230.

publico consilio: 'by resolution of the senate'.

16. **tamen . . .:** 'yet to prevent the senators from doing so by the edicts of your magistracy would have remained a case of intolerable cruelty'. The variant *crudelitatis tuae potestatis* is impossible. Madvig deleted *potestatis* and read *per interdicta tua*; but Cicero is emphasizing that Piso misused the authority of the consulship.

17. **erat:** indicative because the act was in fact cruel; its cruelty is not dependent on the fulfilment of the protasis. In other words, *si* has concessive force. See K.–S. ii. 402, S. A. Handford, *Latin Subjunctive*, p. 129.

19. **popina:** cf. § 13.

saltatrice: Gabinius; he is described as a dancer (i.e. a solo performer at riotous parties) at § 22, *in sen.* 13, *dom.* 60, *Planc.* 87. Macr. *sat.* iii. 14. 15 calls him an accomplished dancer, but he may simply depend on Cicero. The charge may be the exaggeration of an isolated incident at a symposium. Such accusations are

78

COMMENTARY [§ 18

conventional, and Cicero is rightly indignant when his own clients are accused. See *Mur.* 13 'saltatorem appellat L. Murenam Cato. maledictum est, si vere obicitur, vehementis accusatoris, sin falso, maledici conviciatoris. qua re cum ista sis auctoritate, non debes, M. Cato, adripere maledictum ex trivio aut ex scurrarum aliquo convicio, neque temere consulem populi Romani saltatorem vocare'; cf. also *Deiot.* 26. For dancing at Rome see Legrand, D.–S. iv. 1050 ff., Warnecke, *RE* ivA. 2247.

For the contemptuous feminine termination see Fraenkel on Aesch. *Ag.* 1625, Pease on *nat. d.* i. 93; add *Verr.* ii. 192 'muliercula', *prov. cons.* 9 'Semiramis illa', *Att.* iv. 11. 2 'illa populi Appuleia', *Phil.* xiii. 25 'venefica haec'.

20. **tonsa:** possibly 'trim'. This seems to be the interpretation of Servius auct. on Virg. *georg.* iii. 21 ('tonsae foliis ornatus olivae'); see the testimonia. Elsewhere Cicero mentions Gabinius's *cincinni* (§ 25), but the two pictures are not necessarily inconsistent, as *cincinni* could have been neatly trimmed.

    senatum populi Romani: cf. § 70 'senatorem populi Romani'.

22. **suo:** emphatic, like *meis* below.

23. **quasi vero . . .:** 'as if—I say nothing about myself, who had so often gone to the rescue of others—but as if anybody was ever so friendless as to suppose that he would be more secure with such a champion, or even better off for having him as supporter in court or assistant in a contract'.

    multis saepe: a common pleonasm; cf. Löfstedt, *Syntactica*, ii. 177 f.

24. **fuissem** is as good in sense as *fuerim*; Cicero had already at that time rescued many. The clausula produced by *fuissem* is far better, and *fuerim* might have been caused by *fuerit* below. However, the perfect tense is found in a similar context at *Planc.* 87 'nam profecto, praesertim tam bona in causa, numquam, quo ceteri saepe *abundarunt*, id mihi ipsi auxilium meum defuisset'.

25. **advocato:** a person who attended a court to give the accused moral support or legal advice (Mommsen, *Strafrecht*, p. 377). In the Republican period he did not make a speech.

26. **adstipulatore:** the *stipulatio*, a kind of Roman contract, took the following form. Maevius (the *stipulator*): 'Titi, decem mihi dari spondes ?' Titius (the *promissor*) 'spondeo'. Sometimes the *stipulator* was supported by an *adstipulator* who said 'Titi, eadem decem mihi dari spondes ?' Titius again replied 'spondeo'. For the purpose of this curious procedure see F. Schulz, *Classical Roman Law*, pp. 491 ff., F. de Zulueta, *Institutes of Gaius*, ii. 160.

79

§§ 19–20]   COMMENTARY

§ **19.** 1. **eiecto:** of an unwanted corpse, denied proper burial, and thrown out of the premises (*Thes. L.L.* v. 2. 303. 83).

2. **consulem inquam:** for *geminatio* cf. E. Wölfflin, *Sitz. Bayer. Akad.*, 1882, iii. 432 f. (= *Ausgewählte Schriften*, p. 291), P. Parzinger, *Beiträge*, i. 59, L.–H., pp. 833 f.

3. **maiali:** this word is found in Varro (= *sus castratus*), and in Pomponius and Titinius; it must have been used more often in speech than in literature, for it survives in the modern Italian word 'maiale' (= 'a pig' or 'pork', also a term of abuse). See *Novum Glossarium Mediae Latinitatis*, s.v.

5. **stipes:** literally a wooden post which could support a *titulus* or notice; but the word is also used colloquially for a fool, like *truncus* and *caudex*; cf. Hofmann, *Umgangssprache*, p. 88, Otto, p. 332, Seyffert–Müller, *Laelius*, p. 332.

8. **consulum** is a better reading than *consulis*. There is no reason why after *consularis* Cicero should mention only one consul; cf. also *consulibus* below. As *cos* could stand for both singular and plural, corruption was easy.

9. **erat . . . conversum:** 'had on the contrary been directed'.

10. **si consilium . . .:** 'if you ask my purpose' (in withdrawing into exile).

12. **bustuario gladiatore:** Clodius. Gladiators sometimes fought at funeral ceremonies; probably the custom was Etruscan in origin, and a modified form of human sacrifice (*RE* Suppl. iii. 760). Cicero means that Clodius's activities took place in an atmosphere of death and fire.

§ **20.** 14. **Q. Metelli:** Q. Caecilius Metellus Numidicus, cos. 109, commanded in the Jugurthine war 109–107, until he was displaced by Marius. In 100 the tribune Saturninus introduced a *lex agraria* which contained a clause requiring senators to swear obedience; he had for a time the support of Marius, then consul for the sixth time. Metellus refused to swear, and withdrew into exile; he was recalled in 99. Cicero often compares Metellus's experience with his own (*Sest.* 37 with Holden's note); hence he gives Piso the nickname 'Calventius Marius' (*Q.f.* iii. 1. 11).

quem ego civem: Cicero brings a noun in apposition inside a following relative clause: cf. K.–S. ii. 313, L.–H., p. 711.

15. **deorum:** for the comparison of men with gods in the Republican period cf. A. Alföldi, *Mus. Helv.* xi, 1954, 145 ff.

laude: note the compendious comparison (K.–S. ii. 566). In this construction the principal idea is normally expressed in full, the thing with which it is compared abbreviated. Here it is the other way round; cf. *Tusc.* v. 73 'huic . . . non multum differenti a iudicio ferarum'.

80

COMMENTARY [§ 20

16. **et sextum consuli:** *et* = *atque adeo*; cf. Parzinger, *Beiträge*, i. 65 ff., K.–S. ii. 26.

invictis: fresh from their victories over the Teutoni at Aquae Sextiae (102), and the Cimbri at Vercellae (101).

19. **barbaro** refers to Piso's alleged Gallic ancestry (frag. ix) and his lack of culture; as it sometimes implies 'non-Greek' (*Verr.* v. 148) it makes an oxymoron either with *Epicuro* or *Epicureo* (see next note). *barbato* (cod. Pithoei) is clearly an emendation or mistake. *barbatus* is sometimes used to describe stern old Romans of former days (*Cael.* 33, *Mur.* 26, *fin.* iv. 62), but a consul in the late Republic would not wear a beard (Mau, *RE* iii. 33). Cicero says (*Sest.* 19) that Piso *looks* like 'unum aliquem ex barbatis illis'; but it would be much more difficult to *call* him *barbatus* as a metaphorical equivalent for 'severe-looking'. Moreover, Epicurus himself is portrayed with a beard, and many Greek Epicureans must have worn beards in the manner of philosophers; but in sobriquets of this kind something is attributed to the noun which is literally inappropriate (see below).

Epicuro: the 'barbarian Epicurus' is Piso; cf. § 37 'Epicure noster'. For sobriquets of the type 'barbaro Epicuro' cf. *dom.* 72 'felicem Catilinam', *Cael.* 18 'Palatinam Medeam', Caelius frag. 26 (Malcovati, *ORF²*) 'quadrantariam Clytaemestram', frag. 37 'Pelia cincinnatus', Sall. *hist.* i. 55. 5 'scaevos Romulus', Ps. Sall. *in Cic.* 7 'Romule Arpinas', Vell. ii. 33. 4 'Xerxen togatum', Juv. 4. 38 'calvo Neroni', ibid. 7. 214 'Ciceronem Allobroga', Suet. *Calig.* 23. 2 'Ulixem stolatum'. *Epicureo* is the reading of all MSS. of any consequence (including *P*); but it is much flatter than *Epicuro*, and gives a less common clausula. In its favour, however, one might quote *fam.* xv. 16. 1 'Catius, Insuber Epicureus' (I suggest this punctuation).

20. **lanternario:** i.e. Gabinius. Roman streets were not lit at night; so lamp-slaves were used to light the way (*RE* xii. 569, Dio xxxix. 31. 1). Cicero means that Gabinius in his youth was a companion in Catiline's nocturnal adventures; cf. Val. Max. vi. 8. 1 'cuius (M. Antonii) in iudicio accusatores servum in quaestionem perseverantissime postulabant, quod ab eo cum ad stuprum iret lanternam praelatam contenderent'. For other remarks on Gabinius and Catiline cf. *in sen.* 10, 12, *dom.* 62, *Planc.* 87.

neque hercule ego: this is the normal word-order in comedy; cf. E. Kellerhoff in Studemund, *Studien*, ii. 60 f., A. Gagnér, *De hercule mehercle* (Gryphiswaldae, 1920), p. 138.

21. **crotala:** 'castanets', appropriate to a dancing-girl; for illustrations see D.–S. i. 1571. Cf. Scipio Aemilianus frag. 30 (Malcovati, *ORF²*) 'vidi . . . puerum bullatum . . . cum crotalis saltare

5993   H   81

§§ 20–21] COMMENTARY

quam saltationem impudicus servulus saltare non posset'. The reading *crotalia* ('ear-rings') must surely be a corruption of *crotala*. *cymbala* gives an inferior clausula.

1. **nubeculam** describes Piso's sullen frown; cf. Soph. *Ant.* 528 νεφέλη δ' ὀφρύων ὕπερ with Jebb's note, Eurip. *Elect.* 1078, *Phoen.* 1307, Anaxandrides 58, Hor. *epist.* i. 18. 94 'deme supercilio nubem', Sil. viii. 611, Quintil. xi. 3. 75. *nubeculam* and *spiritum* ('breeze' in verse) keep up the nautical metaphor. For an interesting reminiscence in Sedulius Scottus see introd., p. xxii.

§ 21. 2. **alios . . . ventos:** the threat from Caesar's army; cf. *Sest.* 36–41, introd., p. xi.

3. **non cessi:** = *non dicam me cessisse*. Cicero is denying that *cedere* is the right verb to describe his action; cf. *Phil.* v. 24 'non profectus est, sed profugit, paludatus'. *tempestatibus* is dative.

4. **[his]:** this word is too emphatic, and Wunder's deletion is the simplest solution. Mommsen proposed *bis*. Cicero sometimes claimed to have saved the state twice, first in 63, then by withdrawing in 58; cf. *Sest.* 49 'unus rem publicam bis servavi', *dom.* 76, 99, *Pis.* 78. But here one would expect *bis me unum* (as A. Klotz points out); besides, *bis* would have to mean *iterum*, an unparalleled use in classical Latin.

As an alternative to deletion I have considered *eis*; the two pronouns are constantly confused even in the oldest MSS. (cf. 35. 7, *Thes. L.L.* vi. 2692. 25). It may be objected that Cicero is rejecting the single word *cessi* and not the whole clause *aliis . . . cessi*, and that therefore *tempestatibus* must be taken with *obtuli* as well as with *cessi*. But a slight pause may perhaps be admitted after *tempestatibus* while Cicero feels for the right word; then by an anacoluthon *tempestatibus* is replaced by *eis*.

5. **discessu . . . meo:** Cicero often describes his exile thus; his enemies called it *fuga*. *tum* should be taken with *exciderunt* (thus K.–S. i. 220). Others take *tum* closely with *discessu*, meaning 'my departure at that time' (L.–H., p. 467), but this would surely require *meo tum discessu*.

7. **templa gemerent:** for the attribution to buildings of human emotions cf. § 52, *leg. agr.* ii. 9, *Sest.* 53, *Marc.* 10, *off.* ii. 29, Plin. *paneg.* 50. 4, *paneg. Lat.* xi (iii). 11. 3.

8. **complexus es . . . :** 'you embraced that fatal monster (Clodius), compounded of evil debaucheries and civil bloodshed, the cruelty of every crime and the vileness of every sin, and in the same consecrated spot, at the same point of space and moment of time, you carried off your fee not only for my funeral but for Rome's'. At the same time that his bill *de capite civis Romani* was

82

COMMENTARY [§ 21]

passed, Clodius carried another bill which gave Piso his reward, the province of Macedonia (introd., p. x).

9. omni: this reading is as legitimate as *omnium*; for such transferred epithets cf. Löfstedt, *Syntactica*, ii. 110 n. 2, Fraenkel on Aesch. *Ag.* 504.

10. et flagitiorum impuritate: *impuritas* is found only twice elsewhere in Cicero (*Phil.* ii. 6, v. 16) and after that not till Tertullian; but it suits *flagitiorum* and *concretum* well. The assonance with *importunitate* is in Cicero's manner; cf. *Phil.* xii. 13 'importuno atque impuro', frag. viii n. The word's resemblance to *importunitate* might have caused an omission both in *P* and in α. The reading *impunitate* does not suit *concretum*, though *impunitas* is applied elsewhere to Clodius (*dom.* 3, *har. resp.* 33). A. Klotz suggested *ex omnium scelerum et flagitiorum impuritate*, or *ex omni scelerum impuritate* (cf. *praef.*, p. xlii). But *impuritate* goes less well with *scelerum* (political crimes) than with *flagitiorum* (personal vices); for the distinction cf. Tac. *Germ.* 12. 1, H. Usener, *Kleine Schriften*, iv. 360. *importunitate* goes convincingly with *scelerum*; cf. *har. resp.* 4 'illud scelus tam importunum'. If the reading adopted here is correct, *importunitate* and *impuritate* correspond to *cruore* and *stupris*; a chiasmus is thus formed.

concretum: *concretus ex* means 'compounded of'; see *nat. d.* iii. 30, iii. 34, *Tusc.* i. 62, *Clu.* 72 'ex fraude et mendacio factus' (cf. *Cael.* 12 *conflatum*, *Phil.* iii. 28 *conglutinatus*). The variant *conceptum* might seem to be supported by *Sest.* 15 'ille nefarius ex omnium scelerum conluvione natus'. On the other hand *conceptum ex stupris* could only refer to Clodius's parentage, whereas Cicero is thinking of Clodius's own behaviour.

11. templo: the *rostra*. The word need not refer to a building, but can describe any place where the auspices were taken; cf. *imp. Pomp.* 70, *Vat.* 18, 24, S. Weinstock, *RE* vA. 484.

et loci: Halm remarks that with this reading one would expect *eodem vestigio et loci et temporis*. On the contrary, *vestigio* is most idiomatically placed after the first genitive; cf. K.–S. ii. 620, Seyffert–Müller, *Laelius*, pp. 12, 230. For *et loci et temporis* cf. *off.* i. 144, Plin. *epist.* iii. 18. 1, *paneg. Lat.* xi (iii). 15. 1.

vestigio: used of time *Caecil.* 57 *e vestigio* ('instantly'), Caes. *b. G.* vii. 25. 1 'illo vestigio temporis', *b.c.* ii. 7. 3 'eodem vestigio', ibid. ii. 26. 2 'vestigio temporis'. No parallel for *loci vestigio* presents itself.

arbitria funeris: properly an undertaker's fee, so called because the sum was decided by an arbitrator (Ulp. *dig.* xi. 7. 12. 5) to keep the heirs from being too mean. Cicero means that Piso buried the republic and received Macedonia as his reward; for the same metaphor cf. *in sen.* 18, *dom.* 98.

83

§ 22]   COMMENTARY

§§ **22–31**: *Cicero describes the events of Piso's consulship after his own withdrawal into exile. He concentrates on the theme that Piso and Gabinius do not deserve to be called consuls.*

§ **22.** 13. **epulas:** also mentioned *dom.* 62, *Sest.* 54, 111. Piso and Gabinius may have celebrated their appointment to provinces, but the details are obviously fictitious. P. Boyancé, *REL* xxxiii, 1955, 118 f., suggests that Cicero is alluding to an Epicurean dinner, held according to the usual custom on the twentieth day of the month (cf. 67. 13 n.). This theory depends on the view that Cicero left Rome on 19 March (Drumann–Groebe, ii. 552), but that date is too late (G. De Benedetti, *Historia*, iii, 1929, 568).

gratulationem: 'rejoicing'.

14. **gregibus:** Piso's Epicurean friends (67. 19 n.).

17. **in publico:** Piso may in fact have been ill; cf. 13. 7 n.

cum . . .: these clauses, which describe Gabinius, are loosely attached to the previous questions (cf. 29. 20, K.–S. ii. 345 f., L.–H., p. 750). At l. 20 (*hic autem*) Cicero describes Piso's activities in three clauses which balance the three clauses referring to Gabinius. But the construction changes slightly, and Cicero now uses main verbs.

18. **saltaret:** for Gabinius's dancing see 18. 19 n.

19. **saltatorium . . . orbem:** possibly a sort of hoop used by dancing-girls (D.–S. v. 493). The phrase is repeated by Arnobius, *adv. nat.* ii. 42 'lasciviens multitudo incompositos corporum dissolveretur in motus, saltitaret et cantaret, orbes saltatorios verteret . . .'; perhaps he thought that the *orbis saltatorius* was a circular motion of the body. Abram quotes the Byzantine Georgios Pisides *de vanitate vitae* (Migne, *Patrol. Gr.* xcii. 1594. ll. 173 ff.) ἡ γὰρ παρ' ἄλλοις ὠνομασμένη τύχη εἰκών τίς ἐστιν ἀπρεποῦς ὀρχηστρίδος ἐν τοῖς ἑαυτῆς ἀντικλωμένης στρόφοις. But no parallel presents itself for *versare* with an internal accusative such as *orbem*; and the comparison with the wheel of Fortune is perhaps easier if the *orbis* is a material object.

20. **fortunae rotam:** the first surviving instance of this expression, but the idea was not new; cf. Soph. frag. 787 Nauck (= 871 Pearson), Pacuvius, *trag.* 366 ff. For many other parallels see A. Doren, *Vorträge der Bibliothek Warburg*, 1922–3, i. 80 ff., D. M. Robinson, *CP* xli, 1946, 207 ff. Tacitus, *dial.* 23. 1, mentions 'rotam fortunae' as a phrase in Cicero which met with criticism; as Cicero did not invent the image of the 'wheel of Fortune', Tacitus may not be referring to the image in itself, but to the comparison with the *orbis saltatorius*.

hic . . . musicus: 'this less elegant and less musical glutton', i.e. Piso.

84

COMMENTARY [§§ 22–23

22. atque vino: there was a short lacuna in *P* at this point, but traces of *atque vino* were seen by Ströbel (*Philol.* lxx, 1911, 443). Recent editors have accepted *C*'s *et caeno*, but readings found only in *C* ought to be regarded with great suspicion. *atque vino* gives a convincing clausula.

quod ... ferebatur: 'this banquet of his ... was the talk of the town, as if it were some feast of Lapiths or Centaurs'.

23. aut: Sauppe proposed *et*, which is more logical and perhaps right; in the legend the Centaurs got drunk at the Lapiths' banquet; cf. Lucian, *symp.* 45 Λαπίθας οὖν καὶ Κενταύρους εἶδες ἄν, Jul. Valer. i. 13 'prorsus ut nihilum de Centaurorum Lapitharumque convivio demutaret'. Wunder deleted *aut Centaurorum* (cf. Lucian's dialogue Συμπόσιον ἢ Λαπίθαι); this solution would have the merit of shortening a somewhat lengthy clause.

24. nemo potest dicere ...: for insults of this pattern cf. *prov. cons.* 8 'ut nemo posset utrum posterior an infelicior esset iudicare', *Phil.* ii. 99 'quis interpretari potest impudentiorne ... an impurior ... an crudelior ... ?', Sall. *hist.* iv frag. 1, Ps. Cic. *inv. in Sall.* 14, Suet. *Calig.* 25. 1, Amm. Marc. xx. 1. 2, Sidon. *epist.* iii. 13. 4.

1. [an vomuerit]: if these words are kept then *effuderit* would have to mean *minxerit*. However, Wunder plausibly deleted *an vomuerit* as a gloss, and took *effuderit* to mean *vomuerit*. *aut vomuerit*, the reading of α, might seem to support the theory of a gloss, but as both *P* and *X* read *an*, it is unlikely that *aut* represents a genuine tradition. Zielinski deleted *an effuderit*, but it is not clear that this improves the clausula.

§ 23. 2. consulatus tui: in *P tui* may simply have dropped out by accident after *-tus*. Yet *P*'s reading could be defended; the sentence might mean 'will you so much as mention the consulship (in general), or say (in particular) that you were consul ?'

3. in toga [et] praetexta: for the asyndeton cf. *off.* i. 38 'cum Celtiberis, cum Cimbris' with Holden's note (in his supplement). However, Garatoni's *et in toga praetexta* may be right. *et praetexta* is also possible, though *praetexta* (without *toga*) is found only once in Cicero (*Cat.* ii. 4).

4. quae ornamenta ...: Cicero argues that a man does not show himself a consul simply by the external trappings of his office. Even an inferior person like Sex. Cloelius, when he held the *ludi compitalicii* in 58, was entitled to a *toga praetexta* (8. 2 n.) and lictors (*St.-R.* i³. 391).

Cloelio: Shackleton Bailey's emendation for *Clodio*; cf. 8. 2 n.

5. huius ... Clodiani canis: 'this jackal of P. Clodius's'. *canis* suggests a shameless and rapacious attendant, and perfectly suits

85

§ 23] COMMENTARY

Cloelius, the henchman of Clodius. Cf. *har. resp.* 59 '(did the poets ever describe) tam eminentibus canibus Scyllam tamque ieiunis quam quibus istum (Clodium) videtis, Gelliis Cloeliis Titiis rostra ipsa mandentem ?', *Att.* vi. 3. 6 'Gavius . . . P. Clodi canis'. Lambinus proposed *his tu, Clodiane canis, insignibus*; Kayser, who followed him, took 'quae ornamenta . . . declarari putas ?' as one sentence. But the epithet *Clodianus canis* suits Cloelius much better than Piso.

7. **vigilantia:** one of the attributes of a good consul; cf. *Cat.* i. 8, *Planc.* 90, *fam.* vii. 30. 1 'fuit enim mirifica vigilantia, qui suo toto consulatu somnum non viderit'.

8. **omni officio:** 'by every service in his power'; cf. *Balb.* 58, *fam.* i. 1. 1, *epist. ad Brut.* 3 [ii. 3]. 6.

9. **rei publicae consulendo:** 'by consulting the interests of the republic'; cf. Accius, *praetext.* 39 'qui recte consulat consul cluat', Carbo ap. *de or.* ii. 165 'si consul est qui consulit patriae, quid aliud fecit Opimius ?', *Thes. L.L.* iv. 562. 8. *consul* is really derived from *consulere* in its other sense: the consuls consulted the senate. For arguments from etymology cf. Volkmann, p. 224.

an ego . . .: cf. *de or.* iii. 4 'cum (L. Crassus) sibi illum consulem esse negaret cui senator ipse non esset', *Phil.* ii. 10. (Note the many parallels to our speech in the *de oratore*, which was also written in 55 B.C.).

12. **reges:** cf. *rep.* ii. 14, *Phil.* iii. 9, *RE* Suppl. vi. 667.

etenim: this word, if right, seems to introduce Cicero's justification for speaking the previous sentence or sentences (cf. *Planc.* 18, *Thes. L.L.* v. 2. 918. 54): he says that he has now finished with Piso's drinking-bouts and has turned to his political crimes. Müller proposed *ut enim alia iam omittam*; this gives excellent sense, but is somewhat remote from the MSS.

cum . . .: for these events see § 11.

13. **haberentur:** the plural suits the rhetorical exaggeration here, though the singular is found in the parallel passages (*Sest.* 34, *Pis.* 11).

in templum: cf. *dom.* 54 'cum arma in aedem Castoris comportabas'. The variant *templo* is seriously considered by Madvig, *Opusc. acad.*², p. 354; cf. *Sest.* 34 'arma in templo (templum *Naugerius*) Castoris palam comportabantur', *Thes. L.L.* vii. 1. 775. 8. But even if this construction is permissible in Cicero (which is very doubtful), in our passage the accusative has slightly better manuscript support.

14. **luce [et] palam:** the normal expression is *luce palam*; cf. *Sest.* 83, *off.* iii. 93, S. Preuss, *De bimembris dissoluti apud scriptores Romanos usu sollemni* (Edenkoben, 1881), p. 58. In favour of

86

COMMENTARY [§§ 23-24

luce et palam A. Klotz quotes Caes. *b.c.* iii. 30. 3 'Pompeius clam et noctu, Caesar palam atque interdiu', Amm. Marc. xxiv. 4. 21 'dumque haec luce agerentur ac palam'; neither is a satisfactory parallel.

15. **reliquiis:** Cicero maintained that Clodius was supported by the remnants of the Catilinarian conspirators; cf. 11. 9 n.

16. **Catilinae praevaricatore quondam:** 'the man who was once collusive prosecutor of Catiline', i.e. Clodius. Catiline was tried in 65 for extortion; he was acquitted, it was believed, through the collusion of his prosecutor Clodius (*Att.* i. 2. 1, Asc. 78 KS, *RE* iv. 82). Such collusion was common because after an acquittal one could not be tried again on the same charge; cf. Macer, *dig.* xlviii. 2. 11. 2 'ab alio delatum alius deferre non potest', Greenidge, *Legal Procedure*, pp. 470 f. For the attachment of the adverb to the noun cf. 7. 12 n.

17. **equites:** cf. introd., p. x. Lamia was probably the only *eques* banished (64. 10 n., *in sen.* 12, *fam.* xi. 16. 2, Asc. 9 KS, Dio xxxviii. 16. 4). The plural is also found at *in sen.* 32, *Sest.* 35, 52, but in every case is presumably rhetorical; cf. Löfstedt, *Syntactica*, i². 38 ff.

19. **lugere:** cf. introd., p. x.

20. **conservatorem:** cf. 34. 21 n.

21. **nullo more:** 'without precedent'; cf. § 30.

§ **24.** 24. **qui latrones . . .:** for similar types of argument cf. *paradox.* 30 'cur hostis Spartacus si tu civis ?', ibid. 40 'quae servitus est si haec libertas existimari potest ?', *Phil.* iv. 8 'si consul Antonius, Brutus hostis', Aug. *civ. D.* ii. 4 'quae sunt sacrilegia si illa sunt sacra ?'

1. **non capiunt . . . tui:** 'your mean spirit is not big enough (for such grandeur)'. The object of *capiunt* and *recipit* is *magnum nomen*, etc., understood from the previous clause; cf. *in sen.* 10 'sed fuerunt ii consules quorum mentes angustae humiles parvae . . . nomen ipsum consulatus, splendorem illius honoris, magnitudinem tanti imperi nec intueri nec sustinere nec capere potuerunt'. Alternatively one might suppose that *capiunt* and *recipit*, as well as *sustinet*, govern *personam*; but *capiunt* and *pectoris* do not suit *personam* well. Editors put a semicolon after *animi*; this destroys the parallelism of *non egestas animi* and *non infirmitas ingeni*.

4. **Seplasia:** a street in Capua famous for its *unguentarii*; cf. *leg. agr.* ii. 94, *Sest.* 19, Varr. *Menipp.* 511 'hic narium Seplasiae, hic ἡδύχους Neapolis', Petr. 76. 6 *seplasium* (= perfume), Philipp, *RE* iiA. 1546. See also J. Beloch, *Campanien*², 1890, pp. 338 f. (who quotes epitaphs of *unguentarii* of Capua).

5. **Campanum consulem:** Piso was a *duumvir* at the new

87

§§ 24–25]   COMMENTARY

colonia of Capua in 58, the year of his consulship at Rome; so in a sense he was a 'Capuan consul'. Cicero chooses this expression because he is thinking of the events of 216 B.C., when the Capuans asked that one of the Roman consuls should be a Capuan; the demand was rejected with contempt, Capua revolted and was crushed. One would expect a 'Capuan consul' to be welcome to the Capuans, yet they rejected Piso. See Liv. xxiii. 6. 6, *leg. agr.* ii. 93, ii. 95, *in sen.* 17, *dom.* 60, Sil. Ital. xi. 123 f. 'veniet quondam felicior aetas cum pia Campano gaudebit consule Roma'; cf. below pp. 187 f.

ut dici audiebam refers not just to the fact that Capua repudiated Piso, but to the use of the expression *Seplasia Campanum consulem repudiavit*. Cicero sometimes attributed his own jokes to the public (Quintil. vi. 3. 4, vi. 3. 55); for possible instances see *Verr.* II. i. 121, iv. 95, *Sest.* 72, 126; cf. *de or.* ii. 240.

6. **audierat:** 'had heard of' (*Thes. L.L.* ii. 1274. 10).

Decios Magios: in 216 B.C. Decius Magius belonged to the pro-Roman party at Capua; when the city went over to Hannibal he was sent to Carthage, but escaped to Egypt, where he died (Liv. xxiii. 7–10, Münzer, *RE* xiv. 438). The plural here means 'men like Decius Magius'.

Taurea . . . Vibellio: in the second Punic War Cerrinus Vibellius Taurea was a Capuan who favoured Carthage (Liv. xxiii. 8. 5); he fought a memorable single combat (ibid. xxiii. 46–47), and committed suicide when Capua was reconquered by the Romans in 211 (xxvi. 15. 15); cf. *leg. agr.* ii. 93. For the position of *cognomen* before *nomen* cf. H. L. Axtell, *CP* x, 1915, 392 f.

7. **moderatio:** for the proverbial arrogance of Capua cf. *leg. agr.* ii. 91–97, E. Wölfflin, *ALL* vii. 341.

§ **25.** 10. **vestri:** 'of you and your fellow-Capuans'.

11. **madentes:** i.e. with unguents (cf. p. 194).

12. **fimbriae:** normally the fringe of a garment, here locks of hair; cf. Titinius 112 'quasi hermaphroditus fimbriatum frontem gestas'.

fluentes: 'flabby' (with self-indulgence); cf. Nägelsbach, pp. 576 f. Some translate 'dripping with cosmetics' here and at *in sen.* 13 (also of Gabinius); but this explanation does not suit *de or.* ii. 266 'eiecta lingua fluentibus buccis' (of the picture of a Gaul on a shield).

purpurissataeque: cf. Plaut. *Truc.* 290 'quiaque bucculas tam belle purpurissatas habes', Marquardt, *Privatleben*², p. 788. Haplography of *purpur-* could have caused the corruption to *pulsataeque*. The trochaic rhythms from *compti* to *buccae* suggest that Cicero may be paraphrasing a comic poet; for quotations not specifically acknowledged cf. W. Zillinger, *Cicero und die altrömischen*

88

COMMENTARY [§ 25

Dichter (Würzburg, 1911), p. 80. If this assumption is incorrect, the trochaic rhythm caused by *purpurissataeque* would be disturbing. I have considered *fucataeque*, but this would be a much less attractive emendation palaeographically.

13. **haec quidem:** Caesar's new colony at Capua, founded in 59. For the care to avoid giving offence cf. frag. x n.

16. **praetextatum:** wearing the *toga praetexta* of a Roman consul. Cicero avoids saying *consulem* as he refuses to admit that Piso was one. *te* is emphatic in opposition to *mei*.

18. **illam ipsam urbem:** in 63 Cicero sent Q. Pompeius Rufus and Sestius with a military force to Capua. It was a danger-spot because of its gladiatorial *ludi*; Spartacus had begun his revolt there, and the risk was increased in 63 when gladiators were moved there from Rome (Sall. *Cat.* 30. 7, *Sest.* 9, *RE* iii. 1558).

inaurata statua: a bronze statue covered with gold-leaf. Cf. *Phil.* ix. 13, Catull. 81. 4 'inaurata pallidior statua', Liv. xl. 34. 5, H. Blümner, *Technologie*, iv. 309, D.–S. iv. 2. 1483 n. 1.

19. **patronum:** towns in Italy and the provinces sometimes honoured benefactors with this title; cf. M. Gelzer, *Die Nobilität der römischen Republik* (Berlin, 1912), pp. 70 ff., L. Harmand, *Le Patronat sur les collectivités publiques* (Paris, 1957).

a me . . . vitam: cf. *Att.* i. 14. 3, *Phil.* ii. 12, Suet. *Aug.* 98. 2.

20. **praesentem:** in the spring of 58 when Cicero was in danger but still in Rome. *absentem*: early in 57 the local council at Capua, on the motion of Pompey, who was *duumvir*, passed a motion in favour of Cicero's recall (introd., p. xiii).

22. **principe:** 'first'. The resolution at Capua was the first of many throughout Italy; cf. *in sen.* 29 (of Pompey) 'princepsque Italiae totius praesidium ad meam salutem implorandum putarit'. In our passage it is a little awkward to interpret *principe* as 'first in Italy' rather than 'first in Capua'; but the difficulty is lessened if the word is taken with *revellente* as well as with *referente*.

referente: see 14. 21 n., and for municipal contexts *RE* iv. 2333. 20. Mommsen, *St.-R.* iii. 952 n. 1 says that the word is used here incorrectly; this is not so, since Pompey was *duumvir* at Capua at the time.

23. **revocarunt:** Lambinus's *revocarant* would imply that Capua had still an opportunity of seeing Piso (cf. *aspexit* above) after Pompey's *relatio*. But Pompey's duumvirate probably belonged to 57 (cf. *in sen.* 29, *Mil.* 39); and Piso had left Italy by that time. Even if the duumvirate belonged to 58 (as some have supposed), Pompey was in retirement from August to December (*Sest.* 69), and could only have made his *relatio* in December; by that time Piso had probably gone (31. 7 n.).

89

§§ 26–27]   COMMENTARY

§ 26. 25. ecquod: this, rather than *et quod*, is probably the correct form; cf. *Thes. L.L.* v. 2. 52.

maius: one expects Cicero to say 'All fires as big as this were fought by consuls'; it is weaker to argue 'All bigger fires were fought by consuls'. One might, it is true, interpret *maius* as 'fairly big'; yet *ecquod* and *umquam* are elsewhere found in such contexts with true comparatives. Perhaps Cicero's thought is confused, and the point which he is trying to make would have been correctly conveyed by *tantum*.

26. **consul**: for fire-fighting in the Republic see Paulus, *dig.* i. 15. 1, who mentions in this connexion *triumviri nocturni*, aediles, and tribunes of the plebs.

1. **socrum**: Asconius 9 KS has an interesting note for prosopographers: 'socrus Pisonis quae fuerit invenire non potui, videlicet quod auctores rerum non perinde in domibus ac familiis feminarum, nisi illustrium, ac virorum nomina tradiderunt'. This lady's husband was Rutilius Nudus (introd., p. v). For the episode described here cf. *dom.* 62 'columnae marmoreae ex aedibus meis . . . ad socrum consulis portabantur'.

prope . . .: the reading found in the MSS. of Asconius should be rejected. *prope a meis aedibus* gives a convincing clausula, and contains information which is unlikely to have been invented. The divergence in Asconius in the next clause is to be explained by the loss of *ad meam domum* after *domum*, and consequent patching. The repetition *domum . . . domum* is unobjectionable (Landgraf on *Sex. Rosc.* 99).

3. **furiis**: this word is often applied by Cicero to his enemies (e.g. § 8), but here is particularly appropriate because the Furies carried torches (frag. iv, § 46).

6. **adsurrexit**: for this token of respect cf. *St.-R.* i³. 398, *RE* Suppl. vi. 706.

7. **respondendum**: a senator, when asked his *sententia* by the presiding consul, was obliged to reply (*RE* Suppl. vi. 713).

8. **iudicia conticuissent**: cf. § 32, *in sen.* 6 'nihil iudices sententiis, nihil populus suffragiis, nihil hic ordo auctoritate declaravit'. Cicero's language is no doubt greatly exaggerated.

§ 27. 12. caeso if genuine, is a term of abuse of unknown meaning; the MSS. are supported by two testimonia, and so are unlikely to be corrupt. The word looks like a conflation ('portmanteauword') of the names *Caesoninus* and *Piso*; but it would only make sense here if it could be a term of abuse as well. Paul. Fest. 50L notes 'caesones appellantur ex utero matris exsecti', but this information is of no help. It is perhaps worth suggesting that the word might mean τομίας (cf. § 18 *maiali*).

90

COMMENTARY [§§ 27–28

However, *Caesonine* might be right, though a proper name rings oddly here; for adjectives qualifying proper names cf. K.–S. i. 226 f. R. Klotz proposed *quaeso* (from the *deteriores* of Donatus); but the word-order then would be unconvincing.

13. **cum . . . :** cf. *dom.* 25 'excitatus aliquando C. Pompei nimium diu reconditus et penitus abstrusus animi dolor', introd., p. xii. *experta* is a late Latin form of *experrecta* (*Thes. L.L.* v. 2. 1649. 55).

17. **tamen:** the contrast is between Piso and Gabinius. The punctuation of modern editors obscures this.

18. **[Gabinius]:** the name would be an anticlimax here. Cicero elsewhere refers to Gabinius in an allusive way; cf. § 14 'ille homo dignissimus tuis laudibus', § 18 'illo suo pari', *in sen.* 17 'tuo illo pari'.

conlegit . . . tamen: cf. *Cael.* 76 'fecit me invito . . . sed tamen fecit', *Att.* xiii. 48. 1, *Phil.* xii. 11, *paradox.* 37, *fin.* v. 3.

22. **aequitas:** 'impartiality'. The metaphor in this and the next sentence comes from gladiatorial shows; *pari* = 'a pair of gladiators'.

uter: = *utercumque* ('whichever of the two'); cf. *Sest.* 92 'horum utro uti nolumus, altero est utendum'. *perisset* corresponds to the future-perfect *perierit* of direct speech. For the thought cf. Antony ap. *Phil.* xiii. 40 'quibus, utri nostrum ceciderint, lucro futurum est, quod spectaculum adhuc ipsa Fortuna vitavit, ne videret unius corporis duas acies lanista Cicerone dimicantis'.

§ 28. 1. **agebat aliquid:** 'was achieving something'; cf. *Thes. L.L.* i. 1381. 73.

4. **meo sanguine:** at the ratification of a *foedus* a pig was sacrificed (Marquardt, *St.-V.* iii². 425 f.). Cicero sees himself as the victim; cf. *Sest.* 24 with Holden's note. For this *pactio* cf. introd., p. x.

5. **sororius adulter:** Clodius; the charge was made about his three sisters (*RE* iv. 107 f.). Such accusations were conventional in invective; the evidence which L. Lucullus obtained by torturing his wife's slaves (*Mil.* 73) is not conclusive.

6. **pecuniam:** cf. p. 172.

7. **visceribus:** cf. *dom.* 23, 124, *Q.f.* i. 3. 7.

ut: for the repetition of *ut* see K.–S. ii. 589, L.–H., p. 829.

9. **fracti fasces:** Gabinius's (Dio xxxviii. 30. 2); for the breaking of *fasces* on other occasions cf. Dio xxxvi. 39. 3, xxxviii. 6. 3. *RE* xiii. 511. *ictus ipse* refers to Gabinius; this fact is not recorded elsewhere. Cicero uses this staccato style in passages of vivid narrative or description. Its characteristics are a series of short sentences, the omission of *est* and *sunt*, especially with perfect passives, rows

91

§§ 28–30] COMMENTARY

of nouns without verbs, sometimes the historic infinitive. Cf. § 67, *Sest.* 74, *Q.f.* ii. 3. 2, *Att.* iv. 3. 3–4.

fugae: the rioters scattered the populace; cf. *dom.* 67 'quas lapidationes, quas fugas fecerit'.

10. **ad senatum:** in the vestibule of the temple of Castor, where the senate was sitting (*Mil.* 18–19, introd., p. xii, *Thes. L.L.* i. 520. 72).

§ **29.** 12. **actionem:** 'statement in the senate' (*Thes. L.L.* i. 441. 40). *relationem*: cf. 14. 21 n.

14. **qui . . . servarat:** Cicero; cf. *Sest.* 53.

idemque: this word is corrupt. *is se* would make sense, but does not explain the corruption. *idem se* seems possible in spite of the lack of balance with *is se* below. *is denique* is an easy change, but the use of *denique* would be doubtful for Cicero. *is domi se aut denique* (Madvig) is clumsy. I have considered *is quidem*; this has also been suggested independently both by Mr. Williams and Professor Watt.

Clark reads *is denique in Italia* after *publico*. This is certainly wrong; Clark did not see that the first relative clause refers to Cicero, the second to Pompey (cf. *har. resp.* 6, 38, Cic. *orat. frag.* p. 454 Schoell). A. Klotz argues that *in Italia tuto statuit esse non posse* does not suit Cicero; but cf. *dom.* 8 'cum ego me existimassem tuto omnino in civitate esse non posse'. Klotz himself proposed *is coactus est relinquere Italiam*; this spoils the balance between *in Italia* and *in publico*.

15. **qui . . . devinxerat:** Pompey. He won three triumphs (about 80, in 71, and in 61) after victories in Africa over Iarbas and the Marians, in Spain over Sertorius, and in the East over Mithradates. This was a triumph from every continent; cf. *Sest.* 129, *Balb.* 9, 16. The juxtaposition of two parts of *omnis* is common (L.–H., p. 799, P. Parzinger, *Beiträge*, i. 44 f.).

16. **in publico:** cf. introd., p. xii. Cicero absurdly suggests that Pompey's humiliation was worse than his own.

17. **verbum facere:** *verba facere* = 'to make a statement in the senate', as opposed to *referre*, 'to lay a matter before the senate for discussion'; cf. *St.-R.* iii. 957 f. Here Cicero uses the singular *verbum* because Piso was not allowed to utter a word.

19. **nihil . . . acturos:** cf. introd., p. xiii, *St.-R.* iii. 942.

21. **lege impediri:** cf. introd., p. xii, Greenidge, *Legal Procedure*, p. 366, *St.-R.* iii. 361.

§ **30.** 22. **inusta:** literally 'branded' (understand *rei publicae* or *nobis*). This reading is strongly supported by *Mil.* 33 'quas ille leges, si leges nominandae sunt ac non faces urbis, pestes rei publicae, fuerit impositurus nobis omnibus atque inusturus'. Ernesti

92

COMMENTARY [§§ 30–31

objected that in our passage the metaphorical *inusta* is much more striking than *incisa* and *imposita*; he accordingly proposed *iussa* (*iubere legem* is the technical term for 'to pass a law'). But *iussa* is somewhat tame, and spoils the series of compounds beginning with *in-*.

24. **contra omnis leges:** the *lex de exsilio Ciceronis* was, according to Cicero, a *privilegium* (i.e. a law directed against a single individual, contrary to the Twelve Tables). Though it dealt with the *caput* of a citizen, it was not passed at the *comitia centuriata*. There had been no prosecution and no trial. The illegality is less certain than Cicero claims; cf. Greenidge, *Legal Procedure*, pp. 361 ff., P. Wuilleumier, op. cit. [p. xxxi], pp. 13 f.

25. **consules:** probably accusative, though the pause comes after *consules* rather than *dicerent*. For the thought cf. *Sest.* 69 'cum in senatu privati ut de me sententias dicerent flagitabant, legem illi se Clodiam timere dicebant'.

26. **fasti:** cf. *Sest.* 33 'si appellandi sunt consules quos nemo est quin non modo ex memoria sed etiam ex fastis evellendos putet', *Phil.* xiii. 26. There is no evidence in the Republic for the erasure of a consul's name from the *fasti*; the first known case is the removal of Antony's name after Actium (*St.-R.* iii. 1190 f.).

28. **proscriptio:** tribunes normally denounced proscriptions; so there is something paradoxical and epigrammatic in describing a *proscriptio* as *tribunicia*. See also p. 196.

3. **sin:** for the *complexio* or dilemma cf. Volkmann, p. 228.

6. **voltis esse:** 'you claim to be'.

§ **31. 7. paludati:** a proconsul setting out for his province wore the purple *paludamentum* (*St.-R.* i³. 64, *RE* xviii. 3. 281); hence *proficisci paludatus* means 'to set out for one's province'. For the splendour of such occasions cf. Liv. xlii. 49. 2 'semper quidem ea res cum magna dignitate ac maiestate geritur'. For Piso's departure cf. *Sest.* 71 'exierunt malis ominibus atque exsecrationibus duo vulturii paludati'.

Piso and Gabinius probably left Rome before 10 December, when the new tribunes entered office (*Sest.* 71–72); it was quite common for consuls to leave Rome before their year had expired (J. P. V. D. Balsdon, *JRS* xxix, 1939, 62). Cicero, writing from Thessalonica in November, is already awaiting the arrival of Piso's soldiers (*Att.* iii. 22. 1). See also § 57.

8. **emptas . . . ereptas:** for this assonance cf. *Verr.* iv. 10, iv. 37.

9. **credo:** ironic.

11. **tristissimis:** cf. Ateius Capito's cursing of Crassus when he left for Syria in 55 (Pease on *div.* 1. 29). A. D. Simpson, *TAPA*

93

§§ 31–33] COMMENTARY

lxix, 1938, 532 ff. regards the cursing of Crassus as a fiction, modelled on the episode described here, but this is very unlikely. See further pp. 201 f.

§§ 31–33. *Cicero, in describing Piso's consulship, has now come to his departure for his province. This leads naturally to a comparison with his own departure into exile.*

§ 31. 14. **in maledicti ... loco ponere:** 'to treat as a subject for slander'. In such phrases Cicero uses both *in loco* and *loco* (Krebs, *Antibarbarus*, ii. 31, K.–S. i. 19, i. 349). Halm added *in* here to make the construction the same as in l. 20.

16. **non admurmuratione:** cf. *Verr.* I. 45 'non strepitu sed maximo clamore', 5. 20 n.

17. **abiecti ... ac semivivi:** 'broken and demoralized'; cf. *Verr.* ii. 189 'vix vivum relinquo', *Att.* vii. 2. 8 'Bibulum semivivum reliquerunt'. A *codex deterior* reads *semiviri*; this word is not found in Republican Latin, does not combine well with *abiecti*, and would suit Gabinius better than Piso.

§ 32. 19. **taciturnitatem:** cf. § 26.

21. **volnera inflixit:** the 'wounds' were inflicted on Rome by Cicero's enemies when they compelled him to withdraw into exile; cf. *Sest.* 31 'illam meam cladem vos ... maximum esse rei publicae volnus iudicastis'. Bake proposed *inflixerit*; he comments 'non ipse Cicero praedicabat se volnera inflixisse rei publicae; erat hoc in Pisonis maledictis'. But *volnera* cannot be taken as a quotation from Piso, since *luctum, desiderium*, etc. describe the situation from Cicero's own point of view.

22. **calamitosissimus:** i.e. to Cicero.

24. **ille ...:** Cicero must mean that only (*dumtaxat*) the suffering was his, while the disgrace belonged to Piso and Gabinius. Yet *dumtaxat* in this position seems to qualify not *dolor* but *meus*, and this gives the wrong sense. Perhaps one should emend to *ille dolor dumtaxat meus*.

2. **duco:** Bake's emendation *dico* (*schol. hypomnem.* iv. 303) is more emphatic than *duco*, and may well be right, in spite of *non duco* above. *duco* is very rare where a judgement is being made about the past (Madvig, *Opusc. acad.*[2], p. 331, *Thes. L.L.* v. 1. 2157. 46). For the thought cf. *Sest.* 128 'ut verear ne quis me studio gloriae putet idcirco exisse ut ita redirem', *dom.* 76.

§ 33. 7. **male precarentur:** 'cursed'. Wunder proposed *mala* (cf. § 43 'mala precarer'); but see Plaut. *Merc.* 235 'male mihi precatur', *Thes. L.L.* viii. 239. 54.

8. **unam:** they hoped that this would be Piso's last journey, and that he would never come back. For *perpetuam* cf. Turpilius,

94

COMMENTARY [§§ 33-34

com. 207 'age age egredere atque istuc utinam perpetuum itiner sit tibi'. For the collocation of *unam* and *perpetuam* cf. *Verr.* iv. 119 'una via lata perpetua', Catull. 5. 6 'nox est perpetua una dormienda', *paneg. Lat.* ii (xii). 26. 5 'bona nostra ad aerarium una et perpetua via ibant'.

9. **mortalium:** Cicero uses *mortales* as a solemn synonym for *homines* only with *omnes*, *multi*, or *cuncti*; cf. F. Cramer, *ALL* vi. 342 f. Of course when the word means the opposite of *immortales* its use is unrestricted.

§§ **33–36:** *Cicero now describes what happened during his own exile before turning to a comparison with Piso's proconsulship. By confining his account to the honours which he received he is able to claim superiority even here. For the historical allusions see introd., p. xiii.*

§ **34.** 14. [**vestrum**]: *ef* can hardly have any authority for omitting this word (against the consensus of *PVE*), but they may be right by accident. Professor Watt, before he knew of this omission, suggested to me that *vestrum* should be deleted and *rei publicae* taken as genitive; cf. § 18 'occasum atque interitum rei publicae'. If right, *vestrum* would have to refer to the senate; but Cicero has just been addressing Piso in l. 13 and addresses him again in l. 19. It is true that one sometimes finds abrupt switches of person (2. 6 n.), but the present case would be unusually difficult. *X*'s *nostrum* has no authority against the consensus of *PVE*; and Cicero would hardly have referred to his own humiliation in such terms.

15. **concursu Italiae:** Francken deleted; he argued that in January 57 only deputations had come from Italy (cf. *Sest.* 72 'qui concursu legatorum ex Italia cuncta'). But in our passage rhetorical exaggeration is surely possible. Francken also had doubts about the construction, but cf. *Arch.* 3 'hoc concursu hominum litteratissimorum', *Verr.* v. 16, *Att.* iv. 1. 4, Tac. *dial.* 39. 5 'constat C. Cornelium et M. Scaurum ... concursu totius civitatis et accusatos et defensos', Nägelsbach, p. 415. It might also be objected that *concursu Italiae* breaks up the natural sequence *senatus referente consule.* But the parallel of *Sest.* 72 argues against deletion.

16. **P. Lentulo:** P. Cornelius Lentulus Spinther, cos. 57, when he took a leading part in Cicero's recall; for Cicero's gratitude cf. *in sen.* 8 'P. Lentulus, parens ac deus nostrae vitae fortunae memoriae nominis', *Sest.* 144. For his part in the Egyptian question see p. 190. He was killed after Pharsalus on Caesar's orders.

17. **consentiente atque una voce:** *consentiente* refers to internal unanimity (cf. *Deiot.* 11 'senatus consentientis auctoritate'), not to

95

§§ 34–35] COMMENTARY

agreement with Lentulus. For similar expressions cf. *Pis.* 7 'una voce et consensu', *har. resp.* 18 'una atque constanti haruspicum voce', *acad.* i. 17 'una et consentiens . . . philosophiae forma', Suet. *Galb.* 13 'consentiente voce'. But here the word-order is a little strange; one might have expected *una et consentiente*. Müller deleted *consentiente atque*, F. Schoell proposed *consentiente mente atque*. I have considered *consentiente conlega, una voce* (for the agreement of Lentulus's colleague Metellus Nepos cf. *Sest.* 72), but am not convinced that change is needed.

18. **exteris nationibus:** the *liberae civitates* of Greece, e.g. Dyrrachium. Sometimes the expression is used of the provincials in general (*St.-R.* iii. 599 n. 2).

auctoritate sua: 'resolution' rather than 'authority'; a concrete expression is needed to balance *litteris*.

19. **consularibus** gives a better clausula than *consularibusque*.

Insuber: a certain emendation. Piso, considering his mother's origin (frag. ix), was not in a position to accuse Cicero of not being a *civis*.

21. **servatorem:** the nearest Latin equivalent of σωτήρ (cf. A. Alföldi, *Mus. Helv.* ix, 1952, 221 ff.). Cicero is quoting the senate's letter, and the style is solemn. *servatorem* (*PV*) is much better attested here than the commoner *conservatorem* (Ω); Cicero uses both words in similar contexts (§ 23, *dom.* 26, 101). For adjectival *servator* cf. *dom.* 26 *civis . . . conservatoris rei publicae*, J. Wackernagel, *Vorlesungen*, ii. 54, L.–H., pp. 458 f. A. Klotz objects that the omission of *que* spoils the contrast between *orbatum patria* and *civem*; but perhaps Cicero is saying 'not only was I not *orbatus patria* but I was the citizen who saved the nation'.

23. **qui . . . vellent:** a phrase from Lentulus's letter, also quoted *in sen.* 24, *dom.* 73, *Sest.* 128. This formula was spoken by a consul when summoning the people to action (cf. Serv. *Aen.* viii. 1); it had been used by Marius in 100 (*Rab. perd.* 20) and by C. Piso in 67 (Asc. 67 KS). Then the consul had addressed the people of Rome; in 57 for the first time a similar message was given to all Italy (*in sen.* 24).

4. **gratissimae:** welcome to the people; cf. *Att.* iv. 15. 6 'ludi magnifici et grati'.

§ **35.** 5. **auctore:** author of the proposal (*St.-R.* iii. 977 f.). *principe* means that Pompey was the first to speak in favour of the proposal (cf. *dom.* 10, *Balb.* 61). For similar uses of the word cf. H. Wagenvoort, *Philol.* xci, 1936, 208 ff.

6. **in hostium numero:** for such decrees cf. *St.-R.* i³. 283 n. 3.

9. **perscripta:** the technical term for recording a resolution of the senate.

96

COMMENTARY [§§ 35–36

omnes magistratus: seven praetors out of eight and eight tribunes out of ten signed the proposal; for their names see *in sen.* 19–23. The missing praetor was Appius Claudius, brother of P. Clodius. The missing tribunes were Sex. Atilius Serranus and Q. Numerius Rufus (*Sest.* 72, Asc. 10 KS). The latter appears later as a legate of Caesar's in Illyricum (*CIL* i². 2. 759); this inscription comes from Lissus, only a few miles from Piso's province.

11. **de lapide:** the platform on which slaves stood when being sold. Cf. Plaut. *Bacch.* 814 f. 'nescis nunc venire te; atque in eopse astas lapide, ut praeco praedicat', Colum. iii. 3. 8 'vel de lapide noxium posse comparari putat', Pollux iii. 78 and 126 πρατῆρ λίθος.

12. **comitiis centuriatis:** the proper assembly for dealing with the *caput* of a citizen (*Sest.* 73, *rep.* ii. 61, *leg.* iii. 44). With its strong bias in favour of the propertied classes it could be relied on to support Cicero (L. R. Taylor, *Party Politics in the Age of Caesar*, pp. 55 ff.).

de . . . sententia: 'with the approval of'. Elsewhere Cicero describes Metellus Nepos as an *adscriptor* (*legis*) (*in sen.* 9, 26).

13. **eadem res publica:** 'the same public interest'; Nepos and Cicero, who had clashed in 63 (6. 5 n.), were reconciled by P. Servilius Vatia Isauricus (*in sen.* 25, *Sest.* 130, *prov. cons.* 22), and no doubt also by Pompey. For the form of expression cf. *prov. cons.* 21 'quibus eum eadem res publica reconciliavit quae alienarat', *Deiot.* 39, *fam.* v. 7. 2.

15. **viri:** Nepos himself; if Servilius had been meant he would have been named, with a reference to his *gravitas* or *auctoritas* rather than to his *iustitia*.

§ 36. 17. **nemini civi . . . :** 'no citizen thought any excuse reasonable enough to justify his absence'; cf. *Sest.* 112 'nemo sibi nec valetudinis excusationem nec senectutis satis iustam putavit'.

20. **video:** contrasted with *audio*, on the principle that eyes are more trustworthy than ears.

tabulae publicae: particulars about elections were entered in the public records (*St.-R.* ii³. 546 f.).

rogatores: in the days of oral voting *rogatores* put the question to the voters; in Cicero's time, when votes were written, they presumably supervised. The *diribitores* (from *dis-habeo*, with intervocalic *s* changed to *r*) separated the votes, i.e. counted them. The *custodes* guarded the *tabulae* on which the votes were entered; in the *lex Malacitana* they were the same as the *diribitores* (*ILS* 6089. lv), and perhaps this was the case in the Roman *comitia* also. These duties were undertaken by men of substance (cf. Plin. *n.h.* xxxiii. 31), who on this occasion were particularly distinguished senators; cf. *in sen.* 28 'quando illa dignitate rogatores diribitores

5993   I   97

§§ 36–37]   COMMENTARY

custodesque vidistis ?' See further *St.-R.* iii. 403, 406, Botsford, *Roman Assemblies*, pp. 389, 467.

21. **tabularum:** tablets on which voting totals for each *centuria* were recorded; cf. § 11 'tabulam praerogativae', [Q. Cic.] *comm. pet.* 8 'cum ad tabulam quos poneret non haberet', Varr. *r.r.* iii. 5. 18 'ad tabulam, cum diriberent', *St.-R.* iii. 407 n. 4. *tabellarum* ('voting-tablets') is a reading reported by Lallemand, but it gives a less common clausula, and the parallels tell against it. *tabulae* is used above in a different sense, but such repetitions are common; cf. *honoribus . . . honoris* below, Seyffert–Müller, *Laelius*, p. 284, L.-H., p. 841.

in honoribus: at elections it was a mark of favour to act as *custos* for a candidate (11. 16 n.).

23. **honoris:** 'rank'; cf. *Sull.* 26 'me . . . neque honoris neque aetatis excusatio vindicat a labore'.

nullo: *nemine* is rare in Latin and not used by Cicero; cf. Neue–Wagener, *Formenlehre*, i³. 745 f., ii³. 524 ff., J. Wackernagel, *Vorlesungen*, ii. 270 f.

§§ 37–50. *Cicero discusses Piso's absence in Macedonia as proconsul. He mentions his failure to send dispatches* (§§ 38–39), *his defeats* (§ 40), *his demobilization of his army* (§§ 46–48); *but the account lacks detail and precision. There are two digressions on Gabinius's proconsulship of Syria* (§§ 41, 48–50).

§ 37. 24. Epicure noster: i.e. Piso; cf. § 39 'Paule noster', *rhet. ad Her.* iv. 46 'Agamemnon noster', 17. 4 n., 20. 19 n.

ex hara . . .: 'the product of the sty, not of the philosophy-school'. The Epicureans pointed to animals to show that the primary aim of all creatures was ἡδονή; their enemies accused them of putting men on a level with the beasts (*fin.* ii. 32, ii. 109, Epicurus frag. 398 Usener). Hence Epicureans were often compared with animals, especially pigs; cf. Hor. *epist.* i. 4. 16 'Epicuri de grege porcum', Plut. *mor.* 1091C ὥστε μήτε συῶν ἀπολείπεσθαι μήτε προβάτων εὐδαιμονίᾳ, ibid. 1094A, Aug. *enarr. psalm.* 73. 25 '(Epicurus) quem ipsi etiam philosophi porcum nominaverunt', R. Hoyer, *de Antiocho Ascalonita* (Bonn, 1883), p. 46 n. 1. On a silver cup from Boscoreale Epicurus is portrayed with a pig (A. Héron de Villefosse, *Monuments et mémoires* (Fondation Piot), v, 1899, 62 and pl. viii). Ennodius, *opusc.* ii. 9 (p. 290. 8 Hartel) imitates our passage: 'sed redeamus ad gravem et venerabilem, non solum ex hara productam, sed mephiticam propositionem'.

2. **lex generi tui:** Caesar's comprehensive *lex Julia repetundarum*, passed in 59. Besides restricting extortion (§ 90) it limited governors' powers to intervene in *liberae civitates*, and forbade

98

COMMENTARY [§§ 37-38

them to wage war on their own responsibility (§ 50). See *dig*. xlviii. 11, Berger, *RE* xii. 2389 ff., Tyrrell and Purser, *Correspondence of Cicero*, iii². 327 f., A. N. Sherwin-White, *PBSR* xvii, 1949, 12 ff.

3. **lege:** the *lex Clodia* which gave Piso and Gabinius their provinces. Piso was given authority to intervene in the *liberae civitates* of Greece (pp. 172 ff.).

5. **Achaia:** sometimes this word is applied to the Peloponnese, sometimes to Greece as a whole, even in Republican Latin (G. F. Hertzberg, *Geschichte Griechenlands unter der Herrschaft der Römer*, i. 289). Here the former, as *Graecia* is the comprehensive term. The present passage suggests that a substantial part of the Peloponnese was free.

Thessalia: left free in 146 (S. Accame, *Il Dominio romano in Grecia*, pp. 217 ff.), and still free in 58, as appears from our passage. After Pharsalus Caesar 'restored Thessaly's freedom' (Plut. *Caes*. 48. 1, App. *b.c.* ii. 88), but it is not clear when it had been lost. Accame, pp. 224 f., suggests that Sulla imposed tribute which was remitted by Caesar, but the sources talk of freedom, not immunity; perhaps Caesar simply restored the state of affairs which had existed before his war with Pompey.

Athenae: a *civitas libera et foederata* (Accame, op. cit., pp. 163 ff.).

Graecia: named beside Achaia at *Verr*. v. 127, *imp*. *Pomp*. 35, *dom*. 60, *prov*. *cons*. 7. *Graecia* sometimes refers to central Greece north of the Isthmus (A. Klotz, *Gött*. *Gel*. *Anz*. clxxii, 1910, 483 f.). But here with *cuncta* it seems to be used in a wider sense.

6. **exercitum:** normally the senate voted an army; in Piso's case the *lex Clodia* made provision (p. 172). Cicero also emphasizes that the *lex Clodia* was passed not by the *populus* but by the *plebs*; this is simply a debating point, since the difference at this date was not important.

7. **libido:** cf. *Att*. vii. 9. 4 'praeteriit tempus non legis sed libidinis tuae'.

8. **aerarium:** cf. p. 172.

§ 38. 9. **consulari:** to be taken with all three nouns.

10. **statim:** for aposiopesis cf. Volkmann, pp. 503 f., Hofmann, *Umgangssprache*, pp. 53 ff.; for similar cases of anacoluthon, cf. § 50, *Mil*. 76, K.–S. ii. 587. Lagomarsini marked a lacuna after *statim*, unnecessarily.

11. **pecunias:** cf. p. 175.

12. **hospitum:** Plator (§ 83).

15. **conferam:** perhaps *confero* might be suggested; note that the previous word ends in -*am*.

§§ 38–39]   COMMENTARY

17. **litteras:** provincial governors normally sent dispatches to the Senate (P. Willems, *Le Sénat*, ii. 656 ff., *St.-R.* iii. 1107, 1216).

20. **fines:** cf. Ps. Plut. *apophth. Lac.* 217E (a saying of Antalcidas) τείχη δὲ ἔλεγεν εἶναι τῆς Σπάρτης τοὺς νέους, ὅρια δὲ τὰς ἐπιδορατίδας, ibid. 210E, 218F, Plut. *quaest. Rom.* 267C (= chapter 15). Here the picturesque phrase contains a historical truth: the northern frontier of Macedonia was fluid.

ex qua . . .: 'from which, leaving aside some governors with only pro-praetorian *imperium*, none with proconsular *imperium* has returned, and has escaped conviction, who has not triumphed'. For *triumphatores* from Macedonia see p. 177. Ap. Claudius Pulcher (procos. 78–76) and C. Octavius (procos. 60–59) died before their return (*rediit* is significant). C. Porcius Cato (cos. 114) and C. Antonius (procos. 62–60) were convicted; by the restrictive clause *qui incolumis fuerit* Cicero excludes them. But some other proconsuls did not triumph, Cn. Cornelius Sisenna (118), Q. Fabius Maximus Eburnus (115), Memmius (103), L. Julius Caesar (94), L. Manlius Torquatus (64–63). The first four are unimportant; the date was remote, and our information about their status is in some cases imprecise. The case of Torquatus is more difficult, since he was present in the senate during Cicero's speech (§ 47); yet it is clear from § 44 that he did not triumph, perhaps because of the Catilinarian crisis.

22. **hoc** refers to Piso's failure to send dispatches. *illud* points forward, and refers to his even more extraordinary silence after he had been hailed as *imperator*.

23. **volturius:** cf. Aemilius Scaurus frag. 9 (Malcovati, *ORF²*) 'nefarius volturius', frag. 10 'volturius rei publicae', *Sest.* 71 'duo volturii paludati' (Piso and Gabinius), Otto, s.v.

si dis placet expresses indignation = 'would you believe it?' See Landgraf on *Sex. Rosc.* 102, E. Fraenkel, *Studi italiani di filol. class.* xxvii–xxviii, 1956, 123 f.

24. **imperator:** after a governor had won a victory he might be hailed as *imperator* by his troops. The victory theoretically had to be important, though the honour was sometimes given after trifling engagements (*St.-R.* i³. 124 f., Rosenberg, *RE* ix. 1139 ff.). Cicero often alludes derisively to Piso's title. For an inscription referring to Piso as αὐτοκράτωρ see 89. 13 n.

§ 39. 24. **Paule noster:** L. Aemilius Paulus, because of his victory at Pydna in 168, was the supreme example of a Roman general who had won glory in Macedonia.

25. **laurea:** dispatches announcing victory had a laurel attached; cf. v. Premerstein, *RE* xii. 1014, M. B. Ogle, *AJP* xxxi, 1910,

100

COMMENTARY [§§ 39–41

295 n. 1. For messages of victory see L. Halkin, op. cit. [6. 2 n.], pp. 80 ff.

4. **haud scio an . . .**: 'on the whole I should prefer people to think that you were quite brazen in sending dispatches, but that your friends were more discreet and more sensible'. It seems best to delete the second *an* with Graevius (note *am-* following and *an amici* above); *et* (Lambinus) and *at* (Clark) are also possible; *sed* would be good in itself, but is not an easy change. *haud scio an* means 'probably' (K.–S. ii. 520 ff.); it is not used to introduce alternative possibilities, and the two clauses here are not alternatives. Nor can one easily take *an* as an instance of rhetorical repetition (*haud scio an malim A et haud scio an malim B*).

6. **pudentiorem**: this reading suits *pudore* above, and involves a greater insult than *prudentiorem*; the point is not the same in *prov. cons.* 14 'amicos habet prudentiores quam Gabinius'.

§ **40.** 13. **Thessalonicae**: a free city, though it was the residence of the governor of Macedonia. For the campaigns mentioned in this sentence cf. pp. 178 f.

14. **militaris viae**: the vital *via Egnatia* ran from Dyrrachium and Apollonia by way of Lychnidus, Heraclea, and Pella. Strabo says that it ended at Thessalonica (vii frag. 13); but elsewhere he comments that it was laid out with milestones as far as Cypsela on the Hebrus (vii. 7. 4). It is evident that the road in some form reached the Hellespont (*prov. cons.* 4 'via illa nostra quae per Macedoniam est usque ad Hellespontum militaris', cf. Strabo vii frag. 57); and it is significant that the Chersonese was attached to Macedonia (*Pis.* 86). See Oberhummer, *RE* v. 1988 ff., P. Collart, *BCH* lix, 1935, 395 ff., E. Gren, *Kleinasien und der Ostbalkan* (Uppsala, 1941), p. 31.

interitus ferro: for the construction cf. 7. 12 n.

§ **41.** 18. **natus abdomini suo**: cf. *hist. Aug.* xxiii. 16. 1 'natus abdomini et voluptatibus'.

cum equites . . .: for Gabinius's proconsulship see pp. 190 f.

19. **nobiscum**: with the senate.

22. **ausus est . . .**: cf. *Phil.* ii. 16 'ausus es—quid autem est quod tu non audeas ?'

23. **supplicationem**: cf. 6. 2 n. Gabinius was no doubt fully entitled to a *supplicatio*. Cicero in 50 made a similar request from Cilicia, probably with less justification (*fam.* xv. 10, xv. 13).

24. **tune etiam . . .**: Cicero first speaks to Piso, then corrects himself and addresses his remarks to the absent Gabinius as well. *etiam* expresses indignation (cf. § 2).

25. **voragines scopulique**: cf. *de or.* iii. 163 'deinde videndum

101

§§ 41–42]   COMMENTARY

est ne longe simile sit ductum: "Syrtim patrimoni"; scopulum libentius dixerim; "Charybdim bonorum"; voraginem potius'.

meam fortunam: Cicero's exile.

28. **publicanorum:** for their relations with Cicero see H. Strasburger, *Concordia ordinum* (Leipzig, 1931), pp. 46 f.

29. **conlegiorum:** business corporations; cf. *dom.* 74, *Sest.* 32, *Vat.* 8.

1. **numquam auderem:** 'should never have dared'. For the imperfect subjunctive referring to past time cf. S. A. Handford, *Latin Subjunctive*, p. 124.

3. **notas:** Piso had been recalled, Gabinius's request for a *supplicatio* had been rejected.

§ **42.** 5. **famae:** *laceratione* is understood (K.–S. i. 418, D. R. Shackleton Bailey, *Propertiana*, pp. 77 f.).

nullum . . .: either *nullum* or *nihil* is possible in such sentences; cf. *leg.* i. 49 'ut . . . nullam virtutem nisi malitiam putent', K.–S. i. 34 f. Cicero is arguing that crucifixion, etc., can happen even to good men; true punishment lies in the consciousness of guilt. For the theme cf. Plat. *Theaet.* 176d ἀγνοοῦσι γὰρ ζημίαν ἀδικίας, ὃ δεῖ ἥκιστα ἀγνοεῖν. οὐ γάρ ἐστιν ἣν δοκοῦσιν, πληγαί τε καὶ θάνατοι, ὧν ἐνίοτε πάσχουσιν οὐδὲν ἀδικοῦντες, ἀλλὰ ἣν ἀδύνατον ἐκφυγεῖν, *Pis.* 43, 95, 99, *leg.* ii. 43.

7. **voluptarii:** Epicurean philosophers.

8. **utinam audires:** 'would that you made a habit of listening to them'. In classical Latin *utinam* with the imperfect subjunctive is said always to refer to present time, never to past time (K.–S. i. 184). Below Cicero says *ut erant audiendi*, not *ut sunt audiendi*, because his wish cannot now be fulfilled.

numquam . . .: 'never in that case'. The protasis is supplied from the context; cf. Kühner–Gerth, *Griech. Grammatik*, ii. 483 f.

9. **te . . . ingurgitasses:** 'plunged yourself'; cf. Ambr. *enarr. psalm.* 35. 15 'qui se flagitiis ingurgitaveriᵗ', Hegesipp. iv. 7. 1 'ubi se flagitiis ingurgitarunt'.

praesepibus: properly animals' stalls, here the dens of vice frequented by Piso.

10. **in cibo et vino:** 'over your food and wine'; cf. *Verr.* iii. 62, Catull. 12. 2, Jerome, *epist.* 22. 35. 4 'nullus in cibo strepitus'.

sed: resumptive after the parenthesis *quos . . . vino*.

qui mala dolore . . .: 'who confine the bad to what is painful, the good to what is pleasurable'. For the construction cf. *Tusc.* v. 73 'cum praesertim omne malum dolore definiat', *de amic.* 58. For Epicurus's views on pain and pleasure cf. frags. 398 ff. Usener, N. W. DeWitt, *Epicurus and his Philosophy* (Minneapolis, 1954), pp. 216 ff.

COMMENTARY [§§ 42–43]

12. **Phalaridis tauro:** Phalaris was tyrant of Acragas about 560; according to the story, his victims were placed in the brazen bull, a fire was lit under it, and their groans resembled the animal's bellowing. The first allusion in literature is Pind. *Pyth.* 1. 95; see further Th. Lenschau, *RE* xix. 1650 f., Otto, pp. 277 f., A. Sonny, *ALL* ix. 73. Scipio Aemilianus captured in Carthage a brazen bull which he thought was Phalaris's, and set it up at Agrigentum (cf. F. W. Walbank, *CR* lix, 1945, 39 ff.); Cicero must often have seen it there.

13. **suave:** Epicurus says something quite different (ap. Diog. Laert. x. 118): κἂν στρεβλωθῇ δ' ὁ σοφός, εἶναι αὐτὸν εὐδαίμονα ... ὅτε μέντοι στρεβλοῦται, ἔνθα καὶ μύζει καὶ οἰμώζει. It is one thing to be 'happy' on the rack, another to claim that torture is pleasurable. Cicero's mistake can hardly be intentional, for even in his serious discussions he accuses Epicurus of the same absurdity (*Tusc.* ii. 17, v. 31, *fin.* ii. 88, cf. Epicurus frag. 601 Usener). For the theme cf. also Arist. *Nic. eth.* 1153ᵇ19 οἱ δὲ τὸν τροχιζόμενον ... εὐδαίμονα φάσκοντες εἶναι (cf. Plat. *Gorg.* 473c) ἢ ἑκόντες ἢ ἄκοντες οὐδὲν λέγουσι. Greg. Naz. *epist.* 32 (=von Arnim, *Stoic. Vet. Frag.* iii, p. 154) quotes a Stoic saying εἶναι τὸν σπουδαῖον μακάριον, κἂν ὁ Φαλάριδος ταῦρος ἔχῃ καιόμενον.

§ **43.** 15. **quae est ...:** for the use of *quae* rather than *quid* cf. 42. 5 n., R. G. Nisbet, *de domo*, pp. 199 ff.

17. **suscepta fraus:** 'to have assumed the burden of wrong-doing'. Cicero is arguing in philosophical vein that the very act of wrong-doing is its own punishment (cf. 42. 5 n., 46. 14 n.).

impedita: burdened by conscience; cf. *Cael.* 60 'fortissimi viri mentio ... mentem dolore impedivit', Sen. *Thy.* 440 'evince quicquid obstat et mentem impedit' (conquer your fears). After *mens* Ω adds *conscientia*; cf. § 39 'conscientia oppressus scelerum', § 44 'infrenatum conscientia scelerum'. But here the word gives a bad word-order, and is presumably a gloss. The double-cretic clausula -*dita et oppressa mens* looks genuine.

18. **inusta:** Faernus's emendation suits *nota* excellently, and accounts for the readings of the MSS. Yet *nota inusta senatus* sounds like a hexameter-ending, especially after *bonorum odium*; moreover, the genitive *senatus* does not suit *inusta* particularly well. Faernus actually proposed *nota inusta a senatu*, but *a senatu* is clumsy and spoils the balance with *bonorum odium*. Perhaps one might read simply *nota senatus*. Alternatively one could delete the whole phrase, as Mr. Williams suggests; it certainly refers to Piso more specifically than the parallel phrases *suscepta fraus*, etc.

19. **Regulus:** M. Atilius Regulus was captured by the Carthaginians in 255, and about 250 was sent on parole to Rome to

103

§ 43]   COMMENTARY

negotiate an exchange of prisoners (or perhaps peace); he advised
against acceptance, and returned to Carthage, where he died. The
story of the *barbarus tortor* is not in Polybius and is probably
unhistorical (Klebs, *RE* ii. 2086 ff.); for a more favourable view
cf. T. 'Frank, *CP* xxi, 1926, 311 ff. For the use of historical *exempla*
see Volkmann, pp. 233 ff., H. Schoenberger, *Beispiele aus der
Geschichte* (Augsburg, 1911), H. W. Litchfield, *Harvard Studies
in Class. Phil.* xxv, 1914, 1 ff.

   resectis palpebris: cf. Val. Max. ix. 2 ext. 1 'Karthaginienses
Atilium Regulum palpebris resectis machinae in qua undique prae-
acuti stimuli eminebant inclusum vigilantia pariter et continuo
tractu doloris necaverunt'. The two passages are apparently derived from an earlier historian, or possibly a collection of *exempla*
(for such collections cf. C. Bosch, *Die Quellen des Valerius
Maximus*, Stuttgart, 1929). See also *off.* iii. 100 'vigilando neca-
batur', Oros. iv. 10. 1 'resectis . . . necaverunt' as in our passage,
Aug. *civ. D.* i. 15 'vigilando peremerunt'. The accounts of Regulus
by Tuditanus and Tubero (cf. Gell. vii. 4) use different phraseology.

   20. vigilando: 'through insomnia'. The gerund here does not
describe an action of the subject of the sentence, but is used as a
verbal noun = *vigilantia*; cf. Lebreton, p. 394.

   21. C. Marius: saved Italy in 102–101 (20. 16 n.) and preserved
the province of Africa by defeating Jugurtha (107–105). In 88,
when Sulla marched on Rome, Marius fled, hid in the marshes at
Minturnae, and arrived in Africa after many adventures. Cicero
had heard Marius himself telling the story (*quir.* 20); it is often
repeated by later poets and rhetoricians. See App. *b.c.* i. 61–62,
Plut. *Mar.* 37 ff., M. Bang, *Klio*, x, 1910, 178 ff., Weynand, *RE*
Suppl. vi. 1411. For Cicero's attitude to Marius cf. R. Gnauk,
Die Bedeutung des Marius und Cato maior für Cicero (Berlin, 1936).

   22. Minturnensium: *V* spells *Men-*, a form which is found sometimes in the MSS. of Cicero and other authors. Inscriptions with
late or unimportant exceptions read *Min-* (*RE* Suppl. vii. 459,
CIL x, p. 595).

   expulsum: 'driven from Rome', not 'cast up by the sea'
(contrast 43. 2 n.); cf. *fin.* ii. 105 '(Marius) expulsus egens in
palude demersus'.

   25. si . . . precarer: 'if I had ever been going to curse you.'
precarer has future reference; Cicero puts the conditional in an
unreal form (*precarer* rather than *precer*) because there is no need
for his curses now that Piso and Gabinius have been ruined
(A. Klotz). See S. A. Handford, *Latin Subjunctive*, p. 122,
H. C. Nutting, *Univ. California publ. in class. phil.* viii, 1926, 240.
Nutting, op. cit., p. 64 n. 4 gives a different explanation: *precarer*

104

COMMENTARY [§§ 43–44

refers to past time, but is illogically corrected ('if I had cursed you, which I have often done'). For such a construction cf. Landgraf on *Sex. Rosc.* 22, P. Parzinger, *Beiträge*, ii. 23, J. Vahlen, *Opusc. acad.* ii. 329 f. But the repetition of the unreal *precarer* after the correction perhaps argues against this explanation.

26. **audierunt:** the form *audiverunt* for the third person plural is doubtful for Cicero (cf. Neue–Wagener, *Formenlehre*, iii³. 450 ff., *Thes. L.L.* ii. 1262. 28).

1. **Thyestea . . . :** 'it is a curse worthy of Thyestes, the work of a poet who moves the minds of the vulgar, not of the wise, to pray that cast up by a shipwreck somewhere, impaled on the rough rocks and disembowelled, you should have hung by your ribs, as Ennius says, spattering the rocks with putrefaction, gore, and black blood'. Thyestes, in Ennius's play of that name, cursed Atreus in a famous speech (*scaen.* 362 ff. Vahlen, 309 ff. Ribbeck), quoted more fully at *Tusc.* i. 107: 'ipse summis saxis fixus asperis eviscera-tus | latere pendens saxa spargens tabo sanie et sanguine atro' (trochaic octonarii), followed a little later by 'neque sepulchrum quo recipiat habeat portum corporis, | ubi remissa humana vita corpus requiescat malis' (trochaic septenarii). A curse of Thyestes is given by Aesch. *Ag.* 1601, but nothing is said there about drowning; Ennius's curse probably comes from Euripides's *Thyestes* (Fraenkel ad loc.). Horace, *epod.* 5. 86, refers to 'Thyesteas preces'. For prayers that one's enemies may be drowned and cast up cf. Archi-lochus frag. 79a (Diehl³), Hor. *epod.* 10. 21 f. For the use by orators of verse-quotations cf. Volkmann, p. 238, W. Zillinger, op. cit. [supra 25. 12 n.].

2. **naufragio . . . uspiam:** these words probably do not belong to the quotation. They could in theory be the end of a trochaic septenarius, but the absence of a diaeresis at the end of the fourth foot is relatively rare. Cicero, *Tusc.* i. 106, says 'exsecratur . . . primum ut naufragio pereat Atreus'; this implies that the ship-wreck is described with more elaboration than in 'naufragio expulsus'. *ipse* in Ennius seems to be contrasted with a previous mention of the ship (Vahlen).

expulsus means 'cast up on the shore'; cf. Sen. *cont.* viii. 6 'naufragio expulsus est in divitis fundum', *Thes. L.L.* v. 2. 1637. 69. Latin says 'cast out of the sea' (cf. *eiectus*, etc.); see E. Wistrand, *Nach innen oder nach aussen?* (Göteborg, 1946).

3. **penderes:** Cicero uses the unreal form because there is now no need to curse Piso; cf. *precarer* above.

§ **44.** 4. **non ferrem . . . :** 'I should rejoice, it is true'. *omnino* (like *quidem* often) looks forward to the following adversative; cf. 82. 4 n.

105

§ 44] COMMENTARY

5. humanum: the sort of thing that could happen to anybody; cf. ἀνθρώπινος.

6. M. Marcellus: cos. 166, 155, 152, triumphed 166, 155, drowned in 148 on an embassy to Africa (*RE* iii. 2758 ff.). The *praenomen* is omitted by haplography in V^1 and the MSS. of Asconius; it would not have been given correctly by Ω unless it were genuine.

summa virtute: a proper name is sometimes followed immediately by an ablative of quality without the addition of *vir* or *homo* (K.–S. i. 227, Lebreton, p. 83).

7. periit: *perit* has overwhelming support, but this form of the perfect is not certainly attested in classical prose (Neue–Wagener, *Formenlehre*, iii³. 447).

in mari: regarded in the ancient world as a particularly horrible death.

gloria et laude vivit: 'lives on by means of honour and glory' (cf. *Phil.* xiii. 7 'si non spiritu, at virtutis laude vivemus'). *gloriae laude* is a possible reading (cf. *Planc.* 89, *Lig.* 37); for though *laus et gloria* is common, *gloria et laus* is unusual. Yet as *et* is found both in *V* and Asconius it should perhaps be accepted. *V* reads *in gloria et laude*, but this would rather mean 'surrounded by honour and glory'; cf. *fam.* xv. 6. 1 'qui ipsi in laude vixerunt'.

8. putanda: = *numeranda*, *habenda*; cf. § 35 'in hostium numero putaretur'.

9. saxa: Cicero is no doubt partly thinking of the 'rocks' in his quotation from Ennius. But it is also relevant that criminals were thrown from the Tarpeian rock, on the Capitoline, in view of the forum; cf. *Att.* xiv. 16. 2 'proposita cruce aut saxo', Lucr. iii. 1016 'carcer et horribilis de saxo iactu' deorsum', Mommsen, *Strafrecht*, pp. 931 ff.

10. esse duos . . .: Cicero is arguing that true punishment lies not in execution but in feelings of guilt and loss of dignity. Instead of making the point in general terms (as in § 43), he refers specifically to Piso's feelings of guilt and Gabinius's loss of dignity. The clause *esse . . . imperatores* is merely preliminary, and in logic is subordinate to what follows. At *horum alterum* Piso's situation is described; Cicero takes longer over this than he originally envisaged, and the construction changes from the accusative and infinitive to finite verbs.

11. infrenatum: not found elsewhere in Republican prose, but see *Verr.* iii. 130 'cum eius animum . . . conscientia sceleris . . . refrenaret' (cf. *Pis.* 43 *impedita*).

13. ex omnibus una: cf. *Lig.* 24 'provinciam unam ex omnibus huic victoriae maxime infensam', *de or.* i. 99, *orat.* 69.

106

COMMENTARY [§§ 44-46

14. nullam ... litteram: not a single letter of the alphabet; cf. *Att.* ii. 2. 2, *fam.* ii. 17. 6.

15. Torquatus: L. Manlius Torquatus, cos. 65 (Hor. *carm.* iii. 21. 1 'o nata mecum consule Manlio'), proconsul in Macedonia 64–63 (Cicero made the *relatio* mentioned here as consul in 63). He supported Cicero in 58 (§ 77), and again in 55 at the time of this speech (§§ 47, 92). He was a man of judgement and taste (*Brut.* 239), and like his son, the Torquatus of the *de finibus*, an Epicurean (*fin.* i. 39). See also 38. 20 n., 78. 11 n.

16. ab senatu: *imperatores* (38. 24 n.) could be created by the senate (*St.-R.* i³. 124); *ab senatu* is contrasted with *ad senatum* below. The form *ab* is occasionally found before *senatu*. *absens* would have little point here.

17. Cn. Dolabellae ...: for these *triumphatores* see p. 177.

18. iustissimos: *iustus* is applied to triumphs which have fulfilled the requisite conditions; cf. §§ 57, 59, *Planc.* 89, Hor. *carm.* i. 12. 54.

19. altero: Gabinius; cf. § 41.

§ 45. 21. nemo: when Gabinius's request for a *supplicatio* was turned down, Procilius said that such a thing had never happened before (*Q.f.* ii. 7. 1, cf. *Phil.* xiv. 24). This is inaccurate; for the case of Albucius see *prov. cons.* 15 (where Cicero draws a distinction); for other apparent instances cf. L. Halkin, op. cit. [6. 2 n.], pp. 94 ff.

24. numero dierum: before 63 we know of no *supplicatio* which lasted more than five days. Pompey was given ten days in 63, twelve in 62, Caesar fifteen in 57, twenty in 55 (for the date cf. p. 201). See Halkin, op. cit., pp. 105 ff.

genere verborum: importance was attached to honorific phraseology; cf. § 35, *prov. cons.* 27.

5. qui ... meminerit: cf. *Phil.* ii. 16 'quis ullius ordinis qui se civem esse meminisset ... ?'

6. auribus respuat: a common phrase; cf. Gudeman on Tac. *dial.* 9. 2.

recordatione: 'at the memory' (cf. *Sest.* 51, *har. resp.* 2). *perhorrescere* is usually transitive in Cicero, but occasionally intransitive (cf. *Caecil.* 41, etc.). *recordatione* has much stronger authority than *recordationem*, and is intrinsically a little better.

§ 46. 8. plura etiam ...: cf. *Phil.* ii. 1 'mihi poenarum illi plus quam optarem dederunt', *leg.* ii. 44, Dem. xxi. 103.

9. amitteretis: for Piso's military difficulties see pp. 178 f. Gabinius suffered a reverse early in his proconsulship (p. 190); but Cicero's language is greatly exaggerated.

107

§§ 46–47]　　　COMMENTARY

10. **illud** points to what follows, the madness of Piso and Gabinius.

optatum: consciously formulated prayer, as opposed to unformulated wish (*voluntate*).

11. **mihi:** emphatic, like *me* below.

veniret in mentem: 'would have occurred' (cf. 41. 1 n.). Latin normally says *numquam putavi* rather than *numquam putassem* or *putarem* (cf. K.–S. i. 172, Holden on *Sest.* 22); but for the latter cf. *Mil.* 94 'mihi umquam bonorum praesidium defuturum putarem?'

14. **certissimas:** Ω adds *constitutas*, a word often found with *poena* (*Thes. L.L.* iv. 522. 47); cf. *har. resp.* 39 'das eas poenas quae solae sunt hominum sceleri a dis immortalibus constitutae'. But here the genitive *deorum immortalium* does not suit *constitutas* well (Halm). A. C. Clark, *Descent of Manuscripts*, p. 294, defends *constitutas* by quoting other places where *V* has omitted words of eleven letters; but this kind of argument is unsafe.

nolite . . . : cf. Aeschines, *Tim.* 190–1 μὴ γὰρ οἴεσθε . . . τοὺς ἠσεβηκότας, καθάπερ ἐν ταῖς τραγῳδίαις, Ποινὰς ἐλαύνειν καὶ κολάζειν δᾳσὶν ἡμμέναις· ἀλλ' αἱ προπετεῖς τοῦ σώματος ἡδοναὶ καὶ τὸ μηδὲν ἱκανὸν ἡγεῖσθαι, ταῦτα πληροῖ τὰ λῃστήρια, ταῦτ' εἰς τὸν ἐπακτροκέλητα ἐμβιβάζει, ταῦτά ἐστιν ἑκάστῳ Ποινή . . . , *Sex. Rosc.* 67 'nolite enim putare, quem ad modum in fabulis saepe numero videtis, eos qui aliquid impie scelerateque commiserint agitari et perterreri Furiarum taedis ardentibus. sua quemque fraus et suus terror maxime vexat, suum quemque scelus agitat amentiaque adficit, suae malae cogitationes conscientiaeque animi terrent; hae sunt impiis adsiduae domesticaeque Furiae quae dies noctesque parentium poenas a consceleratissimis filiis repetant' (the more elaborate style of this passage is a sign of Cicero's early exuberance). For similar references to the Furies cf. frag. iv, *har. resp.* 39, *leg.* i. 40, *paradox.* 18, Lucr. iii. 1011, Ps. Quintil. *decl. min.* p. 236 (Ritter), Juv. 13. 195 and Mayor's note. For the view that madness is a consequence of crime cf. *Verr.* v. 73, v. 139, *dom.* 3, Lycurgus, *Leocr.* 92.

15. **ita** looks forward to the following accusative and infinitive (K.–S. ii. 572 f.).

16. **furialibus:** the reading *furiarum* is supported by the parallel passage *Sex. Rosc.* 67 'Furiarum taedis ardentibus'; cf. Suet. *Ner.* 34. 4 'verberibus Furiarum ac taedis ardentibus'. But *furialibus* can be defended as a poetic equivalent for *Furiarum*; cf. Ps. Quintil. *decl. mai.* iv. 16 'furiales faces', ibid. iv. 20, Löfstedt, *Syntactica*, i². 121 ff.

§ **47.** 20. **Oreste:** proverbially a madman; Varro wrote *Orestes de insania* (cf. Otto, pp. 258 f.); he was a favourite topic of the

108

COMMENTARY [§ 47

rhetorical schools (Mayor on Juv. 8. 215) and in philosophical discussions (Waszink on Tert. *de anima* 17. 9). For Athamas's madness cf. *har. resp.* 39; it was caused by the Furies (Ov. *fast.* vi. 489); Ennius and Accius wrote plays about him.

22. **caput:** the important point.

paulo ante: earlier in the debate which led to the *in Pisonem*. For Torquatus see 44. 15 n.

gravissimo et sanctissimo: A. Klotz quotes *Flacc.* 5, *Planc.* 27 for this word-order (cf. *quir.* 18, *Deiot.* 10); on the other hand *Cat.* i. 9 has 'sanctissimo gravissimoque' (applied to the senate).

26. **dimittendi:** it was customary for a proconsul to consult the senate before demobilizing his army, but he was probably not bound to do so (*St.-R.* iii. 1082). For the play on words with *amissa* cf. *Caecin.* 75.

28. **quid est aliud furere ? . . . :** 'what is madness if not this (i.e. the unauthorized demobilization of an army) ? Is it failure to recognize people ? No, it is failure to recognize the laws, the senate, the state. Is it mutilation of one's own body ? This injury to one's own life, reputation, and security is more serious.'

quid est aliud . . . ? is a formula of everyday speech, expressing indignation (Hand, iv. 249 f.). The more usual construction would be *quid est aliud furere nisi hoc facere?*; but sometimes the *nisi* clause must be understood from the context (*Phil.* i. 22, ii. 7, v. 5, x. 5, Catull. 29. 15). Here Cicero follows his original question by mentioning two symptoms of insanity, but in each case he pretends to regard Piso's actions as more serious symptoms. The punctuation is due to Madvig (on *fin.* v. 31), as modified by A. Klotz; the construction with question and answer is admittedly unparalleled after *quid est aliud . . . ?*

The crucial point is that *non cognoscere homines*, failure to recognize people, is one of the symptoms of insanity (Plaut. *Men.* 961, Sen. *cont.* ii. 4. 2, Juv. 10. 234, Plut. *mor.* 167C; in particular see Eur. *Or.* 264 for Orestes, Ov. *met.* iv. 512 ff. for Athamas, Tert. *de anima* 17. 9 for both). *non cognoscere homines* cannot refer to Piso, who was not literally mad (*in sen.* 13 'non cognoscendorum hominum studium' describes unsociability, not insanity). Therefore it is not co-ordinate with *non cognoscere leges*, which does refer to Piso. The construction is only possible because Latin says not 'what is this if not madness ?' but 'what is madness if not this ?'

Löfstedt, *Syntactica*, ii. 168 and Hofmann, *Lat. Gramm.*, p. 654 take *quid est . . . civitatem?* as one interrogative sentence (= 'quid est aliud quam furere non cognoscere homines . . . ?'). This construction, even if possible elsewhere in Cicero (which is doubtful),

109

§§ 47–48]   COMMENTARY

is impossible here, as it involves taking *non cognoscere homines* as co-ordinate with *non cognoscere leges*. Clark and others read *non cognoscere homines . . . civitatem?* as a single interrogative sentence; this is open to the same objection, and the logic of the question is obscure. Professor Watt suggests reading *immo non cognoscere leges*; this would make Cicero's argument easier to follow.

2. **cruentare corpus suum?:** self-mutilation was a sign of madness; cf. the cases of Lycurgus (Roscher, *Lexikon*, ii. 2194) and Cleomenes (Herod. vi. 75. 3); add Sen. *cont.* iii exc. 7 'furenti et membra sua lianti'. *V* reads *cruentare corpus suum leve est*; cf. *Verr.* iv. 25 'me cum dico leve est'. But *PΩ*, a weighty combination, omit *leve est*; and Marius Victorinus quotes only *quid est . . . corpus suum?*, though admittedly he misunderstands the argument. Moreover the clausula *-are corpus suum* is excellent; but when *leve est* is added the distribution of words causes doubt (cf. Zielinski, p. 122). It may be objected that *leve est* is needed to balance *maior*; yet Cicero often varies his constructions a little (cf. perhaps 15. 3).

§ 48. 3. si familiam . . .: *argumentum a minore*; cf. 18. 14 n. *familiam* refers to slaves.

5. **amici:** cf. *Tusc.* ii. 48 'constringatur amicorum propinquorumque custodiis', Catull. 41. 6, Prop. i. 1. 25, iii. 24. 9. In law an insane person fell into the *potestas* of his *proximus adgnatus* (F. Schulz, *Classical Roman Law*, p. 197). The *amici* were presumably called in by this relative as a *consilium* to give advice (cf. *RE* iv. 915 f.).

rei publicae: the reading *populi Romani* is less likely in itself, and particularly awkward as *populi* occurs below. *P.R.* and *R.P.* are often confused, even in ancient MSS.

6. **populi Romani:** there are 14 instances in Cicero of *iussu* or *iniussu* with *populi*, but no certain instances with *populi Romani*; in two cases the MSS. differ (here and at 50. 5). The consensus of *PV* does not formally eliminate a variant in Ω; yet one is reluctant to reject so well-attested a reading without decisive reasons. A. Klotz argues that the adjective is always omitted when domestic affairs are being dealt with; this certainly goes too far (cf. *Mur.* 1).

7. **ecce tibi alter . . .:** Cicero turns again to Gabinius, whose actions show that he too has gone mad. *ecce* marks a lively transition (Hand, ii. 348, Seyffert, *Scholae Latinae*, i. 54). *tibi* is ethic dative.

11. **partim etiam . . .:** 'when part had been eaten up by the purchases which he made even in those distant lands where he plundered everything, part by bills of exchange which he used to erect this mountain of a Tusculan villa here in Italy'.

in illis locis: even in Syria, where Gabinius looted so much that one would not expect him to have to buy anything.

110

COMMENTARY [§ 48

12. **partim permutationes:** the layout in *V* is as follows (cf.
A. C. Clark, *Descent of Manuscripts*, pp. 145, 295):

it emptiones <i>partim</i>
<small>mutationes ad hunc</small>
tus<i>culani</i> || || || ||
montem exstruen

The letters italicized are in an erasure; after *tusculani* there is an
erasure which would hold six letters; *mutationes ad hunc* is added
by a second but contemporary hand. Probably *V*[1] read *emptiones
ad hunc*.

Gabinius in Syria would use *permutationes* or 'bills of exchange'
to pay for building expenses in Italy; the omission of *partim permutationes* after *emptiones* might have taken place both in *P* and
V[1]. *ad . . . exstruendum* must be taken only with *permutationes*
and not with *emptiones*; otherwise the contrast between *illis* and
hunc is obscured.

mutationes (*V*[2]) is meaningless. Havet proposed *mutuationes*,
but it would be odd to say that 'borrowings' used up Gabinius's
booty if the expense of interest were meant. *P*'s omission might
be right; *emptiones* would suit the lavish purchase of something
bulky like marble. Yet the rare and technical *permutationes* must
go back to the ancient world, and it describes exactly the method
which Gabinius would have used to pay his bills.

13. **Tusculani montem:** for Gabinius's huge villa see *dom.*
124, *Sest.* 93; it was embellished in 58 with objects of art from
Cicero's Tusculanum (*in sen.* 18, *dom.* 62). *Tusculanum montem*
would also make sense; but as this reading is contradicted by *P V*[2]α
it cannot have any authority. Garatoni proposed *Tusculano in
monte montem* (based on the confused reading in α); but the play
on the two *montes* is clumsy. Clark proposed *Tusculi immanem
montem*, but one would need *immanem Tusculi montem*.

14. **intermissa:** 'interrupted'; less final than *constitisset*, 'had
come to a halt'.

se ipsum . . .: for Gabinius's Egyptian expedition and the
Sibylline oracle which he defied see p. 190.

15. **numen interdictumque:** in spite of this pious talk Cicero in
private took a more cynical view of the oracle; cf. *fam.* i. 4. 2 'nomen
inductum fictae religionis'.

16. **sacerdotum:** the *custodes* of the Sibylline books (*RE* iiA.
2106).

auctoritatem: this term was applied to a decree of the senate
which, in spite of being vetoed, was formally recorded. In January
56 the senate made a guarded pronouncement: 'cum multitudine
(regem Alexandrinum) reduci periculosum rei publicae videri'

III

§§ 48–51] COMMENTARY

(*Q.f.* ii. 2. 3). Later it voted 'ut ne quis omnino regem reduceret' (*fam.* i. 7. 4); this latter decree was vetoed, but recorded as an *auctoritas*. It was described by Cicero ad loc. as 'magis iratorum hominum studium quam constantis senatus consilium'.

17. **iussa populi:** Cicero is followed by Dio xxxix. 56. 4 ἀπειρη-κότος δὲ καὶ τοῦ δήμου τῆς τε Σιβύλλης μὴ καταχθῆναι τὸν ἄνδρα. The tribune C. Cato agitated against the restoration of the king, but there is no mention elsewhere of an explicit law; it would surely have been mentioned in *fam.* i. 7 if it had existed in July 56. Probably Cicero means that as a result of the oracle the people rescinded their previous decisions about the king (Dio xxxix. 15. 3). It is unlikely that he is thinking of the general provisions of the *leges Cornelia* and *Julia* (50. 6 n.).

§ **49.** 18. **finis:** cf. p. 189.

21. **qui licuit:** 'how was it permissible ?'; cf. Landgraf on *Sex. Rosc.* 116.

23. **venit** = *iit.* The perfect of *ire* is hardly ever used by Cicero (Löfstedt, *Syntactica*, ii. 40 f.).

25. **nisi ut...:** Cicero is mocking Gabinius's previous letter to the senate (41. 24). But he sent no dispatches this time (Dio xxxix. 59. 1).

§ **50.** 1. **si mentis . . .:** 'if he had been in his right mind'; cf. *Thes. L.L.* viii. 718. 20.

5. **populi Romani . . .:** cf. 48. 6 n. *ac* rather than *aut* is regular in this formula; cf. *St.-R.* iii. 1256.

6. **lex Cornelia:** Sulla's law (Kübler, *RE* xiv. 547 f.) also enacted that governors should leave their provinces within thirty days of the arrival of their successors (*fam.* iii. 6. 3). For the *lex Julia* cf. 37. 2 n.

8. **auderet** = *ausus esset* (l. 3); cf. 41. 1 n.

P. Lentulus: 34. 16 n.

10. **sorte:** Cicero may mean that the restoration of Ptolemy was entrusted to the proconsul of Cilicia, and that Lentulus had previously obtained that office by lot.

interposita religione: 'when a religious objection was brought forward'. *sine ulla dubitatione* is flagrantly untrue; see *fam.* i. 7. 5, where Cicero advises Lentulus to be careful: 'nos quidem hoc sentimus, si exploratum tibi sit posse te illius regni potiri, non esse cunctandum, si dubium sit, non esse conandum'.

§§ **51–63.** *Cicero compares his own triumphant return from exile (§§ 51–52) with Piso's inglorious return from his province (§§ 53–55). He ridicules Piso's claim to have scorned a triumph (§§ 56–63).*

§ **51.** 14. **et quoniam...:** a common transition when the speaker

112

COMMENTARY [§§ 51–52]

is reminded of a fresh point; cf. *leg. agr.* ii. 92, *Sest.* 118, *Vat.* 35, Juv. 3. 114 'et quoniam coepit Graecorum mentio', Seyffert, *Scholae Latinae*, i. 13, 26.

15. **praecidit:** i.e. Gabinius by his crimes has made it impossible for himself ever to return. In fact Cicero had tried unsuccessfully to have him recalled (88. 4 n.). Gabinius came back in the end in September 54 (p. 191).

16. **os ut videam:** Cicero looks forward to seeing Gabinius's impudent face; cf. *Rab. Post.* 35 'nec mihi longius quicquam est, iudices, quam videre hominum voltus', Ter. *eun.* 597 'tum equidem istuc os tuum impudens videre nimium vellem'.

17. **meus . . . :** for Cicero's return cf. introd.; p. xiv.

18. **agmen perpetuum:** delegations from the towns of Italy welcomed Cicero in such rapid succession that they seemed to form a continuous procession.

viderit: the subject is *agmen*; the object (*reditum*) can easily be supplied. Garatoni suggested that *reditus* is the subject, but he produced no parallel for such a usage; in any case, Cicero is saying that many people saw his own return, whereas nobody saw Piso's (§ 53 'quod te municipium vidit ?').

19. **municipium:** a self-governing community which had entered the Roman state, administered by *quattuorviri*. A *colonia* in origin was a settlement planted by the Romans, and was administered by *duumviri*. A *praefectura* was a less organized region, where originally there was more interference by Roman magistrates; about the time of this speech such areas in Italy were being transformed into *municipia* (A. N. Sherwin-White, *The Roman Citizenship*, pp. 143 f.). *municipia et coloniae* is a phrase often used for 'the towns of Italy'; the three types of community are mentioned together at *Sest.* 32, *Phil.* ii. 58, iv. 7, [Q. Cic.] *comm. pet.* 30, *ILS* 6085. 89 (*tab. Heracl.*). See further E. G. Hardy, *Roman Laws and Charters* (Oxford, 1912), pp. 143 ff., H. J. Cunningham, *CQ* viii, 1914, 132 f., ix, 1915, 57 ff.

20. **publice:** in delegations from the local *curiae* (town-councils). Cf. *Att.* viii. 16. 2 'quas fieri censes ἀπαντήσεις ex oppidis, quos honores' (for Caesar).

21. **adventus:** arrival at different places in succession; cf. *Arch.* 4 'sic eius adventus celebrabantur'.

§ 52. 25. instar: 'equivalent to'; cf. *Brut.* 191 'Plato . . . unus instar est centum milium'. *instar* in classical Latin refers to quantity, size, etc.; later it is used also of other forms of resemblance. See E. Wölfflin, *ALL* ii. 581 ff.

quo should probably be preferred here to *cum*. This clause defines *dies*; the *cum* clauses below elaborate the situation. Cf.

5993   **K**   113

§§ 52–53] COMMENTARY

dom. 76 (describing the same events) 'itaque ille unus dies quo die . . .'.

26. **egressum:** the senate went outside the city gate to meet Cicero. This honour was paid by the senate at triumphs (Joseph. *b.J.* vii. 125), and often to important citizens on other occasions (*fam.* xvi. 11. 2, *Phil.* ii. 78).

27. **convulsa:** cf. *Planc.* 96 'cum ipsa paene insula mihi sese obviam ferre vellet', *Rab. perd.* 8, *paneg. Lat.* v (viii). 1. 1 'si Flavia Aeduorum . . . commovere se funditus atque huc venire potuisset'.

4. **tecta . . .:** a companion picture to § 21 'templa gemerent, tecta urbis ipsa lugerent'.

me: emphatic, underlining the contrast between Cicero and Piso.

5. **domo:** Cicero's house on the Palatine; cf. 11. 11 n., introd., p. xiv.

7. **conlocaverunt:** cf. *dom.* 147 (the last sentence of the speech) 'quaeso obtestorque vos, pontifices, ut me . . . in sedibus meis conlocetis'.

ante me nemini: Asconius ad loc. mentions other cases of private houses built at the public expense; but Cicero's house was the only one which had been *rebuilt* with public money.

§ **53.** 9. **habes . . .:** 'now you know about my return'; cf. *Thes. L.L.* vi. 2433. 43.

10. **os** suggests impudence; cf. *Flacc.* 46 '(cum) haberet nihil praeter illam impudentiam quam videtis'.

12. **laureatis:** after a governor had been hailed as *imperator* his lictors tied laurel round their *fasces*, and perhaps wore laurel themselves (Kübler, *RE* xiii. 508 f., M. B. Ogle, *AJP* xxxi, 1910, 292, Pease on *div.* i. 59).

maeandros: 'meanderings'; cf. Strabo xii. 8. 15 (of the river Maeander) σκολιὸς ὢν εἰς ὑπερβολήν, ὥστε ἐξ ἐκείνου τὰς σκολιότητας ἁπάσας μαιάνδρους καλεῖσθαι, Gell. xvi. 8. 17, Amm. Marc. xxx. 1. 12. For the windings of the river cf. Herod. ii. 29. 3, Ov. *her.* 9. 55 with Palmer's note, Sen. *epist.* 104. 15 'Maeander, poetarum omnium exercitatio et ludus'. Piso returned by an unusual route, but he may have had business elsewhere (92. 4 n.); Cicero's account is an amusing invention.

dum omnis . . .: 'while you threaded your way through every uninhabited district'.

15. **nonne tibi . . .:** cf. *Clu.* 193 (on Sassia) 'itaque nullo in oppido consistendi potestas ei fuit, nemo ex tot hospitibus inventus est qui non contagionem aspectus fugeret; nocti se potius ac solitudini quam ulli aut urbi aut hospiti committebat'. The theme was no doubt conventional.

COMMENTARY [§§ 53–54

17. **efferri:** 'carried out to burial'; a fifteenth-century emendation. *referri* (codd.) can hardly be right; the emphatic position of *redire* at the beginning of the clause shows that the infinitives are contrasted as well as the nouns (A. Klotz). Funerals of the young, and apparently of *infames*, took place at night; cf. Marquardt, *Privatleben²*, p. 343, H. J. Rose, *CQ* xvii, 1923, 191 ff. For the insult cf. *Phil*. ii. 106 'at iste operta lectica latus per oppidum est ut mortuus'.

18. **Romam . . . ipsam:** the object of *ingressus es*, as it appears in Arusianus's citation. *foedavit adventus tuus* is irrelevant to the argument, breaks up the series of questions, and leaves *ingressus es* below without an object. It is presumably an ancient interpolation (*V*'s omission of *foedavit* is perhaps without significance); the interpolator seems not to have understood why *Romam* was in the accusative.

o . . . dedecus: Piso is a disgrace not only to his father's distinguished family, the Calpurnii, but even to his mother's undistinguished one, the Calventii of Placentia (frag. ix n.). For this topic in invective cf. p. 194.

20. **bracatae:** trousers were a barbarian garment (D.–S. i. 746, *RE* i. 2100); *Gallia bracata* was an old name for Narbonensis (*Thes. L.L.* ii. 2155. 68); cf. *Font.* 33, *fam.* ix. 15. 2, Suet. *Jul.* 80. 2. For the pretence that Piso's grandfather was Transalpine in origin cf. frag. ix n.

21. **ingressus es:** thus Arusianus, who quotes specifically to show that *ingredior* can take a direct object. The MSS. of Cicero read *venisti*, which gives an inferior clausula; this reading may have been influenced by *venit* at the end of the next sentence.

22. **horum:** *senatorum.*

legatorum: Piso's former legates ought to have welcomed him. They were Flaccus and Marcius (below), and C. Vergilius (*prov. cons.* 7); for a fourth legate, unnamed, cf. 86. 6 n. The normal number of legates was three, but exceptions occurred (*St.-R.* ii³. 684 f.); or one legate may have replaced another. Piso had appointed his legates against the senate's wishes (*Sest.* 33, *Vat.* 36), but Cicero claims that they were now hostile to him. When Piso left Macedonia, the senior members of his staff were ex-aediles (88. 6); therefore Flaccus and Vergilius, who were ex-praetors, had already left. Marcius perhaps stayed with Piso to the end; but he seems to have reached Rome before Piso, whose route was circuitous.

§ 54. 23. **L. Flaccus:** praetor in 63, when he helped Cicero against Catiline and arrested the Allobrogian envoys (*Cat.* iii. 5). He was propraetor of Asia in 62, and was defended by Cicero when tried for extortion in 59. He is described by Sallust, *Cat.* 45. 2 as a *homo militaris.*

115

§§ 54-55]   COMMENTARY

1. **errantem:** taking a devious route; cf. § 53.

in primis should, I suggest, be taken with *peritum* rather than with *fortem*; cf. *Font.* 41 'usu quoque bellorum gerendorum in primis eorum hominum qui nunc sunt exercitatus'. *vir fortis* is a conventional compliment to all soldiers, like 'gallant' in Parliament; Marcius's special distinction lay not in courage but in generalship.

2. **Q. Marcium:** presumably Q. Marcius Crispus, who fought for Caesar in the civil wars, was proconsul of Bithynia in 45, and in 43 handed over his army to Cassius in Syria. *Homines militares* like Flaccus and Marcius were invaluable to proconsuls who had no military experience.

3. **quorum . . .:** 'one of the legates thanks to whom'. Kraffert proposed *unum ex eis quorum*, but this is perhaps unnecessary; cf. Tac. *ann.* vi. 12. 1 'Caninius Gallus quindecimvirum', K.–S. i. 424, W. Kroll, *Wissenschaftliche Syntax*[3] (Berlin, 1925), p. 24; so in inscriptions 'P. Manlius duovirum', etc. (F. Buecheler, *Kleine Schriften*, i. 68).

5. **numero:** *V*'s reading avoids the dactylic rhythm of *sed quid ego enumero.*

§ **55.** 6. **cui:** *obviam* must be understood from the context. With Jeep's *quin* (*qui* Ω) the meaning would be 'why don't I say?'; cf. *rep.* vi. 15 'quin huc ad vos venire propero ?' But this lively idiom is unsuitable here. Or one might take *quin* to mean 'nay more', and read the sentence as a statement; but such a statement would not cohere well with the preceding question. Ernesti suggested that the word should be deleted, and this might be right.

officiosissima: cf. *Mur.* 69 'illa officiosissima, quae neminem patitur non honeste in urbem introire, tota natio candidatorum'. The candidates for magistracies were zealous in paying courtesies to prominent citizens, and at the time of Piso's arrival the elections had not yet taken place (p. 200). *natio* is contemptuous ('tribe').

7. **volgo:** 'indiscriminately'. *admoniti*: for such invitations by a returning governor cf. *Mur.* 69.

8. **togulae:** lictors wore a toga in the city, a red *sagum* outside (*St.-R.* i[3]. 64, 375, *RE* xiii. 508). They probably had to put on civilian clothes before recrossing the *pomerium*, when their master lost his *imperium*. Cicero pretends that Piso's lictors then passed themselves off as citizens who had come to meet Piso (cf. 61. 14).

9. **quibus illi acceptis:** for the placing of the subject in the middle of the ablative absolute cf. L.–H., p. 613.

11. **tanta provincia:** *exercitus* is often combined with *provincia* (§ 28, *Thes. L.L.* v. 2. 1392. 23). *V* reads *tantae provinciae*; cf. *exercitus Africae*, etc., in imperial inscriptions (ibid. 1395. 27).

116

COMMENTARY [§§ 55–56

triennio post: 'three years after he had set out'. The event that happened three years before is not specifically stated; cf. *Phil.* viii. 32 'cum in spem libertatis sexennio post sumus ingressi'. For Piso's *triennium* see p. 200.

13. **in quo:** 'in connexion with this matter'; cf. 90. 26 n.

14. **reprendit:** pronounced as a trisyllable here, as is clear from the rhythm (cf. Zielinski, p. 177); of course Cicero's spelling is quite uncertain.

15. **Caelimontana:** Piso did not come home by the *via Appia* and *porta Capena*, but by the *porta Esquilina* (cf. 92. 4 n.). Earlier in the debate, or perhaps in the spoken as opposed to the written version of the *in Pisonem* (p. 202), Cicero had said 'Caelimontana' in mistake for 'Esquilina'. He was confused because Piso at this time lived near the *porta Caelimontana* (§ 61). Here he retrieves his mistake brilliantly. The *porta Esquilina* perhaps stood on the site of the later *arcus Gallieni*, a little south-east of S. Maria Maggiore (Platner and Ashby, *Top. Dict.* s.v.). The *porta Caelimontana* perhaps stood on the site of the *arcus Dolabellae et Silani* (cf. A. M. Colini, *Atti Pont. Accad.* mem. vii, 1944, 33 ff. and 439).

sponsione . . .: 'he bet me that he had come in by the Esquiline gate'. A *sponsio* was a challenge used in certain legal procedures, here made jokingly (Greenidge, *Legal Procedure*, p. 54 n. 1). The assertion of the *stipulator* (challenger) is introduced by *ni* because the thought is 'If I didn't enter by the Esquiline gate I promise to pay you such-and-such.' *ni* rather than *nisi* is regularly used in *sponsiones*.

16. **homo promptus:** 'quick-witted as he was'; so *de or.* i. 85. For this use of *homo* see R. G. Nisbet on *dom.* 14.

17. **quisquam** is legitimate as the sentence is quasi-negative; cf. § 18, K.–S. i. 638.

18. **modo ne triumphali:** 'provided that it was not by the triumphal gate'. The *porta triumphalis* was probably not a gate in the city wall (E. Makin, *JRS* xi, 1921, 29 ff., using Joseph. *b.J.* vii. 124–30). Perhaps it was an entrance to the *circus Flaminius* (M. P. Nilsson, *Corolla archeologica Gustavo Adolpho dedicata* (Lund, 1932), pp. 133 f.). *introieris* here might seem to imply a gate in the city wall; but Cicero may be straining the words to score a point. See further Kähler, *RE* viiA. 374 ff.

19. **consulibus:** sometimes found for 'proconsuls' (*Thes. L.L.* iv. 564. 12, *St.-R.* ii³. 240 n. 5).

tu inventus es: Orelli proposed *tu unus inventus es*, unnecessarily; cf. *Verr.* iii. 21 'Verres . . . inventus est', *Clu.* 32.

§ 56. 22. **philosophi:** Epicureans claimed to despise glory; cf. frags. 548 ff. Usener, P. DeLacy, *TAPA* lxxii, 1941, 53 ff.

117

§§ 56–57]   COMMENTARY

23. **scelus:** 'scoundrel'.

1. **qui:** for the absence of an antecedent cf. K.–S. ii. 281 f.

3. **celare:** for the combination with *tegere* A. Klotz compares *Verr.* I. 21 'cupiebam animi dolorem vultu tegere et taciturnitate celare'. *velare* is only used in this sense after the Augustan period.

    Silanus: D. Junius Silanus, cos. 62, now dead; nothing is known about his province. For C. Antonius, Cicero's colleague in 63, see 5. 13 n.

4. **neque enim potest quisquam:** this word-order is very convincing; cf. E. Fraenkel, *Iktus und Akzent*, pp. 88 f.; cf. also *Sull.* 69 'neque enim potest quisquam', *fin.* iii. 73 'nec vero potest quisquam'.

5. **ut non praetexat . . . :** 'without giving as an excuse a desire for a triumph'.

§ 57. 6. **quod si:** 'even if'; *cum vero* (l. 14) introduces the real facts.

8. **tamen erat . . . :** 'yet it would have remained the act of a small and abject spirit'. For the mood of *erat* see 18. 17 n.

10. **nam ut . . . :** 'it is certainly the sign of a frivolous mind always to be on the look-out for unjustified approbation, and to run after every semblance of glory, even when undeserved; but equally it is the mark of a spirit which shrinks from the lustre of the light to spurn the well-deserved glory which is the noblest reward of genuine merit'. Cicero is thinking in Aristotelian terms: one should seek glory neither too much nor too little.

11. **falsae gloriae:** cf. Aug. *in evang. Joh.* 100. 2 (Migne, *PL* xxxv. 1891) 'est . . . falsa gloria quando laudantes errore falluntur'.

12. **est [levis] animi:** *levis* is intolerably clumsy after *levitatis*. It seems simpler to omit the word altogether rather than to emend to something like Lehmann's *tenuis*.

    lucem . . . fugientis: cf. the adjective *lucifugus* (*fin.* i. 61), which was later applied to the Christians (Min. Fel. 8. 4, Rutil. Namat. i. 440).

13. **fructus . . . virtutis:** cf. Arist. *Nic. eth.* 1123^{b}35 τῆς ἀρετῆς γὰρ ἆθλον ἡ τιμὴ καὶ ἀπονέμεται τοῖς ἀγαθοῖς. The thought is a commonplace in Cicero, and explains much about the politics of his time (*de or.* i. 194, *Tusc.* i. 109, iii. 3, *Phil.* i. 29–30, *off.* ii. 36, etc.); add Hor. *epist.* i. 17.41 f., *Thes. L.L.* vi. 2063. 82. For Roman ideas on glory see U. Knoche, *Philol.* lxxxix, 1934, 102 ff., F. A. Sullivan, *TAPA* lxxii, 1941, 382 ff., A. D. Leeman, *Gloria* (Rotterdam, 1949).

16. **libero:** Cicero pretends that the *lex Clodia* was passed by slaves who had no right to vote; cf. § 30 'inusta per servos', § 64.

118

COMMENTARY [§§ 57–58

17. **cumque omnium . . .:** 'since in all your crimes this is the bargain that was struck'.

20. **finibus:** cf. p. 172.

21. **iuventute:** cf. *prov. cons.* 5 'exercitus noster ille superbissimo dilectu et durissima conquisitione conlectus'. The Roman army was conscripted at this date from Italy; Piso may have taken exceptional measures, but allowance must be made for exaggeration.

22. **hieme:** Piso probably left for his province before 10 December (31. 7 n.). Vegetius, *de re mil.* iv. 39, says that from 11 November to 10 March the seas were closed (he is thinking of the transport of armies). Of course many individual voyages took place in winter, but they were unwelcome; cf. E. de Saint-Denis, *REL* xxv, 1947, 196 ff., J. Rougé, *REA* liv, 1952, 316 ff.

§ 58. 24. non est integrum . . .: 'Pompey is no longer free to take your advice.' Cicero ironically rebukes a number of senators for having triumphed; he begins with Pompey, one of the consuls of the year.

26. **ter:** cf. 29. 15 n.

Crasse: the other consul. Unlike Pompey he is addressed in the vocative; probably he was presiding in the senate when Cicero delivered the speech (pp. 200 f.).

1. **lauream:** Crassus defeated the forces of Spartacus in 71; he was given an *ovatio*, not a triumph, since the war had been fought against slaves. Whereupon 'murteam coronam' (appropriate to an *ovatio*) 'insolenter aspernatus est, senatusque consultum faciundum per gratiam curavit ut lauro non murto coronaretur' (Gell. v. 6. 23, cf. Plin. *n.h.* xv. 125). Cicero's politeness to Crassus is insincere; relations were strained at this time (*fam.* i. 9. 20, Dio xxxix. 60. 1). Indeed, our passage may be slightly malicious, as Crassus's behaviour cannot have been universally approved.

2. **P. Servili . . .:** P. Servilius Vatia Isauricus, cos. 79, cens. 55, triumphed 88, and again in 74 (*de Isauris*). Q. Metellus Creticus, cos. 69, triumphed 62 (Crete). C. Scribonius Curio, cos. 76, triumphed 72 (*de Dardanis*). L. Afranius, cos. 60, triumphed perhaps about 70, perhaps from Spain (A. Degrassi, *Inscr. Ital.* xiii. 1. 85, 565). Cicero is probably referring to all living *triumphatores*. Triumphs were won by M. Pupius Piso and M. Lucullus; but Pupius Piso is last heard of in 61 (the reference in *Flacc.* frag. Bob. x may be posthumous). M. Lucullus is last mentioned in 56 (*prov. cons.* 22); as he was a friend of Cicero's (§ 77) and an outstanding general in Thrace (p. 177) one would expect him to have been present if alive and in good health.

4. **C. ipsi Pomptino:** a common word-order (K.–S. ii. 135). Pomptinus was praetor in 63, when with Flaccus (§ 54) he arrested

119

§§ 58–59]   COMMENTARY

the Allobrogian envoys. As governor of Transalpine Gaul 62–61 he crushed a revolt of the Allobroges. He was denied his triumph, in theory because of some unknown religious difficulty, in fact because of objections from Caesar's friends (Schol. Bob. p. 149 Stangl). Cicero does not address him in the vocative, as he lingered many years outside the *pomerium*, until he gained his triumph in 54. In 51–50 he was one of Cicero's legates in Cilicia.

5. **religionibus:** 'for it is only because he has incurred religious objections that he is being debarred (from holding a triumph)'.

7. **Paulum:** 39. 24 n.

rusticum: a simple countryman from Arpinum (cf. *Tusc.* ii. 53 where he is called *rusticanus vir*, Mayor on Juv. 8. 246), and therefore too unsophisticated to despise a triumph.

8. **patres:** Cn. Pompeius Strabo triumphed in the Social War in 89, P. Licinius Crassus over the Lusitani in 93.

§ **59.** 10. **sed quoniam . . . :** nothing can be done about the senators who have already triumphed. Why does Piso not dissuade his own son-in-law, Caesar, who is at this moment winning great victories in Gaul? The irony, with a few interruptions, is sustained till the end of § 61.

praeterita . . . : a sententious commonplace, wittily used in addressing a would-be moralist; cf. Orelli⁴ on Hor. *carm.* iii. 29. 48, Otto, p. 286.

11. **homullus . . . :** according to the legend, man was fashioned from clay by Prometheus; moralists used the story to illustrate the unimportance of human affairs and the vanity of ambition. Here Cicero humorously applies the trite description not to mankind in general, but to the sermonizing Piso in particular. Though *lutum* is often used in similar contexts to mean 'clay' (Otto, p. 202), here there seems to be a hint of the meaning 'mud' or 'dirt'.

[**Epicurus**] could mean 'an Epicurus' and refer to Piso (cf. §§ 20, 37); after *fictus* it produces an excellent clausula. Yet this insult is somewhat confusing here, and weakens the force of Cicero's main point. Müller plausibly deleted the word as a stupid gloss (Priscian's quotation ends at *fictus*). *homullus* and *ex luto fictus* go excellently together, since they belong to the same type of moralizing discourse; cf. Symmachus, *epist.* iv. 33. 2 'homullus Promethei manu fictus'.

13. **fertur . . . gloria:** 'is swept on by ambition'.

flagrat ardet: Baiter deleted *ardet*. But for the asyndeton cf. *Verr.* iii. 155 'dare profundere', *Flacc.* 103 'putavi speravi', *dom.* 113 'disturbaretur diriperetur', Nägelsbach, pp. 704 f., K.–S. ii. 151.

14. **didicit:** often used of learning philosophical doctrines; cf.

120

COMMENTARY [§ 59

Hor. *serm.* i. 5. 101 'namque deos didici securum agere aevum', Cic. *fin.* ii. 26, *Tusc.* i. 39.

15. **mitte:** not only 'send' but 'dedicate'; cf. *fin.* i. 8 'libro quem ad me de virtute misisti', with Reid's note. For Essays on Glory cf. *Arch.* 26 'ipsi illi philosophi etiam in eis libellis quos de contemnenda gloria scribunt nomen suum inscribunt'.

18. **apud indoctum eruditus:** ironic, like the rest; Cicero regarded Piso as uncultured (§ 1, *in sen.* 13), but had a great respect for Caesar's learning (*Brut.* 252).

19. **ut es:** 'being as you are'; cf. K.–S. ii. 451 f., H. S. Anton, *Studien zur lateinischen Grammatik* (Erfurt, 1873), ii. 31 ff.

20. **factus ad:** 'with a natural gift for'; cf. *Verr.* II. i. 64, *Att.* xiv. 18. 2, *off.* i. 103.

concinnus: 'elegant', referring to the harmonious structure of Piso's style; cf. *orat.* 20 'alii (oratores) concinniores', *fin.* v. 13 'concinnus . . . et elegans . . . Aristo'.

perfectus: 'a consummate stylist'. Dobree wished to delete, but for the collocation with *perpolitus* cf. *de or.* i. 58 'perfectos iam homines in dicendo et perpolitos'. N. W. DeWitt, *Epicurus and his Philosophy*, p. 100, thinks that Cicero is mocking an Epicurean view that perfection is attainable. But surely he is using the jargon of literary criticism rather than of philosophy.

politus ex schola: 'freshly polished in the philosophy-school'. Cicero is ridiculing not only Piso but the Epicureans in general for their lack of culture; cf. 70. 26 n.

21. **quid est, Caesar . . .:** note the rhetorical and sententious language; Cicero is parodying a moralizing treatise. For *prosopopoeia*, the invention of imaginary speeches, see Volkmann, pp. 489 f.

supplicationes: see 6. 2 n., 45. 24 n. *totiens* is difficult; cf. p. 201.

22. **delectent:** after *quid est quod* Cicero normally uses the subjunctive; for the indicative (here supported by Ω and a testimonium) cf. *Verr.* iv. 43 'quid erat quod confirmabat se abs te argentum esse repetiturum'. See K.–S. ii. 271, Lebreton, pp. 318 f.

in quibus . . . quas: where the relative is used as a connective such repetition is rare; yet see *Verr.* iv. 122, *dom.* 89, Caes. *b.G.* i. 28. 5.

24. **divinus:** the Epicureans treated Epicurus as divine; cf. Lucr. v. 8 'deus ille fuit', *nat. d.* i. 43 with Pease's note. Here a malicious touch: the Epicureans made their gods so remote that they were accused of virtual atheism (Pease on *nat. d.* i. 123); so it is paradoxical that they should have treated their founder as a god.

neque propitii . . .: cf. Epicurus, *Κ.Δ.* i (Diog. Laert. x. 139) τὸ μακάριον καὶ ἄφθαρτον οὔτε αὐτὸ πράγματα ἔχει οὔτε ἄλλῳ παρέχει·

121

§§ 59–61]   COMMENTARY

ὥστε οὔτε ὀργαῖς οὔτε χάρισι συνέχεται, frags. 363–6 Usener, Lucr. ii. 651 'nec bene promeritis capitur neque tangitur ira', *nat. d.* i. 45 with Pease's note. *propitius* and *iratus* are contrasted at *Cael.* 42, *Att.* viii. 16. 2, *nat. d.* ii. 145.

1. **non facies fidem:** 'you will not be believed'.

2. **tibi . . . iratos:** an unfortunate man was said to be *dis iratis natus* (Mayor on Juv. 10. 129). For a similar joke cf. Ar. *equ.* 32 ff. *ΔΗΜ.* ἐτεὸν ἡγεῖ γὰρ θεούς; | *ΝΙΚ.* ἔγωγε. *Δ.* ποίῳ χρώμενος τεκμηρίῳ; | *Ν.* ὁτιὴ θεοῖσιν ἐχθρός εἰμ'· οὐκ εἰκότως; So also Diog. Laert. ii. 102 (a saying of Theodorus), vi. 42 (a saying of Diogenes).

§ 60. 2. **alteram scholam:** 'your second lecture' (cf. Kühner on *Tusc.* i. 8).

3. **quid tandem habet . . .:** 'what is the good of . . . ?' A vivid sketch of a triumph: the prisoners in chains in front of the triumphal car (*RE* viiA. 503. 47), pictures of captured towns, gold and silver booty (ibid. 503. 1), officers on horseback (509. 3), the ribaldry of the soldiers (509. 50), the applause of the crowd (502. 50). The passage is amusingly rhetorical; one may note in particular the regularity of the clausulae.

6. **pompa:** 'procession'.

inania: κενός was a word much used by Epicurus.

7. **paene puerorum:** 'one might almost say of children' (for *paene* cf. K.–S. i. 219, H. S. Anton, *Studien zu lateinischen Grammatik*, ii. 130). The Epicureans often spoke contemptuously of their opponents (Pease on *nat. d.* i. 18); in particular they called them puerile (*fin.* i. 72, *nat. d.* i. 34; cf. παιδαριώδης in Philodemus, *rhet.* i. 356. 7, ii. 279 frag. xxiii).

8. **vehi' per urbem:** during the daytime carriages were not permitted inside the city except at triumphs and other ceremonial occasions (*St.-R.* i³. 393 ff., Marquardt, *Privatleben²*, pp. 728 ff.).

conspici: whereas Epicurus recommended τὸ λανθάνειν (cf. frag. 551 Usener).

9. **voluptatem** gives a malicious twist to the argument (cf. 69. 21 n.). From this point the parody is dropped, and Piso is made to put his own case in the worst possible light.

§ 61. 10. **quin tu me vides . . . ?:** 'why don't you look at me?' (cf. K.–S. ii. 496). Professor Watt suggests *vide* (K.–S. i. 201 f.).

T. Flamininus: triumphed in 194 (Cynoscephalae), L. Aemilius Paulus in 167 (Pydna), Q. Metellus Macedonicus in 146, T. Didius perhaps in 100 (cf. Degrassi, *Inscr. Ital.* xiii. 1. 562). For other *triumphatores* from Macedonia see p. 177.

11. **levitate:** cf. *Sest.* 119 'levitate me ductum'. The variant *levi cupiditate* would seem to mean 'a slight desire', which would be nonsense here.

122

COMMENTARY [§ 61

13. **lauream conculcarim:** the laurel on the *fasces* of an *imperator* (cf. 53. 12 n., § 74). Piso ought to have laid it on the image of Jupiter in his Capitoline temple (M. B. Ogle, *AJP* xxxi, 1910, 292 n. 1). This was the custom for *imperatores* even if they were not triumphing (Obsequens 61a).

14. **duodecim:** Piso's lictors had made a quick change into civilian clothes (§ 55), and a proconsul had 12 lictors (*St.-R.* i³. 382). *quindecim* could perhaps be defended as a round number including other attendants besides lictors. But the joke is sharper with *duodecim*: though Piso's lictors have disguised themselves as friends who have come to meet him, they betray themselves by their number. Authority favours *quindecim* (the consensus of *VEX* eliminates *ef*); but *xv* and *xii* are easily confused, and an accidental corruption in *ef* might be right. I had conjectured *xii* before I knew the reading of *ef*.

Caelimontanam: Piso proceeded inside the city to the *porta Caelimontana* (55. 15 n.), near where he had obtained a house. It has been supposed that the permanent home of the Pisones stood on the Caelian (Münzer, *RE* Suppl. i. 272), but our passage suggests that a new, and perhaps temporary, house is meant. Piso destroyed a *sacellum* of Diana *in Caeliculo* during his consulship (*har. resp.* 32), but that does not prove that he lived there at that time. There is no reason to see any relevance in a water-pipe from the Caelian with the inscription L. PISO[NIS] (*CIL* xv. 7513).

15. **sitiens:** like an unimportant traveller after a long and tiring journey.

16. **ex hac die:** *dies* is normally feminine when it marks the beginning or end of a space of time, hence often in legal contracts, etc.; cf. E. Fraenkel, *Glotta*, viii, 1917, 24 ff., J. B. Hofmann, *Philol.* xciii, 1938, 265 ff.

17. **campo Martiali:** an open space on the Mons Caelus, perhaps outside the *porta Caelimontana* (Platner and Ashby, *Top. Dict.*, pp. 90, 94). *Martio* is much less appropriate; Piso was on the other side of the city from the Campus Martius.

18. **mi Caesar:** *P*'s *mi*, with its affable tone, is a wittier reading than *VΩ*'s *mihi*. Besides, *mihi* may be a little too emphatic; if it were unemphatic the word-order would be *nummus mihi interea* (frag. iv n.). The corruption of *mi* to *mihi* is common (*Thes. L.L.* viii. 914. 28), and *mihi* occurs immediately above. *mihi* is not essential here; cf. *Verr.* II. i. 51 'cur ea . . . tam diu domi fuerunt?'

ferculis: litters on which were carried the spoils of war, representations of captured cities (cf. § 60), images of the gods, etc. (*RE* vi. 2206, illustrations in D.–S. ii. 1041).

123

§ 61] COMMENTARY

19. **manet et manebit:** for the repetition of a verb in a different tense cf. P. Parzinger, *Beiträge*, i. 27 ff., L.–H., p. 799.

20. **rettuli:** *referre rationes* is the normal expression for handing in accounts to the Treasury. *deferre rationes* is read by the MSS. at *fam.* v. 20. 2. The *lex Julia* (37. 2 n.) required that accounts should be recorded both in Rome and in the province (*St.-R.* i³. 703 f.). Great detail was not expected (A. H. M. Jones, *JRS* xl, 1950, 22); for an excessively brief specimen see *Verr.* II. i. 36. For ancient accounts in general see G. E. M. de Ste Croix in *Studies in the History of Accounting* (ed. A. C. Littleton and B. S. Yamey, London, 1956), pp. 14 ff.

22. **litteras:** 'education'; Piso's accounts were a work of art. *prodesse*, like ὠφελεῖν, was a word used by critics who maintained that literature was of moral benefit (cf. Hor. *a.p.* 333 'aut prodesse volunt aut delectare poetae'); Cicero uses the word satirically of material benefit.

ita enim sunt . . . : 'they are made out with such expertise and literary flair that the secretary at the treasury who entered them, when he had copied out the accounts, scratched his head with his left hand and muttered to himself: "The accounts are quite clear; it's the money that has gone."'

ita goes with *scite et litterate*; for the hyperbaton cf. Löfstedt, *Syntactica*, ii. 398, *Pis.* 17. 8 n.

23. **scriba ad aerarium:** these words probably go together (Francken); cf. *CIL* vi. 1932 'viator ad aerarium', *ILS* 964 'pr. ad aerar.'. One must understand *in tabulas* with *rettulit*. For the important *scribae quaestorii* see *St.-R.* i³. 346 ff., Kornemann, *RE* iiA. 850 f., A. H. M. Jones, *JRS* xxxix, 1949, 41 f., E. Fraenkel, *Horace*, pp. 14 f.

Alternatively one might take *ad aerarium* with *rettulit*. But this gives a less satisfactory rhythm; besides, a *scriba* who was himself at the treasury could hardly be said *referre ad aerarium*. Or one might suppose that the *scriba* was a treasury official seconded to Piso's staff (cf. *St.-R.* i³. 348); then *ad aerarium* could be taken with *rettulit*. But the man's bewilderment is much more natural if he is seeing Piso's accounts for the first time.

perscriptis rationibus: these words are awkward after *perscriptae* (*rationes*). The lacuna in *P* at this point consisted of 9 lines of perhaps 18–21 letters; this passage contains 157 letters in the present text. Therefore it is likely that *perscriptis rationibus* or something of similar length stood also in *P*. Schütz deleted; I have considered *perspectis*, but *sinistra* suits *perscriptis* (see below).

24. **caput . . . perfricans:** out of bewilderment; cf. Lejay on Hor. *serm.* i. 10. 71. *sinistra* is a characteristically vivid touch; the secretary's right hand was holding a pen.

124

COMMENTARY [§§ 61–62]

25. **ratio . . .:** in Plautus's *Trinummus* Lesbonicus has been asking his slave Stasimus how some money has disappeared, and Stasimus has mentioned various extravagances. Lesbonicus then says 'nequaquam argenti ratio comparet tamen', 'it isn't evident how the account adds up'. Stasimus replies 'The account is evident all right, it's the money that has gone'; he is playing on *comparet*, which could mean 'is clear' or 'is visible'. Some editors of Plautus suppose that the second half of the line simply explains the first ('the accounts are quite clear: the money has gone'). But above (l. 414) Stasimus has said 'non tibi illud apparere, si sumas, potest' ('the money can't be in evidence if you use it up'). This suggests that in our line Plautus is drawing a contrast between the *ratio* (which *apparet*) and the money (which *non apparet*).

It is noteworthy that of Cicero's five verbal quotations from Plautus four come from the *Trinummus*; cf. Zillinger, op. cit. [25. 12 n.], p. 97.

26. **οἴχεται:** for this colloquial use cf. *Att.* vi. 1. 1 'quare non οἴχεται tua industria'. For other Greek words in the speeches cf. *Verr.* ii. 50, v. 148, both, like this, special cases. Ω's reading *et doctum te thece* is extraordinary. Presumably *te thece* is a corruption of *oechete*. The humanists emended *et doctum* to *decoctum*, which could be regarded as a gloss on οἴχεται; but this conjecture is more ingenious than convincing. *doctum* can hardly be a gloss on *argutum* (α's reading for *argentum*).

escendentem in currum: 'mounting the triumphal car'. For *escendere (in) currum* cf. Plaut. *merc.* 931, Lucr. v. 1301. A. Klotz reads *ascendere* in such contexts in Cicero (cf. his note on *in sen.* 12); but it is by no means certain that the rarer *escendere* should always be rejected (cf. *Thes. L.L.* v. 2. 856. 63).

§ 62. 1. **tenebrae** alludes to the squalid obscurity of Piso's life. For *lutum* cf. Plaut. *Pers.* 406 'lutum lenonium', etc., Catull. 42. 13 'o lutum, lupanar'.

o paterni . . .: for this sort of invective cf. p. 194.

2. **ita nescio quid . . .:** 'for something broken-down, mean, abject, and squalid about you is too low even to seem worthy of your grandfather, the auctioneer from Milan'.

ita means literally 'in such a way'; for this type of explanatory sentence with asyndeton cf. K.–S. ii. 159, Nägelsbach, p. 760, Hand, iii. 487 f. *nescioquid . . . sordidum* is the subject, *inferius* the predicate. *nescioquid* implies that Cicero cannot fully analyse Piso's distasteful qualities; cf. *Arch.* 15 'illud nescioquid praeclarum'.

4. **L. Crassus:** the greatest Roman orator before Cicero, a man of wide culture and *humanitas*, and as such the leading character

125

§ 62] COMMENTARY

in the *de oratore* (see especially iii. 1–16). He and his colleague Q. Mucius Scaevola (*pontifex*) are described as 'duo consules omnium quos nos vidimus sapientissimi' (*Corn.* i, frag. 21). As consul in 95 he suppressed bandits in Cisalpine Gaul and asked for a triumph; Scaevola in the same year interposed his consular veto (Asc. 13 KS, *inv.* ii. 111, *St.-R.* i³. 282).

5. **specillis**: 'probes'. Crassus prodded the Alps as thoroughly as a doctor using a probe; *prope* marks the metaphor. *specillum* is used literally at *nat. d.* iii. 57; for the metaphor cf. *Att.* xii. 51. 2 τοῦτο δὲ μηλώσῃ ('probe'). For ancient probes see J. S. Milne, *Surgical Instruments in Greek and Roman Times* (Oxford, 1907), pp. 51 ff.

specillis is Madvig's brilliant emendation (ap. Orelli II². ii. 1453). *pecullis* is meaningless, but close to *specillis* (note the preceding *s*). *spiculis* is unsatisfactory. One could say that Crassus searched the Alps with metaphorical spear-points only if real spear-points were used in some kinds of searching or probing operation.

8. **C. Cotta**: cos. 75, procos. Cisalpine Gaul 74; he was awarded a triumph, but died of an old wound before the day (Asc. 13 KS). He and Sulpicius were the leading orators after the deaths of Crassus and Antonius; he is one of the characters in the *de oratore*. His house is the scene of the *de natura deorum*; he maintains the sceptical (Academic) thesis in the third book.

nullo certo hoste: ablative absolute. Guerilla warfare did not justify a triumph (*St.-R.* i³. 133).

9. **peremit**: cf. *Planc.* 90 'quod peremptum esset mea morte id exemplum'. *praeripuit* gives an inferior clausula. *ademit* is possible; A. Klotz objects 'adimuntur honores quos quis habet' (cf. *Planc.* 101), but see *Phil.* xiv. 12 'imperatorium nomen adimemus?' (= 'withhold'). Yet *peremit* has better authority and is the rarer word.

10. **M. Pisonis**: M. Pupius Piso, triumphed from Spain 69, cos. 61, 'iners, somni plenus' (*Att.* i. 14. 6). He was deeply learned in Greek philosophy, and taught Cicero (*Brut.* 236, Asc. 14 KS); he maintains the Peripatetic thesis in book V of the *de finibus*. He was now probably dead (58. 2 n.).

11. **qui ...**: a good instance of Cicero's skill in drawing the wrong conclusion with a plausible air.

13. **tu eruditior . . .**: cf. *Verr.* iii. 43 'tu innocentior quam Metellus?' I suggest that our sentence should be regarded as interrogative.

15. **idiotae**: 'laymen', here of non-philosophers (so § 65, *Sest.* 110); cf. *Verr.* iv. 4 'quos iste idiotas appellat', of those without knowledge about art. For Greek words in Cicero cf. P. Oksala, *Die*

126

COMMENTARY [§§ 62–64

griechischen Lehnwörter in den Prosaschriften Ciceros (Helsinki, 1953).

§ 63. 20. **Themista:** a female pupil of Epicurus with whom he exchanged letters (Diog. Laert. x. 5); cf. *fin.* ii. 68 'nonne melius est de his aliquid quam tantis voluminibus de Themista loqui ?' It is a probable, though not a necessary, inference that some of these writings dealt with glory. The Epicureans were criticized for admitting women to their school; cf. *nat. d.* i. 93, A.-J. Festugière, *Épicure et ses dieux*, p. 40 (English edition p. 29), N. W. DeWitt, *Epicurus and his Philosophy*, pp. 95 f.

21. **ferreum:** 'brazen'; cf. L. Crassus frag. 37 (Malcovati, *ORF²*) 'cui os ferreum, cor plumbeum esset', Catull. 42. 16 f. 'ruborem | ferreo canis exprimamus ore'.

§§ **63–67:** '*Piso's present life is also inferior to Cicero's [here the long comparison between Cicero and Piso ends]. If Piso goes to Pompey's games he will see how much he is despised. To be sure, he may go to the banquet associated with the games—for the sake of the food: for he is a pleasure-loving Epicurean. But there is nothing elegant about his pleasures, as is clear from the dinners he gives.*'

§ 64. 2. **adsidua:** perhaps 'settled in one place' (i.e. Rome); cf. *Caecin.* 63 'adsiduis ac domesticis', H. Nettleship, *Contributions to Latin Lexicography*, p. 320. One might wish to interpret the word as 'constant', as *cotidianus* and *adsiduus* are combined elsewhere (*Sest.* 24); but it is not clear that *adsidua* in this sense would suit *vita*. Baiter deleted *adsidua*; I should rather omit *cotidiana*.

3. **splendorem:** cf. Ps. Sall. *in Cic.* 2 'splendor domesticus tibi animos tollit'. *celebritatem*: throngs of clients and visitors; cf. Marquardt, *Privatleben²*, pp. 228, 259. *operam forensem*: activity in the courts; cf. *div.* ii. 142 'intermissionem forensis operae', Hor. *epist.* i. 7. 8 'opella forensis'.

5. **cuiquam:** cf. *Caecil.* 59 'quid habes quod possis dicere quam ob rem non modo mihi sed cuiquam anteponare?'

6. **despicatissimo** (*var. Junt.*, cf. 1. 22 n.); for the superlative cf. *Verr.* iii. 98 (where *despectissimi* is a variant), *Sest.* 36. The MSS., including *PV*, read *desperatissimo* ('irredeemable'), but this word does not suit *infimo* or the context in general. *despectissimo*, a fifteenth-century emendation, is also possible, though the *Thesaurus* quotes no instance of this superlative before Tacitus.

8. **sed omnino:** 'but actually'; cf. Hand, iv. 377.

9. **videre:** 'look at'. *non possunt* = 'cannot endure to'; cf. *dom.* 65 'quos videre improbi non poterant'. *V* has *nolunt non possunt*, and hence A. Klotz reads *nolunt* (cf. *Sest.* 111 'te nemo

127

§§ 64–65] COMMENTARY

tuorum videre vult', *Verr.* iii. 23, *fam.* x. 31. 2); but *nolunt* is more
likely to be a gloss than *non possunt*.

10. **L. Aelius:** L. Aelius Lamia led the agitation of the *equites* on
Cicero's behalf in 58; as a result he was banished by Gabinius
(introd., p. x). For Cicero's friendship with him see *fam.* xi. 16. 2,
xii. 29. He was probably the father of Horace's friend Lamia
(*carm.* i. 26, iii. 17).

13. **decreta:** at the time of Cicero's exile; cf. *Sest.* 32.

§ 65. 14. **fac . . . :** 'test by experiment this . . . hatred'.

16. **ludi:** given by Pompey in 55 at the dedication of his theatre
(Asc. 1 KS, 14 KS, *fam.* vii. 1. 2–3, Dio xxxix. 38, Drumann–
Groebe, iv. 529 f.); for the date cf. p. 199. In private Cicero was less
enthusiastic about these games; cf. *fam.* vii. 1. 2 'ludi apparatissimi,
sed non tui stomachi; coniecturam enim facio de meo'. When an
important personage arrived at a spectacle of this kind the reaction
of the crowd was thought significant (*Sest.* 115–27, *Att.* i. 16. 11,
ii. 19. 3, F. F. Abbott, *TAPA* xxxviii, 1907, 49 ff.).

18. **da te populo:** 'hand yourself over to the people's verdict';
cf. *Sest.* 124 'se populo dedit'. For *committere se* (with similar
meaning) cf. *dom.* 49, *Sest.* 116, *Mil.* 61. Ernesti proposed *committe te*, but when one reflexive verb follows another the pronoun
need not be repeated; cf. *Q.f.* i. 3. 5 'erige te et confirma'.

19. **ubi sunt . . . ?:** 'have you forgotten your Epicurean lectures?'
For *scholae* cf. 60. 2 n. *vestrae* means 'of you and your fellow-
Epicureans'. For Epicurus's contempt for the crowd see Vat. frag.
29, 67 (C. Bailey, *Epicurus*, pp. 110, 116).

ne . . . times ?: in Cicero *adclamare* normally refers to hostile
shouting (for a possible exception cf. *inv.* i. 25). Perhaps one
should omit *times* with Ω (*P* is not available), and understand
metuis from above. In that case one could read below *adferantur
times*, which has the strong support of *P*Ω. Yet here *V*'s *ne
adclametur times* seems a little more natural.

ne id . . . : 'it is the part of a philosopher not to care about that
either'. *ne . . . quidem*, like οὐδέ, can mean 'not either' as well as
'not even'; that is to say, it need not introduce a climax.

21. **dolor:** to the Epicureans pain (λύπη, *dolor*) was the greatest
evil, just as pleasure (ἡδονή, *voluptas*) was the greatest good (cf.
42. 10 n.).

dedecus: Rinkes proposed *decus*; this would make a pair
with *existimatio*, which usually refers to good reputation. But
Cicero may be progressing from *existimatio* (which is sometimes
neutral in sense, cf. *Verr.* iv. 45) to a climax in *turpitudo*.

22. **verba:** 'mere words', 'just talk'. See *fin.* ii. 48 'si ad honestatem omnia referant neque in ea voluptatem dicant inesse,

128

COMMENTARY [§§ 65-66

(Epicurus) ait eos voce inani sonare; his enim ipsis verbis utitur', Epicur. frags. 69, 511 Usener, Hor. *epist.* i. 6. 31 'virtutem verba putas', Dio xlvii. 49. 2 (Brutus's last words, quoting a lost play) ὦ τλῆμον ἀρετή, λόγος ἄρ' ἦσθ', ἐγὼ δέ σε | ὡς ἔργον ἤσκουν.

23. **convivium publicum:** a state banquet for senators, held in conjunction with games, triumphs, etc.; cf. Suet. *Aug.* 35. 2 'servavit publice epulandi ius' (for senators), *ILS* 6085. 139 (*tab. Heracl.*) 'neve convivium publicum is inito' (of persons not eligible to be members of municipal *curiae*), Marquardt, *St.-V.* iii². 350.

non dignitatis causa: 'not for the sake of prestige'.

24. **patribus conscriptis:** Cicero comments ironically 'unless of course in order to dine with the senators'. The senators would attend a *convivium publicum* (see l. 23 n.), and dining with them would normally bring a man prestige. But Piso could have no such motive, since they would show their distaste for him (cf. § 64 *senatus odit te*).

Naugerius proposed *P. Clodio*, which has been widely accepted. The thought would then be: 'unless he thinks it will bring him prestige to dine with Clodius (the only senator who will talk to him)'. But one cannot believe that *P. Clodio* was abbreviated to *P.C.* in the ancient world; and an accidental corruption of this kind does not seem very likely.

1. **amatoribus:** if this reading is right it means 'supporters', and is ironic; for *amator = fautor* cf. *Att.* i. 14. 6, etc. It is unusual to find *hoc est* followed by an ironic remark; but the oddity is justifiable here, where the irony of the clause has been signalled by *nisi forte*.

maioribus could only mean 'ancestors', which would be absurd; it could not mean 'superiors' here. The emendation *amoribus* is necessary if one reads *P. Clodio* above; otherwise it has no merit. One might wish to delete *hoc est . . . suis* as a gloss; but an explanatory clause is natural here, and deletion would spoil the clausula.

sed . . . causa: 'but simply to gratify his taste for pleasure'; for *animi* cf. *Thes. L.L.* ii. 96. 80.

2. **idiotis:** cf. 62. 15 n.

§ **66.** 3. **abdominis voluptates:** cf. Epicurus, frag. 409 Usener ἀρχὴ καὶ ῥίζα παντὸς ἀγαθοῦ ἡ τῆς γαστρὸς ἡδονή (for parallels see Usener, loc. cit., and Pease on *nat. d.* i. 113). Epicurus meant that the ἀπονία of the stomach was a prerequisite to the ἀταραξία of the mind; his critics, ignoring his praises of frugality (*epist. ad Men.* 130–2), accused him of making the pleasure of the stomach the main object of life (C. Bailey, *Epicurus*, p. 397).

4. **nam quod . . . videatur:** 'in case he seems to you . . .'. This potential subjunctive is commoner in early than in classical Latin;

5993 L 129

§ 66]   COMMENTARY

but cf. *Verr.* ii. 15 'quod . . . audierit', v. 175 'quod . . . cogites',
K.–S. ii. 277 f., S. A. Handford, *Latin Subjunctive*, p. 114, C. F. W.
Müller, *Rh. Mus.* xx, 1865, 479 n. 1.

   5. **olim:** before he obtained a province.

   quod sordidus . . .: the other adjectives in the sentence
seem to break up into pairs of synonyms (*contumax superbus, fallax
perfidiosus, impudens audax*, not to mention the pairs at the beginning and end). This pattern is unlikely to be accidental; if it is
deliberate it must be sustained throughout the sentence. I therefore suggest that something may have fallen out before or after
quod sordidus, for instance *quod contemptus*.

   8. **posterius:** 'morally worse'; cf. *Sex. Rosc.* 137 'homines
postremi' with Landgraf's note, Löfstedt, *Syntactica*, ii. 204 f. Add
perhaps *prov. cons.* 8 (also of Piso) 'cuius ut provinciam tetigit sic
fortuna cum improbitate certavit, ut nemo posset utrum posterior
an infelicior esset iudicare'; there recent editors accept the emendation *protervior*, which does not correspond well with the more
general *improbitate*. For the combination of *posterius* and *nequius*
cf. the striking parallel in C. Gracchus frag. 27 (Malcovati, *ORF²*)
'si ulla meretrix domum meam introivit . . . omnium nationum
postremissimum nequissimumque existimatote'. In the present
passage *posterius* is wider in meaning than one might wish (Cicero
is emphasizing that Piso was a voluptuary), but it may take its tone
from *nequius* (which refers to *luxus vitae prodigus*, cf. Gell. vi.
11. 7).

   The reading *protervius* deserves very serious consideration, but
it does not seem to combine so well as *posterius* with the more
general word *nequius*. In this context it would naturally be taken
as a synonym for *libidinosius*; this perhaps diverts the reader too
much from the central theme of gluttony.

   9. **luxuriem:** Cicero goes off on a fresh tack; though Piso thinks
too much of the pleasures of the table, he does not have the good
taste which partly excuses such self-indulgence. The theme was
topical in 55 B.C., when Pompey and Crassus introduced a sump-
tuary law which was resisted by Hortensius (Dio xxxix. 37. 2–3).
For the contrast between the gross and elegant kinds of *luxuries*
cf. *fin.* ii. 23.

   hanc: 'of the following sort'; for *enim* after such a *hic* see
K.–S. ii. 122, Hand, ii. 379. Yet the position of *hanc* here seems
a little unusual. Besides, after so short a sentence one hardly looks
for a fresh start; one might sooner have expected *nolite in isto eam
cogitare quae . . . .* Faernus suspected that something has fallen out
after *hanc*; in that case *hanc* would mean 'which we see around us'.
But proposed supplements are unsatisfactory. *solitam* (Orelli) and

130

COMMENTARY [§§ 66–67]

vulgarem (R. Klotz) cohere badly with *quaedam*, which does not suggest that this better sort of *luxuries* was particularly common. *lautam* (Orelli) and *nobilium hominum* (A. Klotz) are too complimentary in view of *vitiosa atque turpis* below. R. Sydow suggested *concessam* (*Philol.* xcii, 1937, 234), but this does not specify the kind of *luxuries* clearly enough.

Though *P* breaks off after *nolite* one can be fairly certain that its reading here agreed with that of the later MSS. Ströbel was able to distinguish the top of *-tare est* (*Festschrift* [supra, p. xxi], p. 28); these letters therefore belonged to the first line after the tear. But *P* had only about 18–21 letters to the line; therefore it can have contained nothing between *hanc* and *cogitare*.

§ 67. 10. **quaedam:** *V* reads *quaedam quae*, which would necessitate reading *est tamen* below with Clark; but *quae* may simply be a dittography before *quamquam*.

quamquam . . .: 'though every sort is . . .'; cf. *Phil.* x. 19 'omnis est misera servitus; sed fuerit quaedam necessaria'. This is more pointed than taking *omnis* to mean 'entirely'.

11. **ingenuo . . . dignior:** 'more worthy of a free-born man and a free man' (i.e. anybody who is not a slave). This is faint praise; cf. § 22 'agentem aliquid quod esset libero dignum', § 75, *amic.* 89 'adsentatio . . . quae non modo amico, sed ne libero quidem digna est'.

12. **laudabo inimicum . . .:** 'to do him justice, nothing even very expensive—except his lusts'. *laudabo inimicum* points to what follows: Cicero pretends to concede something to Piso, but the concession simply leads to the gibe *praeter libidines*. After *inimicum V* adds *cui*, which is probably a dittography of *-cum*. Halm emended to *quin* (introducing a climax). But then *laudabo inimicum* could only refer to what precedes; and this is impossible as *nihil . . . exquisitum* is not a compliment. *magno opere* is to be taken closely with *exquisitum*; for the hyperbaton see 17. 8 n.

13. **toreuma nullum . . .:** for ἐνάργεια or realistic description see Volkmann, p. 442; for the clipped sentences see 28. 9 n. Cicero says below (§ 70) that he knows about Piso's dinners from the epigrams of Philodemus; and it looks as if this passage is a satiric adaptation of one of these epigrams. This poem seems to have described a dinner at Piso's house in honour of Epicurus; compare *anth. Pal.* xi. 44 (quoted p. 184), which describes a similar dinner at Philodemus's house. Such celebrations took place every year on Epicurus's birthday, and also on the εἰκάδες or twentieth day of each month (Diog. Laert. x. 18, A.-J. Festugière, *Épicure et ses dieux*, pp. 31 ff. (English edition, pp. 22 f.), N. W. DeWitt, *Epicurus and his Philosophy*, pp. 104 f.). Cicero portrays the

131

§ 67] COMMENTARY

simplicity of the occasion as squalor; yet Catullus talks of Piso's *convivia lauta* (p. 180). Piso no doubt tried to combine Epicurean geniality with senatorial dignity; Cicero represents the one as a taste for low company, the other as stand-offishness (*ipse solus*).

toreuma: an embossed cup or other piece of plate, particularly of silver; cf. G. Lippold, *RE* viA. 1750 ff., Marquardt, *Privatleben²*, pp. 696 ff.

14. **et hi:** 'and what is more'. *et ei* would have been more normal, and on such a point the evidence of MSS. is quite unreliable. Yet one cannot rule out *et hi*; cf. *Thes. L.L.* v. 2. 875. 22, vi. 2725. 5.

ne contemnere . . .: 'to show his regard for his countrymen, made in Placentia' (and evidently of an inferior type). Piso's maternal grandfather came from Placentia (frag. ix n.).

15. **conchyliis:** Macrob. *sat.* iii. 13. 12 preserves the astonishing menu of a late Republican *cena pontificum*; it contains many kinds of fish and shellfish. See further Marquardt, *Privatleben²*, pp. 432 ff., H. Blümner, *Privataltertümer*, pp. 180 ff.

17. **senes:** instead of *formosi pueri* (*fin.* ii. 23); see Mayor on Juv. 5. 56.

idem coquus . . .: 'the same man is both cook and steward'.

pistor: wealthy Roman houses baked their own bread; cf. H. J. Loane, *Industry and Commerce of City of Rome* (Baltimore, 1938), pp. 67 f. It was a matter of pride in the ancient world to provide one's own supplies; cf. Fraenkel on Aesch. *Ag.* 961.

18. **panis . . .:** 'bread from the retailer, wine from the barrel'. For the word-order cf. *Verr.* II. i. 6 'multa enim et in deos et in homines impie nefarieque commisit', II. i. 33, *de or.* iii. 12, *Mil.* 28, 68, *Tusc.* i. 2 and Dougan, Tac. *ann.* i. 69. 1 and Nipperdey, Plin. *paneg.* 40. 4, 44. 7, Apul. *apol.* 24.

cupa: a large barrel made of wood (Keune, *RE* Suppl. iii. 345, illustrations in D.–S. s.v.). Instead of maturing choice vintages in his own cellar, Piso bought inferior wine in bulk.

Scaliger took *cupa* here as another spelling of *copa* (the hostess of an inn); the spelling *cupa* is found in the MSS. of Charisius, *GL* i. 63. But *de cupa* could only mean 'from the barrel'; cf. Aug. *quaest. hept.* iv. 32 'de dolio, de cupa'. Emendation to *copa* would be easy, but *de* would be strange, especially after *a propola*. *cupa* corresponds to *cella* (both things) as *propola* to *pistor* (both people).

19. **Graeci:** Piso's Epicurean friends. For the importance attached by the Epicureans to friendship cf. *fin.* i. 65, A.-J. Festugière, *Épicure et ses dieux*, pp. 36 ff. (pp. 27 ff. in English edition).

quini: normally there were no more than three diners on one couch, but compare Hor. *serm.* i. 4. 86 'saepe tribus lectis videas cenare quaternos'. There were at least 14 people at Trimalchio's

132

COMMENTARY [§§ 67–68]

triclinium (Friedländer on Petronius, *cena* 31); see also Marquardt, *Privatleben*², p. 305 n. 2.

lectulis: the diminutive suits the humour of the passage (so *Mur.* 75), is the *difficilior lectio*, and gives a better clausula.

20. **solio:** the meaning 'tub' yields no satisfactory sense. Editors generally read *dolio*; this was a large earthenware vessel containing new, and hence inferior, wine (*Brut.* 288, H. Blümner, *Privatalter-tümer*, p. 148). Cicero might (*a*) be emphasizing the large quantity drunk: perhaps the guests were finally served straight from the *dolium* without the use of mixing-bowl or *cyathus*. Or (*b*) he might be suggesting that as the evening wore on the quality of the wine grew worse; see St. John's Gospel ii. 10 πᾶς ἄνθρωπος πρῶτον τὸν καλὸν οἶνον τίθησι, καὶ ὅταν μεθυσθῶσι τὸν ἐλάσσω (cf. H. Windisch, *Zeitschrift f. d. neutest. Wissenschaft*, xiv, 1913, 248 ff.).

Yet this reading causes doubt. Cicero has just said that Piso's wine came from the *cupa*; and there is no evidence that wine *de dolio* was worse than wine *de cupa*. But on interpretation (*a*) there is no inconsistency: the wine could be delivered to the house in wooden *cupae* and stored thereafter in *dolia*. Secondly, the subjunctive *ministretur*, with its suggestion of purpose, creates difficulties; it would only be convincing if drinking *de dolio* had been a predictable stage in a long symposium.

Some scholars have tried to introduce a reference to 'scraping the bottom of the barrel'; but *de dolio imo* (Baden) and *de solido* (Jeep) are extremely implausible. At one time I considered *dum soli ministretur* (i.e. Piso aims to out-drink the Greeks); but it must be admitted that *de* goes convincingly with *ministretur*.

galli: Cicero is punning on *gallus* 'a cock' and *Gallus* 'a Gaul', with reference to the supposed origin of Piso's grandfather (frag. ix n.). For the same pun cf. Varro, *Menipp.* 379 'ille ales gallus qui suscitabat Atticarum Musarum scriptores an hic' (L. Plotius Gallus) 'qui gregem rabularum', Suet. *Ner.* 45. 2 'ascriptum et columnis iam Gallos eum cantando excitasse', *Thes. L.L.* vi. 1687. 61. For Cicero's puns cf. H. Holst, op. cit. [frag. viii n.].

cantum: Cicero seems to see a resemblance between the crowing of a cock and the proclamation of an auctioneer (the alleged trade of Piso's grandfather).

21. **mensam tolli:** at the end of a Roman dinner the table was removed.

§§ **68–72.** *Cicero explains that he knows all about life in Piso's house from the epigrams of the Greek philosopher and poet Philodemus: there follows a witty travesty of their relationship.*

§ **68.** 22. **dicet aliquis:** for formulae of *occupatio* (anticipated

133

§ 68] COMMENTARY

objection) cf. Seyffert, *Scholae Latinae*, i. 140 ff. For the use of the figure in similar contexts cf. Catull. 67. 37 'dixerit hic aliquis: quid? tu istaec, ianua, nosti . . . ?' Sen. *apocol.* 1 'si quis quaesiverit unde sciam . . .'.

me hercules: Cicero himself says 'libentius dixerim . . . mehercule quam mehercules' (*orat.* 157). *mehercules* is found six times in the MSS. of the speeches (four times 69 B.C. or earlier); *mehercule* is much more common. See Hofmann, *Umgangssprache*, p. 29, A. Gagnér, *De hercle mehercle* (Greifswald, 1920), pp. 30 ff.

23. **contumeliae causa:** cf. *Verr.* I. 18 'quem ego hominem honoris potius quam contumeliae causa nominatum volo', *Phil.* ii. 113 'quam ego sine contumelia describo'. As often, *describere* means 'to depict unfavourably'.

24. **ne . . . possum:** for *ne quidem* surrounding two words cf. K.–S. ii. 55. For the mood of *possum* cf. Lebreton, p. 358.

1. **Graecus:** Asconius explains that this was Philodemus. See Appendix III.

cum isto vivit: this may only imply close association; one need not assume that Philodemus lived in Piso's house. See *fam.* xiii. 24. 2 'Lyso vero cum mecum prope cotidie esset unaque viveret', *Brut.* 309 'qui cum habitavisset apud me mecumque vixisset', *acad.* ii. 115 'Diodoto . . . qui mecum vivit tot annos, qui habitat apud me' (cf. Reid's note). Philodemus had a house of his own (p. 184).

2. **vere ut dicam:** for the word-order cf. K.–S. ii. 615, J. Marouzeau, *L'Ordre des mots*, iii (Paris, 1949), 121 ff.

humanus: Philodemus is a civilized and cultivated man—except when he is with Piso.

4. **iam tum:** *iam tum cum* is possible, but unnecessary; cf. *dom.* 99 'et senatum et omnis bonos . . . mutata veste vidi'. Pluygers proposed *iam cum*, but *tum* is necessary.

distracta fronte: this expression does not seem to occur elsewhere; it presumably means the opposite of *contracta fronte*, and refers to Piso's raised eyebrows (cf. 14. 17). At *Sest.* 19 Cicero describes Piso's *contractio frontis*; but he may have been in the habit both of frowning and raising his eyebrows. *dis irata fronte* is unconvincing. Sometimes *iratus* is used to describe the attitude of the gods to men (§ 59); hence some suppose that Cicero is joking at the anti-religious views of the Epicureans, and that he paradoxically describes Piso as 'angry at the gods' (cf. Ov. *met.* xiii. 186 'divisque irascitur ipsis', Sen. *contr.* exc. viii. 1 'irata, inquit, dis, sacrilegium potuit committere', Sen. *de ira* iii. 31. 1 'dis quoque irascimur'). But *dis irata* is clumsy when combined with *fronte*. Besides, Cicero is making excuses for Philodemus, who was

134

COMMENTARY [§§ 68–69]

deceived by Piso's false air of gravity (§ 70); it would be quite another thing to say that he was attracted by Piso's *dis irata fronte*.

5. praesertim: to be taken with *cum*; for the word-order cf. *Verr.* iii. 68, *Caecin.* 15, *Balb.* 60, *Phil.* i. 27, *fin.* ii. 22.

8. eruditissimorum: for similar compliments to the audience cf. *Mur.* 61 'et quoniam non est nobis haec oratio habenda aut in imperita multitudine aut in aliquo conventu agrestium'. The insincerity of such remarks is shown by *fin.* iv. 74 (referring to the *pro Murena*) 'apud imperitos tum illa dicta sunt'. In the following passage Cicero pretends not to know too much about philosophy (69. 21 *ut opinor*, 70. 26 *dicunt*, 71. 19 *ut fertur*). For similar εἰρωνεία about Greek art and history see Thomas on *Verr.* iv. 4, Holden on *Sest.* 48; for pretended ignorance of pontifical law see *dom.* 39, 121.

10. voluptate metiri: cf. Dem. xviii. 296 τῇ γαστρὶ μετροῦντες καὶ τοῖς αἰσχίστοις τὴν εὐδαιμονίαν, Pease on *nat. d.* i. 113.

rectene an secus: cf. *off.* iii. 11 'rectene . . . an secus', *inv.* ii. 70 'rectene an contra', *de or.* iii. 66 'vere an secus nihil ad hoc tempus', Plin. *epist.* vii. 17. 12 'recte an secus nihil ad me'.

11. sed tamen: resumptive after a digression; cf. K.–S. ii. 76.

13. et: this emendation makes *lubricum* and *praeceps* co-ordinate as at *Flacc.* 105, *rep.* i. 44, *Phil.* v. 50. The omission of *est* is natural in an expression of opinion of this kind, and harmonizes with the abbreviated style of the previous sentence.

§ 69. 13. admissarius iste: 'that stallion', i.e. Piso; cf. Plaut. *Mil.* 1112 'ad equas fuisti scitus admissarius'.

14. nihil expiscatus est: Piso made no investigations into Epicurus's real meaning. *expiscari* is colloquial; cf. Ter. *Phorm.* 382, *Att.* ii. 17. 3, *fam.* ix. 19. 1. One might object to the incongruity of *expiscatus* between the two horse metaphors *admissarius* and *adhinnivit* (cf. Madvig, *Adv. crit.* ii. 228), but the derivation from *piscis* need not have been keenly felt; for mixed metaphor cf. *prov. cons.* 31 *redundare . . . recisas*, *de or.* ii. 162. Müller suggested *aliud nihil*, unnecessarily.

15. suos . . . illius: there is a slight contrast between these words, which are both emphatic.

17. arbitraretur: Francken proposed *arbitrari videretur*: the consequence of Piso's 'neighing' was not his opinions but a belief about his opinions. But the reading of the MSS. is unobjectionable; for the brachylogy Müller compares § 82 'qui te ita gesseris ut timeres', *leg. agr.* ii. 53 'is enim sic se gerit ut sibi iam decemvir designatus esse videatur'.

Graecus . . . : 'the Greek (Philodemus) at first drew distinctions and split hairs about the meaning of those doctrines. Piso,

135

§ 69] COMMENTARY

like the proverbial lame man with the ball, hung on to what he had received, solemnly swore it was true, was ready to sign a deposition on the subject, pronounced magisterially that Epicurus was a clever fellow. Yet after all Epicurus says (I am given to understand) that he can conceive of no good when the pleasures of the body have been taken away.'

18. **distinguere et dividere:** the so-called 'historic' infinitive gives a rapid and vivid effect, like the use of nouns without verbs. See E. Wölfflin, *ALL* x. 177 ff., P. Perrochat, *L'Infinitive de narration en latin* (Paris, 1932) and *REL* x, 1932, 187 ff., L.–H., p. 591. The construction is rare in Cicero's speeches.

dividere is used, as often, of logical distinctions. No doubt Philodemus pointed out that the 'pleasure' of Epicurus was not to be understood in too limited a sense; but Piso failed to understand such subtleties. Cf. *Sest.* 23 '(Piso) eos (philosophos) laudabat maxime qui dicuntur praeter ceteros esse auctores et laudatores voluptatis: cuius et quo tempore et quo modo non quaerebat.' For such misapprehensions about Epicureanism cf. *in sen.* 14 (also on Piso), Sen. *dial.* vii. 12. 4.

illa: the subject of *dicerentur*, not the object of *dividere* (*dividere illa* would give a hexameter-ending in the clausula).

19. **claudus ... pilam:** the lame man cannot manœuvre the ball, but can only 'hang on to it'. The game described seems to have contained an element of running; for such games cf. K. Schneider, *RE* vii. 2405 ff., E. N. Gardiner, *Athletics in the Ancient World* (Oxford, 1930), pp. 230 ff. For *accipere* of catching a ball cf. Mart. xii. 82. 4. Some old editors understood *pilam*, 'a pillar'; but this interpretation does not suit *quod acceperat*, and gives an inferior clausula.

iste is the subject and *retinere* the verb; *claudus ... pilam* is a parenthesis, with *claudus* in apposition to *iste*, and *pilam* corresponding to *quod acceperat*. For this way of quoting proverbs cf. *de or.* ii. 233 'docebo, sus ut aiunt, oratorem eum ...', *fam.* ix. 3. 2; see also the interesting article by P. Shorey, *CP* iv, 1909, 433 ff. Modern editors take *iste ... pilam* as a self-contained sentence, but it would be strange to have the proverb attached to a single word like *iste*. Some older editors ended the sentence at *retinere*; but this leaves *quod acceperat* unintelligible, and *pilam retinere* gives a poor clausula.

quem ad modum is not normally used in quoting proverbs; *Verr.* v. 53 is an unsatisfactory parallel ('et ut hoc beneficium quem ad modum dicitur trabali clavo figeret'). In our passage with its clipped style the expression is clumsy, particularly as it occurs above. In quoting proverbs Latin authors usually say *ut aiunt*

136

COMMENTARY [§ 69]

(common in Cicero), or *quod aiunt* (*de sen.* 21); I have considered reading the latter here. Alternatively one might read *claudus aiunt pilam* (which is found in some *recentiores*, e.g. the Bodleian MS. Laud lat. 48). For this usage, which does not occur elsewhere in Cicero, cf. φασί in Greek proverbs, Ter. *Andr.* 805 'ut quimus, aiunt, quando ut volumus non licet', *Phorm.* 419, Hor. *serm.* ii. 2. 64 'hac urget lupus, hac canis, aiunt'.

20. **testificari:** Piso spoke solemnly and with conviction, as if giving evidence in a court of law; cf. *fin.* ii. 51 'ut nos intuens quasi testificarere laudari honestatem et iustitiam aliquando ab Epicuro'.

tabellas obsignare: Piso subscribed to Epicureanism as if he were witnessing a legal document; cf. *Tusc.* v. 33 'tu quidem tabellis obsignatis agis mecum et testificaris quid dixerim aliquando aut scripserim', Sen. *cont.* ix. 5. 11 'tantum non tabellis signatis denuntiare'. The seals of *obsignatores* were superimposed on a thread which went round the *tabulae ceratae*; see D.–S. iv. 1329, Bruns, *Fontes*[7], i. 274 f., 423, *CIL* iv, Supp. 1, pp. 277 f.

disertum decernere: *disertum* means 'a clever fellow'; cf. Ter. *eun.* 1011 'at etiam primo callidum et disertum credidi hominem'. *decernere* ('pronounced') refers to Piso's dogmatic assertions; for *decretum* of a philosopher's dogma cf. *acad.* ii. 27 'de suis decretis quae philosophi vocant δόγματα' with Reid's note, *Thes. L.L.* v. 1. 155. 64. For the double accusative cf. Ter. *hec.* 212 'qui illum decrerunt dignum suos quoi liberos committerent', *Thes. L.L.* v. 1. 141. 17. *disertum dicere* would also be a possible reading; but *decernere* gives more point and a better clausula. Besides, if *dicere* were read here, *dicit* in the next sentence, which has a different subject, would be confusing.

Francken proposed *diserte id dicere* as an accusative and infinitive after *tabellas obsignare*. But *diserte* (α) is eliminated by the consensus of *V* and *X*, and the infinitive would be misleading after the historic infinitives. Madvig (on *fin.* ii. 7) proposed *desertum dicere*; he explained 'desertum Epicurum clamabat ab iis qui dogma de corporis voluptate non tenerent'. But it would be impossible to understand all this from the context; in any case it was not for the stupid Piso to say whether Epicurus was rightly understood or not. Clark proposed *diserte dicere existimare* (continuing *dicit autem opinor*). But the collocation of *dicere* and *existimare* is unattractive, *existimare* is intolerably flat, and the proposal involves far too much change.

21. **et tamen:** this reading has strong support; the only variant is *V*'s meaningless *est tamen*. Cicero is adding a malicious afterthought; Epicurus may have been *disertus*, but the fact remains that his doctrines were outrageous. A. Klotz proposed *is tamen*,

137

§§ 69–70]   COMMENTARY

and indeed one might expect a pronoun to mark the subject as Epicurus; but there is no real ambiguity (cf. Seyffert–Müller, *Laelius*, p. 246 for abrupt changes of subject). Müller proposed *is autem*, 'now Epicurus . . .'; this is idiomatic, but too great a change. Below *dicit ut opinor* is supported by the clausula, and is surely right.

se nullum bonum . . .: cf. Epicurus, frag. 67 Usener οὐ γὰρ ἔγωγε ἔχω τί νοήσω τἀγαθόν, ἀφαιρῶν μὲν τὰς διὰ χυλῶν ἡδονάς, ἀφαιρῶν δὲ τὰς δι' ἀφροδισίων, ἀφαιρῶν δὲ τὰς δι' ἀκροαμάτων, ἀφαιρῶν δὲ καὶ τὰς διὰ μορφῆς κατ' ὄψιν ἡδείας κινήσεις. Cicero often refers to this passage; see *nat. d.* i. 111 with Pease's note, *fin.* ii. 7 with Reid's note, and especially *Tusc.* iii. 41, which gives a longer and fairer version than the surviving Greek quotation. For an account of Epicurean hedonism see N. W. DeWitt, *Epicurus and his Philosophy*, pp. 216 ff.

§ 70. 23. venustus refers to charm and grace, and is a dubious compliment when applied to a man; cf. *off.* i. 130 'venustatem muliebrem ducere debemus'.

senatorem: the variant *imperatorem* is untenable; Piso did not become an *imperator* till his proconsulship (§ 38). C. Cichorius, *Römische Studien*, p. 295, actually assigns Piso's meeting with Philodemus to his proconsulship; but this is contradicted by *adulescentem* (§ 68).

25. fere ceteros: Orelli deleted *ceteros*, but the repetition *ceteris . . . ceteros* is unobjectionable. *fere ceteri* is found at *Verr.* iv. 86, *fin.* v. 9; cf. *Thes. L.L.* vi. 495. 58.

26. neglegere: cf. Epicurus ap. Diog. Laert. x. 120 μόνον τε τὸν σοφὸν ὀρθῶς ἂν περί τε μουσικῆς καὶ ποιητικῆς διαλέξασθαι· ποιήματά τε ἐνεργείᾳ οὐκ ἂν ποιῆσαι. Epicurus rejected the arts, as not contributing to happiness; cf. frag. 163 Usener παιδείαν δὲ πᾶσαν, μακάριε, φεῦγε τἀκάτιον ἀράμενος, Pease on *nat. d.* i. 72, Reid on *fin.* i. 26, i. 72. Yet some of this may be regarded as a criticism of the narrow educational curriculum of his day (N. W. DeWitt, op. cit., pp. 12 ff., 44, 106 ff.). Epicurus and most of his followers neglected ornaments of style, and regarded clarity as enough (Pease on *nat. d.* i. 58).

poema: not 'a poem' but 'poetry'; so *leg.* i. 5, *orat.* 67, *de opt. gen.* 1, *acad.* i. 9.

1. festivum: 'charming'.

nihil ut: this word-order is idiomatic (68. 2 n.).

2. argutius: 'cleverer'.

3. modo leviter: 'only not too seriously'.

4. impurum: it seems best to follow *V*'s word-order. *impurum* is the strongest of the three adjectives, and makes a witty contrast

138

COMMENTARY [§§ 70-71

with *poetam*, especially in view of what Cicero goes on to say about Philodemus's poetry.

9. **ad istum de isto:** for the polyptoton cf. *Phil*. ii. 6 'et de te et a te latas', *fam*. ix. 8. 2 'de nobis inter nos', *de amic*. 80 'per se et propter se'. Ernesti's emendation *de ipso* seems unnecessary. After *isto* V adds *quoque*; this is perhaps right, as *de isto* adds an emphatic new point. Yet *-o quoque scripsit* gives a hexameter-ending in the clausula. (An open short syllable at the end of a word before *sc-* etc. remains short in prose. See *Verr*. iv. 35 'ede mihi scriptum', *Sull*. 42 'celeritate scribendi', *Pis*. 28 'ipse sceleratus', *Phil*. ii. 44 'vulgare scortum'; cf. Gell. i. 7. 19.)

10. **hominis:** omitted by *V*, but idiomatic, and almost required by the sense (*eius* comes very late). *hominis* could easily have fallen out after *omnis*; the two words are often confused.

conviviorumque in this position gives an idiomatic word-order and a good clausula.

11. **delicatissimis** hints at impropriety; cf. Catull. 50. 3 'ut convenerat esse delicatos'. Yet see Plin. *epist*. v. 3. 5 for a list of distinguished Romans who wrote *versiculi parum severi*: it begins with M. Tullius himself.

§ 71. 12. **tamquam in speculo:** i.e. reproduced with clarity and accuracy. See Fraenkel on Aesch. *Ag*. 838 ff., who quotes among other passages Alcidamas ap. Arist. *rhet*. 1406ᵇ12 τὴν 'Οδύσσειαν καλὸν ἀνθρωπίνου βίου κάτοπτρον, Cic. ap. Donat. *de com*. 5. 1 'comoediam esse imitationem vitae, speculum consuetudinis, imaginem veritatis'. See also *fin*. ii. 32, v. 61, Marx on Lucil. 1029.

13. **multa a multis:** such repetition of *multus* is very common in Latin; cf. Landgraf on Sex. Rosc. 130.

14. **ni vererer:** for *ni* with *vererer* cf. *Verr*. iv. 55, *fam*. vi. 6. 4, *off*. ii. 67. For a similar apology cf. *Verr*. iv. 109 'iam dudum vereor ne oratio mea aliena ab iudiciorum ratione et a cotidiana dicendi consuetudine esse videatur'. Orators often claim to keep silence because of modesty; cf. *Verr*. I. 14, II. i. 32, ii. 180, *Flacc*. 34, *Phil*. ii. 47, xi. 9, Volkmann, p. 504.

16. **nil volo:** cf. *Planc*. 52 'nihil est . . . de te detractum'.

21. **mihi sustinere:** this word-order gives unemphatic *mihi* its normal position, second word in the clause (cf. frag. iv n.).

§§ **72–82.** *Cicero here starts a new line of thought. Piso had jocularly remarked that Cicero had been exiled because of his poem* de consulatu suo, *which had offended Pompey. Cicero rejects this charge, and proceeds to an account of his relationship with Pompey* (§§ 76–77) *and with Caesar* (§§ 79–82). *The passage is brilliant, but completely misleading.*

139

§ 72] COMMENTARY

§ 72. 26. **laudatio:** *conlaudatio* is found in classical Latin only in rhetorical treatises (*inv.* ii. 125, *rhet. ad Her.* ii. 13, ii. 15). For the compound *conlaudasset* followed by the simple *laudatio* cf. W. Clausen, *AJP* lxxvi, 1955, 49 ff., who collects passages where a compound verb is followed by the simple form.

paene turpis: for the theme 'it is a disgrace to be praised by you' cf. *Vat.* 29, 41, *har. resp.* 46, 51–52, *Phil.* ii. 18; contrast Naevius, *trag.* 15 'laetus sum laudari me abs te, pater, a laudato viro'.

27. **non illa ... invidia** means *non illarum rerum invidia*; so *Mil.* 75 *qua invidia = cuius rei invidia*. See Seyffert–Müller, *Laelius*, p. 17, Kühner on *Tusc.* i. 45, Mayor on *nat. d.* ii. 27. *non ulla* is occasionally found in Cicero (Madvig on *fin.* iii. 50), but here would make the sequence of thought less clear than *non illa*.

1. **sive ... libero:** 'a poet who was, if you like, bad, or, let us rather say, bold'. Cicero argues that the worst he had done, on the most hostile interpretation, was to write bad poetry; he himself would rather say that he had simply used a poetical figure of speech (73. 15). The second *sive* introduces a weaker expression, which Cicero personally prefers; cf. *prov. cons.* 42 'sive iratus mihi ... sive exoratus', *Mil.* 91 'in hac Milonis sive invidia sive fortuna'. For *libero* cf. *de or.* i. 70 '(poeta) verborum licentia liberior', iii. 153 '(inusitata verba) sunt poetarum licentiae liberiora quam nostrae', *orat.* 202 '(sunt) liberiores poetae' (cf. J. E. B. Mayor, *J. Phil.* viii, 1879, 260). The word is admittedly unusual here, in that it is not predicative, as in the other examples.

Some interpret *libero* as 'a free man', with the derogatory implication of 'even the humblest citizen who is not actually a slave' (cf. 67. 11 n.). But this meaning does not correspond well with *malo poetae*; and it would be absurd to suggest that exile should never be inflicted on any free man.

2. **cedant ...:** 'cedant arma togae, concedat laurea laudi' is a line from Cicero's poem *de consulatu suo* (Schanz–Hosius, *Gesch. der röm. Lit.* i. 536).

quid tum?: 'what if I did?', 'why do you say that?' *quid ergo?* and *quid postea?* are similarly used.

4. **sepulcro rei publicae:** the *aedes Libertatis* erected by Clodius on the site of Cicero's house (introd., p. xi). Cf. *dom.* 100 'illud non monumentum virtutis sed sepulcrum, inimico nomine inscriptum'; for another gibe cf. *dom.* 131 where Clodius's Statue of Liberty is called 'simulacrum Licentiae'. *elogium* ('epitaph') suits the metaphor of *sepulcro*; Clodius inscribed on his shrine the text of his bill *de exsilio Ciceronis*.

5. **VELITIS ...:** 'is it your desire and pleasure that whereas

140

COMMENTARY [§§ 72–73

M. Cicero has written a line of verse . . . ?' The preamble to Clodius's bill read 'whereas M. Cicero has put to death uncondemned citizens', but of course said nothing about his verses; Cicero is pretending to take seriously Piso's remark that he was exiled because of his poem.

velitis iubeatis is the regular formula at the beginning of a bill; the mood depends perhaps on an unexpressed *rogo*. For other extracts from this bill cf. *dom.* 50 'QVOD M. TVLLIVS FALSVM SENATVS CONSVLTVM RETTVLERIT', ibid. 47 'VT M. TVLLIO AQVA ET IGNI INTERDICTVM SIT'.

6. **VINDICARIT:** this ought to be a quotation from Clodius's bill; yet the word is perhaps not the most appropriate for a punishment which was unjustified (as Clodius maintained). Perhaps Clodius wrote *interfecerit* or something similar, and Cicero has craftily substituted a word more favourable to himself (P. Manutius).

§ **73.** 7. **quoniam te . . .:** 'since we have in you not an Aristarchus but a Phalaris for our schoolmaster'. When the Alexandrian critic Aristarchus came to a line in Homer which he judged unworthy, he obelized it (*notam apposuit*) as a sign that it was spurious. Cicero is joking at this capricious method of textual criticism; cf. *fam.* iii. 11. 5 'ut enim Aristarchus Homeri versum negat quem non probat', *fam.* ix. 10. 1 'profert alter, opinor, duobis versiculis expensum Niciae; alter Aristarchus hos ὀβελίζει'.

Phalarim: this is the spelling of the MSS., including V (where *Phalarin* is reported by editors). Phalaris, tyrant of Acragas, was proverbial for his cruelty (42. 12 n.). Cicero is referring to his quarrel with the poet Stesichorus (Ar. *rhet.* 1393^b, Maas, *RE* iiiA. 2459 f.). For his use of arms against Stesichorus see the letters of Phalaris, especially nos. 92, 93, 103, 108, 109; though these are late forgeries they contain older material.

11. **summum imperatorem:** according to Piso, Cicero meant by *cedant arma togae* that Pompey's victories were less important than his own suppression of the Catilinarians. Cicero retorts that he simply meant 'let war give way to peace'. Cicero's explanation is refuted by the latter part of the line, *concedat laurea laudi*; for *laurea* must refer to the exploits of Roman generals. The correct interpretation is implied by *off.* i. 77 'quae res igitur gesta umquam in bello tanta ? qui triumphus conferendus ?', Cassius, *fam.* xii. 13. 1 'est enim tua toga omnium armis felicior'; for the wrong interpretation cf. *Phil.* ii. 20 ' "cedant arma togae". quid ? tum nonne cesserunt ? at postea tuis armis cessit toga'.

Cicero can hardly have intended an explicit comparison between Pompey and himself; but as Pompey in 63 was winning great glory in the East, the line was tactless. At the end of 63 Cicero had sent

141

§§ 73-74] COMMENTARY

a long letter to Pompey boasting of his achievements (*Planc.* 85, *Sull.* 67); he offended Pompey 'quod quadam superbiore iactantia omnibus se gloriosis ducibus anteponeret' (Schol. Bob. p. 167 Stangl). Pompey's reply was not cordial (cf. *fam.* v. 7).

12. **asine:** i.e. stupid, obstinate, and uncultured; cf. the proverb ὄνος λύρας (Otto, pp. 40 f., who also quotes Lucil. 765 'uti litteras doceas lutum'). The image is sustained by *fustibus* in the next sentence; cf. Plaut. *Pseud.* 136 'neque ego homines magis asinos numquam vidi, ita plagis costae callent'. In classical Latin *asinus* is normally a term of abuse; the animal is *asellus* (Housman, *CQ* xxiv, 1930, 11).

13. **arma:** I have considered deleting this word as a gloss on *scutum et gladium* (see next note); but deletion would spoil the pattern *togam . . . arma . . . toga . . . arma.* Alternatively one might read at the beginning of the sentence *non dixi togam hanc togam.* This repetition sounds a little clumsy; but Cicero is adopting the weary tones of a schoolmaster expounding the obvious to a stupid pupil. Yet one cannot be sure that the inconcinnity of the MSS. is impossible.

scutum et gladium: for this phrase as an equivalent for *arma* cf. *Caecin.* 62 'si tu solus aut quivis unus cum scuto et gladio impetum in me fecisset . . . auderesne dicere interdictum esse de hominibus armatis, hic autem hominem armatum unum fuisse ?', ibid. 64 'an armatos non fuisse eos qui sine scutis sineque ferro fuerint', Juv. 8. 123 'scutum gladiumque relinques', Hegesipp. v. 16. 1 'scuta et gladios parastis'. These parallels tell against *V*'s reading *scutum aut gladium*, though the negative in our passage makes some difference.

14. **quia pacis est . . . :** in *de or.* iii. 167 Cicero gives as instances of metonymy 'togam pro pace, arma ac tela pro bello'. As this work was also written in 55 B.C. he was clearly trying to justify his own line. See also Serv. *Aen.* i. 1 'ut Cicero cedant arma togae, id est bellum paci'.

15. **poetarum more locutus:** perhaps the best reading, in spite of the hexameter-ending *more locutus. conlocutus* is the wrong word; *tum locutus* is weak. *more poetarum locutus* would give a better rhythm, but one prefers the emphatic *poetarum* to come first (thus *de or.* ii. 352).

§ **74.** 17. **poeta:** Philodemus; cf. Appendix III.

18. **genus ipsum:** the category to which the expression belongs, as opposed to the particular instance; so *nat. d.* ii. 126 'multa eiusmodi proferre possum, sed genus ipsum videtis', *Verr.* iv. 1 'genus ipsum prius cognoscite, iudices'.

20. **laudi:** this reading is confirmed by l. 24, and also has the

142

COMMENTARY [§§ 74-75

best manuscript authority at *off.* i. 77. *linguae* is read by Ps. Sall. *in Cic.* 6, Plin. *n.h.* vii. 117, Quintil. xi. 1. 24 (cf. *laus Pis.* 36 'laurea facundis, cesserunt arma togatis', Plut. *comp. Dem. et Cic.* 2. 1 γλώττῃ). *laus* is appropriate to the glory of a civilian magistrate (Seyffert–Müller, *Laelius*, p. 149); *lingua* in Cicero sometimes has a disparaging note. It seems that *concedat laurea linguae* is a satiric adaptation of Cicero's line; it is strange that it should have deceived Quintilian. Some suppose that Cicero originally wrote *linguae* and then changed it to the less offensive *laudi*. But in that case every time he quoted the line with *laudi* he would have reminded people of his original blunder.

22. cruentis fascibus: stained with the blood of the provincials. *V* reads *e cruentis*, but *detraho* in classical Latin takes a dative in such contexts (*Thes. L.L.* v. 1. 824). There is no real exception at *Verr.* II. i. 54, 'ex ipsa Diana quod habebat auri detractum atque ablatum esse dico'; there *ablatum* makes a difference.

23. abiecisti: cf. 61. 13 n.

iudicasti: 'you pronounced', not simply 'you thought'; cf. *Balb.* 42 'hospitium fecit ut et civitate illum mutatum esse fateretur, et huius civitatis honore dignissimum iudicaret' with Müller's note, *Tusc.* v. 61 'hic . . . tyrannus ipse iudicavit quam esset beatus' with Kühner's note. In our passage *indicasti* is found in a *codex deterior*; for *indicare* used of 'giving the show away' cf. *Vat.* 3 'paulo ante imprudens indicasti'.

non modo amplissimae . . .: i.e. Piso yielded even to Cicero's modest fame; for such self-disparagement (*deminutio*) cf. Volkmann, pp. 499 f. *non modo*, as often, has the sense of *non dico* (K.–S. ii. 57).

26. mihi, like *Pompeium*, is indignantly emphatic; if it had been unemphatic the order would have been *Pompeium mihi inimicum* (frag. iv n.).

§ 75. 2. multis . . . orationibus: cf. especially *de imperio Cn. Pompeii*, the lost digression in *pro Cornelio* i (cf. frag. 47 Schoell), *de lege agraria*, the lost speech proposing a *supplicatio* for Pompey (*prov. cons.* 27). For *multis saepe* cf. 18. 23 n.

4. sit offensus primo: 'let us suppose that he was displeased at first'.

5. quod si est commotus: 'supposing he *was* made angry'. Cicero is making a further concession to an imaginary opponent, just as in *sit offensus* above. Schütz emended to *esset*, but an unreal condition ('supposing he had been made angry') is rhetorically weaker. Müller kept *est* here and read *fuit* for *fuisset* at the end of the sentence; this implies that Pompey was in fact cruel, which Cicero would not publicly admit.

143

§§ 75–76] COMMENTARY

6. **ad perniciemne . . .:** 'would he have been stirred to the destruction—I shall not say of a close friend, of one who had done so much for his own (Pompey's) glory and the national interest, I shall not say of a consular, of a senator, of a citizen, of a free man— would he have been so savage against the life of any human being simply because of a line of verse ?' The genitives form a series; each describes somebody with less claim on Pompey than the last. For *liberi* cf. 67. 11 n. After *ad perniciemne* one might have expected *incitatus esset*, or something of the kind, but at *in hominis caput* the construction changes.

9. **tu quid . . .:** cf. Hor. *epist.* i. 18. 68 'quid de quoque viro et cui dicas saepe videto', Quintil. xi. 1. 43 'nec tantum quis et pro quo sed etiam apud quem dicas interest'.

10. **complecti . . . ad:** 'involve in'. The construction with *ad* seems to be unparalleled (*Thes. L.L.* iii. 2085. 28), but Francken's *socios complecti* is no improvement.

amplissimos viros: Caesar and Pompey, who are also *eos* in l. 13.

12. **eis:** Piso and Gabinius. *quos despicerem*: Piso no doubt said *qui minus valent* or something of the kind, but Cicero substitutes a more contemptuous expression. Piso's observation was perfectly justified.

15. **una causa omnium:** one expects the emphatic *una* to come first; cf. also *Att.* ii. 19. 3 'una vox omnium'. In spite of the deliberately vague *omnium* Cicero is only thinking of Pompey and Caesar; there is a touch of malice in the suggestion that their interests are not identical.

§ 76. 16. **eius:** cf. K.–S. i. 601.

19. **vestrae fraudes . . .:** 'it was your trickery, your crime, your charges wickedly invented that I was plotting and that Pompey was in danger, at the same time the charges of those persons who with the privilege of friendship had established a home for their own wicked talk in his ears at your instigation, it was your longing for provinces which brought it about that I was excluded'.

Cicero alleges that Piso and Gabinius told Pompey that Cicero was plotting against him; for this story cf. *dom.* 28, *Sest.* 41, 67, 133, though Piso and Gabinius are not named in those passages. One may compare the similar accusations made by Vettius in 59 (*Att.* ii. 24. 3, *Vat.* 24 ff.). Caesar may have been behind some of these slanders, as he needed to separate Cicero from Pompey (cf. W. C. McDermott, *TAPA* lxxx, 1949, 351 ff., W. Allen, *TAPA* lxxxi, 1950, 153 ff.). Yet Pompey could not have been afraid of a personal attack by Cicero; he tried to avoid an interview with Cicero simply to save himself embarrassment. Cicero now makes excuses on his

144

COMMENTARY [§§ 76–77]

behalf; he cannot state the truth, that Pompey had betrayed him.

22. **eorum:** Vatinius was one of the authors of this slander, according to *Sest.* 133; yet he would perhaps not have been called a friend of Pompey's. Cicero is no doubt aware that his vague hints could be applied by the malevolent to Caesar himself.

24. **vestrae ... effecerunt:** this phrase does not occur here in the MSS., which at this point include *P*. It comes in Ω in l. 21 after *mearum*, where it makes complete nonsense. In *P* there was a lacuna from l. 19 -*simum atque* to l. 22 *eorum qui fa-*; it contained nine lines, with about 18–21 letters to the line. If we posit that *vestrae ... effecerunt* stood in the lacuna then everything fits exactly; otherwise the lacuna would be about two lines too long.

Angelius placed the phrase where it stands in this text. According to this suggestion, after mentioning in three clauses the wicked slanders of Piso and Gabinius, Cicero as a climax gives their real motive, namely their longing for provinces.

Halm completely deleted the phrase. According to this interpretation the main verb never comes; at l. 27 instead of the expected *omnia haec perfecerunt* Cicero changes the construction and says *quibus rebus est perfectum*. On this assumption *ut ego excluderer ...* would be a final clause, which is somewhat unnatural.

Neither of these theories explains *P*'s reading satisfactorily. *P* must have contained the phrase, or something equivalent; yet it is hard to believe that the nonsensical reading of the later MSS. was widely diffused in the ancient world. But no other solution presents itself. One can hardly insert the phrase elsewhere in the lacuna, since *cupiditates* seems to be a climax after *criminationes*; and *effecerunt* must surely belong to the last of the parallel *vestrae* clauses.

25. **ut ego excluderer:** when Cicero called, Pompey escaped by a back-door to avoid the awkward interview (Plut. *Cic.* 31. 3). Yet it seems that Pompey saw Cicero at some stage; cf. *Att.* x. 4. 3 'is qui nos sibi quondam ad pedes stratos ne sublevabat quidem'.

§ 77. 28. **plane suo stare iudicio:** 'rely altogether on his own judgement'. *P* reads *plane stare in suo iudicio*; but the separation of *suo* from *iudicio* is idiomatic and likely to be right. Besides, *stare* in this sense elsewhere takes a plain ablative; cf. *Sull.* 22 'non suo stare iudicio', *Tusc.* ii. 63 'eius iudicio stare nolim', ibid. v. 81 'suis stare iudiciis', *Att.* xii. 21. 5, *off.* iii. 110. *stare in* seems to mean 'to remain in' rather than 'to rely on' (*stare in fide, in sententia*, etc., cf. K.–S. i. 400). A. Klotz, who follows *P*, maintains that both *plane* and *suo* are emphatic, and must therefore be separated; but *plane* need not be emphatic, and indeed cannot be if *illi*, as seems likely, is emphasized.

5993   M   145

§§ 77–78] COMMENTARY

29. **retardassent:** cf. *Sest.* 67 'Cn. Pompeius . . . excitavit illam suam non sopitam sed suspicione aliqua retardatam consuetudinem rei publicae bene gerendae'. Cicero is too forgiving.

30. **nonne . . . non:** this is the normal construction; *nonne . . . nonne* is rarer but possible (§ 86, K.–S. ii. 516).

Lentulus: L. Cornelius Lentulus Crus was the chief accuser of Clodius in 61 at the Bona Dea trial, praetor in 58, an intransigent consul in 49; he was murdered in Egypt soon after Pompey. Q. Fabius Sanga helped Cicero in 63 in his negotiations with the Allobrogian envoys (Sall. *Cat.* 41. 4). For Torquatus see 44. 15 n. M. Terentius Varro Lucullus, the brother of L. Lucullus, was consul in 73, proconsul of Macedonia 72–71 (p. 177, 58. 2 n.).

2. **multique mortales:** Francken objected that this implies that Lentulus, etc., were not *mortales*; he proposed *multique undique mortales*. This ignores an idiom; cf. *Brut.* 310 'commentabar . . . cum M. Pisone et cum Q. Pompeio aut cum aliquo cotidie', K.–S. i. 636, ii. 25, Seyffert–Müller, *Laelius*, p. 247, Page on Eur. *Med.* 1172.

Albanum: for Pompey's famous estate near the Alban Lake cf. Drumann–Groebe, iv. 542; for the site cf. G. Lugli, *Bull. Arch. Com.* xlii, 1914, 281 ff., *Notizie degli Scavi*, vii, 1946, 60 ff.

3. **ut ne:** cf. 17. 6 n.

4. **ut causam . . .:** deliberately misleading (so *Sest.* 41); Pompey was simply trying to pass the responsibility.

6. **publico consilio:** 'a resolution of the senate'.

7. **consulibus:** emphatic, to contrast with the emphatic *se* at the beginning of the previous clause. So *P*'s *se consulibus* is impossible.

§ 78. 9. **omnes quidem:** understand *furebant*; cf. *Tusc.* i. 38 'itaque credo equidem etiam alios tot saeculis, sed, quod litteris exstet, Pherecydes Syrius primum dixit'.

11. **ipse Torquatus:** also called *fortis* at *Sull.* 11, 30, *fin.* ii. 62. In 65 there was an alleged plot to murder the consuls Torquatus and Cotta; Catiline was suspected at the time, and later writers implausibly accused Caesar and Crassus. Torquatus himself disbelieved in the plot (*Sull.* 81), probably rightly. See R. Syme, *JRS* xxxiv, 1944, 96 f., H. Frisch, *Classica et Mediaevalia*, ix, 1948, 10 ff.

nihil . . . armis: not 'arms were superfluous' but 'arms were unavailing'; cf. Liv. xliii. 19. 4 'nihil Oaeneo capto opus esse ait nisi in potestate et Draudacum sit'. E. Wölfflin, *ALL* iv. 325, connects the usage with a supposed derivation from *opis*, but this is unlikely.

14. **se:** for the change from second to third person cf. 2. 6 n.

15. **defuturum:** A. Klotz thought that *non defuturum* might be right. But he was wrong in supposing that this is *E*'s reading (see

146

COMMENTARY [§§ 78–80

app. crit.); in any case such a pleonasm would be impossible in Cicero.

hic: 'under these circumstances', 'and now' (indignant); cf. Hand, iii. 80, Landgraf on *Sex. Rosc.* 132.

§ **79.** 16. **C. Caesarem:** for Cicero's analysis of his attitude to Caesar cf. introd., p. xvi.

17. **quae me scio:** cf. K.–S. i. 719.

20. **detulit:** understand *honores* (for these offers see introd., pp. viii f.). I have considered beginning a new sentence at *detulit* and reading a colon at *rogavit*. Francken wrongly supposed that *me* is the object of *detulit*. It is true that *deferre aliquem* can mean 'to hand in somebody's name at the *aerarium* for a reward or office' (cf. *Arch.* 11, *Balb.* 63); but Cicero did not allow his name to go forward in this way.

non sum . . .: for the position of *sum* in the unemphatic second place cf. *Verr.* II. i. 16 'in Siciliam sum inquirendi causa profectus', frag. iv n., L.–H., p. 612.

24. **adducta res . . .:** 'in your consulship things seemed to have come to a struggle which would decide whether Caesar's deeds of the previous year were to stand or be annulled'. Domitius and Memmius were threatening Caesar's legislation of 59 (introd., p. x).

§ **80.** 1. **omitto:** perhaps preferable to *mitto*; Cicero several times says *praeterita omittamus* (*Phil.* ii. 112, v. 31, vi. 9, *Att.* xiv. 14. 3).

Pompeius: for his efforts on Cicero's behalf in the spring of 57 see introd., p. xiii.

3. **fidem:** 'protection'; cf. E. Fraenkel, *Rh. Mus.* lxxi, 1916, 193 ff., R. Heinze, *Hermes*, lxiv, 1929, 153 ff.

4. **frequens:** cf. K.–S. i. 236.

adsideret: 'sat in conference with'; cf. *dom.* 30 'hic (Pompeius) tuis, P. Lentule, . . . consiliis omnibus interfuit'. For the use by consuls of an unofficial advisory *consilium* cf. *in tog. cand.* ap. Asc. 79 KS, *Sull.* 11, 13, *rep.* iii. 28, *Att.* xvi. 16c. 11, *St.-R.* i³. 311, J. A. Crook, *Consilium Principis* (Cambridge, 1955), pp. 6 f.

senatus sententiam praestaret (*P*): 'gave the weight of his support to the resolution of the senate'. *praestaret* seems to mean 'underwrote', 'supported by his authority'; cf. Madvig, *Opusc. Acad.²*, p. 122 n. 3, who quotes *Sest.* 38 'ut meum factum semper omnes praestare tuerique deberent'. *sententiam* refers to the senate's resolution of July 57; cf. *dom.* 30, a closely parallel passage, 'hic in senatu princeps sententiae fuit', *Pis.* 35, *Sest.* 129. A. Klotz interprets 'efficeret ut senatus idem sentiret quod ipse', but Cicero could not suggest that the senate's support depended on Pompey. The Ω group reads *senatui*. The meaning would then be 'gave

147

§§ 80-81]   COMMENTARY

the senate the authority of his opinion'; cf. *de or.* iii. 134 'idemque in senatu et apud populum . . . consilium suum fidemque praestabant'. But *praestare* suits *consilium* better than the more concrete *sententiam*; besides, on this interpretation one would expect *sententiam suam*.

There is an evident parallelism between the senate and the *contiones*, and this would be brought out clearly by the reading *senatui*. But if *senatus* is read, and interpreted as above, the balance of the sentence is not impaired: Pompey 'underwrote the resolution of the senate' in the senate itself, not elsewhere.

11. **alter . . . alter:** Pompey . . . Caesar.

12. **aliquando sibi:** *sibi aliquando* would make *sibi* too strong; *aliquando* like *semper* is the emphatic word. Before Bake editors took *meminero semper* and *obliviscar aliquando* together; but the latter phrase ('I shall forget one day') is too hostile to Caesar.

§ 81. 16. **habet hoc:** 'has this characteristic'.

17. **de facie:** 'by sight'; so Apul. *apol.* 98. *facie nosse* is also found (Aug. *civ. D.* v. 17).

18. **[posita]:** this word is intolerable here. It is left out by a Bodleian MS., Laud lat. 48; this must be either an accidental omission or an emendation. Cf. *amic.* 29 'quodsi tanta vis probitatis est ut eam . . . in hoste etiam diligamus'. See also Hegesipp. iii. 17. 1 'tanta est enim virtutis gratia ut frequenter etiam hostem delectet'; but this passage throws no light on the text here.

Francken considered, but rejected, *proposita*. *proponere* sometimes means 'to put on view as an object for admiration and imitation'; cf. *Rab. Post.* 42 'multas equidem C. Caesaris virtutes . . . cognovi, sed sunt ceterae maioribus quasi theatris propositae', *Phil.* x. 5 'propones illi exempla ad imitandum'. Francken also considered *exposita*; cf. *Phil.* ii. 114 '(quod factum) expositum ad imitandum est', *acad.* ii frag. 5 'vitam suam exponere ad imitandum iuventuti'. Francken himself preferred *conspecta*, which Müller improved to *perspecta*; but these conjectures are not close enough to the MSS.

20. **saepe iam dixi:** especially in the *de provinciis consularibus*.

21. **si semper aspernaretur:** *semper* is omitted by Ω, but can be defended, as *implacabilem* below also describes a permanent attitude.

24. **non amicus:** cf. *prov. cons.* 24 'nemini ego possum esse bene merenti de re publica non amicus', *fam.* ix. 24. 1.

25. **Alpium vallum:** cf. Serv. *Aen.* x. 13 'Alpes quae secundum Catonem (frag. 85 Peter) et Livium (xxi. 35. 9) muri vice tuebantur Italiam', Polyb. iii. 54. 2 ὥστε ἀκροπόλεως φαίνεσθαι διάθεσιν ἔχειν

148

COMMENTARY [§§ 81–82]

τὰς Ἄλπεις τῆς ὅλης Ἰταλίας, Cic. *prov. cons.* 34, *Phil.* v. 37, Herodian. ii. 11. 8, *paneg. Lat.* xi (iii). 2. 4, Hegesipp. v. 46. 1, Rutil. Namat. ii. 33 ff., Isid. *etym.* xiv. 8. 18.

26. **Rheni fossam:** 'the moat of the Rhine' (keeping up the imagery of *vallum*). In the summer of 55 Caesar bridged the Rhine for the first time; cf. Caes. *b.G.* iv. 17–19, Catull. 11. 10 f. 'Caesaris visens monumenta magni, Gallicum Rhenum . . .'. It is not certain that Cicero knew of this exploit when he delivered the speech (pp. 199 f.).

gurgitibus: 'floods' (not necessarily whirlpools). Cicero is using colourful, almost poetical, language; cf. *amnes* below.

§ 82. 28. si montes . . .: cf. *prov. cons.* 34 'quae (Alpes) iam licet considant; nihil est enim ultra illam altitudinem montium usque ad Oceanum quod sit Italiae pertimescendum', Plin. *paneg.* 16. 5 'omnia haec tam prona tamque cedentia virtutibus tuis sentiet ut subsedisse montes flumina exaruisse . . . arbitretur', *paneg. Lat.* x (ii). 7. 7 'licet Rhenus arescat . . . nullus inde metus est', ibid. vi (vii). 11. 1 'neque enim iam Rheni gurgitibus, sed nominis tui terrore munimur. quamlibet ille aut arescat aestu aut resistat gelu, neutro hostis audebit uti vado', Hegesipp. ii. 9. 1 '(Romani) quorum improviso adventu consedisse montes Germania credidit, Rhenum exaruisse', ibid. v. 46. 1 'Romanae itaque virtuti consederunt montes, amnes exaruerunt'.

1. **tuis inimicitiis:** 'will you by means of your feuds bring me back to a state of enmity (with Caesar)?' *tuis inimicitiis* is parallel to *tuis sceleribus* in the next clause. The reading of the MSS., *a tuis inimicitiis*, would suggest that Piso was diverting Cicero from his quarrel with himself to a quarrel with Caesar. But *revocare* is a strange verb to use if one is diverting somebody from a closer to a more remote relationship with oneself; it does not mean the same as *depellere*.

If *a* is retained *simultatem* must be qualified in order to obtain a contrast with *tuis*; hence Lambinus proposed *simultatem C. Caesaris*, Pluygers *depositam simultatem*, Clark *simultatem veterem* (he read *vocabis* instead of *revocabis*). If *a* is deleted there is probably no need for an insertion. The clausula *-em revocabis*, though not common, is possible; such clausulae are most objectionable when the last word is a disyllable or a trisyllable (F. W. Shipley, *CP* vi, 1911, 410 ff.).

2. **sic:** *sicine* is often used indignantly, especially in early Latin (in Cicero only perhaps at *Flacc.* 81, cf. Liv. vi. 16. 2, vii. 15. 1); it seems possible that *sic* is so used here, though no satisfactory parallel presents itself. The fact that *sic* is not found in the balancing clause *tu me . . .* is also a difficulty, though perhaps not insuperable.

149

§ 82]   COMMENTARY

If the word is thought too strange, deletion is the easiest cure (thus Pluygers).

fata refricabis: i.e. renew the disagreements of 59–58. *refricare* 'to open an old wound' is often used in metaphorical contexts. Here Cicero says not *vulnera*, which would be too critical of Caesar, but the more euphemistic *fata*.

3. **quod quidem . . .:** 'as for the fact that you scoffed, though knowing well my close relationship with Caesar, when you asked me, with quivering lips to be sure, why I did not prosecute you—let me tell you that although as far as I myself am concerned "I shall never lessen your anxiety by making you denials", yet I have to consider how great a weight of worry I impose on my friend Caesar, when he is involved in such grave affairs of state and so important a war'.

If the punctuation adopted here is right, *eludebas* is intransitive; *quamquam* introduces Cicero's retort (thus Pluygers). Editors generally put a full stop after *requirebas*; *quod eludebas* would then mean 'you scoffed at this thing' (i.e. the opening up of old wounds). But *quod* would be strange, and *eludebas* would not refer directly (as one expects) to Piso's invitation to prosecute. Besides, on this interpretation one would look for a connective (e.g. *sed*) before *quamquam*.

4. **omnino:** concessive; cf. Nägelsbach, pp. 778 f., du Mesnil on *Flacc.* 71.

5. **cur:** Cicero did not prosecute Piso because Caesar would not have allowed him. Cicero's own explanation can have deceived nobody.

6. **numquam . . .:** Asconius comments: 'prope notius est quam ut indicandum sit hunc versum esse L. Acci poetae [*Atreus* 234] et dici a Thyeste Atreo.' Duentzer emended Asconius to 'ab Atreo Thyesti'; the line may have come in where Thyestes begins to suspect that he is eating his children. But we know too little of the play to guess. For other allusions to the line see *in sen.* 33, *Sest.* 8; for many references in Cicero to the play see W. Zillinger, op. cit. [25. 12 n.], pp. 133 f.

10. **iuventus:** prosecutions were usually conducted by young men who had still a name to make; cf. *Cael.* 73, Quintil. xii. 6. 1, Tac. *dial.* 34. 7, Apul. *apol.* 66, Plut. *Luculli.* 1. 3, M. Gelzer, *Die Nobilität der römischen Republik*, pp. 68 f. It was thought unduly quarrelsome for an older man to incur *inimicitiae* so lightly (cf. *off.* ii. 49 'laudabilior est defensio').

11. **debebat** refers to present time (K.–S. i. 173).

12. **abiectum:** 'discarded', of corpses thrown out without burial; but the meaning 'abject' is also present here.

150

COMMENTARY [§§ 82–83

consularibus spoliis: spoils taken from a consular; so Tac. *hist.* iv. 42. 4 'raptis consularibus spoliis'. One suspects that *consularia spolia* naturally meant 'spoils won and dedicated by a consul'; if so the phrase is used satirically here.

13. **inopi:** 'friendless'; *inops* and *infirmus* are combined elsewhere (*Mur.* 45, *Att.* vii. 8. 5). *opimum praeda* can mean 'rich in booty' (*Verr.* II. i. 132), and Horace hopes that his enemy's corpse will be *opima praeda* for the gulls (*epod.* 10. 21); but *opimo* does not harmonize with the other adjectives here.

14. **ut timeres:** 'that you seemed to be afraid'; cf. 69. 17 n.

15. **eius:** Clodius.

§§ **83–94.** *Cicero in* § 82 *has said that he is not going to prosecute Piso: he now explains that his reason is not lack of material. This leads to a summary of Piso's crimes in Macedonia: first cases of* crudelitas (§§ 83–85), *then of* avaritia (§§ 86–88), *finally events at the end of Piso's proconsulship* (§§ 88–93). *In* § 94 *Cicero warns Piso that he will prosecute when the time is ripe. For a discussion of Cicero's charges see pp.* 175 *ff.*

§ **83.** 19. **ingressus:** 'steps'.

volutationibus: this word is literally used of pigs rolling in mud, and hence suits the boar-hunting metaphor of *vestigiis* and *odorantes*; metaphorically it suggests 'wallowing in vice' (*har. resp.* 42, 59, *rep.* ii. 68). Cf. *Verr.* iv. 53 'Verre quem in luto volutatum totius corporis vestigiis invenimus' (with a pun on *verres*, 'a boar'); in our passage Cicero is thinking of the pig-like qualities of the Epicurean Piso (37. 24 n.). I have considered reading *totius* here (cf. *Verr.* loc. cit.), but *totis* is defensible (21. 9 n.).

20. **cubilibus** suggests the lairs of an animal; cf. *Verr.* ii. 190 'ut omnes mortales istius avaritiae non iam vestigia, sed ipsa cubilia videre possint', *Clu.* 82. The ambiguity of *volutationibus* is sustained.

et is not normally used by Cicero as an equivalent for *etiam*. Here it probably points forward to another *et* ('both . . . and'); but the construction changes, and the second *et* never comes. See Madvig, *de finibus*, excursus i, *Thes. L.L.* v. 2. 887. 1.

21. **adventu:** often used of the arrival of a magistrate in his province.

accepta pecunia: cf. *dig.* xlviii. 11. 3 'lege Iulia repetundarum tenetur qui cum aliquam potestatem haberet, pecuniam ob iudicandum vel non iudicandum decernendumve acceperit'.

Dyrrachinis: Dyrrachium was a free city (*fam.* xiv. 1. 7), perhaps protected by a *foedus* (cf. Liv. xlii. 48. 6–8).

22. **Platoris:** the name, like *Pleuratus*, is Illyrian (*RE* s.v.).

151

§ 83] COMMENTARY

Cicero says elsewhere (*har. resp.* 35) that Plator was a *homo clarus* from Orestis, a free area in central Macedonia; he went to Thessalonica as a *legatus* (from Orestis, one assumes, as Dyrrachium is not there mentioned), and was executed because he refused to give Piso money. Cicero's two accounts are not quite consistent, but here *fide tua* and *Pleuratus eius comes* (l. 2) suit the story of a deputation. Plator may have resisted interference by Piso in Orestis.

devertisti: 'lodged at'; Mommsen's emendation is certain. Piso no doubt billeted himself on Plator, but Cicero suggests that he was bound by the most sacred ties (cf. *Verr.* v. 108). By using the pluperfect *addixeras* he implies that Piso had decided to execute Plator before he went to his house; this increases the odium of the charge, but is obviously implausible. One would naturally assume from the context that Piso stayed with Plator at Dyrrachium. But as he might have been expected to find a more reliable *hospes* in this important city, it is possible that he stayed with him in Orestis.

23. symphoniacis: rich men sometimes had private musicians in their retinue; cf. Marquardt, *Privatleben*², p. 151, Abert, *RE* ivA. 1169.

26. maiorum . . . more: execution by beheading, normally preceded by flogging (*Verr.* v. 133, *RE* Suppl. vii. 1615). The use of the phrase to describe flogging to death is exceptional (Suet. *Ner.* 49).

27. cervices: always plural in Ciceronian prose (P. Maas, *ALL* xii. 501).

gestiret: describes passionate longing, here used with irony of Plator's modest wish.

medico: for doctors in proconsuls' retinues see *Verr.* ii. 27, iii. 28, iii. 137 (cf. Suet. *Jul.* 4).

28. [tu]: this word is too emphatic. Perhaps it should be deleted, as Naugerius proposed (dittography after *cŭ*), or perhaps one should read *tum* with Halm. K. Busche, *W.Kl.Ph.* xxxv, 1918, 16 proposed *quem tecum in comitatu eduxeras*, but this is much too speculative.

eduxeras: this verb is often used of taking *comites* to a province.

venas incideret: this was a common method of suicide under the Empire; cf. also Suet. *Ner.* 37 'medicos admovebat qui cunctantes continuo curarent (ita enim vocabatur venas mortis gratia incidere)'. Even if Cicero's account is not fictitious, this method of execution avoided the pain and publicity of the *mos maiorum*, and must be considered a concession to Plator. But Cicero can excite indignation at Piso's use of a doctor; cf. *har. resp.* 35 (of the same

COMMENTARY [§§ 83-84]

incident) 'qualis hunc carnifices putamus habere, qui etiam medicis suis non ad salutem sed ad necem utatur'.

§ 84. 3. **Bessicae gentis:** the Bessi were a large Thracian tribe living in the area of the Hebrus. Cicero's sympathy is misplaced; they had fought M. Lucullus in 72, C. Octavius in 60 (Eutrop. 6. 10, Suet. *Aug.* 3), and Strabo says of them καὶ ὑπὸ τῶν ληστῶν λησταὶ προσαγορεύονται (vii. 5. 12). They were finally subdued by Piso's son about 12-10 B.C.; cf. Antipater of Thessalonica, addressing the younger Piso, Σοί με, Θρηικίης σκυληφόρε, Θεσσαλονίκη μήτηρ ἡ πάσης πέμψε Μακηδονίης. ἀείδω δ᾽ ὑπὸ σοὶ δεδμημένον Ἄρεα Βεσσῶν (*anth. Pal.* ix. 428).

4. **principem:** perhaps not 'the chief' but 'a leading man'; the chief of the tribe might not have come himself as a *legatus*.

Cotto: probably King of the Astae, who lived in the eastern corner of Thrace towards the Bosporus, and not of the Odrysae as some suppose; for Bizye, which was the capital of the Astae, was the home of this family (A. H. M. Jones, *Cities of Eastern Roman Provinces*, p. 378 n. 11). The Bessi seem to have extended as far east as the Astae (Jones, op. cit., pp. 13, 379 n. 18). For Piso's movements at this time see pp. 178 f.

The spelling of the name is doubtful, but emendation to *Cotyi* is unwarranted. Cf. Caes. *b.c.* iii. 4. 3 *Cotus* (probably the same man), iii. 36. 4 *Cotti* (or *Cottis*), Nep. xi. 3. 4 *Coti*, xiii. 1. 2 *Cotum*. For various Thracian princes of this name see A. Salač, *BCH* lv, 1931, 43 ff.

6. **praesidia et auxilia:** α omits *et*; hence Baiter proposed deleting *auxilia* and Halm *praesidia*. Yet such simple words hardly need a gloss. Thracian auxiliaries were used e.g. by Sulla (M. Holleaux, *REG* xxxii, 1919, 320 ff.) and by Pompey (Caes. *b.c.* iii. 4. 3); but Piso may have distrusted the Bessi, or they may have imposed intolerable conditions.

9. **Denseletis:** the Denseletae lived in the upper Strymon valley. C. Sentius was governor of Macedonia 93-87 (Münzer, *RE* iiA. 1509 f.). He had to contend with serious Thracian incursions, which Cicero here connects with the general revolt against Rome at the time of the Mithradatic War (p. 177). Cicero's belief in the fidelity of the Denseletae is unjustified; cf. Gran. Lic. 35 (of Sulla in 85) 'Dardanos et Denseletas caesis hostibus qui Macedoniam vexabant in deditionem recepit'. They were, it is true, allies of Rome in 29 B.C. (Dio li. 23. 4), but Strabo includes them in a list of ληστρικώτατα ἔθνη (vii. 5. 12).

14. **praedatores:** this reading is supported by § 96 'vexatorem praedonem'; the variant *perditores* is supported by *Vat.* 7 'perditorem et vexatorem rei publicae'.

153

§§ 84–86]   COMMENTARY

16. **familias abripuerunt:** 'they kidnapped their slaves'.

17. **oppido:** the dative is legitimate with *desperare*; cf. § 89, *Thes. L.L.* v. 1. 741. 38.

 munire arcem: cf. *prov. cons.* 4 'ut Thessalonicenses . . . relinquere oppidum et arcem munire cogantur', *Pis.* 40. The acropolis of Salonika is 140 metres high (*RE* viA. 160).

§ 85. 18. **Zbelsurdi:** J. H. Mordtmann, *Rev. Arch.* xxxvi, 1878, ii. 302, emended *velsuri* of the MSS. to *Svelsurdi*; the emendation is in principle certain, though Cicero's spelling is very doubtful. Zbelsurdos was a Thracian god whose name has been found in a number of inscriptions, usually dedications Διὶ Ζβελσούρδῳ. Three of these inscriptions were found in the upper Strymon valley (in SW. Bulgaria), exactly the region where Piso was operating (§ 84). They may even have come from the site of the temple mentioned here (G. Kazarow, *Rev. Arch.* iv série, xxi, 1913, i. 340 ff.). For details and bibliography see Keune in Roscher, *Lexikon*, vi. 559 ff. (cf. *ILS* 4077); add Kazarow, *RE* viA. 515 f., D. Detschew, *Festschrift für Rudolf Egger*, i (Klagenfurt, 1952), 20 ff.

 Turnebus's emendation *Urii* has been generally accepted; Ζεὺς Οὔριος had a temple in Macedonia, at least in the second century B.C. (*Verr.* iv. 129). Yet he was a Greek and not a barbarian god.

19. **direptum est:** Cicero was not always so sympathetic to foreign religions; cf. *Flacc.* 68 (why Pompey did not loot the temple at Jerusalem) 'non enim credo religionem et Iudaeorum et hostium impedimento praestantissimo imperatori, sed pudorem fuisse' (dislike of being thought avaricious).

 scelera . . .: cf. *prov. cons.* 5 'scelus imperatoris in poenam exercitus expiatum' (*expiatum* van de Coppello, *expetitum* or *expetitus* codd.).

20. **novo:** if *uno* of the MSS. were right, Cicero would be emphasizing that Piso's army suffered from an epidemic; cf. *hist. Aug.* xxiii. 5. 5 'ut uno die quinque milia hominum pari morbo perirent'. Yet there *quinque milia* makes a considerable difference; so here it is probably best to accept Müller's *novo*. At *Rab. Post.* 16 *novam* is corrupted to *unam*.

23. **atque:** Cicero in his speeches seldom uses *atque* before a consonant, except in the clausula; cf. J. Wolff, *Jahrb.* Supp. xxvi, 1901, 637 ff., B. Axelson, *Unpoetische Wörter* (Lund, 1945), pp. 83 ff.

25. **cognoscis:** Professor Watt suggests *agnoscis*; cf. § 12 'ipse certe agnoscet'.

§ 86. 26. **avaritiae:** one might have expected *avaritiae tuae*, but the MSS. are supported by Priscian. *tuae* must be understood from

154

COMMENTARY [§ 86

crudelitatis tuae above; therefore editors are wrong in joining *cognoscis . . . universum* to the previous paragraph.

27. **generatim:** so Cicero says that he can only discuss Verres's crimes by categories (*Verr.* iii. 53, 58, etc.).

28. **centiens et octogiens:** 18,000,000 sesterces. This sum seems very large, but it is hard to interpret its exact significance. Pompey, as proconsul of Spain from 54 to 49, drew 1,000 talents a year, or about 25,000,000 sesterces (Plut. *Caes.* 28. 5); he was given 6,000 talents against the pirates (App. *Mith.* 94). The cost of keeping a legion for a year has been estimated at 4,000,000 sesterces (T. Frank, *Economic Survey of Ancient Rome* (Baltimore, 1933), i. 326 ff.); but even if this figure is accurate, we do not known the relation between equipment-money and the normal grant. Mommsen suggested that Cicero deliberately confused the two (*St.-R.* i³. 296 n. 4), but this is quite uncertain.

1. **quasi vasari nomine:** 'under the heading, as was pretended, of equipment-money'. *nomine* is a book-keeping expression, and does not in itself contain a suggestion of pretence, which is supplied by *quasi. vasa* was a military term for baggage (*vasa colligere*, etc.); *vasarium* (only here in this sense) was apparently 'equipment-money' (*St.-R.* i³. 296). No doubt the word was normally applied to the equipment-money of individual soldiers; in the present context, where it refers to the grant for a whole army, it is probably derisive rather than technical.

2. **in quaestu:** 'earning interest'; cf. *imp. Pomp.* 37 'quid hunc hominem magnum aut amplum de republica cogitare qui pecuniam ex aerario depromptam ad bellum administrandum . . . propter avaritiam Romae in quaestu reliquerit ?'

4. **Fufidium:** a friend of Cicero's, and like him a native of Arpinum (*Q.f.* iii. 1. 3, *RE* vii. 200 f.). He is presumably the same person, or at least one of the same family, as the rapacious banker in Hor. *serm.* i. 2. 12 ff. 'Fufidius vappae famam timet ac nebulonis, dives agris dives positis in fenore nummis. quinas hic capiti mercedes exsecat, atque quanto perditior quisque est tanto acrius urget.' Fufidius had lent money to Apollonia, no doubt at exorbitant interest, and Piso had reduced the debt; cf. *Sest.* 94 'eundemque (Pisonem) bona creditorum civium Romanorum cum debitoribus Graecis divisisse', below, p. 174. For loans to communities cf. J. Hatzfeld, *Les Trafiquants italiens dans l'orient hellénique* (Paris, 1919), 203 ff., J. A. O. Larsen in T. Frank's *Economic Survey*, iv. 372 ff.; for Piso's reduction of the debt compare the similar action by L. Lucullus in Asia (Plut. *Luc.* 20. 3).

6. **suis:** cf. 16. 14 n.

addixisti: when a magistrate 'made over' a debtor to a

155

§ 86] COMMENTARY

creditor, the creditor could privately imprison him. The word is used here paradoxically to excite pity for the creditor whose claims have been refused.

hiberna: Cicero is thinking notably of Byzantium, where Piso's soldiers, billeted in winter-quarters, caused offence by their licentious behaviour (*prov. cons.* 5–6). For cities' anxiety to escape *hiberna* cf. *Att.* v. 21. 7; the *lex Antonia de Termessibus* (*ILS* 38) says that such inflictions are not to be imposed except with the consent of the senate. See further R. O. Jolliffe, *Phases of Corruption in Roman Administration* (Wisconsin, 1919), pp. 7 ff., M. Rostovtzeff, *Soc. Econ. Hist. Hell. World*, p. 1561, T. R. S. Broughton in T. Frank's *Economic Survey*, iv. 575.

legato praefectoque: one person, with the rank of *legatus*, the function of *praefectus* (*St.-R.* ii³. 700). Cf. *prov. cons.* 5 'iis praeposuit quos putavit fore diligentissimos satellites scelerum, ministros cupiditatum suarum'. So the legate cannot be Flaccus, Marcius, or Vergilius, since Cicero approves of all of them (§ 54, *prov. cons.* 7).

9. qui modus . . . : 'where did you draw the line in accepting money in lieu of corn ?' Governors could compulsorily purchase *frumentum in cellam* for their armies (not just for their staffs: cf. A. H. M. Jones, *The Greek City*, p. 323 n. 59); the price was determined by the senate (*Verr.* iii. 188), and the amount limited (iii. 225). Governors often accepted money in lieu of this corn; this was called *aestimare frumentum* ('setting a price on corn'). See further J. Carcopino, *La Loi de Hiéron* (Paris, 1914), pp. 192 ff.

10. honorarii (sc. *frumenti*): 'complimentary gifts of corn'; cf. Cato, *orat.* frag. 132 (Malcovati, *ORF*²) 'cum essem in provincia legatus, quam plures ad praetores et consules vinum honorarium dabant'.

si quidem . . . : for this kind of rhetorical point cf. *Verr.* iv. 40, *Clu.* 34, *Planc.* 70, *Sest.* 33, *Mil.* 33, *Phil.* iii. 20, etc. The figure is called ἀφορισμός or διορισμός (Julius Rufinianus 14 = Halm, *Rhet. Lat. Min.*, p. 42).

12. Boeotii: Boeotia was a fertile area, and one which suffered under Piso (§ 96). Madvig objected that Boeotia was free at this date (*Adv. crit.* ii. 229); but this is untrue (p. 173), and in any case irrelevant (Byzantium and Thessalonica were free, but not excused from contributions). The real difficulty is that Boeotia was much more remote from the Thracian front than the other places mentioned. Yet Cicero says *tota in provincia* below (though this may refer simply to Macedonia proper). Besides, it was profitable to demand corn from a distant area; if money were paid in lieu, the cost of transport could be taken into account. Madvig himself

156

COMMENTARY [§§ 86–87]

proposed *Bottiaei*; these people occupied the plain west of the Axius, but are little mentioned in the Roman period. This emendation may be right, but is not certain.

Byzantii: Byzantium was a *civitas libera* (*prov. cons.* 7) *et foederata* (Tac. *ann.* xii. 62).

Cherronensus: the Thracian Chersonese included both *ager publicus* and *liberae civitates* (A. H. M. Jones, *Cities of Eastern Roman Provinces*, pp. 15 f.). It was probably not strictly a part of Macedonia (cf. U. Kahrstedt, *Beiträge zur Geschichte der thrakischen Chersones*, pp. 50 ff.), but an area where Piso had authority to intervene. The MSS. read *Cherronenses*, a form found in late writers (*Thes. L.L.* onomast. ii. 389. 71); but a place name is desirable to balance *Thessalonica*.

§ 87. 15. **reorum pactiones:** 'bargains involving accused persons'. Cicero suggests that in negotiations with third parties Piso promised to convict prisoners. *reorum* is also to be taken with *redemptiones*, etc.

16. **libidinosissimas:** 'highly capricious'.

17. **tantum locum aliquem:** 'simply some topic'; when Cicero has mentioned the category of crime he will leave Piso to think of specific instances.

20. **pellium nomine:** hides were needed for tents, shields, boots, etc. (*RE* xix. 1. 371 f.); for such requisitioning cf. *Verr.* II. i. 95 'cum iste civitatibus frumentum coria cilicia saccos imperaret'. *nomine* implies that Piso's reason was not the whole truth; cattle were lucrative in other ways.

22. **bello Italico:** the Social War; it is not called *bellum sociale* in Republican Latin (A. v. Domaszewski, *Wien. Akad. Sitzungsb.* cci, 1 Abh., 1924, 3 ff.).

23. **pater:** cf. introd., p. v. For this sort of invective cf. p. 194.

24. **vectigalem . . .:** 'do you remember that, when you imposed a fixed duty on every separate article that was destined for sale, a province which paid *vectigalia* to Rome was ⟨handed over⟩ to your slaves?'

provinciam: Clark inserted *populi Romani* (*p.r.*) before this word, an easy change, but unnecessary.

25. **portorio:** a tax levied on goods passing a control-point, which need not necessarily be a harbour or frontier-town (S. J. de Laet, *Portorium* (Brugge, 1949), p. 16). Piso also transferred the *portorium* of Dyrrachium to his own use (p. 175). For his use of his own agents rather than *publicani* compare the action of Gabinius in Syria (p. 191).

Here Rostovtzeff interprets *portorium* as an ἐπώνιον or sales-tax (*Soc. Econ. Hist. Hell. World*, pp. 987, 1574), but I have found no clear instance of such a use. The point of *quaecumque venirent*

157

§§ 87–88] COMMENTARY

may simply be that the *portorium* was only levied on articles destined for sale; cf. Tac. *ann.* xiii. 51 'militibus immunitas servaretur nisi in eis quae veno exercerent', *codex Just.* iv. 61. 5 (a tax levied on things) 'quae negotiationis gratia portantur', R. Cagnat, *Étude historique sur les impôts indirects chez les Romains* (Paris, 1882), pp. 104 f. In Liv. xxxii. 7. 3 the MSS. read '(censores) portoria venalicium Capuae Puteolisque . . . locarunt'; but no certain inference can be made as the passage appears to be corrupt (cf. de Laet, op. cit., pp. 55 f.).

servis . . .: *publicanis* is meaningless and should be deleted (Bake). For *factam* I have considered *patefactam* or something like *traditam*; Professor Watt suggests that *factam* is genuine, and that a predicative adjective (something like *quaestuosam*) has fallen out before *a te*. Clark proposed *servam tuis publicanis a te factam*; cf. *Verr.* iii. 50 'Veneriosque servos, quod isto praetore fuit novum genus publicanorum'; but in our passage Piso's agents could not be called his *publicani* without explanation. A. Klotz reads *servis tuis a te factam*, and interprets 'Macedonia was made tax-paying to your slaves'. But *vectigalem* cannot be predicative; it must refer to the well-known fact that Macedonia paid *vectigalia* to Rome.

§ 88. 26. centuriatus . . . venditos: cf. *imp. Pomp.* 37 'quem enim imperatorem possumus ullo in numero putare, cuius in exercitu centuriatus veneant atque venierint ?', Jolliffe, op. cit. [86. 6 n.], pp. 17 f.

27. tuum servolum: an official on Piso's staff. Probably he was an experienced freedman, like Q. Cicero's Statius (*Q.f.* i. 2). For *servus* used abusively in this way cf. *Mil.* 87 and Asconius ad loc., perhaps also *Pis.* 11, 30.

ordines adsignatos: usually the *tribuni militum* appointed centurions (*St.-R.* i³. 120 n. 4, Marquardt, *St.-V.* ii². 369). For the system of promotion cf. H. M. D. Parker, *The Roman Legions* (Oxford, 1928), pp. 31 ff., Kromayer–Veith, *Heerwesen*, pp. 319 ff., 400 ff. *adsignare* is the technical term for awarding ranks.

1. stipendium: the cities of Macedonia paid Piso's army, though this money should have been provided by Piso from the *ornatio* of his province. *mensis* means 'banking-tables' (τράπεζαι).

2. illa . . . profectio: cf. p. 179. The construction changes illogically from the accusative (after *meministi*) to the nominative.

4. praetoria nuntiata: in June 56 the senate discussed the provinces which the consuls of 55 were to govern in 54. Servilius Isauricus proposed Macedonia and Syria; Cicero suggested further that these provinces should be governed by praetors in 55, i.e. that Piso and Gabinius should be recalled a year earlier. In the end it was decided that Syria should be given to one of the consuls of 55

158

COMMENTARY [§§ 88–89]

in 54, and Macedonia to one of the praetors of 56 in 55; i.e. Piso was to be recalled a year earlier than Gabinius. See Butler and Cary's edition of *prov. cons.* p. 13, *St.-R.* ii³. 218 n. 2, E. G. Hardy, *CR* xxxi, 1917, 13.

6. quaestor . . .: with *praepositus* understand *provinciae*; *aediliciis reiectis* is ablative absolute. When a governor left his province he put one of his staff in charge to await the arrival of his successor. He normally chose his quaestor, who as the holder of an elective office was technically superior to a legate; but if a legate had held higher office his claims might be difficult to resist. Cicero himself chose his quaestor; cf. *fam.* ii. 15. 4 ' "puerum" inquis. at quaestorem, at nobilem adulescentem, at omnium fere exemplo. neque erat superiore honore usus quem praeficerem', *fam.* ii. 18. 2, *Att.* vi. 3. 1, *St.-R.* i³. 682 f.

Of Piso's known legates (54. 22 n.) Flaccus and Vergilius were ex-praetors; Marcius Crispus may have been an ex-aedile (R. Syme, *CP* l, 1955, 135). *aediliciis reiectis* seems to imply that Piso had two ex-aediles on his staff (for a fourth legate cf. 86. 6 n.), unless indeed the plural is rhetorical. *aedilicio reiecto* would be a possible reading, but is less close to *aedilicius reiectus* of the MSS. One might also consider *aedilicius reiectus, quaestor praepositus*; but Cicero is giving a list of Piso's offences, and nobody could criticize the appointment of a quaestor *per se*.

7. violatus: 'insulted'; Piso disregarded their *dignitas*. For his stern treatment of his staff see p. 182.

8. non recepti: not admitted to his presence.

§ 89. 10. sordibus: 'mourning' (*RE* viA. 2229). Romans when threatened with prosecution often assumed mourning; but the account here has all the appearance of fiction.

populari . . . sacerdoti: Clodius. Cicero calls him elsewhere 'sacerdos bonae deae' (*Att.* ii. 4. 2) and 'stuprorum sacerdote' (*Sest.* 39); cf. also *dom.* 77 'ubi tu te popularem, nisi cum pro populo fecisti, potes dicere?' He also calls him a *sacerdos* in connexion with the consecration of his own house (*dom.* 103, 111, *har. resp.* 9). In our passage and at *Sest.* 66 he uses the expression 'popularis sacerdos' without making his exact reference clear; after the Bona Dea incident he must have made the joke so many times that the name had stuck.

11. sescentos: an indefinite large number, which seems to have originated in a duodecimal system of counting (E. Wölfflin, *ALL* ix. 178 ff., 527 ff.).

ad bestias: when Clodius, as aedile, gave the Megalesian games in April 56 his friend Piso supplied human victims; in the same way Caelius, when aedile, hoped that Cicero, the proconsul

159

§ 89] COMMENTARY

of Cilicia, would provide him with panthers (*fam.* viii. 4. 5). The victims were presumably criminals; the same form of execution had been used by Aemilius Paulus and Scipio Aemilianus on provincials or allies who had gone over to the enemy (Val. Max. ii. 7. 13 f.). See Mommsen, *Strafrecht*, pp. 925 f., *Sex. Rosc.* 71.

amicos sociosque: the provincials. A. Klotz argues that with this reading *populi Romani* would be necessary (Cicero is not referring to Piso's personal friends); but there is no ambiguity in so common a phrase (here used maliciously). The reading of Asconius, *socios stipendiariosque*, is rhetorically less effective.

12. **decessionis:** here used, as often, of the departure of a governor from his province.

13. **Samothraciam:** an inscription to Piso has been found at Samothrace on the base of a statue: [ἡ βουλὴ καὶ ὁ δῆμος Λεύκιον Καλπόρνιον] Λευκίου υ[ἱὸν Πείσ]ωνα τὸν αὐτοκράτορ[α καὶ πάτ]ρωνα τῆς πόλεως (H. Bloch, *AJA* xliv, 1940, 485 ff.). Bloch suggests that Piso visited Samothrace to be initiated in the mysteries; but his position as patron is sufficient reason for a farewell visit (cf. 89. 20 n. for a similar visit to Beroea, L. Harmand, op. cit. [25. 19 n.], pp. 138 ff.). Clearly the Samothracians did not make Piso their patron at the end of his proconsulship, when his usefulness had passed. The statue was probably erected in 56, after Piso had been hailed as *imperator* (αὐτοκράτωρ), and before his supersession.

post inde: for such pleonasms cf. K.–S. ii. 573 f.

14. **saltatoribus:** similarly Antony had *saltatores* in his retinue (*Phil.* v. 15); cf. H. Blümner, *Die römischen Privataltertümer*, p. 616. In Greece actors, musicians, etc. ('technitae of Dionysus'), had a privileged position (Poland, *RE* vA. 2473 ff.), and might well have been found in the entourage of a phil-Hellene proconsul.

Autobulo . . .: by quoting these obscure names, which he no doubt pronounced with distaste or amusement, Cicero shows how much he knows about the details of Piso's life.

[et]: deleted by Madvig (*fin.* iv. 56); where three co-ordinate words are on the same level Cicero does not use the pattern 'A B et C' (K.–S. ii. 32, *Thes. L.L.* v. 2. 877. 1).

15. **formosis fratribus:** presumably these people were brothers of one another, entertainers in Piso's retinue. H. Bloch, op. cit., suggests that *fratribus* means 'fellow initiates of Piso' (cf. *Thes. L.L.* vi. 1257. 28). But a reference to initiation would be obscure, especially as Thasus and *saltatores* are mentioned after Samothrace. *formosis* sometimes has the ironic meaning of 'fine'; cf. *leg. agr.* ii. 53 'cum suis formosis finitoribus auctionantem'. Yet in view of *teneris* above it surely means 'beautiful' here; Cicero suggests that Piso associated with effeminate Greeks.

160

COMMENTARY [§§ 89–90

16. **Euhadiae:** a possible name (from ἀνδάνω), though it is not actually quoted by W. Pape, *Wörterbuch der griechischen Eigennamen.* The variant *Euchadiae* is unlikely; *Euadnae* (Halm) is the most plausible emendation.

17. **obsoletus:** in shabby clothes, as a sign of mourning; cf. *Verr.* II. i. 152 'obsoletius vestitum'.

18. **venisti:** 'went'; cf. 49. 23 n.

20. **Beroam:** a town about 40 miles west of Thessalonica (*RE* iii. 304 ff.); the spelling Βερόη is found as well as Βέροια. It was far from being an *oppidum devium*, and was visited by St. Paul (Acts xvii. 10). Piso was patron of Beroea, which explains his farewell visit (cf. 89. 13 n. on Samothrace). See J. M. R. Cormack, *AJA* xlviii, 1944, 76 f., quoting the following inscription: Λεύκιον Καλπόρνιον Πίσωνα ἀνθύπατον Βεροιαῖοι καὶ οἱ ἐνκεκτημένοι Ῥωμαῖοι τὸν ἑατῶν πάτρωνα. The subject of the inscription is identified by some with Piso's son, cos. 15 B.C., proconsul of Thrace; but there is no evidence that he was proconsul of Macedonia.

21. **quod:** 'in that'. Logically one would expect *esset successurus* or *esse successurum putabas*; but cf. the common conflation in causal sentences (K.–S. ii. 200 f.).

Q. Ancharius: praetor 56, succeeded Piso as governor of Macedonia in 55 (*RE* i. 2102, *SIG*3 748 n. 14, H. Pomtow, *Klio*, xv, 1917, 70); his appointment must have been an affront to Caesar, whom he had opposed in 59. Ancharius was available towards the end of 56, but does not seem to have arrived in Macedonia till the summer of 55 (cf. p. 200). Perhaps Caesar arranged that Piso should not be unduly hurried.

23. **renovasti:** cf. *de or.* ii. 199 'animos equitum Romanorum ... ad Q. Caepionis odium . . . renovabam atque revocabam' (though the text is doubtful). *innovasti* (codd.) is not found elsewhere till the second century A.D. Professor Watt suggests *revocasti*.

§ 90. 23. aurum coronarium: in origin this was a gift of gold for a general's triumphal crown; in practice it became a contribution of money which he could turn to his own use (Marquardt, *St.-V.* ii². 295, Kubitschek, *RE* ii. 2552). Rullus in his agrarian bill in 63 had required generals to hand over such money to the State; then Cicero was indignant (*leg. agr.* i. 12, ii. 59). The *lex Julia repetundarum* in 59 (37. 2 n.) attempted to restrict such donations; for the extension of *leges repetundarum* beyond their original scope cf. A. N. Sherwin-White, *PBSR* xvii, 1949, 14.

25. **te:** many editors omit, as the *lex Julia* obviously did not name Piso. Yet the word is rhetorically effective.

26. **in quo** means 'in connexion with this', and refers to the

§§ 90–91] COMMENTARY

previous sentence as a whole; cf. J. K. Schönberger, *Tulliana* (Augsburg, 1911), pp. 29 f.

acceptam tamen . . . pecuniam: Abram emended from the ablative to the accusative, since *evomere* needs an object. *tamen*, if genuine, seems to point a contrast between the money which caused Piso perplexity and the money which he had actually received; Abram deleted the word; R. Klotz proposed *iam*.

1. **evomere:** cf. Plaut. *Curc.* 688 'argentum vomere'; so ἐξεμεῖν (Ar. *Ach.* 6, *equ.* 1148).

vocabula . . . mutabas: 'you simply changed the descriptions and categories of the money' (co-ordinate with *tu . . . non poteras*).

2. **diplomata:** certificates given by Piso to officials or friends, entitling them to free hospitality and transport. Cf. Cato, *orat.* frag. 173 (Malcovati, *ORF²*) 'numquam ego evectionem datavi quo amici mei per symbolos pecunias magnas caperent', Wünsch, *RE* v. 1158 f., A. H. M. Jones, *The Greek City*, pp. 323 n. 59, 328 n. 90.

3. **numerum navium:** the Romans relied on the provincials to provide a navy (Jones, op. cit., p. 323 n. 60, Rostovtzeff, *Soc. Econ. Hist. Hell. World*, pp. 963, 1562 n. 23, Broughton in T. Frank's *Economic Survey*, iv. 571 ff.). Cicero alleges that Piso violated a provision of the *lex Julia* restricting the number of ships levied. Such action might be a cloak for illicit gain (*Verr.* v. 60 f., *Flacc.* 27 ff., Jolliffe, op. cit. [86. 6 n.], pp. 34 ff.); yet Cicero's brevity here suggests that the charge may have been false. In any case Piso might have quoted Cicero's own words (*Flacc.* 27): 'proximum est ergo ut opus fuerit classe necne quaeramus. utrum igitur hoc Graeci statuent . . . an nostri praetores, nostri duces, nostri imperatores ?'

4. **praedae:** generals were allowed to expend booty in the national interest without a close audit, but not to appropriate it (Mommsen, *Strafrecht*, p. 765, Marquardt, *St.-V.* ii². 285 ff., Jolliffe, op. cit., pp. 19 ff.).

rationem: 'calculation', in the literal arithmetical sense.

§ 91. 7. **Aetoliam:** this area probably still enjoyed a measure of independence (S. Accame, *Il Dominio romano in Grecia*, pp. 211 ff.). Piso's action in expelling the Agraei (91. 13 n.) proves nothing about the constitutional position of the area; his powers were exceptional, and he presumably was supported by the neighbouring cities.

8. **in sinu pacis:** cf. Plin. *paneg.* 56. 4 'in hoc urbis otio et intimo sinu pacis'.

9. **gremio:** cf. *prov. cons.* 4 'Thessalonicenses positi in gremio imperi nostri'.

Poena: = Ποινή; cf. *Clu.* 171.

162

COMMENTARY [§§ 91–92]

10. **decedens:** 'when leaving your province'. Cicero's phraseology is misleading; Piso's action, which is alleged to have caused the outbreak, took place two years earlier.

11. **ut . . . indicasti:** perhaps in Piso's *altercatio* in the senate with Torquatus (§ 92). These words refer only to *nobilis urbis atque plenas*. Cicero no doubt exaggerates; for the decline of Aetolia in the following period see U. Kahrstedt, *Historia*, i, 1950, 554 f.

12. **nempe eis:** for the combination of question and answer (διαλεκτικόν) cf. Quintil. ix. 2. 14, Volkmann, pp. 492 f.; for *nempe* introducing a reply cf. *Lig.* 7, 25, *Phil.* x. 6, Hand, iv. 162.

13. **sedens:** 'taking up your quarters', evidently with a military force. For Ambracia see 96. 25 n.

Agraeorum: cf. § 96 'Dolopes finitimique montani oppidis atque agris exterminati'. Lambinus's emendation suits admirably. The Agraei lived in the mountains east of the Ambracian Gulf (north of Stratus); but the exact extent of their territory is unknown (cf. W. J. Woodhouse, *Aetolia* (Oxford, 1897), pp. 81 ff., A. Philippson, *Die griechischen Landschaften*, ii, teil 1, 187). The Agrianes were a Thracian people and cannot be meant here; however, it is possible that Cicero himself was confused about the name.

14. **Dolopum:** these people lived in the mountainous area between Aetolia and Thessaly (*RE* v. 1290 f., viA. 108 f.). When Piso ejected them from their homes they must have moved south; otherwise they would have been too far from the lowland cities of Aetolia. By the time of Augustus they had ceased to exist (Paus. x. 8. 3). It was common Roman policy to move wild hill-tribes to settlements in the valleys; cf. Agrippa's action in Spain (Dio liv. 11. 5), perhaps also the replacement of Bibracte by Augustodunum.

aras et focos: an attempt to evoke pity, which may have been undeserved.

17. **dimisisti:** cf. 47. 26 n.

19. **cognosci:** this emendation gives a slightly smoother sentence than Madvig's *quam quemquam . . . cognoscere*. Cobet compared Liv. xxxix. 20 'consul . . . ne quantum deminutae copiae forent appareret in locis pacatis exercitum dimisit'. One could only defend the reading of the MSS. as a rhetorical extravagance: Piso will not acknowledge the facts even to himself. But it is more to Cicero's purpose to say that he is concealing the truth from the senate and people.

§ 92. 21. **Albucius:** T. Albucius (*RE* i. 1330 f.), as propraetor of Sardinia about 104, celebrated a kind of private triumph there; for such 'triumphs' outside Rome cf. the celebration of Cn. Domitius in Gaul in 120 (Suet. *Ner.* 2. 1), and of Antony in Alexandria in 34 (Dio xlix. 40. 3). Albucius was refused a *supplicatio* by the senate,

163

§ 92] COMMENTARY

convicted of extortion, and exiled. He wrote Epicurean treatises (*nat. d.* i. 93), and Cicero describes him as 'perfectus Epicureus' (*Brut.* 131). For his phil-Hellenism cf. especially Lucilius 88 ff., where Scaevola grects him in Greek: ' "chaere" inquam "Tite". lictores turma omnis chorusque | "chaere Tite". hinc hostis mi Albucius, hinc inimicus.'

22. exspectaret: cf. *prov. cons.* 16 'eius exitum exspectet' (of Gabinius and Albucius).

23. tropaea: such monuments had been erected by Sulla at Chaeronea and by Pompey in the Pyrenees; cf. G. C. Picard, *Les Trophées romains* (Paris, 1957).

25. praeposterus: 'paradoxical'; his behaviour was the exact opposite of what you would expect. Cf. *fam.* xv. 17. 1 'praeposteros habes tabellarios', of messengers who ask for letters but bring none.

26. ad ... dedecus: cf. *dom.* 103 'doloris mei defixum indicium ad memoriam omnium gentium sempiternam' with R. G. Nisbet's note, *Thes. L.L.* i. 538. 61.

30. Torquato: cf. 44. 15 n., 47. 22.

3. nocte intempesta: 'at dead of night'. *intempesta* literally means 'unseasonable', 'when nothing can be done'. Censorinus regards *intempesta nox* as the part of the night between *concubium* and *media nox* (*de die natal.* 24. 6); cf. Sidon. *epist.* ii. 2. 14.

crepidatus: wearing Greek sandals, suitable for a phil-Hellene, unseemly for a proconsul; cf. 13. 6 n., Gell. xiii. 22. For such gibes cf. Pers. 1. 127 'qui in crepidas Graiorum ludere gestit', *St.-R.* iii. 220 n. 1, below, p. 194. Yet when Rabirius Postumus was maligned for wearing Greek clothes Cicero's defence was unanswerable: 'L. vero Scipionis, qui bellum in Asia gessit Antiochumque devicit, non solum cum chlamyde sed etiam cum crepidis in Capitolio statuam videtis' (*Rab. Post.* 27).

veste servili: obvious fiction, part of the stock-in-trade of escape stories; cf. Val. Max. ix. 8. 2, App. *b.c.* ii. 22. For the ablative cf. K.–S. i. 408, L.–H., p. 430.

4. ultimas Hadriani maris oras: Cicero's language could be taken to mean that Piso sailed to the north of the Adriatic. Yet he returned to Rome by the *porta Esquilina* (§ 55), where the *via Praenestina* and *via Labicana* entered the city. This does not suit a journey to the north, but he may have made a detour to visit some estate near Rome.

It does not seem to have been pointed out that certain inscriptions from Pola may have a bearing on this passage. See *Inscr. Ital.* x. 1. 65 (= *CIL* i². 2. 2512) 'L. Calpu[rnius L.f.] Piso Ca[esoninus] cos'. The name *Caesoninus* points to the consul of 58 (though

164

COMMENTARY [§§ 92-94

cf. 14. 16 n.); *cos* points to the year 58 (this is the reading of A. Gnirs, *Jahresh. des österr. archäol. Inst.* xiii, 1910, Beibl. 196, though the -*s* is not visible in his photograph).

A second inscription, on the *porta Herculis*, refers to L. Cassius C.f. Longinus and L. Calpurnius L.f. Piso as *duumviri* (*Inscr. Ital.* x. 1. 81 = *CIL* v. 54; see also A. Degrassi, *Il Confine nord-orientale dell'Italia romana*, Bern, 1954, pp. 65 f.). As the colony probably belonged to the triumviral period this Piso may be the son of Cicero's enemy. Some scholars have believed that Cicero's enemy was *duumvir* in his old age; but one would expect so eminent a personage to have been mentioned before his colleague.

A third inscription reads simply '[Cal]purn[   ]son[' (*Inscr. Ital.* x. 1. 708). -*son*- may be part of *Pison-* and not *Caesonin-*; therefore there is no reason to suppose that this inscription refers to the consul of 58.

A fourth inscription records a *senatusconsultum*, mentioning soldiers and ships (*Inscr. Ital.* x. 1. 64). One of the consuls named is ']us Q.f. Metellus', perhaps the consul of 57 B.C. (thus Groag, *PIR*² C 64); yet for a later date cf. Polaschek, *RE* xxi. 1246.

The first three of these inscriptions show that the Pisones had an interest in the Pola area; perhaps they inherited property from Calventius (frag. ix n.); Degrassi notes the number of Calpurnii in Histria. It may also be relevant that Piso's son-in-law, Caesar, was governor of Cisalpine Gaul and Illyricum; perhaps the Romans were showing a particular interest at the time in this important strategic area (cf. p. 174, Degrassi, *Il Confine nord-orientale*, pp. 31 ff.). If the fourth inscription quoted above could be firmly attached to 57 it would support such a view.

§ 93. 8. **crepidatum imperatorem:** the expression is humorously incongruous.

9. **statuam:** for the destruction of statues cf. *Verr.* ii. 158 ff., Juv. 10. 58 ff. 'descendunt statuae restemque sequuntur' with Mayor's note.

10. **memoria moreretur:** for the same assonance cf. *in sen.* 3, *off.* ii. 56.

12. **id:** for the pleonasm cf. K.–S. i. 625.

§ 94. 14. **excellent:** Priscian, *GL* ii. 444 f. shows that this verb sometimes belonged to the second conjugation; he quotes from a lost letter of Cicero's 'elabora ut excelleas'. For other instances cf. *Thes. L.L.* v. 2. 1212. 70.

15. **turbam:** cf. *de or.* ii. 314 'ut ea quae excellent serventur etiam ad perorandum; si qua erunt mediocria . . . in mediam turbam atque in gregem coniciantur'.

16. **nihil est . . .:** 'you need not exhort me'. Piso had ironically

165

§ 94] COMMENTARY

urged Cicero to prosecute him (cf. § 82); Cicero says that a hint will be enough, but only when the time is ripe.

17. **autem:** cf. K.–S. ii. 93.

18. **tempus:** 'time of opportunity' (καιρός).

19. **ecquid vides . . .:** Cicero suggests that he will prosecute Piso when the jury-system has been reorganized. Nobody can have believed him.

20. **lege iudiciaria lata:** Asconius explains that by the *lex Aurelia* of 70 B.C. *iudices* were drawn from three classes, the senate, equites, and *tribuni aerarii* (cf. H. Last, *CAH* ix. 338 ff., J. D. Denniston on *Phil.* i and ii, appendix ii). He goes on: 'rursus deinde Pompeius in consulatu secundo, quo haec oratio dicta est, promulgavit ut amplissimo ex censu ex centuriis aliter atque antea lecti iudices, aeque tamen ex illis tribus ordinibus, res iudicarent'. That is to say, Pompey kept the three classes of *iudices*, but within each class imposed a stricter property-qualification (cf. Denniston on *Phil.* i. 20). This provision would sufficiently restrict the number of *iudices*; previously a list had been made out by the urban praetor (Greenidge, *Legal Procedure*, pp. 445 f.). Those selected were no longer to be allowed to decline service. Pompey's *lex iudiciaria* was ineffective (Ps. Sall. *epist.* ii. 3. 3); it lasted until Caesar excluded the *tribuni aerarii* from the *iudices* in 46.

21. **neque legetur:** *neque* might have been read as *ñeque*. Hand, i. 198 f., accepts *non aeque*, and suggests that it means 'not to the same extent as at present'. He compares *de or.* iii. 50 'simulac Fufius aut vester aequalis Pomponius agere coepit, non aeque quid dicant . . . intellego'; there *non aeque* is explained by the previous context (cf. *Thes. L.L.* i. 1044. 72). Yet in our passage it seems clumsy.

22. **nulli conicientur . . .:** 'none will be pitched into the order of jurymen, none will be exempted'; cf. *Phil.* v. 15 'totum denique comissationis Antonianae chorum in tertiam decuriam iudicum scitote esse coniectum', *Phil.* i. 20, *Thes. L.L.* iv. 310. 73.

23. **non iniquitas . . .:** this passage is hopelessly corrupt. Lambinus proposed *non iniquitas ad simultatem*; *simultas* is contrasted elsewhere with *gratia* (*de or.* ii. 62, Ps. Sall. *epist.* ii. 11. 1), but suggests lasting hostility rather than bias on a particular occasion. Madvig (*Adv. crit.* iii. 148) suggested *non iniquitas ad aemulationem*; *aemulatio* can mean 'jealousy' (*Tusc.* iv. 17), but gives an inadequate contrast with *gratiam*. Hence Busche (*Jahrb.* cliii, 1896, 570) proposed *non ad iniquitatem aemulatio*; I should prefer *non aemulatio ad iniquitatem*. Professor Watt suggests that *non simultas ad iniquitatem* would give the best contrast.

The verb is also corrupt. *conicientur* of the MSS. comes from

COMMENTARY [§§ 94-95

above; the lost word need not resemble it closely. *conitetur* (Faernus) would mean 'will strive towards', but is unsatisfactory. I have considered *incitabit*.

24. **lex . . . libido:** these words are contrasted at *Verr*. iii. 82, *Att*. vii. 9. 4, Sall. *Jug*. 31. 7, *hist*. orat. Phil. 17, Liv. iii. 9. 5, Ps. Sall. *epist*. ii. 3. 4.

26. **invitum invitabis:** for the play on words cf. Plaut. *rud*. 811, *Trin*. 27.

27. **quod nolim:** because of his pretended friendship with Caesar.

§ **95.** *Cicero gives other unconvincing reasons to explain why he is not prosecuting Piso.* §§ **96–99** *contain a recapitulation of some points made earlier: this was often done at the end of a speech* (*Volkmann*, pp. 262 ff.).

§ **95.** 1. **paulo ante:** cf. §§ 42–44.

6. **P. Rutilio:** P. Rutilius Rufus, cos. 105, legate in Asia (perhaps in 94) where he offended the *publicani*; he was condemned for extortion by an equestrian jury in 92, and retired to Asia, the very province which he was accused of having plundered. He was visited by Cicero at Smyrna in 78. He is called 'exemplum innocentiae' (*de or*. i. 229), 'vir non saeculi sui sed omnis aevi optimus' (Vell. ii. 13. 2), and so often in later writers. His reputation for integrity was fostered by his own memoirs, by anti-equestrian propaganda, and by many references in Cicero, especially after his own exile. See Münzer, *RE* iA. 1269 ff., G. L. Hendrickson, *CP* xxviii, 1933, 153 ff., E. Badian, *Athenaeum*, xxxiv, 1956, 104 ff.

quod: the attraction of gender is normal (K.–S. i. 37).

8. **L. Opimius** as praetor in 125 crushed the revolt of Fregellae, as consul in 121 suppressed C. Gracchus; cf. *Planc*. 70 'cum illum e civitate eiecerunt qui praetor finitimo, consul domestico bello rem publicam liberarat'. He was condemned in 109 for taking bribes from Jugurtha; revenge for 121 was the real reason. One can imagine Cicero's feelings when he was in exile at Dyrrachium and saw Opimius's tomb 'desertissimum in litore' (*Sest*. 140).

e patria: Cicero says *eicere e civitate* eight times in the speeches. With some nouns he occasionally omits the preposition (cf. *Mil*. 87 'multos sedibus ac fortunis eiecerat'), but he offers no close parallel to Asconius's reading *eiectus est patria*.

9. **non in eo . . . :** cf. Plat. *Gorg*. 469c ἐλοίμην ἂν μᾶλλον ἀδικεῖσθαι ἢ ἀδικεῖν, Metellus Numidicus frag. 7 (Malcovati, *ORF²*) 'probi iniuriam facilius accipiunt quam alteri tradunt', *Tusc*. v. 56, *Phil*. xi. 9, Otto, p. 175.

11. **bis Catilina absolutus:** in 65 Catiline was acquitted of extortion (23. 16 n.), in 64 of murder during Sulla's proscriptions.

167

§§ 95–96] COMMENTARY

Cicero made this same point after the acquittal of Clodius (*Att.* i. 16. 9). *est* can be understood from *eiectus est* above, in spite of the sentence which comes between.

emissus: 'let loose', like a caged animal in the arena. Cf. *rhet. ad Her.* iv. 51 'sicut cavea leo emissus', *Sest.* 134, *har. resp.* 37.

ille auctor tuus: Clodius. One would have expected *ille tuus auctor*.

12. **stuprum:** for the Bona Dea incident cf. introd., p. viii. It should not be forgotten that Caesar's former wife was also involved, and more indirectly Caesar's own *dignitas*. Cicero's tactlessness is no doubt deliberate; for a more direct thrust at Caesar cf. *har. resp.* 38 'hominibus iniuria tui stupri inlata in ipsos dolori non fuit'.

pulvinaribus: at certain ceremonies the images of the gods were placed on *pulvinaria*, or sacred couches (G. Wissowa, *Religion und Kultus*², p. 422, A. Hug, *RE* xxiii, 1977). For other allusions to the *pulvinaria* in connexion with the Bona Dea incident cf. *har. resp.* 8, 33, *Mil.* 72.

13. **tanta:** Pluygers proposed *tota*, but cf. *dom.* 108 'civis est nemo tanto in populo', *har. resp.* 11 'sed quae est in hac urbe tantā domus . . . ?', *Rab. Post.* 45 'ecquis est ex tanto populo . . . ?', Catull. 81. 1 'nemone in tanto potuit populo esse, Iuventi, bellus homo quem tu diligere inciperes . . . ?'

14. **pari scelere:** Crassus was said to have bribed the jury at Clodius's trial (cf. *Att.* i. 16. 5). The charge may have been true, but Cicero was perhaps in the habit of saying such things when a verdict displeased him.

§ **96.** 15. **quinque et septuaginta:** there were 75 *iudices* in trials *de repetundis* (Greenidge, *Legal Procedure*, p. 447, J. Lengle, *Zeitschrift Savigny-Stiftung*, Rom. Abt. liii, 1933, 293 f.). For *diribeantur* ('counted') cf. 36. 20 n.

18. **aditu:** cf. *Clu.* 41, *Sest.* 111, *Vat.* 2. **communi:** 'which one gives freely to all men'; cf. Petr. 113 'nec Giton me . . . sermone communi vocabat'. **salutatione:** cf. *Cat.* i. 16, ii. 12.

19. **putat:** the indicative is better than the subjunctive: Cicero is talking about the present attitude to Piso, not about future possibilities. For instances of both moods cf. Housman on Manil. iv. 922.

20. **a re publica detestantur:** 'seek to exorcize from the state'.

21. **fuerunt:** Cicero does not in theory reject the form *fuere*; cf. *orat.* 157 'nec vero reprehenderim "scripsere alii rem" etsi "scripserunt" esse verius sentio, sed consuetudini auribus indulgenti libenter obsequor'. But the form in *-ere* is very seldom found in important MSS. of Cicero. See L.–H., p. 338, Neue–Wagener,

168

COMMENTARY [§§ 96-97]

Formenlehre, iii³. 190 ff., A. Önnerfors, *Pliniana* (Uppsala, 1956), pp. 54 ff.

militum: Orelli's *militares* gives an inferior rhythm.

24. Achaia . . .: cf. 37. 5 n. Cicero's language is exaggerated; no doubt these states felt obliged to contribute to Piso's war fund (cf. p. 173).

25. Dyrrachium: cf. 83. 21 n. *Apollonia:* cf. 86. 4 n.

Ambracia: declared free in 187 (Liv. xxxviii. 44. 4); a Roman garrison was stationed there in 171 (Liv. xlii. 67. 9), and again by Piso (§ 91); but this does not prove that the city had lost its *libertas*.

26. Partheni: a tribe in the hinterland of Dyrrachium (R. Syme, *CQ* xxxi, 1937, 42), occupying a vital position near the *via Egnatia*. They were still dangerous; Pollio triumphed over them in 39. The spelling *Partheni* is occasionally found (*RE* xviii. 2045), and might be right here.

Bullienses: an Illyrian tribe living south of Apollonia. The forms *Bullidenses*, *Byllidenses*, *Bulliones* (*fam.* xiii. 42. 1), and *Bullini* are attested (*Thes. L.L.* ii. 2265. 65); *Bullienses*, which is read by the MSS. here, may also be possible.

Locri: Eastern Locris fought Rome in 147; thereafter it may have been subordinated to the governor of Macedonia. Western Locris remained loyal in 147 (W. A. Oldfather, *AJA* xxvi, 1922, 446 f.); it was *immunis* in the early Empire, and possibly in Piso's time also (Accame, *Il Dominio romano*, pp. 206 ff., Oldfather, *RE* xiii. 1233 f.). Accame refers our passage to Western Locris, and connects it with the sacking of Naupactus (§ 91). But the reference to the Phocii and Boeotii suggests that tax-gathering is meant, and this points to Eastern Locris. Yet in these vague exaggerations one cannot look for precision.

1. Phocii Boeotii: probably subordinate to the governor of Macedonia, with the exception of some free cities; see p. 173, Accame, op. cit., pp. 193 ff.

Acarnania: probably 'free'; in 94 the chief city Thyrreum became a *civitas foederata* (*SIG*³ 732, Accame, op. cit., p. 215).

Amphilochia Perraebia Athamanumque gens: all probably 'free' (Accame, pp. 228 ff.).

3. Aetolia: cf. § 91; *amissa* is an absurd exaggeration. *Dolopes:* cf. § 91.

4. cives Romani: for Italian *negotiatores* in Greece see J. Hatzfeld, op. cit. [86. 4 n.], M. Rostovtzeff, *Soc. Econ. Hist. Hell. World*, pp. 762 ff.

5. unum solum: for the pleonasm cf. *Flacc.* 45 and du Mesnil's note.

§ 97. 7. domesticum iudicium: 'your own personal verdict';

169

§§ 97–98]   COMMENTARY

cf. Caes. *b.c.* iii. 60. 2 'ex domestico iudicio atque animi conscientia intellegebant', Nägelsbach, pp. 330 f. For the thought cf. *Clu.* 59 'suo iudicio . . . est condemnatus'.

sententiae . . . : 'the votes in favour of your conviction are . . .'; i.e. Piso is convicted not by the verdict of 75 jurymen, but by a series of damaging actions on his own part. But the text is doubtful: the genitive after *sententiae* is unparalleled, and the omission of *sunt* is also a little strange. Bake's deletion of *sententiae . . . tuae* is worth consideration; but it seems awkward to take *adventus, iter,* etc., in apposition to *iudicium.* Many editors join *sententiae . . . tuae* to the previous sentence, but this is impossible. A. Klotz, *praefatio,* p. lxii, proposed *nam quid fuerunt nisi sententiae . . . ?* I have followed him in taking *sententiae* as nominative, but his supplement is perhaps unnecessary.

8. **occultus adventus:** cf. § 53.

9. **nullae . . . litterae:** 'the absence of letters' (cf. K.–S. i. 770); see § 38.

10. **trinis aestivis:** cf. p. 200.

12. **seminario:** literally 'a nursery', where young trees could be fostered in favourable conditions; the metaphor is continued in 'arida folia laureae'. For the large number of triumphs from Macedonia see § 38, p. 177.

14. **abiecta:** cf. 61. 13 n.

fecisse videri: the verdict of 'Guilty' in Roman courts was 'fecisse videtur'; cf. Greenidge, *Legal Procedure,* p. 498. Cicero, *acad.* ii. 146 comments on the caution of *videtur*; see also D. Daube, *Forms of Roman Legislation* (Oxford, 1956), pp. 73 ff.

16. **ubi exercitus:** 'what were you doing with your army?'; cf. § 38 'quas res gessisti imperio exercitu provincia ?' For this use of *ubi* cf. *Verr.* v. 83 'ubi quaestores ?'

18. **speraveras:** for *aliquid sperare* cf. *Sull.* 34, *Att.* vii. 3. 8, Holden on *off.* i. 35. *sperare volueras* (codd.) can hardly be right; hopes are not a matter for wish or decision, and the clausula is unconvincing. *sperare potueras* (Madvig) is weak in sense, and gives the same clausula.

cogitaras: Naugerius proposed *si cogitaras,* but *si* may not be necessary; cf. F. Leo, *Plautinische Forschungen*[2], p. 272 n. 4.

§ 98. 23. **eventis:** 'results'; cf. *Rab. Post.* 1 'hoc plerumque facimus ut consilia eventis ponderemus', Ov. *her.* 2. 85 f. 'exitus acta probat. careat successibus, opto, quisquis ab eventu facta notanda putat', Otto, pp. 126 f.

24. **[dicere audes]:** these words, meaningless here, come from 97. 12.

26. **[te]:** Garatoni deleted; the word is inconsistent with *se* in l. 5.

170

COMMENTARY [§§ 98–99

3. **[non apud equites Romanos]**: these words are impossible here, after the more general *non apud ullum ordinem*. Garatoni's transposition is possible (cf. § 45 'hic ordo . . . equites Romani . . . ceteri ordines'). But the next clause has only two members ('non in urbe, non in Italia'); so two members are better than three here also.

5. **ad ignoscendum**: Halm's deletion might seem to be supported by the confusion in X; yet for a similar pleonasm cf. *part. or.* 131 'ignoscendi petenda venia est'. The clausula is better if the words are kept.

se ipsum oderit: *ipsum* is justified instead of *ipse*, as there is a contrast with the accusative *omnis*; though even in such circumstances *ipse* is possible (K.–S. i. 632, Nägelsbach, pp. 395 f., Lebreton, pp. 145 ff.). Below *se ipse condemnet* is required by Latin usage, and confirmed by the clausula.

§ 99. 8. quod . . . commune: these words belong together; for the thought cf. 42. 5 n. The subjunctive *posset* is oblique; Cicero is describing his own attitude in the past ('that punishment which could, as I knew . . .'). But Bake's *potest* may be right.

11. **quicquid increpuisset**: cf. *Cat.* i. 18 'quicquid increpuerit Catilinam timeri', Sall. *Jug.* 72. 2 'circumspectare omnia et omni strepitu pavescere', Virg. *Aen.* ii. 728, Hor. *carm.* i. 23. 5 ff., Sen. *epist.* 56. 13, 90. 43, Juv. 10. 21 with Mayor's note. The subjunctive is probably oblique (L.–H., p. 709), and corresponds to a future-perfect in direct speech ('quicquid increpuerit pertimesces'). It is less likely to be iterative, as Cicero normally uses the indicative in such circumstances; yet cf. *de or.* iii. 60 'quam se cumque in partem dedisset', K.–S. ii. 206 f.

19. **sordidum**: dirty, i.e. contemptible. *sordidatum*: wearing the mourning of an accused man.

APPENDIX I

PISO'S PROCONSULSHIP OF MACEDONIA
57–55 B.C.

PISO was created proconsul of Macedonia by the *concilium plebis* in defiance of the senate. Long-term appointments[1] to extraordinary commands had occasionally been made by popular assemblies; the *lex Vatinia* of 59 had broken new ground by appointing Caesar to an ordinary province in this way. Piso's minimum term of office must have been stated in the *lex Clodia*; otherwise the senate would have superseded him at the first opportunity.[2] It seems to have been legally possible, even if not easy, to replace him at the end of 56 (88. 4 n.); but a tenure of two years seems short for a command of this kind. Perhaps the law named a term of three years, or even longer, but provided for a reduction of this period if the Thracian war were finished sooner.

Piso was voted at the same time a large sum of money, which was made available from Caesar's resettlement fund.[3] His allowance for equipment amounted to 18,000,000 sesterces, but it is difficult to interpret the significance of this sum (86. 28 n.). He was authorized to conscript an army of unusual size (§§ 37, 57, *prov. cons.* 5). He was also given special powers, which are described as *infinitum imperium* (*dom.* 55); this is not a precise term of constitutional law but a vague rhetorical insult.[4] Perhaps he was permitted to make war and install garrisons in the Thracian and Black Sea sectors; Cicero complains to Clodius 'cum alteri . . . Macedoniam omnemque barbariam . . . condonasses' (*dom.* 60). But the chief offence of the provision, in Cicero's eyes, was that it gave Piso undue authority in the *liberae civitates* of Greece (§§ 37, 90, *dom.* 23, 60).

The constitutional status of Greece (the later province of Achaea) is obscure at this date.[5] Some at least of the states defeated in 146

---

[1] A. E. R. Boak, *Amer. Hist. Rev.* xxiv, 1918, 1 ff., J. P. V. D. Balsdon, *JRS* xxix, 1939, 68 ff.

[2] The half-hearted attempt to recall Piso in 57 (*prov. cons.* 13) may have been based on the assumption that the *lex Clodia* was invalid.

[3] *dom.* 23, *Pis.* 28, 37, 57; for such grants cf. P. Willems, *Le Sénat*, ii. 424. [4] J. Béranger, *Mélanges Marouzeau* (Paris, 1948), pp. 19 ff.

[5] See Marquardt, *St.-V.* i². 321 ff., and especially S. Accame, *Il Dominio romano in Grecia*, with the reviews by F. W. Walbank, *JRS* xxxvii, 1947, 205 ff. and M. Gelzer, *Gnomon*, xxi, 1949, 20 ff.

APPENDICES

had lost their liberty; one may include in this category, for example, Megara, Eastern Locris, Phocis, Boeotia, Chalcis (Accame, op. cit., p. 8). Other areas were left nominally free,[1] for instance Athens, Thessaly, and much of the Peloponnese (37. 5 n.), Aetolia (91. 7 n), Western Locris, Acarnania, Amphilochia, Perrhaebia, Athamania (96. 1 n.). Other states farther north were also free, notably Thessalonica, Byzantium (86. 12 n.), Dyrrachium (83. 21 n.), Apollonia, Thasos, Samothrace (Plin. *n.h.* iv. 73).

It is not clear what taxes were normally exacted from these areas.[2] Pausanias, speaking of the events of 146, says φόρος ἐτάχθη τῇ Ἑλλάδι (vii. 16. 9), but he is not necessarily reliable. The territory of Corinth was *ager publicus* (*leg. agr.* i. 5), and tax-farming is recorded both in Euboea[3] and Boeotia;[4] most of Phocis probably also paid tribute (cf. Paus. x. 34. 2). Even *liberae civitates* had no constitutional right to immunity from taxes;[5] they had often paid them under Hellenistic kings, and Macedonia between 168 and 146 was both free and tribute-paying (Liv. xlv. 29. 4). In some crisis, perhaps during M. Antonius's campaign in 102 against the pirates, the free city of Messene paid a 2 per cent. property tax.[6] During the operations against the pirates in 74–71 payments were made by the free city of Gythium.[7] Some states were recognized to be immune from tribute, but even they would be expected to do their duty in emergencies.

The *lex Clodia* seems to have regularized Piso's authority to impose taxes on the free cities of Greece; previously the senate's permission may have been necessary;[8] besides, the *lex Julia* had very recently restricted the powers of governors (§ 90). Piso was in an odd position, as he had quarrelled with the senate; he might be obstructed by it if he demanded financial support from the

[1] Caes. *b.c.* iii. 3. 2, Zonaras ix. 31; this meant little (*SIG³* 684).
[2] Rostovtzeff, *Soc. Econ. Hist. Hell. World*, pp. 748 f., J. A. O. Larsen in Frank's *Economic Survey*, iv. 307, H. Hill, *CP* xli, 1946, 35 ff.
[3] *CIL* i.² 588 (*S.C. de Ascl.*).
[4] *nat. d.* iii. 49, *SIG³* 747 (*S.C. de Amph.*).
[5] A. H. M. Jones, *Anatolian Studies presented to W. H. Buckler* (Manchester, 1939), pp. 103 ff. For the status of *liberae civitates* see A. N. Sherwin-White, *The Roman Citizenship*, pp. 149 ff.
[6] *IG* v. 1432–3, A. Wilhelm, *Jahreshefte*, xvii, 1914, 1 ff., Rostovtzeff, op. cit., pp. 750 ff., Accame, pp. 136 ff.
[7] *SIG³* 748, Rostovtzeff, pp. 951 ff., Accame, pp. 131 f.
[8] Cf. Polyb. xxviii. 13 and Liv. xliii. 17; the rule was invoked by Rhodes against Cassius (App. *b.c.* iv. 66).

173

APPENDICES

liberae civitates. Again, governors sometimes needed a supplementary allocation from the senate;[1] Piso, who had not been financed in the first place by the senate, was unlikely to be given a fair hearing. He needed the resources of a large province to sustain him.

Piso was also given unusual rights of jurisdiction in *liberae civitates*. A recent *senatusconsultum* had forbidden governors to intervene when Roman financiers tried to recover their loans to these cities; Cicero sympathized with Atticus when he was thus prevented from applying pressure to Sicyon (*Att.* i. 19. 9). This decree had been confirmed by the *lex Julia* of 59, but a clause in the *lex Clodia* had exempted Piso from the rule; Cicero complains 'emisti grandi pecunia ut tibi de pecuniis creditis ius in liberos populos contra senatus consulta et contra legem generis tui dicere liceret' (*prov. cons.* 7). In spite of Cicero's insinuation Piso used this clause in the interests of Apollonia (86. 4 n.); in the only other case mentioned, in Byzantium, no details are given (*prov.. cons.* 6), but it cannot be supposed that Piso at any time showed bias in favour of Roman capitalists.

It is uncertain what other privileges Piso enjoyed. Some have seen significance in an inscription from Delos which is dated directly by his proconsulship, without any mention of the fact that his province was Macedonia;[2] this method of dating is not otherwise found in Achaea till the creation of the new province in 27. Yet as the inscription was set up not by Greeks but by Italian businessmen, the method of dating may have no great significance. Nor can one be sure of the purpose behind the *lex Clodia*. It could be argued that administrative arrangements in Greece were chaotic, and the activities of *publicani* and bankers detrimental to the provincials; perhaps certain statesmen of vision, including Caesar himself, saw the need for a stronger and more centralized government. Besides, there were strategic issues. The position on the Thracian frontier was intolerable, and the resources of the peninsula could have been employed more effectively. It is even possible, though on the whole unlikely, that the menace of the Dacian Burebista[3] was already

[1] *prov. cons.* 28, *Balb.* 61, *St.-R.* iii. 1098 n. 1.

[2] Inscr. de Délos 1737 (= F. Durrbach, *Choix*, 164): L. Cal[pu]rnio L.f. Pisone proco[s ἐ]πὶ [ἀ]νθυπάτου Λ[ευκίου] Καλπορνίου τοῦ Λ[ευκίου Πε]ίσωνος οἱ ʽΕρμαισταὶ τὸν ναὸ[ν κ]αὶ τὰ ἀγαλματα ʽΕρμε[ῖ]. See also J. Hatzfeld, *BCH* xxxiii, 1909, 522 ff.

[3] Carcopino associates the *lex Vatinia* with Burebista's movements (*Hist. rom.* II. ii[4], Paris, 1950, pp. 739 f.).

174

APPENDICES

being felt; with Caesar's legate in Illyricum and Piso in Macedonia was Balkan policy now being coordinated ?[1] Yet one must be cautious in positing grandiose schemes of this kind; 'infinitum imperium' can be explained, at least in part, by the need to compensate a governor who could expect no backing from the senate.

To turn to the details[2] of Piso's proconsulship, Cicero first alleges that he embezzled the money voted to equip his army (§ 86); he would no doubt have given particulars if any had been available. Piso levied an annual εἰσφορά from the Achaeans (*Sest.* 94, *prov. cons.* 5), as well as a lump sum of 100 talents (§ 90); but as has been seen, such temporary exactions had precedents in time of war. A *portorium* was introduced, which was collected by Piso's own officials rather than by the *publicani* (87. 25 n.); the local[3] *portorium* at Dyrrachium was transferred to the central government of the province (*prov. cons.* 5). Cicero states that the soldiers' pay was exacted from the province (§ 88), though even so they were not paid in full (§ 92); this is likely enough, but only proves that the administration needed money. Piso is also said to have accepted payment when centurions were appointed (§ 88), and to have kept too much war-booty for himself (§ 90).

Piso requisitioned large quantities of grain (86. 9 n.); rightly so, seeing that Roman legionaries were starving to death (§ 40). He rounded up cattle, since essential military equipment was made of leather (§ 87); persons with cattle to sell would have preferred to let prices find their natural level in a free market. Piso was also said to have levied warships beyond the legal number (90. 3 n.). He billeted troops in the towns during the winter, a harsh but necessary proceeding (86. 6 n.); it is unreasonable to ascribe the excesses of the garrison in Byzantium to the proconsul in person (*prov. cons.* 6). According to the regular practice he supplied many persons with certificates entitling them to free lodging and transport (90. 2 n.). He acquired statues and pictures from Byzantium and the temples of Greece (*prov. cons.* 6–7, *Sest.* 94); Rostovtzeff suggests that they were seized as security for the payment of a capital levy, but this for once may be too charitable a view.[4]

---

[1] Cf. perhaps 92. 4 n. (Piso's activities in the north Adriatic).
[2] Rostovtzeff, pp. 987 f., 1574 f., R. O. Jolliffe, op. cit. [supra 86. 6 n.].
[3] For such taxes cf. S. J. de Laet, *Portorium*, pp. 89 ff.
[4] Yet it is not certain that the Herculaneum bronzes belonged to Piso (p. 187).

APPENDICES

It was alleged that Piso had been bribed to execute a chieftain of the Bessi (below, p. 178); but Cicero could have no knowledge of the circumstances. Another charge is even more absurd: after having been bribed by the Thracians to keep at peace with them, Piso is said to have allowed them to find the money by devastating the province (*Sest.* 94, *prov. cons.* 4). Piso executed two persons from Orestis called Plator and Pleuratus (83. 22 n.); Cicero says again that he was bribed, but they might have been engaged in activities which would have provoked cruel reprisals from any Roman governor. Cicero mentions other corrupt convictions and acquittals (§ 87), but produces no evidence. The case of Apollonia is more significant. Cicero claims that Piso was bribed to give a verdict against Fufidius, but it is clear that he was protecting the Greeks against the extortions of a ruthless financier (86. 4 n.).

It cannot be proved that Piso was a paragon of rectitude; like others of his age and class he may have regarded his province as a source of profit. But Cicero's charges are so vague (contrast the Verrines), and sometimes so unreasonable, that they arouse the greatest scepticism. It is no argument to point out that Cicero, who lived in Dyrrachium in the early part of Piso's proconsulship, was in a position to know the facts; his own bitterness and the conventions of his genre gave him every encouragement to mislead. When Cicero claims that Piso was hated by his staff (§ 88) and the Italian business community (§§ 96, 98), this tells in his favour; Catullus shows that he checked the acquisitiveness of his subordinates (p. 182). His taxes no doubt caused hardship, but they may have been justified by military necessity and the parsimony of the senate. It should not be forgotten that Piso was a phil-Hellene and an Epicurean, the patron of places like Samothrace (89. 13 n.) and Beroea (89. 20 n.), the friend of Greeks like Philodemus and Socration (p. 182).

According to Cicero Piso's direction of the Thracian war was as disastrous as his civil administration. The key to Roman power in the Balkans was the *via Egnatia*, which with its extensions reached from Dyrrachium and Apollonia to the Hellespont (40. 14 n.). This road was also the only overland communication with Asia, yet it was thinly protected, particularly in the Thracian sector. The range of Rhodope, rising to 9,000 feet, interposed a solid barrier to the north; an advance could only be made up the valleys of the Axius

176

APPENDICES

or Hebrus, or to a lesser extent the Strymon.[1] There was no permanent or cohesive frontier: the province was bounded by the tips of the legionaries' javelins (§ 38). The Romans could only control the interior by punitive expeditions and playing off one tribe against another.

So Macedonia became the scene of chronic wars and indecisive victories (*prov. cons.* 4, *Pis.* 38).[2] About 119 Sex. Pompeius, the governor, was killed in action (*SIG*³ 700); in 114 C. Cato was defeated by the Scordisci (Liv. *per.* 63). Triumphs[3] were won by C. Caecilius Metellus Caprarius in 111, by M. Livius Drusus in 110, by M. Minucius Rufus in 106, by T. Didius about 100 (§ 61). Between 91 and 88 Thracians raided the province, and though beaten back for a time by the governor, C. Sentius, they penetrated as far as Dodona (§ 84, Oros. v. 18. 30, Dio frag. 101. 2). The invasion of Mithradates must have had an even more disastrous effect on Roman prestige.

Cn. Cornelius Dolabella, proconsul 80–77, won a triumph (§ 44). His successor, Appius Claudius Pulcher, defeated the tribesmen of Rhodope and occupied the cities of the Bosporus and Propontis, but died in his province in 76 (Oros. v. 23. 19, Amm. Marc. xxvii. 4. 10); Cicero has nothing to say about this governor, the father of his enemy Clodius. C. Scribonius Curio (76–73) took five legions to Macedonia, defeated the Dardani, and broke through to the Danube (Front. *strat.* iv. 1. 43, Eutr. vi. 2), presumably by a bold thrust up the Axius (Vardar) and down the Morava and Timok. M. Lucullus (72–71) marched up the Hebrus valley and defeated the Bessi near the Haemus (Balkan) range; then in a second campaign he won the Greek cities on the Black Sea as far as the Danube (Eutr. vi. 10, Ruf. 9, Strabo vii. 6. 1). His gains were not consolidated, but Rome extended her network of alliances; to this period may belong the treaty with Callatis (*CIL* i². 2. 2676). Curio and Lucullus were awarded triumphs (§§ 44, 58); in spite of their spectacular exploits they are little mentioned in the *in Pisonem*, for Curio was an enemy of Cicero's, and Lucullus was probably dead (58. 2 n.). L. Manlius Torquatus (64–63) was hailed as *imperator*,

[1] For the geography of the country cf. S. Casson, *Macedonia, Thrace, and Illyria* (Oxford, 1926), pp. 3 ff.

[2] Cf. G. Zippel, *Die römische Herrschaft in Illyrien* (Leipzig, 1877), pp. 140 ff., C. Patsch, *Wien. Akad. Sitzungsb.* ccxiv, 1 Abh., 1932, 28 ff., B. Lenk, *RE* viA. 439 ff.

[3] For details cf. A. Degrassi, *Inscr. Ital.* xiii. 561 ff.

APPENDICES

but did not triumph (44. 15); when he attacked Piso's administration in the senate, he no doubt set himself up as a specialist in Macedonian affairs (§§ 47, 92). C. Antonius (62–60) was defeated first by the Dardani on the central Axius front, then by the Bastarnae at Istrus near the mouth of the Danube (Dio xxxviii. 10. 2–3); he seems to have lost all Lucullus's gains, and must have been highly unpopular when he returned to Rome. C. Octavius (60–59), the father of Augustus, was hailed as *imperator* for a victory over the Bessi, but died on the way home (*ILS* 47, Suet. *Aug.* 3). L. Appuleius Saturninus was propraetor in 58, but nothing of interest is recorded of his administration. The province needed a strong governor; Cicero's suggestion that it was peaceful (*prov. cons.* 4–5) is nonsense.

Cicero's account of Piso's campaigns is vague and misleading; there are few indications of chronology, but matters mentioned in the *pro Sestio* or *de provinciis consularibus* must have happened in 57 or early in 56. Piso sent an expedition against the Denseletae, who lived in the upper Strymon valley; Cicero exaggerates the docile manners of these brigands (84. 9 n.). The temple of the Thracian god Zeus Zbelsurdos was destroyed (85. 18 n.); it must have been dangerous to march a column through the narrow Kresna gorge.[1] But the expedition, which was a punitive or warning raid rather than an attempt at conquest, accomplished nothing. The Denseletae swept down the valley and sacked some unspecified towns; one would have expected Cicero to mention names if any place of importance (for instance Amphipolis) had been attacked. The vital *via Egnatia* was cut, or at any rate threatened; in one passage Cicero vividly describes the barbarian encampments which studded the strategic highway (*prov. cons.* 4), but in our speech he uses the less imaginative phrase *obsessio militaris viae* (§ 40). The incursion was taken seriously; even the townspeople of Thessalonica evacuated their homes and fortified the acropolis (*prov. cons.* 4, *Pis.* 40, 84). The Dardani, who lived in the upper Axius valley, also made raids (*Sest.* 94).

Piso may also have operated further east, in the footsteps of M. Lucullus, where the most interesting vistas opened up. Cicero describes how he was offered reinforcements by the Bessi, a troublesome tribe (84. 3 n.) which lived in the Hebrus valley; he retorted by beheading their emissary, one Rabocentus. This, like the attack on the Denseletae, must have happened in 57; for the epidemic sent

[1] For a photograph cf. S. Casson, op. cit., p. 20.

178

APPENDICES

from heaven in retribution (§ 85) is already known to Cicero in June 56 (*prov. cons.* 5). Rabocentus might of course have visited Piso during his campaign against the Denseletae, but a separate operation in the Hebrus valley seems much more likely. This view is supported by the suggestion that Piso was bribed by Cotys, who was probably king of the Astae in Eastern Thrace (84. 4 n.).

In the winter of 57–56 Piso billeted troops in Byzantium, among other places (*prov. cons.* 5, *Pis.* 86). The city was a convenient base for a strategic reserve; besides, it had recently experienced internal conflicts, and Clodius in 58 had given Cato the task of reinstating certain exiles (*dom.* 52, Plut. *Cat.* 34). During this winter the Roman army suffered severely from cold, disease, and shortage of rations (§§ 40, 85, *prov. cons.* 5). Catullus offers bantering condolences to two elegant young aides-de-camp on Piso's staff (p. 180).

But Piso's huge army justified itself in the end. A great victory was won by Q. Marcius and other legates (§ 54), Piso was hailed as *imperator* (§ 38), triumphal monuments were constructed (§ 92). This battle cannot have taken place later than the spring of 56, as Cicero sneers at Piso's title of *imperator* even in the *de provinciis consularibus* (§ 15). Cicero also mentions a futile expedition to the Black Sea (*Pis.* 88); the date of this campaign is probably 56, since it is mentioned in the same context as Piso's supersession. In 55, shortly before Piso's return, there was trouble in Aetolia; the Agraei and Dolopes, wild clansmen who had been ejected from their fastnesses early in 57, broke loose and looted Arsinoe, Stratus, and Naupactus (91. 14 n.). Cicero probably makes too much of the incident.

Piso's campaign was in the long run successful; and though he owed his victory to the professionals on his staff, so did many proconsuls, not least Cicero in Cilicia. Even though short of money he would not have demobilized his army if his province had been in any danger. It is true that Torquatus attacked him for this action (§§ 47, 92), but Torquatus had been a friend of Cicero's since boyhood (Nep. *Att.* 1. 4). Cicero's suggestions of mental derangement are not serious, as Piso was uncommonly level-headed. We hear nothing of trouble in Thrace in the following years, which is some indication that Piso had done his work well. About this time[1] the

---

[1] Between 60 and 48 (*SIG*³ 762). Dio Chrysostom puts his advance about 150 years before he is writing (*orat.* xxxvi. 4); that speech was written after A.D. 96.

APPENDICES

Dacian Burebista over-ran the Greek cities on the Black Sea from Olbia to Apollonia; but if this had happened during Piso's proconsulship Cicero would have said so. In any case the Thracian frontier stood firm and no clash with Rome took place, though Caesar meditated a large-scale expedition (Suet. *Jul.* 44. 3, App. *b.c.* ii. 110, iii. 25). Thrace, it is true, remained unsubdued; the distinction of reducing this bleak and intractable country belonged not least to Piso's son.

APPENDIX II

PISO AND CATULLUS[1]

> Pisonis comites, cohors inanis,
> aptis sarcinulis et expeditis,
> Verani optime tuque mi Fabulle,
> quid rerum geritis ? satisne cum isto
> vappa frigoraque et famem tulistis ?
> ecquidnam in tabulis patet lucelli
> expensum, ut mihi, qui meum secutus
> praetorem refero datum lucello ? . . . .
>
> (Catullus, xxviii. 1–8)

> Porci et Socration, duae sinistrae
> Pisonis, scabies famesque mundi,
> vos Veraniolo meo et Fabullo
> verpus praeposuit Priapus ille ?
> vos convivia lauta sumptuose
> de die facitis, mei sodales
> quaerunt in trivio vocationes ?
>
> (xlvii)

Veranius and Fabullus were on a certain Piso's staff at the same time that Catullus was on Memmius's staff in Bithynia (Catull. 28. 6 ff., cf. 10. 7).[2] Memmius was praetor in 58, therefore probably

[1] See L. Schwabe, *Quaestiones Catullianae*, i. 243 ff., C. L. Neudling, *Prosopography to Catullus* (Iowa Studies in Classical Philology, 1955), pp. 42 ff., R. Syme, *Classica et Mediaevalia*, xvii, 1956, 129 ff.

[2] For such appointments cf. J. van Vliet, *De praetoria atque amicorum cohortibus* (Traiecti ad Rhenum, 1926), pp. 22 ff., W. Allen and P. H. DeLacy, *CP* xxxiv, 1939, 59 f.

APPENDICES

governor of Bithynia in 57. Caesoninus, who was proconsul of Macedonia 57–55, is the only Piso who is known to have been a provincial governor during that period. He was the most important Piso at that date. He was the father-in-law of Caesar, whom Catullus also lampoons. As an Epicurean and a friend of poets he makes a good pair with Memmius, the patron of Lucretius. He is said by Cicero to have given prolonged dinners to Greek favourites (§§ 22, 67); this fits poem xlvii. His distinguished ancestry suits Catullus 28. 13 'pete nobiles amicos' (though admittedly most governors would be *nobiles*). The reference to *frigoraque et famem* coheres with § 40 'exercitus nostri interitus ferro fame frigore'.[1]

Unfortunately Catullus says elsewhere that Veranius and Fabullus went together to Spain (12. 14, cf. 9. 6); he probably means Hispania Citerior, since he mentions Saetaban napkins. The governor of that province in 57 is not known. Theoretically he could have been another Piso;[2] for instance, M. Pupius Piso, proconsul in Spain 71–69 and consul 61, could have held a second proconsulship. Yet Piso Caesoninus fits Catullus's poems so well that it seems best to suppose that Veranius and Fabullus made two journeys together. Syme has pointed out (op. cit., pp. 132 ff.) that Caesoninus could have been governor in Spain in 60–59, after his praetorship; perhaps Veranius and Fabullus went twice in his entourage. But as he himself observes, there is no certainty that Piso governed a province after his praetorship (cf. introd., p. vi).

The date of poem xxviii is presumably 56, after the cold winter of 57–56 (p. 179). Veranius and Fabullus are still in Macedonia ('satisne cum isto . . . ?'), but Catullus may have left Bithynia or be on the point of leaving.[3] Poem xlvii also describes a state of affairs during Piso's proconsulship. After Piso had returned to Rome his

---

[1] Yet *frigora* suits other provinces besides Macedonia: for instance, the interior of Hispania Citerior was cold in winter.

[2] Thus, for example, P. Maas, *CQ* xxxvi, 1942, 80. Maas points out that in 25. 7 Thallus steals 'sudarium Saetabum catagraphosque Thynos'; in xii Marrucinus steals a *sudarium Saetabum* which Veranius and Fabullus have sent from Spain: the poems naturally belong together, about the time of the journey to Spain; what is Catullus doing with Bithynian *catagraphi* if he has not recently been in Bithynia ? Neudling, op. cit., p. 42, suggests that he got them from his brother.

[3] C. Caecilius Cornutus appears on coins of Amisus, evidently as governor of Bithynia and Pontus; cf. *Brit. Mus. Catalogue, Pontus, etc.* (London, 1889), p. 21. As he was praetor in 57 he was probably governor in 56.

181

APPENDICES

staff could not expect many invitations to his house; but if they were excluded from the proconsul's table in Thessalonica they were in a real difficulty. Schwabe and Baehrens thought that Porcius and Socration were so enriched by Piso that they themselves gave lavish dinners in Rome; but the poem loses point if the dinners were given by anybody but Piso.

Porcius looks like a Roman of distinguished family. Neudling, op. cit., pp. 147 f., suggests that he may have been C. Porcius Cato; but Cato could hardly have been in Macedonia in 57–56, and as has been seen, poem xlvii probably describes events in Thessalonica. The name Socratio -onis is attested (*CIL* iii, p. 948, twice), and Galen mentions a doctor called Σωκρατίων (xii. 835); the Latin form of this name would normally be *Socratio*, but could be *Socration* (Neue–Wagener, *Formenlehre*, i³. 246 ff.). Alternatively Socration might stand for Σωκράτιον; this is a possible diminutive of Σωκράτης though it is not found elsewhere. In the latter case it would be a nickname for one of Piso's philosophical friends, perhaps even Philodemus, as Friedrich suggested in his commentary (p. 228). But as Porcius is a real name, Socration is perhaps a real name also. The status of the man is obscure. *sinistrae* suggests that he was a tax-official on Piso's secretariat. But one expects a Greek dining with Piso to be a philosopher or other intellectual; in that case *sinistrae* is simply abusive.

Catullus does not yield much information about Piso. Cicero's picture of a grim hedonist finds a little confirmation, though both writers obviously exaggerate. The obscenities at the end of xxviii mean simply 'Piso has been as niggardly to you as Memmius has been to me';[1] it is important to learn that Piso restricted the depredations of his staff. Catullus's evidence is less valuable when he accuses Piso of theft; even if *duae sinistrae* is not entirely fictitious, Catullus would not distinguish between extortion for personal gain and the imposition of necessary taxes.

[1] Housman, *Hermes*, lxvi, 1931, 408.

APPENDIX III

PISO AND PHILODEMUS[1]

PHILODEMUS, the Epicurean philosopher and poet, was born, like Meleager, at Gadara,[2] perhaps about 110 B.C. He studied at Athens under Zeno of Sidon. He came to Italy about 75 or 70, and found in Piso a sympathetic patron; noblemen with cultural interests, or pretensions, liked to have learned Greeks in their entourage.[3] Piso was then still an *adulescens* (§ 68), or so Cicero contemptuously calls him; yet about the same time or a little later he is described as a senator, which he became about 70. Philodemus need not necessarily have lived in Piso's house (68. 1 n.); at one time he had a house of his own (*a.P.* xi. 44. 1). It has been thought that in later life he worked in a villa at Herculaneum belonging to Piso, but this cannot be decisively proved (Appendix IV). He may have had other important friends,[4] but there seems no reason to doubt that Piso was his principal patron.

Some scholars[5] believe that Philodemus was in Piso's entourage in Macedonia, but Cicero's words *nec fere ab isto umquam discederet* (§ 68) need not be taken so literally. In one of his epigrams Philodemus hopes for a safe journey to the Peiraeus (*a.P.* vi. 349), but the poem cannot be dated. At *a.P.* x. 21. 4 Philodemus talks of himself as τὸν χιόσι ψυχὴν Κελτίσι νειφόμενον, and hence Cichorius suggests that he went with Piso on a visit to Caesar in Gaul; but ψυχήν shows that the Celtic snows are metaphorical. Some have supposed that Philodemus is the Socration who was favoured by Piso in Macedonia (Catull. 47. 1), but this too is uncertain (p. 182).

About thirty of Philodemus's epigrams[6] survive in the Greek

---

[1] For details and bibliography see R. Philippson, *RE* xix. 2444 ff., P. H. and E. A. DeLacy, *Philodemus: on Methods of Inference* (Philadelphia, 1941).

[2] Near the Sea of Galilee, the Gadara of the swine (cf. W. Peek, *Griech. Vers-Inschriften* i. 1070. 3 against Strabo xvi. 2. 29).

[3] Cf. the relationship of Antiochus to Lucullus, Staseas to M. Piso, Diodotus to Cicero.

[4] W. Allen and P. H. DeLacy, *CP* xxxiv, 1939, 59 ff.

[5] C. Cichorius, *Römische Studien*, pp. 295 f.; for a faulty argument see 70. 23 n.

[6] Edited G. Kaibel (Greifswald, 1885).

183

APPENDICES

Anthology, some of outstanding elegance, as Cicero says (§ 70); one may mention especially *a.P.* v. 46, 107, 112, 123, ix. 412, 570. His themes are sometimes Epicurean, friendship (ix. 412, xi. 44), moderate pleasure (xi. 34), the finality of death (ix. 570. 5 *εὕδειν ἀθανάτως πουλὺν χρόνον*). He invites Piso to a simple Epicurean dinner (xi. 44):

> Αὔριον εἰς λιτήν σε καλιάδα, φίλτατε Πείσων,
>   ἐξ ἐνάτης ἕλκει μουσοφιλὴς ἕταρος
> εἰκάδα¹ δειπνίζων ἐνιαύσιον· εἰ δ' ἀπολείψεις
>   οὔθατα καὶ Βρομίου χιογενῆ πρόποσιν,
> ἀλλ' ἑτάρους ὄψει παναληθέας, ἀλλ' ἐπακούσῃ
>   Φαιήκων γαίης πουλὺ μελιχρότερα·
> ἢν δέ ποτε στρέψῃς καὶ ἐς ἡμέας ὄμματα, Πείσων,
>   ἄξομεν ἐκ λιτῆς εἰκάδα πιοτέρην.

Philodemus also seems to have described an Epicurean dinner given by Piso (67. 13 n.).

Some of Philodemus's epigrams are on erotic themes (cf. § 70), but Cicero is wrong in suggesting that he condoned adultery (cf. *a.P.* v. 126, Hor. *serm.* i. 2. 120 ff.). In any case such verses tell nothing about Philodemus's character, as the genre was conventional (70. 11 n.). Besides, Philodemus may have written many of these epigrams before he met Piso. At the age of 37 he talks of his last love-affair (xi. 41), and in another poem claims to have turned to more serious pursuits (v. 112):

> καὶ παίζειν ὅτε καιρός, ἐπαίξαμεν· ἡνίκα καὶ νῦν
>   οὐκέτι, λωιτέρης φροντίδος ἁψόμεθα.

Yet Cicero maliciously pretends that these epigrams describe life in Piso's house (§ 70); of course no Greek, however eminent, would have portrayed a *princeps civitatis* in this way.

Many of Philodemus's philosophical writings were discovered at Herculaneum (p. 186). They cover an astonishing range, and include treatises on the Gods, on Flattery, on Music, on Malice, on Poems, on Rhetoric, on Methods of Inference, on the Good King according to Homer. Philodemus's prose makes a startling contrast

---

¹ i.e. a dinner in honour of Epicurus (cf. 67. 13 n.). P. Boyancé, *REL* xxxiii, 1955, 113 ff., suggests that Ikadium, a slave of Piso's daughter Calpurnia (*carm. epig.* 964), derived her name from this festival.

184

APPENDICES

with his verse; it is arid[1] and technical in the Epicurean manner (cf. 70. 26 n.), and sometimes polemical about matters of no importance. But much Hellenistic philosophy was like this before Cicero humanized the subject again. Philodemus is very painstaking, and acute in scoring small points, but he does not seem to have had a powerful or original mind. His ideas depend mainly on Epicurus and Zeno of Sidon; but he may well have added something of his own in the περὶ ποιημάτων, where he maintains that the aim of poetry is not moral but aesthetic.[2]

Philodemus dedicated to Piso his περὶ τοῦ καθ' Ὅμηρον ἀγαθοῦ βασιλέως. He may have written this essay during Caesar's dictatorship, as after the Ides of March kingship was less admired.[3] One might see significance in the condemnation of civil war (col. x), but it is dangerous to look for topical allusions in so conventional a type of literature.[4] It is even possible that the treatise was written as early as the time of Piso's proconsulship in Macedonia.[5] Philippson sees a reference to Piso in another fragment[6] where he reads εὐθὺς ἔτυχες τῆς ἀνωτάτης συν[ψηφίας] καὶ κλήρου τῶν ἐν[ικῶς πα]ρ' ἀστοῖς τειμωμένων (he compares § 2 'omnes magistratus sine repulsa adsecutum'). But his supplements and interpretation are extremely doubtful. There is a clearer historical allusion in the περὶ θεῶν, where Philodemus seems to criticize both Antony and the Liberators: ὅ[ταν] ὁρᾷ παρωσαμένους ὑφ' ἑνὸς [Ἀ]ντωνίου [χεῖ]ρα[ς τ]ὰ [κα]τ' ἄσ[τ]υ τοὺς [ἐ]ναντίου[ς (i. 25). This suits the latter part of 44 when Piso opposed Antony.[7] It has also been suggested that in this treatise Philodemus criticized the deification of Caesar (iii. 10 τὰ κατασκευαζόμενα πρὸς ἡμῶν εἴδη καὶ τοὺς νέους θεούς). But this is an uncertain interpretation of an obscure and perhaps corrupt passage.[8]

[1] For a defence, perhaps too sympathetic, see Philippson, op. cit., col. 2476.

[2] Op. cit., cols. 2479 ff., A. Rostagni's edition of Horace's *ars poetica*, pp. xciv ff.

[3] A. Momigliano, *JRS* xxxi, 1941, 153.

[4] For the genre cf. M. Rostovtzeff, *Soc. Econ. Hist. Hell. World*, p. 1594.

[5] M. Paolucci, *Aevum*, xxix, 1955, 201 ff.

[6] *RE* xix. 2475, W. Crönert, *Rh. Mus.* lvi, 1901, 618.

[7] H. Diels, *Abhand. Preuss. Akad.* (Phil.-Hist. Kl.), 1915, 7, 99 f., R. Philippson, *Hermes*, liii, 1918, 381 ff., A. Momigliano, op. cit., p. 154.

[8] H. Diels, *Abhand. Preuss. Akad.*, 1916, 6, 34, R. Philippson, *Rh. Mus.* lxxxiii, 1934, 172 ff., G. Freymuth, *Zur Lehre von den Götterbildern in der epikureischen Philosophie* (Akademie-Verlag, Berlin, 1953), pp. 11 f., 17.

APPENDICES

In the *in Pisonem* Cicero is restrained in his criticisms of Philodemus (§§ 68–72). He does not mention him by name, he calls him *eruditus* and *humanus*, he admits that his pernicious doctrines are subject to philosophical qualifications. The pomposity of the rebukes in §§ 71–72 need not be taken too seriously; Cicero is amusing himself at the expense of his Epicurean friends. It has been supposed by some[1] that Philodemus dedicated one of his treatises to Cicero; though this is very uncertain, there is no doubt that Cicero owed much to Philodemus for his knowledge of Epicureanism.[2] He shows his real attitude in the *de finibus*: 'familiares nostros Sironem et Philodemum, cum optimos viros tum homines doctissimos' (ii. 119).

APPENDIX IV

PISO AND THE VILLA OF THE PAPYRI

IN 1750 an exciting discovery was made at Herculaneum.[3] Tunnelling deep under the solid lava the engineers of the King of the Two Sicilies struck a villa of fantastic magnificence; the peristyle round the garden was 100 metres by 37, the *piscina* 66 metres by 7. Two years later hundreds of black briquettes were found inside the villa; they suffered some damage before it was realized that they were not charcoal, but carbonized papyrus rolls. More were destroyed while being split open, until the monk Piaggio devised a slightly less destructive process. Savants eagerly awaited the recovery of some sublime masterpiece of antiquity. At last some scraps were deciphered of Philodemus περὶ μουσικῆς.

The papyri have turned out to be almost entirely Epicurean, and about two-thirds of the identified rolls are by Philodemus. The villa,[4] which was built in the first century B.C., was much too

---

[1] Diels, op. cit. (1915), p. 99.
[2] Cf. Pease's edition of *de natura deorum*, i, pp. 39 ff.
[3] W. Scott, *Fragmenta Herculanensia* (Oxford, 1885), pp. 1 ff., C. Jensen, *Bonner Jahrb.* cxxxv, 1930, 49 ff.
[4] D. Mustilli, *Rendiconti della accademia di archeologia*, Napoli, N.S. xxxi, 1956, 77 ff. The villa is still underground.

186

APPENDICES

grandiose for a philosopher; but early in the nineteenth century it was already being attributed to Philodemus's patron Piso. Comparetti[1] revived the theory in 1879, but used some bad arguments easily refuted by Mommsen;[2] the case has recently been put more persuasively by Herbert Bloch.[3]

One of the papyri suggests that Philodemus had connexions with Herculaneum: ἐδ]όκει δ' ἐπ[ανελθεῖν] μεθ' ἡμῶν εἰς [τὴν Νεά]πολιν πρὸς τὸν [φίλατο]ν Σίρωνα [κ]αὶ τὴν [περὶ αὐτ]ὸν ἐκεῖ διαίτη[σιν καὶ φι]λοσόφους ἐνεργ[ῆσαι ὁμι]λίας Ἡρκλ[ανέωι τε συχνό]τε[ρον παρενδιατρῖψαι].[4] An epigram by Philodemus (a.P. ix. 412) seems to describe an Epicurean *hortulus* near the sea; could it have been at Herculaneum ? At the end of the second book of Cicero's *de finibus* Torquatus says that he will refer the topic under discussion to Siro and Philodemus; it may be significant that the dialogue is set near Naples, at Cicero's Cumanum. There is a well-known tradition that Virgil studied Epicureanism under Siro in the Naples area.[5]

Over eighty busts and statues, mainly in bronze, were found in the villa; they are now to be seen in the Museo Nazionale at Naples.[6] Some are of outstanding merit, and the collection was evidently formed by a connoisseur of great wealth and taste. Cicero specifically alleges that Piso looted statues from Greece (*Sest.* 94, *prov. cons.* 7); of course many Epicureans must have been avid collectors, but the owner of this house was a remarkable representative of the type. There is a bust of Zeno of Sidon, Philodemus's teacher, but this would have been natural enough in any Epicurean's house. Comparetti absurdly claimed to have recognized the features of Piso, as described by Cicero, in the tortured eyes and dishevelled hair of the pseudo-Seneca.

It has been suggested that Piso had an association with Campania. Such a connexion would give special point to his duumvirate at Capua in 58, but the argument has little independent force; Piso,

---

[1] For his fullest account cf. D. Comparetti and G. De Petra, *La Villa ercolanese dei Pisoni* (Torino, 1883).

[2] *Arch. Zeit.* xxxviii, 1880, 32 ff.

[3] *AJA* xliv, 1940, 490 ff.; my debt to this article is obvious.

[4] W. Crönert, *Kolotes und Menedemos, Studien zur Palaeographie und Papyruskunde* (Leipzig, 1906), p. 126, A. Körte, *Gött. Gel. Anz.* clxix, 1907, 264.

[5] Serv. *ecl.* 6. 13, *vita* 6; cf. A. Körte, *Rh. Mus.* xlv, 1890, 172 ff.

[6] De Petra, op. cit. [n. 1], pp. 256 ff., G. Lippold, *Kopien und Umbildungen griechischer Statuen* (München, 1923), pp. 77 ff.

APPENDICES

as consul of the year, might have wished to give a good start to a colony in which Caesar was interested.[1] The Piso of the *laus Pisonis* (*c.* A.D. 60) had associations with Naples (l. 92), but this proves nothing. Mommsen argued that if Piso had lived at Herculaneum we should find Calpurnii in inscriptions; but there are so few inscriptions from Herculaneum that no inference can be drawn (Bloch, op. cit.).

The crux of the problem lies in the character of the papyri themselves. The disproportion of Philodemus's writings is remarkable; yet he was the leading Epicurean of the day and an unflagging writer; he would have been well represented in any Epicurean library. Some of the rolls are duplicates, but any Epicurean centre (for instance Siro's) might have had spare copies. It is more significant that marginal notes in one papyrus seem to be incorporated in the text of another;[2] but though this suggests that the library belonged to Philodemus himself, we do not know what would have become of it after his death. And if he had left it to Piso, as seems reasonable, we cannot be sure what happened after Piso's death; for instance, the Epicurean centre might have transferred itself to another rich patron. The theory that Piso owned the villa is more reasonable than Mommsen made it appear, but it cannot be regarded as proved.

APPENDIX V

GABINIUS[3]

AULUS GABINIUS appears from the first as a Pompeian,[4] and remains so consistently until abandoned by Pompey. His wife was a Lollia, perhaps the daughter of Pompey's partisan M. Lollius Palicanus. As tribune in 67[5] he seems to have moved a law which

[1] For the meaning of *Campanum consulem* see 24. 5 n.

[2] W. Crönert, *Rh. Mus.* lxii, 1907, 624 f., D. Comparetti, *Mélanges Chatelain* (Paris, 1910), pp. 121 ff.

[3] See Drumann–Groebe, iii. 39 ff., Vonder Mühll, *RE* vii. 424 ff., H. E. Butler and M. Cary, *de prov. cons.* appendix ii, E. M. Sanford, *TAPA* lxx, 1939, 64 ff., E. Badian, *Philol.* ciii, 1959, 87 ff.

[4] E. Badian, op. cit., identifies him with the A. Gabinius who was military tribune under Sulla in 86; but Cicero's picture, though a grotesque caricature, seems to suggest a younger man.

[5] The *lex Gabinia de legationibus* is assigned by some to this year, but

188

APPENDICES

prevented the lending of money to provincials at Rome; this measure was designed to protect them from exorbitant rates of interest. In the same year he removed Lucullus from his eastern army, and secured for Pompey his command against the pirates. Pompey wished to make him a legate, and Cicero cordially supported the illegal proposal (*imp. Pomp.* 57–58). In fact he became Pompey's legate under the *lex Manilia*, and served at the Tigris and in Judaea. When he returned to Rome Cicero may have defended him.[1] He became praetor in 61, consul in 58, thanks to Pompey.

Gabinius agreed without demur to Cicero's exile. He was said to have been an associate of Catiline in his youth (20. 20 n.), and P. Gabinius Capito the conspirator was probably a relative; but Pompey's consent to Cicero's removal is explanation enough. In the *lex Clodia de provinciis* he was originally given Cilicia (*dom.* 23, *Sest.* 55), but later was rewarded with Syria instead. Syria had recently been governed by ex-praetors; but a revolt in Judaea looked dangerous, and Gabinius was an outstanding commander who knew the country. Besides, Roman designs on Parthia, and perhaps already also on Egypt, made Syria very important at this time. Gabinius, like Piso, received what Cicero rhetorically calls *infinitum imperium* (*dom.* 55, *Pis.* 49, cf. p. 172); this seems to have given him some power to intervene in client kingdoms, perhaps also in the foreign states across his eastern frontier.[2]

Gabinius and Piso promoted the *lex Gabinia Calpurnia*,[3] which exempted Delos from customs dues; the island had recently suffered a serious decline in prosperity. The bill no doubt won some goodwill for Piso, but Gabinius may have been its chief sponsor. Gabinii are found at Delos at the beginning of the century,[4] and Delos had worked with Pompey against the pirates.[5] In the latter part of 58

is attributed by Carcopino to A. Gabinius, trib. pleb. 139 B.C. (*Mélanges Gustave Glotz*, Paris, 1932, i. 120 ff.).

[1] *quir.* 11 'causam capitis receperam'. Yet this may refer to a threat of prosecution after the tribunate of 67.

[2] *dom.* 60 'alteri Syriam Babylonem Persas . . . tradidisses', ibid. 124 'cui regna omnia Syrorum Arabum Persarumque donaras'.

[3] *Inscr. Délos* 1511 (= *CIL* i². 2. 2500), E. Cuq, *BCH* xlvi, 1922, 198 ff., S. Accame, *Il Dominio romano in Grecia*, p. 185.

[4] Th. Homolle, *BCH* viii, 1884, 143. For other Gabinii in Greek lands cf. *RE* vii. 423 ff. (nos. 6, 8, 10, 13).

[5] The *lex Gabinia Calpurnia* contains a flattering reference to the *lex Gabinia de piratis persequendis*. There was a thiasos of Pompeiastae at Delos (*SIG³* 749).

189

APPENDICES

Gabinius quarrelled with Clodius, here again following Pompey's lead (introd., p. xii).

Soon after his arrival in Syria Gabinius lost some cavalry, no doubt in battle against the Arabs (*prov. cons.* 9, *Sest.* 71). Worse trouble was awaiting him in Judaea.[1] Pompey in 63 had established Hyrcanus as high-priest of the Jews; his brother and rival, Aristobulus, had been taken prisoner to Rome. Now Alexander, Aristobulus's son, had started a rebellion against Hyrcanus; but Gabinius defeated him, killed 3,000 of his men, and captured 3,000 more. He was hailed as *imperator* (*prov. cons.* 15, *Pis.* 44) and asked the senate for a *supplicatio*, to which he was amply entitled; but the senate, which resented his behaviour in 58, rejected the request on 15 May 56 (*Q.f.* ii. 7. 1, *prov. cons.* 14–15, *Pis.* 41, 45). Later[2] Aristobulus himself escaped to Judaea, but was defeated with the loss of 5,000 of his men, and sent back to Rome.

After preparing expeditions against the Arabs (App. *Syr.* 51) and the Parthians (Dio xxxix. 56. 1) Gabinius was diverted by a more enticing prospect.[3] In 58 Ptolemy Auletes, king of Egypt (the father of Cleopatra), had been expelled by his subjects; the senate decided that P. Lentulus Spinther (cos. 57) should restore him. In 56 the statue of Jupiter on the mons Albanus was hit by lightning; and the custodians of the Sibylline books, who were consulted on this portent, conveniently found an oracle forbidding the restoration of the king 'with a multitude' (48. 15 n.). Cicero persuaded Lentulus that it would be imprudent to act without being certain of success (50. 10 n.). But Gabinius was in a much stronger position than Lentulus; in the spring of 55 he invaded Egypt, and after winning a battle he entered Alexandria and restored the king (*Att.* iv. 10. 1, Dio xxxix. 58). His action appeared to violate the laws which forbade a proconsul to leave his province (§ 50), but he claimed to be acting within the powers given him by the *lex Clodia* (*Rab. Post.* 20). He was certainly relying on Pompey's support (Dio xxxix. 55. 3, xxxix. 56. 3), but Cicero conceals this (*Rab. Post.* 21, *Pis.* 49). It was believed that he had been given 240,000,000 sentences by Ptolemy and his agent Rabirius Postumus (*Rab. Post.* 21, *Pis.* 48),

[1] Joseph. *b.J.* i. 160–78, *a.J.* xiv. 82–104, A. H. M. Jones, *The Herods of Judaea* (Oxford, 1938), pp. 22 ff.

[2] Dio xxxix. 56. 6 puts the war against Aristobulus shortly before the invasion of Egypt; but his chronology may not be exact.

[3] *fam.* i. 1–7, Dio xxxix. 12–16, Tyrrell and Purser, *Correspondence of Cicero*, ii². xxix ff.

190

APPENDICES

but he claimed that he had only received expenses (*Rab. Post.* 34). Meanwhile Syria was left unprotected and suffered much from raids by pirates (Dio xxxix. 56. 5, xxxix. 59. 2), and another rebellion by Alexander (Joseph. *a.J.* xiv. 100–2, *b.J.* i. 176–7). When Gabinius returned from Egypt he won a great victory over Alexander, but this may have happened after the delivery of the *in Pisonem*.

Gabinius's domestic administration also caused offence; according to Cicero he enslaved the *publicani* to the Jews and Syrians, nations born to slavery.[1] In more prosaic language, he confirmed the right of some cities to immunity from taxes,[2] and gave new grants to others;[3] he may have arranged to collect taxes directly, and thus exclude the *publicani*;[4] he refused to hear suits brought by *publicani*, and removed the guards from customs control-points (*prov. cons.* 10). Many *publicani* lost money; but when Cicero says 'multos fama vitaque privasset' (§ 41) one must make allowances for the conventions of rhetoric. Gabinius also continued Pompey's reorganization of Judaea. He divided the country into five provinces, and left the high-priest with only spiritual powers. He rebuilt many cities; Samaria became known as Gabinia.[5] This makes a strange contrast with Cicero's talk of devastation (§ 41).

Gabinius's return to Rome, so eagerly awaited by Cicero (§ 51), took place in September 54.[6] The *publicani* were determined on revenge, and when Gabinius called Cicero an *exul* they showed their indignation (*Q.f.* iii. 2. 2). He was prosecuted first on a charge of *maiestas*, for restoring Auletes without authority, but acquitted; it was decided that the Sibyl had meant another king (*Q.f.* iii. 4. 1, iii. 7. 1, Dio xxxix. 62. 3). Then he was tried *de repetundis*; though Cicero was forced to defend him[7] he was convicted and sent into

---

[1] *prov. cons.* 10, Rostovtzeff, *Soc. Econ. Hist. Hell. World*, pp. 981 ff., 1572 f. [2] Probably Tyre was one; cf. *Q.f.* ii. 12 (11). 2.

[3] *prov. cons.* 10 'vectigalis multos ac stipendiarios liberavit'.

[4] Ibid. 'quo in oppido ipse esset aut quo veniret ibi publicanum aut publicani servum esse vetuit'. Cf. Piso's action in Macedonia (*Pis.* 87).

[5] Joseph. *b.J.* i. 165–70, *a.J.* xiv. 87–91, A. H. M. Jones, *Cities of Eastern Roman Provinces*, pp. 259, 455.

[6] *Q.f.* iii. 1. 24 'noctu in urbem introierat . . . nihil illo turpius; proximus tamen est Piso; itaque mirificum embolium cogito in secundum librum meorum temporum includere, dicentem Apollinem in concilio deorum qualis reditus duorum imperatorum futurus esset, quorum alter exercitum perdidisset, alter vendidisset'.

[7] *Rab. Post.* 19 '(Gabinium) quem ex tantis inimicitiis receptum in gratiam summo studio defenderim', ibid. 32 'neque me vero paenitet

191

APPENDICES

exile. Pompey spoke on his behalf at a *contio* (Dio xxxix. 63. 4), but no doubt accepted his departure with his usual phlegm. Gabinius endured his unjustified exile much longer than Cicero; he was recalled by Caesar, and died while acting as his legate in Illyricum in the winter of 48–47 (*bell. Alex.* 42. 4–43. 3).

Gabinius fully deserved his proconsulship; he was a successful general trusted by both Pompey and Caesar.[1] His intervention in Egypt, though it left his province undermanned, was justified not only by Pompey's interest but by Rome's: it was vital that the corn supply should be assured. Cicero's charges of plunder[2] may or may not have been true; yet even a corrupt and energetic governor could do less harm than one who was impeccable and easy-going. Gabinius, however, lacked political judgement; it was a mistake to offend both the senate and the equites, and then trust to Pompey for protection.

Gabinius was extravagant and often in debt,[3] like some other *populares*. Though he was virile enough to command armies on troubled frontiers he seems to have affected a certain foppishness in dress and manner; he was even rumoured to be an expert dancer (18. 19 n.). The story may have had little foundation in fact, but it was worth writing up; and Gabinius the *saltatrix* with his curls and his castanets[4] is one of the most vivid characters in Cicero, and a perfect foil to the grim and ponderous Piso.

APPENDIX VI

THE *IN PISONEM* AS AN INVECTIVE

THE *in Pisonem* exemplifies a type of writing which had widespread ramifications in the Graeco-Roman world. The conventional themes of invective can already be recognized in Archilochus and Alcaeus; the art reaches its peak in Old Comedy and the Attic

mortales inimicitias, sempiternas amicitias habere'; cf. frag. p. 486 Schoell.

[1] Praised by Joseph. *b.J.* i. 160, *a.J.* xiv. 104; cf. *bell. Alex.* 43. 1.
[2] *dom.* 60, *Sest.* 93, *prov. cons.* 9, *Pis.* 48, echoed uncritically by Dio xxxix. 56. 1.
[3] §§ 12, 48, *in sen.* 11, *Sest.* 18, 28, etc.
[4] §§ 20, 25, *in sen.* 12, 13, 16, *Sest.* 18.

192

APPENDICES

orators. The rhetorical theorists reflect the practice of their day. Gorgias thought it the task of an orator 'rem augere posse laudando vituperandoque rursus affligere' (Cic. *Brut.* 47); Thrasymachus was the greatest expert of his day at slandering and refuting slanders (Plat. *Phaedr.* 267 d). For specimen ψόγοι one may consult the compositions on Philip written by Aphthonius (ix ed. Rabe) and Libanius (ed. Foerster viii. 296). Pollux supplies a convenient catalogue of rude names (iv. 35), apparently derived from some textbook.

Invective came easily to the Romans,[1] even before it was fostered by study of the Greek classics; one has only to think of their unflattering proper names, the insulting maledictions forbidden by the Twelve Tables,[2] the ribald songs at weddings and triumphs, the lurid curses of *defixiones*, the abusive epithets of Plautus and Lucilius. The early Roman orators could be as scurrilous as Cicero.[3] Political invective was at its best in the first century B.C.;[4] one remembers the attacks on Caesar by Catullus,[5] Calvus, and others (Suet. *Jul.* 49, 73, 75. 5), Caesar's own *Anticatones* (ibid. 56. 5), the exchange of vituperations between Antony and Octavian. Under the empire libellous pamphlets and scandalous anecdotes continued to circulate; some of their inventions live on in Tacitus and Suetonius. The art-form survived even the advent of Christianity, and distinguished specimens of rhetorical polemic were composed by saints and fathers of the Church.

Under these circumstances it is not surprising that Roman invective often shows more regard for literary convention than for historical truth. Some quotations are given below from the anti-Ciceronian invectives[6] (Pseudo-Sallust, *invectiva in Ciceronem*, and Fufius Calenus's speech in Dio xlvi. 1–28); though they are rhetorical compositions they no doubt contain much genuine material. The falsity or exaggeration of these libels is generally recognized in Cicero's case; Piso deserves as much consideration.

[1] U. E. Paoli, *Vita Romana* (Paris, 1955), chap. xiii.

[2] H. Usener, *Rh. Mus.* lvi, 1900, 1 ff. (= *Kleine Schriften*, iv. 356 ff.), E. Fraenkel, *Gnomon*, i, 1925, 187 ff.

[3] Cf. Cato, frag. 213 (Malcovati, *ORF*[2]), Scipio Aemilianus, frag. 17, C. Gracchus, frags. 43, 58, Titius, frag. 2, Cic. *Font.* 37–39.

[4] See especially R. Syme, *The Roman Revolution*, pp. 149 ff.

[5] H. A. J. Munro, *Criticisms and Elucidations of Catullus*, carm. xxix.

[6] I owe much of what follows to W. Süss, *Ethos* (Leipzig and Berlin, 1910), pp. 245 ff.; he quotes extensively from the *in Pisonem* and the anti-Ciceronian invectives.

APPENDICES

Criticisms of social background are a stock theme. Suggestions of servile origin may be made without even a pretence of plausibility (§ 1 *Syrum*, Süss, p. 247). Imputations of ξενία are even more popular (Süss, p. 248); Piso's grandfather is described as a Gaul (frag. ix n.), but Cicero could be called 'rex peregrinus' (*Sull.* 22), 'inquilinus civis' (Sall. *Cat.* 31. 7), 'reperticius ac paulo ante insitus huic urbi civis' (Ps. Sall. *in Cic.* 1). One's enemy's father should be given a banausic trade (Süss, p. 248), or if he is too well-known, something detrimental may be invented about his mother; it can then be hinted that the child grew up in an unwholesome atmosphere. Euripides's mother was a greengrocer, Aeschines's father a schoolmaster; Piso's maternal grandfather was an auctioneer, a disreputable occupation (frag. ix n.), his father was a war profiteer dealing in leather, an unsavoury commodity (§ 87); Cicero's father was a fuller (Dio xlvi. 4), Octavian's grandfather a baker.[1] It did not matter whether a man's ancestors were distinguished or not; as the textbooks pointed out, he could always be contrasted with them unfavourably (*rhet. ad Her.* iii. 13). Cicero follows this principle in the *in Pisonem*; see § 53 'o familiae non dicam Calpurniae sed Calventiae . . . dedecus', § 62 'o paterni generis oblite, materni vix memor'.

Physical appearance was another stand-by (*de or.* ii. 266). Piso's hairy cheeks and bad teeth are worth a laugh (§ 1); in the same spirit Cicero mocked Vatinius's *struma* (*passim*), and Vatinius mocked Cicero's varicose veins.[2] Eccentricity of dress was another topic (Süss, p. 253). Piso appeared in sandals on unsuitable occasions (13. 6 n., 92. 3 n.); Cicero wore his toga too long (Dio xlvi. 18. 2). Gabinius dripped with unguents (§ 25), but even Cicero might seem too dandified for some tastes; see Dio xlvi. 18. 3 τίς δ' οὐκ ὀσφραίνεται τῶν πολιῶν σου τῶν κατεκτενισμένων;

Cicero makes startling accusations of immorality against his enemies. Such charges are conventional (Süss, pp. 249 f.), and should not be too readily believed; Cicero is indignant when more temperate slanders are made against his friends.[3] Even Cicero did not escape calumny; see *dom.* 93 'cum mihi furta largitiones libidines obiciuntur', Plut. *Cic.* 7. 7, Ps. Sall. *in Cic.* 2, Dio xlvi.

---

[1] For more of these fictions cf. Süss, p. 248, M. Gelzer, *Die Nobilität der römischen Republik*, pp. 11 ff.

[2] Macr. *sat.* ii. 3. 5, cf. Dio xlvi. 18. 2.

[3] *Mur.* 11, *Planc.* 30, *Cael.* 6 'aliud est male dicere, aliud accusare'.

194

APPENDICES

18. 4–6. We hear that Piso was a glutton and a drunkard (§§ 13, 22, 42, 66), Gabinius a 'helluo natus abdomini suo' (§ 41); but Pseudo-Sallust talks of Cicero's *gula immensa* (*in Cic.* 5).[1] Cicero insists that Gabinius was a dancer, but when his own clients are accused of the same vice he is dignified and reproachful (18. 19 n.). If one's enemy lived a blameless life one could charge him with hypocrisy as well as sin; see *de inventione*, ii. 34 'nam eum ante celasse, nunc manifesto teneri', *rhet. ad Her.* ii. 5 'illum ante occultasse sua flagitia', Süss, p. 252. Piso was vulnerable under this heading, if no other (frag. xviii, § 1, *in sen.* 14, *Sest.* 22).

Cicero's attacks on Piso's Epicureanism are equally conventional.[2] Piso was a product of the sty; but Epicureans were often compared with pigs (37. 24 n.). Piso valued the *abdominis voluptates* above all other delights; in the same spirit Timon had portrayed Epicurus as γαστρὶ χαριζόμενος τῆς οὐ λαμυρώτερον οὐδέν (ap. Ath. 279F). The stories of Piso's drinking-bouts (§§ 13, 22, 67), his *stupra* (§§ 42, 70, 83), his fondness for dissipated and sycophantic friends (§§ 22, 67, 70), all follow the familiar pattern. Cicero ridicules the Epicureans for their veneration of Epicurus (59. 24 n.), their contempt for glory (§§ 59–60), their lack of culture (70. 26 n.); all are commonplaces.

Avarice was another popular charge, no doubt more often true than some others. Piso's paternal grandfather was 'homo furacissimus' (frag. ix), Piso himself appears as *latro* (§ 24), *fur* (§ 38), *rapax* (§ 66), and Gabinius was no better (§ 48); yet some said the same of Cicero (Ps. Sall. *in Cic.* 4, 5). Piso is accused of taking bribes (§§ 83, 84, 87); so also Cicero (*in Cic.* 3). Gabinius 'praebuit se mercennarium comitem regi Alexandrino' (§ 49); Cicero himself is called 'mercenarius patronus' (*in Cic.* 5). With rapacity goes extravagance: Cicero attacks Gabinius for his opulent Tusculan villa (48. 13 n.), but his own Tusculan villa (*in Cic.* 4) as well as his Palatine house (*Att.* i. 16. 10, *in Cic.* 2) were equally blameworthy. Lack of means was another conventional reproach (Süss, p. 254): Gabinius's debts are a perennial theme (§ 12, etc.), but Cicero's δανείσματα could also excite comment (Dio xlvi. 18. 3).

Pretentiousness (ἀλαζονεία) was a well-worn topic. Piso is mocked for his stern expression and severe eyebrows (1. 16 n.); for parallels

---

[1] This whole passage is an abusive commonplace derived from Lycurgus; cf. *JRS* xlviii, 1958, 30 ff.

[2] P. DeLacy, *TAPA* lxxii, 1941, 49 ff.

195

APPENDICES

from the Greek orators see Süss, pp. 251 ff. He is also ridiculed for his philosophical interests; Cicero claims to be an 'idiota' (§ 62), unversed in such mysteries (68. 8 n.), yet he himself could be described as σοφιστής and φιλόσοφος (Dio xlvi. 21. 4). Cicero sneers at Piso for his 'Graeci' (§§ 22, 68), but his own enemies called him a 'Graeculus' (Dio xlvi. 18. 1), with good reason.

Cicero's abusive vocabulary can easily be paralleled in other writers, notably the comic poets.[1] Animal names were a favourite form of invective,[2] for instance *belua* (§§ 1, 8), *maialis* (19. 3 n.), *pecus* (§ 19), *canis* (§ 23), *volturius* (§ 38), *admissarius* (§ 69), *asinus* (§ 73). Words suggesting dirt are common; cf. *lutulentus* (§§ 1, 27), *caenum* (§ 13), *o lutum, o sordes* (§ 62), *volutationibus* (§ 83). Among other epithets one may mention *portentum, monstrum, prodigium* (frag. i, § 9, cf. the emperor Claudius, *ILS* 212. ii. 15 'illud palaestricum prodigium'); *pestis, labes, scelus* (§§ 3, 56); *furcifer* (14. 19 n.); *truncus, stipes* (19. 5 n.); *gurges, vorago* (§ 41).

Some catchwords seem to have been particularly common in political contexts. Cicero was called *carnifex* (*in Cic.* 3, cf. *dom.* 21 of Cato) and *tyrannus* (*dom.* 75, *Sest.* 109, *Vat.* 29), and accused of *crudelitas* (14. 18 n.) and *proscriptio* (*in Cic.* 5); he repeats all these taunts against Piso (§§ 11, 18, 30). Both Cicero and Piso might be charged with imposing *servitus* on the city (*in Cic.* 6, *Pis.* 15). Such epithets as *hostis, proditor* (§§ 24, 78), *gladiator* (§§ 19, 28), *praedo* (§ 96) were too trite to have much meaning. Charges of *furor* (μανία) are conventional, especially against *populares* (§§ 21, 26, 47, 50); similarly Cicero calls Piso a *Furia* and *Poena* (§§ 8, 91, cf. ἀλάστωρ). For epigrammatic sobriquets of the type *barbarus Epicurus* see 20. 19 n.

Best of all, one could give an account of the activities of one's enemy which in spite of a wealth of circumstantial detail was largely or completely fictitious; for such *mendaciuncula*, as Cicero calls them, see the quotation from L. Crassus at *de oratore*, ii. 240. Several of the descriptions in the *in Pisonem* belong to this type: Piso's return from his drinking-den (§ 13), his celebration of Cicero's flight (§ 22), his furtive home-coming (§ 53), the delivery of his accounts at the treasury (§ 61), his Epicurean dinner (§ 67), his behaviour when recalled (§§ 89, 92). Such inventions were meant

---

[1] S. Hammer, *Contumeliae quae in Ciceronis invectivis et epistolis occurrunt quatenus Plautinum redoleant sermonem*, Cracow, 1906.

[2] J. B. Hofmann, *Umgangssprache*, p. 88.

196

APPENDICES

to cause pain or hilarity, not to be believed. In the same spirit another writer portrays the boy Cicero handling filthy clothes in the family laundry (Dio xlvi. 5. 1). These embroideries were the fashion of the day; and an instructive parallel has survived from Caelius's speech against Antonius:

'namque ipsum offendunt temulento sopore profligatum, totis praecordiis stertentem, ructuosos spiritus geminare, praeclarasque contubernales ab omnibus spondis transversas incubare et reliquas circumiacere passim; quae tamen exanimatae terrore, hostium adventu percepto, excitare Antonium conabantur, nomen inclamabant, frustra a cervicibus tollebant, blandius alia ad aurem invocabat, vehementius etiam nonnulla feriebat; quarum cum omnium vocem tactumque noscitaret proximae cuiusque collum amplexu petebat, neque dormire excitatus neque vigilare ebrius poterat, sed semisomno sopore inter manus centurionum concubinarumque iactabatur' (*ORF*[2] frag. 17).

Cicero was not the only Roman orator with a lively imagination.

APPENDIX VII

PISO AND THE *INVECTIVA IN CICERONEM*

THE succinct and faintly entertaining brochure known as the *Invectiva in Ciceronem* is attributed by the manuscripts, and by Quintilian, to the historian Sallust. Eduard Schwartz[1] had the ingenious idea that its true author was none other than L. Piso. Following Richard Reitzenstein[2] he dated the work to 54 B.C.: how else could the pamphleteer sneer at Cicero's defence of Vatinius in August 54, and then say nothing about his defence of Gabinius in December? It further transpired that in that self-same year Piso had published a counterblast to the *in Pisonem* (introd., p. xiv). Schwartz suggested that the *invectiva* was an extract from Piso's *in Ciceronem*.

Some features would suit Piso well enough, the expostulations at Cicero's insults (§ 1), the gibes at his municipal origin (§ 1, § 7 'Romule Arpinas') and arrogant poetry (§ 5, cf. *Pis.* 72). But Schwartz's theory is as difficult to maintain as any other which

---

[1] *Hermes*, xxxiii, 1898, 101 ff. [2] Ibid., pp. 87 ff.

197

APPENDICES

regards the *invectiva* as a genuine pamphlet.[1] The work seems too self-contained to be an extract, and if it had been authentic it would have been very much longer. Piso must have tried to rebut the misstatements of the *in Pisonem*; he would not have run short of material. Observations on the venality of the Roman people (§ 1) were inappropriate under the Republic, even for a statesman with Piso's detachment. The attack on Cicero's consulship (§ 5) seems too vigorous for Piso, who had supported Cicero in 63 (*Pis.* 72), even if he disapproved of the execution of the conspirators (*Pis.* 14). Besides, there are chronological difficulties. Piso's pamphlet must have been published in July 54 at the latest, since in September Cicero received Quintus's comments from Britain (*Q.f.* iii. 1. 11); yet Vatinius's trial, which is mentioned in the *invectiva*, took place in August (*Q.f.* ii. 16. 3). The *invectiva* ridicules Cicero's description of the *concilium deorum* (§§ 3, 7); but this graphic scene belonged to the poem *de temporibus suis* (*Q.f.* iii. 1. 24), which in December 54 was not yet known to the world at large (*fam.* i. 9. 23).

It seems likely that the *invectiva* was a rhetorical exercise. It has now been suggested[2] that its author was writing in the character of Piso, and demonstrating the sort of retort which Piso ought to have made to Cicero. But in such circumstances even a prize-essayist might have dealt with some of the points made by Cicero in his classic speech. As the *invectiva* was attributed to Sallust it seems *prima facie* more plausible that its author was trying to write in the character of Sallust. He does not in general imitate Sallust's historical style, which would have been ludicrous in a political pamphlet,[3] but in a few phrases seems to venture a Sallustian tinge.[4] But however that may be, the *invectiva* surely has nothing to do with Piso, nor indeed with any of the famous people to whom it is ascribed from time to time in the learned periodicals.

[1] See F. Schoell, *Rh. Mus.* lvii, 1902, 159 ff., O. Seel, *Klio*, Beiheft xlvii, 1943, 1 ff., G. Jachmann, *Miscellanea Academica Berolinensia*, 1950, pp. 235 ff., F. Oertel, *Rh. Mus.* xciv, 1951, 46 ff.

[2] Tentatively by R. Syme, *JRS* xxxvii, 1947, 201, at greater length by G. Jachmann, op. cit., pp. 262 ff.

[3] E. Fraenkel, *JRS* xli, 1951, 192 ff.

[4] *in Cic.* 1 'iniquo animo paterer', *Jug.* 31. 21 'aequo animo paterer'; *in Cic.* 1 and *Cat.* 11. 4 (cf. 38. 4) 'neque modum neque modestiam'; *in Cic.* 1 'fortunas suas venales habeat', *Cat.* 10. 4 'omnia venalia habere'; *in Cic.* 2 'quod alicui collibuisset', *Cat.* 51. 9 'quae victoribus collibuissent'; *in Cic.* 6 'atque parum quod impune fecisti', *Jug.* 31. 22 'parum est impune male fecisse'.

APPENDIX VIII

THE DATE OF DELIVERY AND PUBLICATION

THERE can be no doubt that the *in Pisonem* in its original form was delivered in 55 B.C. Cicero says (§ 65) 'instant post hominum memoriam apparatissimi magnificentissimique ludi quales non modo numquam fuerunt . . .'; as Asconius points out (1 KS), this refers to Pompey's famous games in 55. Cicero mentions that the fathers of both the consuls had won triumphs (§ 58); this suits Pompey and Crassus, the consuls of 55. He mentions a new *lex iudiciaria*, which will soon begin to operate (§ 94); he must mean Pompey's law of 55. He addresses Crassus in the vocative (§ 58), implying that he is present in the senate; Crassus left for Syria in November 55 (*Att.* iv. 13. 2).

It is more difficult to determine the month when the speech was delivered. Valerius Maximus mentions the heat at Pompey's games: 'Cn. Pompeius ante omnes aquae per semitas decursu aestivum minuit fervorem' (ii. 4. 6). He probably means the lavish games in 55, though Pompey's other games in 70 cannot be entirely excluded. The hottest months in 55, when the calendar was out of order, would be August and September. Perhaps Pompey's games came immediately before the *ludi Romani* (5–19 Sept.), as they had done in 70 (*Verr.* I. 31); after the *ludi Romani* the populace might be jaded. Plutarch (*Pomp.* 52. 5) seems to imply that Pompey held his games about the time when Crassus set out for the East (November), but no cooling arrangements would have been needed then.

In his panegyric of Caesar (§ 81) Cicero does not mention the invasion of Britain; he could not have ignored this exploit if the news had been known. Caesar landed about 4 October, by Groebe's calculation, about 13 September by Le Verrier's.[1] The news would take about a month to reach Rome (cf. *Q.f.* iii. 1. 25); this confirms that the speech was delivered not later than October.

But in § 81 Cicero does mention the Rhine. It is not clear when Caesar made his famous bridge, but it cannot have been much less than two months[2] before the crossing of the Channel, i.e. by about

[1] Cf. Drumann–Groebe, iii. 753 ff., J. Carcopino, *Hist. rom.*[4], p. 736.
[2] Caesar spent 18 days across the Rhine (*b.G.* iv. 19. 4). He then had to march his army to the Channel and prepare his fleet.

199

APPENDICES

the beginning of August (if one uses Groebe's system) or the middle of July (if one uses Le Verrier's). The news would have been known in Rome by about the middle of August (Groebe) or the beginning of August (Le Verrier). Unfortunately it is not clear from Cicero's reference to the Rhine either that he knows of the crossing or that he does not know. In the latter hypothesis (which is perhaps slightly preferable), the speech belongs to early August at the latest; on the former hypothesis September would also be possible. In any event Cicero knows of some of Caesar's operations in the summer of 55.

Piso's successor in Macedonia was Q. Ancharius, praetor in 56; he was appointed at some date after the debate *de provinciis consularibus* in June 56. Piso did not wait for Ancharius to arrive, but left his quaestor in charge (§ 88); though at one time he hoped for a reprieve his hopes were deceived (§ 89). One would therefore expect him to have left at the end of 56, or in the spring of 55, when the voyage would be easier. Yet Cicero says that Piso returned 'triennio post' (§ 55); he controlled the corn supply for three years (§ 86); most difficult of all is § 97 'nulla ex trinis aestivis gratulatio'. This implies that Piso had his army in summer quarters in 55[1] as well as 57 and 56; and even if one makes every allowance for exaggeration he can hardly have left Macedonia before May or June. His journey was circuitous (§ 53), and included perhaps a visit to the North Adriatic and a country estate (92. 4 n.); he can hardly have reached Rome before July.

When Piso arrived in Rome the elections had not yet been held (§ 55 *candidatorum*). In normal circumstances this would suggest a date not later than July. However, in 55 the elections seem to have been postponed; for Cicero writes in November (*Att.* iv. 13. 1) 'comitiorum non nulla opinio est'. So this approach proves nothing.

In § 58 Cicero refers to one consul, Pompey, in the third person, but addresses the other, Crassus, in the vocative. It seems likely that Crassus was in the chair;[2] the presiding consul and other senators could be referred to in either the second or third person,

[1] E. G. Hardy, *CR* xxxi, 1917, 12 n. 3 suggests that Cicero is reckoning from the spring of 58, when the *lex Clodia* gave Piso his province. But *nulla ex trinis aestivis gratulatio* shows that Piso was in his province in person during at least part of three campaigning seasons; and he did not set out for his province till the end of 58 (§ 57).

[2] P. Stein, *Die Senatssitzungen der Ciceronischen Zeit* (Münster, 1930), p. 45 n. 247.

200

APPENDICES

but it is certainly noteworthy that Pompey is nowhere directly addressed. Crassus comes after Pompey in the *fasti* for 55; by the normal custom he should have presided in the even-numbered months (June, August, etc.).[1] But in 55 the consuls did not assume office till late January, or more probably early February. Cicero, writing to his brother at some date after 11 February, says 'Crassum consulem ex senatu domum reduxi' (*Q.f.* ii. 8(7). 2); this seems to refer to the procession home of the newly inaugurated consuls (cf. *St.-R.* i³. 617). In the same letter Cicero mentions arrangements for the forthcoming election of praetors, and it is known that Pompey presided at this election (Plut. *Cat.* 42. 4, *Pomp.* 52. 3). These facts suggest, if anything, that Pompey presided in the even-numbered months, Crassus in the odd-numbered (e.g. July and September).[2] But the argument is very uncertain.

It seems, therefore, that the speech was delivered between July and September 55. Some consequences may be important. In § 59 Cicero says 'quid est, Caesar, quod te supplicationes totiens iam decretae tot dierum tanto opere delectent?' (cf. § 45). One may assume, though it is not mentioned, that Caesar won a *supplicatio* in 61 or 60 for his victories in Spain. In 57 he won a *supplicatio* of 15 days, then a record, for his victories in Gaul (*b.G.* ii. 35. 4). In 55 he won one of 20 days, but this happened after his return from Britain (*b.G.* iv. 38. 5), i.e. after the delivery of the *in Pisonem*. *totiens* is inappropriate if it refers to only two occasions. Perhaps Caesar was awarded a *supplicatio* in 58 or 56, but if so it is strange that he does not mention the fact in the *de bello Gallico*. It is more likely that Cicero rewrote the speech for publication at the end of 55 or beginning of 54, and included the *supplicatio* of 55 by an oversight.[3]

If this is so, it is relevant that in the debate on Caesar's *supplicatio* Cato attacked his Gallic policy (Plut. *Cat.* 51); Cicero's praise of military glory (§§ 56 ff.) could reflect this debate. Again, the description of the execrations at Piso's departure would have added piquancy, and a flavour of malice, after Crassus had been cursed

[1] L. R. Taylor and T. R. S. Broughton, *Mem. Amer. Acad. Rome*, xix, 1949, 1 ff.

[2] P. Stein, op. cit., n. 242, comes to this conclusion, but only because two weak arguments cancel each other.

[3] The difficulty is pointed out by L. Halkin, op. cit. [6. 2 n.], p. 45, but he is wrong in concluding that the speech was delivered late in the year.

201

APPENDICES

in November 55 (31. 11 n.). (The theme, however, is not simply suggested by Crassus's experience, as it is already used at *Sest.* 71, i.e. in 56 B.C.). Again, one may point to a slip of the tongue which Cicero acknowledges in § 55: he had said that Piso had entered the city by the *porta Caelimontana*, and Piso had corrected him. There is no such allusion in our speech before § 55, and Cicero would hardly have entertained the senate with two separate accounts of Piso's return. Perhaps the slip was made in the actual speech, the correction in the published invective.

Asconius (1 KS) mentions an earlier scholar, whose name is lost in the manuscripts, who believed that the *in Pisonem* was Cicero's last speech in 54. It was certainly not the last, but conceivably there was a tradition that the speech was published in that year. However that may be, the fact that Piso's reply was being discussed a year after the delivery of the speech (introd., p. xiv) suggests that there was an interval between delivery and publication.

These are speculations; but it is likely in any case that the published invective was very different from the speech which Cicero delivered. Roman orators often adapted their speeches for publication; cf. *Brut.* 91 'pleraeque enim scribuntur orationes habitae iam, non ut habeantur'.[1] When Piso criticized Cicero in the senate Cicero was no doubt prepared, and would not have refrained from replying. But he might have expanded his reply out of all recognition; a speech that was intended to cause pain and not to influence policy was particularly liable to such treatment. Invectives were often published in the form of a speech; one recalls the Second Philippic, and Piso's rejoinder to Cicero (*Q.f.* iii. 1. 11) is described as an *oratio*. Quintilian, it is true, comments (iii. 7. 2) 'editi in competitores, in L. Pisonem, in Clodium et Curionem libri vituperationem continent, et tamen in senatu loco sunt habiti sententiae'. But this is not good evidence that we possess the speech as spoken. The comparison with the *in toga candida* and *in Clodium et Curionem* suggests just the opposite; for the latter was not delivered (cf. *Att.* iii. 15. 3), and the former was probably much expanded for publication.

[1] See especially Schanz–Hosius, *Röm. Literaturgeschichte*, i. 453, J. Humbert, *Les Plaidoyers écrits et les plaidoiries réelles de Cicéron* (Paris, 1925).

202

INDEX NOMINVM

(The references are to section and line of lemma, or—where there is no relevant note—to section and line of text.)

Acarnania, 96. 1.
Achaia, 37. 5, 90. 1, 96. 24.
Aelius Lamia, L., 23. 17, 64. 10, p. x.
Aemilius Paulus, L., 58. 7, 61. 10; cf. 39. 24.
Aetolia, 91, 96. 3.
Afranius, L., 58. 2.
Agraei, 91. 13.
Albucius, T., 92. 21.
Ambracia, 91. 13, 96. 25.
Amphilochia, 96. 1.
Ancharius, Q., 89. 21.
Antonius, C., 5. 13, 15, 56. 4, p. 178.
Apollonia, 86. 4, 96. 25.
Aristarchus, 73. 7.
Arsinoe, 91. 10.
Athamanes, 96. 1.
Athamas, 47. 20.
Athamas (Graeculus nescioquis), 89. 14.
Athenae, 37. 5, 96. 25.
Atilius Calatinus, A., 14. 15, 58. 6.
Atilius Regulus, M., 43. 19.
Aurelius Cotta, C., 62. 8, 14.
Autobulus, 89. 14.

Baebius, M., 88. 8.
Bero(e)a, 89. 20.
Bessi, 84. 3, 84. 6, pp. 178 f.
Boeotia, 86. 12, 96. 1, p. 173.
Bottiaei (?), 86. 12.
Brundisium, 51. 17, 92. 4.
Bullienses, 96. 26.
Burebista, pp. 174 f., 179 f.
Byzantium, 86. 12, pp. 175, 179.

Caecilius Metellus Celer, Q., 8. 22.
Caecilius Metellus Creticus, Q., 58. 2.
Caecilius Metellus Macedonicus, Q., 61. 10.

Caecilius Metellus Nepos, Q., 6. 5, 35. 13.
Caecilius Metellus Numidicus, Q., 20. 14.
Calpurnia, pp. vi, 184 n. 1.
Calpurnius Piso, L. (Piso's grandfather), frag. ix, p. xvi n. 3.
Calpurnius Piso, L. (Piso's father), frag. ix, xiii, 87. 23, p. v.
Calpurnius Piso, L. (Piso's son), 84. 3, p. xvi.
Calpurnius Piso Frugi, C., frag. xiii, 12. 20, 13. 4.
Calventius, frag. ix, x, xi, xiii, xv, 62. 4, 67. 20; cf. 14. 16, 53. 18, p. xiv.
Capua, 24–25, pp. 187 f.
Cherronensus, 86. 12.
Claudius Marcellus, M., 44. 6.
Claudius Pulcher, Ap., 35. 9.
Clodius, Sex., see Cloelius.
Clodius Pulcher, P., 9–11, 23. 16, 28. 5, 95. 12, &c., pp. vii–xii.
Cloelius, Sex., 8. 2, 23. 4.
Cornelius Dolabella, Cn., 44. 17.
Cornelius Lentulus Crus, L., 77. 30.
Cornelius Lentulus Spinther, P., 34. 16, 1, 35. 12, 50. 8, 80. 3.
Cornelius Lentulus Sura, P., 16. 13.
Cotys (or Cottus), 84. 4, 8.

Delos, pp. 174, 189.
Denseletae, 84. 9, p. 178.
Didius, T., 61. 10.
Dolopes, 91. 14, 96. 3.
Dyrrachium, 83. 21, 92. 29, 93, 96. 25, p. 176.

Epicurus, 59. 24, 69. 20, p. 195; cf. 20. 19, 37. 24.
Epirus, 96. 26.

203

INDEX NOMINVM

Euhadia, 89. 16.
Execestus, 89. 16.

Fabius Sanga, Q., 77. 30.
Fufidius, 86. 4.

Gabinius, A., 27–28, 40–41, 48–50, &c., pp. 188–92.
Gellius Poplicola, L., 6. 27.
Graecia, 37. 5.

Insuber, frag. ix, xv, 34. 19.
Iulius Caesar, C., 3. 23, 21. 2, 59–61, 79–82, pp. viii–xi, xv–xvi.
Iulius Caesar, L., 8. 21.
Iunius Silanus, D., 56. 3.

Lapithae, 22. 23.
Licinius Crassus, L., 62. 4, 15.
Licinius Crassus, M., 58. 26, pp. 200 ff.
Licinius Crassus, P., 58. 8.
Locri, 96. 26.
Lutatius Catulus, Q., 6. 25.

Magius, Decius, 24. 6.
Manlius Torquatus, L., 44. 15, 47. 22, 77–78, 92. 30, p. 179.
Marcius Crispus, Q., 54. 2, 88. 6.
Marcius Figulus, C., 8. 21.
Marius, C., 20. 14, 43. 21, 58. 7.
Mediolanum, 62. 3.
Minturnenses, 43. 22.
Mucius Scaevola, Q., 62. 9.

Naupactus, 91. 10.
Numerius Rufus, Q., 35. 9.

Opimius, L., 95. 8.
Orestes, 47. 20.

Parthini, 96. 26.
Perraebia, 96. 1.
Phalaris, 42. 12, 73. 7.
Philodemus, 68–72, 74. 17, pp. 183–8.

Phocii, 96. 1, p. 173.
Placentia, frag. x, xi, 14. 16, 53. 20, 67. 15.
Plator, 83. 22, 84. 1.
Pleuratus, 84. 2.
Pompeius Magnus, Cn., 16. 13, 25. 22, 27. 21, 28. 10, 29. 15, 34. 2, 35. 5, 58. 24, 74–77, 80. 1, pp. xvi, 192, 200 f.
Pompeius Strabo, Cn., 58. 8.
Pomptinus, C., 58. 4.
Pupius Piso Calpurnianus, M., 62. 10, 13.

Quinctius Flamininus, T., 61. 10.

Rabirius, C., 4. 7.
Rabocentus, 84. 3.
Rhenus, 81. 26, pp. 199 f.
Rutilius Nudus, P., p. v; cf. 26. 1.
Rutilius Rufus, P., 95. 6.

Samothracia, 89. 13, p. 173.
Scribonius Curio, C., 44. 17, 58. 2, p. 177.
Sentius, C., 84. 9, p. 177.
Seplasia, 24. 4, 9.
Sergius Catilina, L., 5. 19, 11. 9, 14–16, 20. 20, 23. 16, 95. 11, p. vii.
Servilius Vatia Isauricus, P., 58. 2.
Stratus, 91. 10.

Terentius Varro Lucullus, M., 44. 18, 77. 1, pp. 119, 177.
Thasus, 89. 13.
Themista, 63. 20.
Thessalia, 37. 5, 96. 24.
Thessalonica, 40. 13, 83. 25, 84. 17, 86. 13, 89. 17.
Thyestes, 43. 1.
Timocles, 89. 14.
Tusculum, 48. 13.

Valerius Flaccus, L., 54. 23.
Vibellius Taurea, Cerrinus, 24. 6.

Zbelsurdus, 85. 18.

INDEX VERBORVM

abstrusus, frag. vii.
adsiduus, 64. 2.
adstipulator, 18. 26.
amator (= *fautor*), 65. 1.
arbitria funeris, 21. 11.
asinus, 73. 12.
aspirare, 11. 17.
atque (before consonants), 85. 23.
auctoritas, 4. 9, 8. 21, 34. 18, 35. 7, 48. 16.
audere, 10. 22.
autem, frag. viii, 91. 12, 94. 17.

bustum, 9. 12, 11. 10, 16. 20, 19. 12.

caeso, 27. 12.
canis, 23. 5.

decernere, 69. 20.
dies (fem.), 61. 16.
diribitores, 36. 20; cf. 96. 16.
distracta frons, 68. 4.
duco (with perf. inf.), 32. 2.
dumtaxat, 32. 24.

emori, 15. 11.
et, 83. 20, 89. 14.
expiscari, 69. 14.
expulsus, 43. 2.

facie, de, 81. 17.
ferculum, 61. 18.
fimbriae, 25. 12.
foris esse, 12. 21.
frequens, 6. 26, 18. 17, 80. 4.
furcifer, 14. 19.

Gallicanus, frag. xi.
gallus, 67. 20.
gurgustium, 13. 5.

hercule, 20. 20, 68. 22.
homo, frag. xiv, 2. 15, 55. 16.

idiota, 62. 15, 65. 2.

impellere in fraudem, 1. 21.
in quo, 90. 26.
inspectante, 9. 5.
instar, 52. 25.
intempestus, 92. 3.
ita, 62. 2.
iudicare, 74. 23.

liber, 67. 11, 72. 1.
luce palam, 23. 14.

maeander, 53. 12.
maialis, 19. 3.

ni, 55. 15, 71. 14.
notio, 10. 21.
notus, &c., 1. 22.
novicius, 1. 18.
nubecula, 20. 1.

obrepere, 1. 4.
omnino, 44. 4, 82. 4.
opus esse, 78. 11.

paludatus, 31. 7.
permutatio, 48. 12.
poema, 70. 26.
portorium, 87. 25.
posterius, 66. 8.
praeposterus, 92. 25.
praestare, 80. 4.
praevaricator, 23. 16.
princeps, 6. 25, 7. 17, 25. 22, 35. 5.
propter ('near'), 6. 27.
pulvinar, 95. 12.

quidam, frag. ix, 9. 9.
quidem, 10. 22, 78. 9.
quid est aliud . . . ?, 47. 28.
quid tum ?, 72. 2.
quin, 3. 24, 61. 10.
quisque (with ordinals), 10. 24.
quod (with subjunctive), 66. 4.

ratio (comitiorum), 4. 13.

INDEX VERBORVM

recordor (with genitive ?), 12. 3.
refricare, 82. 2.
renovare ad, 89. 23.

saltatorius orbis, 22. 19.
scutum et gladius, 73. 13.
sed tamen, 27. 18, 68. 11, 82. 5.
serracum, frag. xvi.
servator, 34. 21.
servolus (of freedman), 88. 27.
sescenti, 89. 11.
sic (*indignantis*), 82. 2.
si dis placet, 38. 23.
specillum, 62. 5.
speculum, 71. 12.
sponsio, 55. 15.
stare, 12. 22, 15. 8, 77. 28.

subitus, frag. ix.

tabellas obsignare, 69. 20.
tanta civitas, &c., 95. 13.
templum, 21. 11.
triduo post, 9. 5.

ubi ?, 65. 19, 97. 16.

vasarium, 86. 1.
venire (= *ire*), 49. 23, 89. 18.
verba, 65. 22.
vestigium temporis, 21. 11.
vir fortis, 54. 1.
volitare, 8. 3, 26. 9.
volturius, 38. 23.

INDEX RERVM

ablative absolute in military citations, 6. 2.
aedes Libertatis, 72. 4, p. xi.
Aeschines imitated, 8. 22, 46. 14.
alliterative phrases, 9. 6.
Alps compared to wall, 81. 25.
army: demobilization, 47. 26; pay, 88. 1; promotion, 88. 27; recruitment, 57. 21; winter quarters, 86. 6.
Asconius, mistakes in, frag. viii, x.
Aurelium tribunal, 11. 3.

bakers, domestic, 67. 17.
brachylogy, 42. 8, 69. 17, 77. 2.

campus Martialis, 61. 17.
capital punishment: beheading, 83. 26, 84. 5; *bestiae*, 89. 11; inflicted by doctor, 83. 27; Tarpeian rock, 44. 9.
Capuan consul, 24. 5.
Castor, temple of, 11. 7, 23. 13.
cedant arma togae, 72–74.
censors, 9. 10, 10. 21, 24.
collegia, 9. 8, 41. 29.
comitia: centuria praerogativa, 11.
16; *comitia centuriata*, 3. 1, 35.
12; *cunctis suffragiis*, 2. 14;
diribitores, &c., 36. 20; *prior
renuntiari*, 2. 14, 3. 27; *tabulae*,
11. 16, 36. 21.
compendious comparison, 20. 15.
conditional sentences, 18. 17, 43.
25, 57. 8, 75. 5.
conscience, 42. 5, 46. 14.
consilium: in cases of insanity,
48. 5; of consul, 80. 4.
consul-designate, *auctoritas* of, 8.
24.
contio, 14. 12, 20.
convivium publicum, 65. 23.
corona: gold, 90. 23; laurel, 58. 1;
oak, 6. 1.
Cyprian imitates Cicero (?), frag.
xvii.

dancing, 18. 19, 20. 21, 22. 19,
89. 14.
drinking customs, 13. 4, 67. 18, 20.

εἰρωνεία about philosophy, 68. 8.
Epicureans: attitude to arts, 70.
26; to crowd, 65. 19; to Epicurus

206

INDEX RERVM

59. 24; to friendship, 67. 19; to glory, 56. 22; to gods, 59. 24; to pleasure, 42. 10, 66. 3, 69. 21; their dinners, 67. 13; in invective, p. 195; happy on rack, 42. 13; resemble pigs, 37. 24.
eyebrows, &c., 1. 16, 14. 17, pp. 195 f.

face reveals thoughts, 1. 20.
fasti, erasure from, 30. 26.
female names applied to men, 18. 19.
fire-fighting by consuls, 26. 26.

games, crowd's reactions at, 65. 16.
glory, Roman views on, 57. 13.
gods compared with men, 20. 15.
Greek words, 61. 26, 62. 15.

Hegesippus imitates Cicero, 81. 18, 82. 28.
human sacrifice, 16. 21, 19. 12.

imagines, sooty, 1. 4.
imperatores, 38. 24, 44. 16.
imperium infinitum, pp. 172, 189.
insanity, symptoms of: failure to recognize people, 47. 28; self-mutilation, 47. 2.
insults of conventional pattern, 3. 24, 8. 22, 18. 10, 22. 24, 24. 24, 72. 26, pp. 194–7.

jokes attributed to public, 24. 5.

lamp-slaves, 20. 20.
laurel, 39. 25, 53. 12, 58. 1, 61. 13.
legates, Piso's, 53. 22, 86. 6, 88. 6.
lex Aelia et Fufia, 9. 6.
lex Clodia de exsilio Ciceronis, 30. 24, 72. 5, p. xi.
lex Cornelia maiestatis, 50. 6.
lex Julia repetundarum, 37. 2, 50. 7, 61. 20, 90. 23, 6.
lex Pompeia iudiciaria, 94. 20.
lex Servilia (Rulli) agraria, 4. 4.
lictors, 23. 4, 53. 12, 55. 8, 61. 14.
ludi compitalicii, 8. 20, 8. 1.

magistri (vicorum), 8. 25.

manes (of individual dead), 16. 18.
metaphor, mixed, 9. 12, 69. 14.
municipia, frag. x, 51. 19.

navigation in winter, 57. 22.

Palatine, Cicero's house on, 11. 11, 26. 24, 52. 5.
panegyric, 82. 28.
parens patriae, 6. 26.
pathetic fallacy applied to buildings, 21. 7.
patrons of towns, 25. 19, 89. 13, 20.
pleonasm, frag. iv, 15. 11, 18. 23, 93. 12, 96. 5.
Pola, Piso at (?), 92. 4.
porta Caelimontana, 55. 15, 61. 14; Esquilina, 55. 15, 61. 13, 74. 23; *triumphalis*, 55. 18.
prosecutions by young men, 82. 10.
proverbs, &c., frag. iii, 1. 20, 38. 20, 59. 10, 11, 69. 19, 95. 9, 98. 23; construction in, 69. 19.
provinces, allocation of, 5. 15, 12. 21, 88. 4.
provincial governors: accounts, 61. 20; dispatches, 38. 17; doctors on staff, 83. 27; leave quaestor in charge, 88. 6.
publicani, 41. 28, 87. 25, p. 191.

repetition of words, 15. 2 (?), 26. 1, 36. 21, 70. 25, 9.
rhetorical terms: *adnominatio*, frag. viii; *argumentum a minore*, 18. 14, 48. 3; *complexio*, 30. 3; *congeries*, 1. 22; *geminatio*, 19. 2; *immutatio*, 3. 1, 73. 14; *occupatio*, 68. 22; *reditus ad propositum*, 17. 27; ἀφορισμός, 86. 10; διαλεκτικόν, 91. 12; ἐνάργεια, 67. 13; κύκλος, 2. 11; προσωποποιία, 59. 21.

sacerdos popularis, 89. 10.
scribae quaestorii, 61. 23.
senate: *frequens*, 6. 26; order of speaking, 11. 17; presiding consul, pp. 200 f.; *princeps senatus*, 6. 25; *referre*, &c., 14. 21, 29. 17; seating, frag. xxi, 6. 27.

207

INDEX RERVM

sobriquets of type *barbarus Epicurus*, 20. 19.
statues: gilt, 25. 18; pulled down, 93. 9.
supplicatio, 6. 2, 41. 23, 45. 21, 24, p. 201.

toga praetexta, 8. 2.
topical themes in 55 B.C., 9. 11, 66. 9, pp. 199–202.
tricolon, 1. 1.
trinum nundinum, 9. 5.
triumphatores alive in 55 B.C., 58. 2.
triumphs: held in province, 92. 21; *iusti*, 44. 18; Macedonian, 38. 20, 61. 10, p. 177; procedure, 55. 18, 60. 3; vetoed by consul, 62. 4.

Veleia and Pisones, frag. ix.
verb 'to be' omitted, 15. 10, 28. 9, 68. 13, 97. 7.
verse-quotations, 25. 12, 43. 1, 61. 25, 82. 6.
verse-rhythms in prose, frag. i, 25. 12.
via Egnatia, 40. 14, p. 176.

walls, Servian, 5. 21.
wheel of Fortune, 22. 20.
word-order: hyperbaton, 14. 23, 17. 8, 18. 11, 54. 1, 56. 4, 61. 22, 67. 12; Wackernagel's law, frag. iv, 71. 21, 79. 20; *et loci vestigio et temporis*, 21. 11; *panis et vinum a propola atque de cupa*, 67. 18; *quibus illi acceptis*, 55. 9.